SELLING OUT

ALSO BY MARK GREEN

Mark Green's Guide to Coping in New York City

The Consumer Bible

The Challenge of Hidden Profits: Reducing Corporate Bureaucracy and Waste
(with John Berry)

Reagan's Reign of Error: The Instant Nostalgia Edition
(with Gail MacColl)

Who Runs Congress?, 4th Edition
(with Michael Waldman)

Winning Back America

Taming the Giant Corporation
(with Ralph Nader and Joel Seligman)

The Other Government: The Unseen Power of Washington Lawyers

The Monopoly Makers

The Closed Enterprise System

EDITED BY MARK GREEN

Changing America: Blueprints for the New Administration

America's Transition: Blueprints for the 1990s

The Big Business Reader, 2nd Edition

Verdicts on Lawyers
(with Ralph Nader)

Corporate Power in America
(with Ralph Nader)

With Justice for Some
(with Bruce Wasserstein)

How Big Corporate Money
Buys Elections,
Rams Through Legislation,
and Betrays Our Democracy

MARK GREEN

ReganBooks
An Imprint of HarperCollinsPublishers

HarperCollins books may be purchased for educational, business, or sales promotional use. For information please write: Special Markets Department, HarperCollins Publishers Inc., 10 East 53rd Street, New York, NY 10022.

FIRST EDITION

Designed by Christine Sullivan

Printed on acid-free paper

Library of Congress Cataloging-in-Publication Data

Green, Mark, 1945-
    Selling out : how big corporate money buys elections, rams through legislation, and betrays our democracy / Mark Green.—1st ed.
        p. cm.
    Includes index
    ISBN 0-06-073582-1
    1. Campaign funds—United States—History. I. Title.

JK1991 .G74 2002
324.7'8'0973—dc21

                                                                    2002031803

          04   05   06   RRD   10   9   8   7   6   5   4   3   2

This book is dedicated to Justices Sandra Day O'Connor and Anthony Kennedy, whose opinions on democracy can revive democracy

Contents

SELLING OUT

THE EVIL OF ACCESS:
An Introduction

*"There are two things you need for success in politics.
Money . . . and I can't think of the other."*
—Senator Mark Hanna (R–OH), 1903

*"Political action committees and moneyed interests are setting the
nation's political agenda. . . . Are we saying that only the rich have
brains in this country? Or only people who have influential friends
who have money can be in the Senate?"*
—Senator Barry Goldwater (R–AZ), 1988

*"The Enron scandal should launch a national movement to leash the
corrupt power of money in politics so that legislators and regulators
can serve the public interest."*
—*The American Prospect*, February 2002

Representative Jim Shannon, a Democrat from Boston's North End—
home to working-class families as far back as the 1848 potato
famine—wasn't happy. As a protégé of Speaker Tip O'Neill, and a
member of the prestigious Ways and Means Committee, he thought
he'd learned all about the culture of Congress, about its blend of high-
minded rhetoric and low-road cynicism. But now he was confronted
with an overbearing business lobbyist, telling him that his client was
disappointed with Shannon's position on an important tax bill while
reminding Shannon that this particular client "makes good PAC contributions to the party." Shannon exploded. "I'm tired of hearing
appeals based on money," he shouted. Looking pained, the lobbyist
responded, "You think I like this any more than you do?"

㋐ ㋑

How do you know when a democracy is in decline? When a bridge collapses, so does the reputation of its engineer. When a plane loses two engines, passengers suddenly lose their lives. A democracy, however, is more like a bather in water slowly getting hotter and hotter: it's hard to notice the change in circumstances until it's too late.

How do you know when a difference in degree becomes a difference in kind, when a democracy goes from warm to scalded?

- ◄○► when the 0.1 percent of Americans who contribute $1000 or more to political candidates have far more influence than the other 99.9 percent;

- ◄○► when, in an election year, it's nearly more likely for an incumbent congressperson to die than to lose;

- ◄○► when senators from the ten largest states have to raise an average of over $34,000 a week, every week, for six years to stay in office;

- ◄○► when the cost of winning a House or Senate seat has risen tenfold in twenty-four years;

- ◄○► when it's far easier for a working-class person to win a seat in the Russian congress than in the American one;

- ◄○► when legislatively interested PAC money goes 7 to 1 for incumbents over challengers—and 98 percent of House incumbents win;

- ◄○► when most other democracies get a 70 to 80 percent turnout of eligible voters, while in the U.S. it's half in presidential elections, a third in congressional elections, and often only a fifth in primaries;

- ◄○► when one senator and one mayor each spend more getting elected than *all* the legislative candidates in Great Britain combined.

It's true, as Václav Havel wrote, that a genuine democracy is the equivalent of a distant horizon we can see but never reach. Still, at minimum a democracy requires that "the people will participate in the process by which their lives are organized," as historian Lawrence Goodwin put it. But is it a democracy if 0.1 percent pay the piper, if 80 percent stay at home in primaries, if 98 percent of incumbents return to a "permanent Congress"?

Selling Out is a book about how big money is sabotaging our democracy—and how to stop it. For despite occasional bursts of reform, the system of checks and balances we studied in high school has steadily evolved instead into a system of checks, checks, and more checks. Warren Beatty's caricatured rants in *Bulworth* about how elected officials care more about their contributors than about their constituents are a far more accurate depiction of Washington and state capitals today than those heard in July 4th speeches.

Indeed, the corporate abuse in mid-2002 was the direct by-product of a corporate Washington filled with those paid to be what Kipling called "shut-eyed sentries." In the view of Joan Claybrook, head of Public Citizen and a veteran of the campaign finance wars, "political money from the Enrons and others bought loopholes, exemptions, lax law enforcement, underfunded regulatory agencies, and the presumption that corporate officials could buy anything they wanted with the shareholders' money."

The basic problem is that candidates regard money as Mark Twain did bourbon: "Too much is not enough." Because the press and public judge a candidacy by its treasury, and because no one can be sure how much will be "enough," candidates feel the pressure to engage in financial overkill, just as the Soviets and Americans did with nuclear missiles in their arms race. And when the Supreme Court in the 1976 *Buckley v. Valeo* decision struck down the Federal Election Campaign Act's spending ceilings, the alms race took off. Then—and now—the sky's the limit.

Yes, we're weary of screeds about money in politics. It's an old story: from Plutarch writing about how money corrupted elections and ruined Rome . . . to the Standard Oil Trust in the 1890s, which, it was said, "did everything to the Pennsylvania Legislature except refine it" . . . to Lyndon Johnson's emergence as a major politician, according to biographer Robert A. Caro, only when he distributed large funds from Texas oil interests to congressional colleagues . . . to Richard Nixon's $2 million contribution from milk interests in 1972, followed by his order to increase milk price supports and thereby milk prices to millions of American families . . . to Charles Keating, of "Keating Five" fame, who, when asked whether his substantial contributions influenced the policy makers receiving them, helpfully replied, "I want to say in the most forceful way I can: I certainly hope so."

We've been so periodically bombarded by small-bore corruption or Watergate-size scandals that money in politics has become like sex in Victorian England—a subject of gossip, amusement, and ultimately indifference. "They all do it," many citizens sigh, with a shrug.

Allow me to be skeptical about cynicism. While money has long been the lifeblood of the body politic, only recently has it metastasized into an authentic crisis due to its volume and impact. While in 1976 it cost an average of $87,000 to win a House seat and $609,000 a U.S. Senate seat, those amounts grew by 2000 like beanstalks to $842,000 for the House and $7.2 million for the Senate—a tenfold leap (or more than threefold in current dollars). And more money brought with it intended leverage. "We're all tainted by this corrupt system," concludes Senator John McCain (R–AZ), a national leader for cleaner elections.

So, although issues such as terrorism, social security, health care, and pollution absorb far more public attention and concern, **the scandal of strings-attached money corrupting politics and government is the most urgent problem in America today—because it makes it harder to solve nearly all our other problems**. How can we produce smart defense, environmental, and health policies if arms contractors, oil firms, and HMOs have such a hammerlock over the committees charged with considering reforms? How can we adequately fund education and child care if special interests win special tax breaks that deplete public resources? How can we attract the best people to be public servants if those who run and serve are increasingly either special-interest hustlers or self-financing multimillionaires?

ॐ ॐ

It was before the firm became a household name, but in early April 2001 the vice president knew to take the call of CEO Kenneth Lay of Enron and to agree to an April 17 private meeting on "energy policy matters." Dick Cheney knew that Enron was President George W. Bush's biggest contributor in his gubernatorial and presidential campaigns and had placed company allies in several key posts—like Thomas White as secretary of the Army, Alberto Gonzalez as White House counsel, Lawrence Lindsay as chief White House economist, Patrick H. Wood III as chair of the Federal Energy Regulatory Commission, and Harvey Pitt, an Enron and Arthur Andersen lawyer, in charge of what he hoped would become a "kinder and gentler" Securities and Exchange Commission (SEC).

As reported by John Nichols of The Nation *magazine, Lay handed Cheney a memorandum at the meeting that said, "The administration should reject any attempt to re-regulate wholesale power markets by adopting price caps," and that included a "wish list" of Enron's policy recommendations. At first, Lay got what he desired: the next day, Cheney came out of hiding to tell the* Los Angeles Times *that price caps were out of the question ("short-term political relief for the politicians," he said); and after a total of six meetings between Cheney, Lay, and aides, the Bush-Cheney energy task force adopted all or significant parts of seven of eight company policy recommendations.**

"There is no company in the country," concluded Representative Henry Waxman, the California Democrat leading the congressional investigation of Enron, "that stood to gain as much from the White House plan as Enron." Agreeing was author Kevin Phillips, who in 2002 wrote in the Los Angeles Times, *"Not in memory has a single major company grown so big in tandem with a presidential dynasty and a corrupted political system."*

After Enron was dragged under by a riptide of fraud and self-dealing, however, Cheney refused to disclose who attended these meetings—and got sued by the General Accounting Office—while President Bush falsely implied that Ken Lay had supported rival Ann Richards in his 1994 Texas gubernatorial campaign.

Then on July 14, 2002, Cheney gave a solemn, strong speech denouncing corporate irresponsibility and saying that their administration "will pursue the wrongdoers."

*For example, "extend federal control of transmission lines, use federal eminent-domain authority to override state decisions or transmission-line siting, expedite permitting for new energy facilities and limit the use of price controls."

◖ ◗

When the McCain-Feingold campaign finance bill narrowly passed the Senate, guaranteeing its enactment, its supporters enjoyed a round of champagne, hugs, and high fives at a Capitol Hill celebration on Wednesday, March 20, 2002. It had been twenty-eight years since the last major campaign finance law, and the victors—especially former Common Causer Fred Wertheimer, who had worked on both bills—felt vindicated.

But like rowdy, uninvited guests at the prom, a prominent front-page story three days later reminded everyone how deeply embedded the pay-to-play system really was.

The New York Post *reported that John Whitehead, Governor George Pataki's appointee to head the nonpartisan Lower Manhattan Development Corporation rebuilding downtown after September 11, would be the headliner at a big-money Republican fund-raiser in April. The reliably Republican* Post *reported that "Whitehead's starring role in the gala event with Gov. Pataki has some businessmen quaking over whether they'll have to pony up donations if they want to get lucrative contracts related to the reconstruction of downtown. That's because Whitehead is set to award over $1 billion in state contracts."*

One businessman requesting anonymity explained the implicit squeeze: "Look, you don't have to be a political genius to know that if you're interested in doing business with Whitehead's agency and you get an invitation like this, you're expected to kick in some cash. But I have to say, there's something really unseemly about doing it when you're looking at something as sacred as the duty of rebuilding the World Trade Center and the surrounding community."

After this publicity, Whitehead withdrew from the event.

◖ ◗

For years tobacco interests had a surprisingly easy time of it in the New York state legislature and pro-health advocates weren't exactly sure why. Then a lawsuit and a New York Times *investigation in 1999 found two smoking guns in the previously sealed files of the Tobacco Institute and Philip Morris: first the institute had secretly funneled $440,000 in a single year to the New York Tavern and Restaurant Association to "carry its baggage," in the words of an internal memo, and lobby for its interests; sec-*

ond, from 1995 to 1997, 115 of the state's 211 legislators had accepted tens of thousands in gifts from Philip Morris, including hotel accommodations, tickets to sporting events, and meals.

After these disclosures, Common Cause, the League of Women Voters, and the New York Public Interest Research Group filed formal complaints, which resulted in a $75,000 penalty, the largest ever imposed in New York for violations of the lobbying law. Those legislators who accepted the illegal gifts suffered no punishment. But embarrassed by the publicity, the legislature did refuse to enact the bill Philip Morris was pushing to prohibit localities from passing smoking restrictions.

ᏛᎦ   ᎦᏛ

Among the staff sharing responsibility with House Speaker Newt Gingrich (R–GA) for an important 1995 telecommunication bill was a telecommunications entrepreneur named Donald Jones. Jones owned 80 percent of Cyberstar, a firm doing cable business in Wisconsin and the Virgin Islands. Ralph Nader filed an ethics complaint, arguing that the arrangement appeared to be an improper in-kind contribution to Gingrich's office—a clear violation of House Rule 45, which prohibits private funding of House offices. "The big problem with such an arrangement," said Gary Ruskin, director of the Congressional Accountability Project, "is that most Americans are shut out of the legislative process while the corporate special interests get the special provisions, exceptions, loopholes, favors, and benefits that they want." At the time, the telecommunications industry spent about $9 million in campaign contributions each federal election.

A passage in Gingrich's book Contract with America calls for "wresting power from special interest groups and returning it to the public."

ᏛᎦ   ᎦᏛ

The Washington Post reported in June 2002 that leading Republican activists, spearheaded by Grover Norquist, were researching the political giving of hundreds of Washington lobbyists in what was called by its compliers "the K Street Project." "[It's] part of a campaign that would deny government access to Democrats. . . . 'What's different this time is you will have this list to control access' to the White House, Congress and federal *agencies, according to a GOP lobbyist working on it. 'That's been very clear from the discussions.' "*

An irate Senate Majority Whip Harry Reid (D–NV) on the chamber floor asked what the list was for: "For intimidation and professional retribution? The President should pick up the phone, call his friend [Grover Norquist and] tell him that George W. Bush won't tolerate what amounts to McCarthyism."

Instead, the White House replied that the President wouldn't condemn the project because "he's not part of it." And Representative Thomas M. Davis III (R–VA), chairman of the National Republican Congressional Committee, predicted that House Republican chairmen would be interested in receiving a copy. Contributions to the wrong party, said Davis, can "buy you enemies. People often don't remember who gave them contributions. But they remember who gave to their opponents."

ᏬᎧ   ᎧᏬ

I should acknowledge a long, personal history on the subject of how private money corrupts public policies. For while there are numerous scholars and candidates who have devoted big chunks of their lives to studying money or raising money, not many have been both a student of and a participant in the process, exposing political money and raising political money.

In 1972, under the auspices of the Nader Congress Project, my book *Who Runs Congress?* (written with James Fallows and David Zwick) described in detail "the golden rule of politics—he who has the gold, rules"—and exhumed Will Rogers's observation that "Congress is the best money can buy." By describing the extent of congressional crime, exposing Congress as a "twig" of government, and showing the links between contributions and votes, we annoyed a lot of members. But we also contributed to the debates that in 1974 produced the Federal Elections Campaign Act amendments and the overthrow of strict seniority in selecting committee chairs.

In the three decades that followed, I advocated for more corporate accountability and cleaner campaigns. In 1977, as the director of Public Citizen's Congress Watch, I was asked by Senator Howard Metzenbaum (D–OH) to join his business-labor-consumer Panel on Corporate Governance to hash out the problems of corporate irresponsibility, CEO self-dealing, directorial independence—and what federal law could do about it. I recall spirited exchanges where Metzenbaum and I would argue that the problem was systemic and required a strong federal response—but duPont chairman Irving Shapiro and U.S. Chamber of Commerce president Richard Lesher would invariably counter that any abuse was rare and undeserving of "more regulation." (They won the political debate in 1977, though our side finally prevailed with enactment of the Sarbanes-Oxley Corporate Accountability Act in July 2002.)

After jousting with Shapiro, I organized the "nickel campaign" to persuade the House of Representatives to vote for a consumer protection agency that would represent consumer interests before regulatory agencies. Since business lobbies were successfully opposing it as "more expensive bureaucracy," we got 40,000 people to send actual nickels to wavering members—because the consumer agency cost only five cents a voter. Members were irate to receive this (symbolic!) payoff—but, in an early harbinger of the coming Reagan revolution, defeated the bill 228–189.

On the theory that if you can't beat 'em, join 'em, in 1980 I ran for Congress on the East Side of Manhattan against Republican Congressman Bill Green (no relation). We agreed to and held to a $320,000 spending ceiling, one of the first such mutually self-imposed limits in a congressional campaign. Then in 1984, as Senator Gary Hart's speechwriter in his presidential campaign, I persuaded him to be the first presidential candidate to refuse all gifts from political action committees (PACs). When Vice President Walter Mondale followed suit, but then allowed some committed delegates to secretly accept $400,000 in PAC funds, Hart blasted Mondale in a speech that ended, "Walter, just give the money back." He did, the next day.

In 1986, I ran an insurgent candidacy for the U.S. Senate in New York against a wealthy heir named John Dyson, who gave himself $7 million—a record amount in a Senate Democratic primary. When I visited the state Democratic chair to tell him I'd be opposing Dyson for the nomination, he asked, "Well, where's your $5 million up front?" Patting my pockets, I gibed, "I was *sure* I had it when I left my office." He didn't laugh.

But when Dyson publicly laughed me off that spring as an opponent who "couldn't raise a dime," I announced a "Mark of Dimes" fund-raising drive and asked, "Where's the wealth test for Senate in the U.S. Constitution?" I refused all PAC gifts, was outspent 10 to 1—yet won the Democratic nomination 54 to 46 percent. Senator Alfonse D'Amato then won the fall election 57 to 41 percent after spending $13 million—at that time the second-largest sum ever spent in a Senate election—compared with my nearly $2 million outlay. (That year, $2 million sounded small, though it was about what D'Amato himself had spent to win the seat just six years before.)

Wearying of running long-shot campaigns and being outspent by multiples—*and* then refusing PAC money—in 1993 and 1997 I ran for New York City public advocate, the number two citywide office, next in line to Mayor Rudolph Giuliani. Under the New York City campaign finance laws providing public matching funds in exchange for agreed-on expenditure limits, I won the election—and re-election. (Since other public advocate candidates those two election years "opted in" to the city's voluntary campaign finance system, no one outspent me.)

The New York City system was good but flawed. So in 1998, I coauthored a municipal campaign finance law that reduced the maximum gift from $8500 to $4500 and increased the public funding match to 4 to 1 for contributions of up to $250 per resident (so $100 became $500 or $250 became $1250), in order to better level the playing field for city candidates.

Then, in 2001, I ran for mayor. After winning the Democratic nomination from among a field of four experienced Democrats—who all spent the same amount of money, because all complied with the expenditure limits of the city's campaign finance system—I began the shortened 3.5-week general election campaign (the delays caused by the September 11 World Trade Center attack) twenty points ahead of a novice Republican candidate in a 4 to 1 Democratic city. But that Republican was Michael Bloomberg, the forty-second wealthiest American (with a worth of $4.2 billion, according to the Forbes 400). He spent a self-financed $73.9 million in all—including $30 million in the final three weeks—to win 49 to 47 percent.

I'll leave all the reasons for this result to more neutral observers. I certainly made my share of mistakes—and some Latino voters were upset after I defeated a strong Latino candidate for the nomination. In a widely held view, *Crain's New York Business* concluded that September 11 both gave Bloomberg a muscular rationale (we need a businessman to rebuild the city) and a hero endorser, Rudy Giuliani (who was "worth sixteen points," according to Bloomberg's media adviser, David Garth). But few doubted Newt Gingrich's observation on C-SPAN that Bloomberg wouldn't have run or won without his unique treasury—i.e., his money was necessary though not sufficient.

At the start of the general election, I asked Mark Mellman, my pollster, under what circumstances I could possibly lose. "Well, not many have lost so far ahead with a few weeks to go," he said, "but then no one's ever won being outspent by $50 million either." There were numerous, ominous signs, as when one friend told me he watched a Bloomberg–Giuliani ad every inning of a Yankee World Series game, then saw the Bloomberg Radio sign at Madison Square Garden, then got five different four-color mailings from him in two weeks—and even heard a Bloomberg-for-Mayor ad when he called Moviefone.

Asked in the spring by *New York* magazine how much of his own money he expected to spend, Bloomberg said "up to $30 million." Anything more, he added, would be "obscene." Seventy-four million later, Bloomberg laughed off his change of mind. "You know, we always talked about spending what was necessary to get our message out," said his senior strategist Bill Cunningham, "and, ultimately, that's exactly what we did."

When our campaigns sent in our final filings after the election, mine included 14,000 contributor names. Bloomberg's contained one—his own.

My expenditure of $16.2 million was the third highest of any non-presidential candidate in the country in 2000–2001. But Bloomberg set the bar so high—spending nearly as much in one city as Bush spent in fifty states winning the Republican presidential nomination—that after the election the *New York Post* referred to my "anemic" war chest.

My whole public life has been buffeted by money. After *Who Runs Congress?* in 1972 and a 1980 piece in the *New York Times,* where I wrote that the combination of "*Buckley* and very expensive campaigns predictably provide electoral advantage to candidates of great personal wealth," in 2001 I lost to the first self-financed $100-a-vote campaign in American history.* Does God have a sense of humor or what?

ᕮ ᕭ

Charles E. Lindblom, Mancur Olson, and William Greider were closer to the mark than James Madison.

A Founding Father, the fourth president, and the primary author of the *Federalist Papers,* Madison famously explained in *Federalist #10* that numerous "factions" would fairly compete for governmental policy and favor—that one faction would be balanced by another. But two centuries later, three authors—Lindblom in *Politics and Markets* (1977), Olson in *The Rise and Decline of Nations* (1982), and Greider in *Who Will Tell the People?* (1992)—showed that all factions weren't created equal, that some economic interests would be able to leverage their special resources, sophistication, and power to obtain special treatment from government.

Since government regulates the modern economy and accounts for one quarter of the GNP, companies will petition their government; that's their First Amendment right. What isn't right is the fact that current campaign rules give producers far more access and power than consumers, organized interests far more access and power than unorganized voters. Because of what economists call the "free rider effect"— which is the difficulty of conscripting supporters to a large advocacy group when they can obtain the same benefits without membership— there is no consumers' PAC, no poor people's PAC, no PAC for the homeless. So auto companies and the United Auto Workers have far more say and sway on CAFE (corporate average fuel efficiency) standards in Congress than car buyers, and coal producers have far more leverage over President Bush's decision to reverse his campaign pledge on carbon dioxide emissions than families who live downwind of polluting plants.

---

*Some apt comparisons: Ken Livingston spent 80 cents a vote winning the mayoralty of London in 2000; Ed Koch, $2 a vote winning the New York mayoralty in 1977; Giuliani, $15 a vote winning reelection in 1997.

It's not enough for these favored special interests to hide behind repeated mantras such as "free speech" or "property rights." Often competing rights have to be balanced. Private property rights are indispensable in a competitive capitalist economy—until they're invoked to protect a monopoly, stop workers from organizing, or force airline pilots to fly back-to-back cross-country trips. So the law intervenes to restrict private property when it collides with certain human and public safety rights. Of course, free speech is a "compelling interest" in our constitutional galaxy; but that doesn't mean it's legal to publish child pornography, to shout "fire" in a crowded theater, to electioneer within 100 feet of a polling place, or to give a speech through a 100-decibel sound system and drown out other speakers in a residential community. Are dollars like decibels? Should special interests be free to make 100-decibel contributions that threaten to monopolize the public conversation?

Creating wealth is good and so is wanting to be wealthy. It's fine for private businessmen to make multimillions and buy other companies. But should we allow unlimited private sector wealth to leach into the public sector, where such money buys not companies but congress-people? Or where such money allows someone to *become* a member of Congress? A key benefit of the complementary systems of capitalism and democracy is that capitalism produces and distributes wealth, while democracy polices the marketplace for abuses and assures minimal standards of safety and justice (police cars, food stamps, SEC investigators). Each system needs the other to survive and thrive. But what does it mean when the private sector seeks to take over the public sector? How then can democracy police capitalism? If elephants are free to dance among the chickens, isn't it clear who's going to get crushed?

If anything, this problem is getting more acute as the wealth gap widens—as fewer people have so much more money and power. When I first investigated company pay scales in the early 1980s, the average Fortune 500 CEO made 40 times more than the average line worker (about $1 million versus $25,000). Now it's grown to *400 times* more—and the top-ten earners make 4300 times more! "The Gilded Age looked positively egalitarian compared with the concentration of wealth now emerging in America," wrote *New York Times* economics columnist Paul Krugman, commenting on *Wealth and Democracy* by

Kevin Phillips. A lifelong Republican, Phillips warns that "the imbalance of wealth and private democracy is unsustainable."

The role of money in politics raises very difficult philosophical questions about freedom, property, and justice. To make necessary distinctions and draw necessary lines requires a preliminary understanding of the costs of the current campaign finance system (which chapter 5 focuses on in more depth):

SPECIAL INTERESTS GET SPECIAL ACCESS AND SPECIAL TREATMENT. "I view money buying access as one of the most threatening aspects of our democracy," said Senator Carl Levin (D–MI), "and it's not hidden but openly sold." Insisting on anonymity, one D.C. lobbyist, himself a liberal Democrat, said in an interview, "When a major lobbyist seeks a meeting with a member, within a few weeks they'll get an invite to the member's next fund-raiser. If he gives, he'll get another meeting, and if he doesn't, he won't—and anyone who doesn't know that shouldn't be hired to be a lobbyist."

One western senator went off the record to admit that "there aren't many conversations about the influence of money, because my colleagues don't want to admit it to others, or themselves. But senators are human calculators who can weigh how much money every vote will cost or gain them." The access that money buys, of course, doesn't guarantee legislative success, but the lack of it probably guarantees failure.

Representative Carolyn Maloney (D–NY) gives a small example of the evil of access. Putting on her green eye shades, she found a federal boondoggle called the Civilian Marksmanship Project. Using a law from 1812 as its justification, the government had a program in place to spend $2.5 million a year to pay for bullets for the National Rifle Association. Calling it "petrified pork," she got the military to admit it wasn't necessary for national defense. "Then the NRA fought back and all hell broke loose," recalls Maloney, sighing. "One southern Democratic colleague said to me, 'I want to be for your amendment, but the NRA just bought five tickets to my fund-raiser.'" Maloney lost.

Here's a bigger example: in 2000, before the collapse of Arthur Andersen and New York Attorney General Eliot Spitzer's lawsuit against Merrill Lynch, SEC Chair Arthur Levitt Jr. proposed rules to stop the conflicts of interest at the (then) Big Five, where auditors were also consultants. Like hell, said an industry that contributed $53 million to federal candidates in the 1990s. Fifty-five of its pals in the Congress, Republicans and Democrats alike, then complained to Levitt, some threatening him with budget cuts if he went ahead to more strictly police the profession. Levitt too lost, in the short term. Two years later *every* complaining member jumped on the bandwagon of reform and voted for a law to stop industry self-dealing after the Enron and WorldCom frauds were exposed.

FUND-RAISING IS A TIME THIEF. Imagine if someone kidnapped all candidates for state and federal office for half a day. The story would be bigger than Gary Condit, and surely lead to calls for tougher penalties against political kidnapping.

Well, there is such a culprit. It's the current system of financing political campaigns, which pits each candidate in a race to raise more than his or her opponents—and enough to feed the broadcasting monster called airtime. And just like professional athletes would see performance diminish if they lost half their training time, elected officials who raise money rather than legislate, read, travel, and meet with constituents will underperform as well.

"Senators used to be here Monday through Friday; now we're lucky to be in mid-Tuesday to Thursday, because Mondays and Fridays are for fund-raisers," complained one midwestern senator, requesting confidentiality. "Also, members are loath to vote on controversial issues because it'll be used against you when you're raising money. And people wonder why nothing much happens in the Senate."

Candidates start to feel like Bill Murray in *Groundhog Day*, trapped in a daily, stultifying repetition they can't escape. As a mayoral candidate I made 30,000 phone calls (that is not a misprint) over two years to lists of potential donors and spoke at 205 of my own fund-raising events. It's hard to overstate the physical and psychological stamina required in such an effort, and how little time and energy it leaves for all else. "I can't think," an exasperated President Bill Clinton once bellowed to his staff. "You want me to issue executive orders, but I can't focus on a thing but the next fund-raiser."

THE "MONEY PRIMARY" WEEDS OUT GOOD CANDIDATES AND GOOD INCUMBENTS. Potential candidates know they have to succeed not in one but two elections: the first, in which contributors "vote" with their dollars, comes long before constituents have their say. And if you don't win round one financially, you might as well not bother with round two; after all, no challenger spending under $900,000 won a House seat in 2000. With odds like those, many women and men of talent never enter the political fray.

The late Judge J. Skelley Wright called them the "silent casualties" of politics—and I know several. One is a friend with a famous name, great skills, and a passion for public service. But he said that he'd never run because he couldn't endure the fund-raising gamut and grind required even of someone so renowned. And the list of public officials who say they left office in large part because they couldn't stomach the incessant fund-raising is long: Senators Tom Eagleton, Charles Mathias, Sam Nunn, Frank Lautenberg, and Fred Thompson, among others.

THE "PAY-TO-PLAY" SYSTEM ESPECIALLY HURTS DEMOCRATIC CANDIDATES AND VALUES. Many Republicans oppose new regulations and taxes out of authentic belief. So they regard the special-interest funding of public elections as a brilliant system: for them, principles and payments go hand in hand.

Not so Democrats, who have to worry about how to raise business PAC funds if they get—however unfairly—an "antibusiness" reputation. How else to explain that, despite the widest gap between rich and poor in forty years, sixty-four congressional Democrats recently voted for capital gains tax cuts and forty-one for abolishing the estate tax, which by definition is paid only by the wealthiest Americans? Robert Reich, the prolific author, former secretary of labor, and candidate for governor in Massachusetts, believes that his party is losing its identity as the champion of the average family "because Democrats became dependent on the rich to finance their campaigns. It is difficult to represent the little fellow when the big fellow pays the tab. The problem is not corruption. The inhibition is more subtle. Democrats have come to sound like Republicans because they rely on the same funders to make the same contacts as the GOP."

Indeed, over the past decade, the group Democracy 21 reports that corporations gave $636 million to Republicans and $449 million to Democrats—and in 1999–2000, $221 million to the former and $161 million to the latter. Ever wonder why so many Americans in polls strongly favor higher minimum wages, prescription drug benefits for Medicare, quality day care, publicly financed congressional campaigns, and stronger environmental protection, even at the cost of higher taxes—yet the political system can't produce any of these? The pay-to-play system is a circuit breaker between popular will and public policy. As Robert Kuttner writes in *The American Prospect*, "Elite opinion is far to the right of mass opinion and the political system is just not offering voters the menu they'd like to see. Political scientist Walter Dean Burnham termed this a 'politics of excluded alternatives.'" So Congress is content to weigh in on the portability of health plans—as long as they're not asked to address their universality.

WEALTH BUYS OFFICE. Wealthy, self-financing candidates usually say that "nobody owns me," "it's my money," or "I needed to spend so much to get known." But it's also wise to remember an observation made by the late Senator Warren Magnuson (D–WA): "All anybody wants in life is an unfair advantage."

Yes, there can be great public servants who happen to be rich (Franklin Roosevelt, John F. Kennedy) and bad ones who happen to be poor. And some recent self-financing winners, such as Jon Corzine and Michael Bloomberg, are smart, capable, and effective. So a person's net worth is, alone, not disqualifying.

But as more and more multimillionaires run and win—the percentage of them in the Senate has risen to over one third, or about the number before senators began being elected by popular vote in 1913—there are three problems. First, a de facto wealth test screens out many quality candidates. Already, innumerable experience-rich candidates are grilled about how they can win against inexperienced but wealthy self-financing candidates. In the spring of 2002, Tony Sanchez, a fifty-nine-year-old oilman and banker, won the Democratic gubernatorial nomination in Texas because he spent $20 million of personal funds in a *primary;* Douglas Forrester won the New Jersey Republican Senate nomination because he spent $3.1 million; and near billionaire businessman Dennis Mehiel was being called the Democrats' "Mehiel ticket" for promising to spend vast amounts to become lieutenant governor of New York, thereby boosting the entire Democratic slate.

Second, when a very wealthy candidate inundates TV, radio, and mailboxes with ads portraying him as a young Abe Lincoln and you as the Manchurian Candidate, the pressure to hustle special-interest money becomes even more intense. For a well-funded charge, unanswered by a well-funded rebuttal, will stick. A lot of good candidates will surrender to temptation if forced to choose between oblivion and, say, Big Oil.

Third, democracy requires diversity in its legislatures in order to reflect popular will. Imagine the outrage if there were a dwindling number of Latinos and women over time because of a particular campaign rule. As superrich candidates begin to crowd out average-income candidates, we'll have a congress of members who relate more to golf clubs than to political clubs. Ellen Miller, a sixteen-year veteran of the Center for Responsive Politics and the Public Campaign, describes what this means: "The problem [with] more and more wealthy people running and winning is that then tax policy, health care policy, education policy are seen through the lens of multimillionaires, people who don't need government services. They are a different class of people, from a different world than most Americans who sit around their kitchen calculating their finances."

VOTING DECLINES. There are many reasons for the desultory fact that of twenty-four Western democracies, we rank twenty-third in voting turnout. Surely one reason is the conclusion that as money has increasingly gone into the system, voters have gone out. If "one person, one vote" really means "one PAC, many votes," some voters might rationally conclude they don't count.

MINORITIES HAVE TO JUMP HIGHER HURDLES. State Senator Byron Brown of Buffalo put it in a nutshell at a May 2002 symposium in New York City on money and minorities. "It's harder for candidates of color to raise money," said the thirty-year-old African American, "because there are fewer wealthier people in communities of color." The existing campaign finance system makes it even more difficult for historically excluded candidates to break into the winner's circle, especially in more expensive statewide or citywide races.

⟨ɢ   ⊙⟩⟩

There have been several excellent books—most notably in the past decade or so, Phil Stern's *The Best Congress Money Can Buy,* Brooks Jackson's *Honest Graft,* and Elizabeth Drew's *The Corruption of American Politics*—that illuminated aspects of how quid pro quo money distorts our political system. If the saga of political money is an old one and a discussed one, however, it's peaking in 2002–2003 with three epic developments. Not since the Watergate scandal and the 1974 campaign finance law have both public attention and the prospect for systemic change been so great.

First, the Enron scandal, which started with questions about corrupt financing practices, moved to questions about corrupt political practices. No matter how often the Bush administration repeated its catechism that this was a business scandal not a political scandal, it was no coincidence that, as noted above, CEO Ken ("Kenny Boy") Lay and Enron were the largest contributors to George W. Bush—and were able to dictate who should be the head of the Federal Energy Regulatory Commission and what should be in the Bush-Cheney energy plan.

Over the past decade, Enron gave $6 million to federal candidates across the country. When it came time, then, for Congress to probe this corporate miscreant, 212 of 248 members on the eleven investigating committees had received money from the company or its accounting firm, Arthur Andersen.

Just as commentators were opining in the spring of 2002 that the Enron scandal had petered out as a political force,* the other shoe

---

*For instance, on June 10, the *New York Times* reported that "Six months after the collapse of Enron, a wave of enthusiasm for overhauling the nation's corporate and accounting laws has ebbed and the toughest proposals for change are all but dead. A powerful group of lobbyists . . . appears to have killed efforts to impose tight new controls on corporate conduct." Four weeks later the U.S. Senate passed just such a bill 97–0—and two weeks after that President Bush signed it into law.

dropped—WorldCom. When the biggest bankruptcy ever was followed by an even bigger bankruptcy, and when the business pages read as if written by muckrakers Ida Tarbell and Lincoln Steffens, the issue of "corporate responsibility" suddenly seemed to make a species jump. With more money now in mutual funds than in banks, Americans who saw their retirement funds shrivel told pollsters and politicians of their outrage. It certainly didn't help President Bush's efforts to distance himself from the scandal when it turned out that WorldCom had contributed $100,000 to his record $30 million June fund-raiser—and that the Republicans wouldn't return the tainted money.

Was the political-press stampede spurred by Enron/Adelphia/Global Crossings/Tyco/WorldCom just another moment in the bubble-bust story of capitalism, or might it lead to a shift in our political zeitgeist? Just as farmer outrage at eastern banks and consumer disgust after Upton Sinclair's *The Jungle* sparked the Progressive Era at the turn of the last century, and the Depression cast Republicans and executives into the darkness for decades, will the current crisis again remind voters why laissez isn't always fair?

It's too early to know whether we're in the midst of another "turning point" in the words of Kevin Phillips. Surely, though, when such a business stalwart as Federal Reserve Board Chair Alan Greenspan, a devotee of Ayn Rand, condemns "infectious greed" and President Bush (his administration "looks, behaves and thinks exactly like the board of a Fortune 500 company," concludes *The Times* of London) says in the Rose Garden "no more easy money for corporate criminals—just hard time," *something* big is happening. And it's probably not good news for antiregulation, anti–campaign reform Republicans. From Reagan to Gingrich, their mantra has been to deregulate, privatize, and allow the "magic of the marketplace" to be free of big government. Yesterday's conservative shibboleths largely evaporated after Ken Lay and Bernie Ebbers became more famous than they intended.

At the least, the corporate governance scandals have helpfully educated the public about civic values—not those of bluenoses more interested in peccadilloes than policies, but those described by Michael Tomasky, who wrote in the *Washington Post*:

"Values" can mean something else now, like integrity in business and government. It means that a president who ran on a
promise of "restoring dignity" to the White House ought to tell
the truth about how long he's known the CEO who has been
his biggest corporate backer. It means that the vice president
should recognize as a simple ethical matter that the people . . .
have a right to know which lobbyists he met with while formulating a major policy, just as Republicans demanded similar
information from Clinton's health policy panel back in 1993.

Based on this broader view of public ethics, rewarding contributors
with a night in the Lincoln Bedroom was embarrassing. But rewarding
contributors with policy in the "Enron Bedroom" is far worse.

The next major development is McCain-Feingold—the first significant campaign finance law in a quarter century. Curiously, when
the bill was first introduced in 1995, banning so-called soft money
(large, unregulated contributions made to parties, not candidates) was
only a peripheral provision. But when Congress stiffened its opposition
to any public financing system just as soft money gifts geometrically
grew, the lead authors shifted their focus. Senator Russell Feingold
(D–WI), an intense, cheerful man who is perfectly in step with Wisconsin's maverick tradition, described how a colleague quietly urged
Feingold on after admitting that he himself had asked a major industry
in his state for a $250,000 soft-money gift—and got it. "I felt like I
needed a shower," said the disgusted senator.

It took a confluence of events to produce even this "modest beginning" of a law, as Feingold himself characterized it: John McCain's
presidential campaign focusing on campaign finance reform; the
Enron scandal, with a story line that shareholders, employees, and
pensioners everywhere could understand; the addition of four new
Democratic senators in favor of the bill; and a broad citizen-labor coalition led by Common Cause and Public Citizen. Even then its enactment was regarded as "remarkable" by Mark Schmitt, an expert on the
subject at the Open Society Institute: "House members never defy
their leadership by signing a discharge petition (they did); the Senate
never passes House bills unchanged (it did); coalitions never stick

together through every amendment (the reform coalition in the House did); Senators never influence House members (John McCain did)."

But just as Enron (epic event 1) helped create McCain-Feingold (epic event 2), this law is now leading to epic event 3—the first Supreme Court decision on the subject since 1976's disastrous *Buckley v. Valeo,* which both allowed and accelerated the current scandal.

By mid-2003 the Court will likely rule on the law's two major provisions—to ban soft money fund-raising by the national parties and to restrict "independently" financed electioneering ads thirty and sixty days before primaries and general elections, respectively. In so doing, it will either reverse or ratify the earlier 6–2 ruling declaring that legislatively enacted "expenditure limits" were an unconstitutional infringement on speech. If *Buckley* had come to a different conclusion, there would be no $2 million House candidates today, no $15 million Senate candidates, no $74 million mayoral candidates.

In other words, the two-hundred-year-long movement to make sure that citizens speak louder than contributors has come to a critical juncture. We are at what Bill Moyers calls "a teachable moment."

⟪◉ ◉⟫

It's referred to as the "revolution of rising expectations." Once a long-endured evil is acknowledged and abated, victims will not be satisfied with half measures. Alexis de Tocqueville observed this paradox when the most fervid advocates of the French Revolution resided where the standard of living had risen the most: "It happens very often that a people who has suffered the most crushing laws without complaining, as if it did not even feel them, jettisons them violently as soon as the oppressive weight is lifted somewhat," de Tocqueville concluded. "The French found their position all the more intolerable as it became better."

Or recall Mikhail Gorbachev's reforms behind the Iron Curtain. He believed he'd win human rights awards for his policies of perestroika and glasnost. Instead, the Soviet Union lost Eastern Europe. Lech Walesa of Poland and Václav Havel of Czechoslovakia wouldn't accept partial freedom when they saw the sunny horizon of full freedom.

Fred Wertheimer of the pro-campaign-reform group Democracy 21 believes that when it comes to campaign finance reforms, 2002 America is now, in effect, 1789 France or 1989 Eastern Europe. "Winning McCain-Feingold will open the door to another round," he says in his downtown Washington, D.C., office, its walls lined with sixty years of Herblock cartoons on money in politics. "And we have put together the best coalition I've ever seen on an issue—from the AARP to the Sierra Club to labor and some businesses."

But overcoming what Pogo once called the "insurmountable opportunities" in any "next round" will be very hard, for the same two big reasons that have long stymied change: there are 535 experts in Congress loath to change the rules that got them there and have kept them there; and there are hundreds of large interests who invest thousands and reap billions, a rate of return unrivaled since IBM and Microsoft went public. Economic interests may not "like" the money chase, to quote Representative Shannon's business lobbyist, but they also don't "like" the regulation and taxation that they believe reduce their profits and bonuses.

In the short term, most observers believe that it will take the confluence of a presidential aspirant again making this tainted political culture a major plank (and then winning the Oval Office) and another scandal or two or three. New presidents are allowed early legislative victories, like Reagan's and Bush's deep tax cuts; and Washington often legislates by headlines, such as the way thalidomide babies led to Senator Kefauver's legislation that improved drug safety and Ryan White's death produced more funding to stop AIDS.

But why do we need more scandals (which will surely occur)? Isn't the recent "corporate crime wave"—to use *Business Week*'s phrase—quite enough? In any event, here the scandal *is* the system—the smoking gun *is* a campaign law that encourages not so much elections as auctions. It was Watergate special prosecutor Archibald Cox, in another context, who observed that the problem isn't what's illegal, but what's legal. The problem today isn't bad people but a bad system that coerces good people to do bad things in order to hold on to office.

Just as pollution inspired Earth Day and then the federal Environmental Protection Agency, a campaign finance system tolerating spending increases of 1000 percent in twenty-five years will at some point explode and collapse—or else lead to a world in which some Democratic state chair will ask a U.S. Senate aspirant in 2020, "Where's your $50 million?"

Two available reforms could cut this golden Gordian knot.

First, a public matching-funds law (discussed at length in chapter 7): given the hundreds of billions lost in the S&L scandals of the 1980s and the corporate crime/accounting scams of 2002, a public financing program costing millions would appear to be quite a bargain. Its rationale is simple: if, say, twenty special interests each give a senator $100,000, they own him or her; if instead a million taxpayers each give $2 in public funds, *we* own him or her. Isn't it preferable for elected officials to be more responsive to all voters than a relatively few donors?

Such a measure has three notable virtues: it has already worked successfully in presidential campaigns and in New York City, Arizona, and Maine elections; it avoids First Amendment arguments, since it *increases* speech; and it is popular—majorities of 70 percent regularly support dramatic reforms, such as creating floors under, and ceilings over, spending. Two conservative senators from Mississippi, Democrat John Stennis (who served from 1947 to 1989) and Republican Thad Cochran (1979 to date) have switched from being adamantly against to ardently for public financing of public elections; if they can do so, so might others.

Second, a future Supreme Court should overturn *Buckley* and uphold the constitutionality of an expenditure ceiling. These two changes would reduce the influence of donors and elevate the influence of citizens; reduce the pressure on candidates to sell their souls to pay for last-minute TV ads, giving them the "freedom not to grovel," in the words of a *New York Times* editorial; and stop multimillionaires from exploiting the "unfair advantage" of being able to buy elections.

Impossible? Not really. The history of America shows a "capacity for self-correction." Obvious abuses often yield to human rights: the three-fifths clause of the Constitution and the 1857 *Dred Scott* decision were reversed by *Brown v. Board of Education* and the 1965 Voting Rights Act. A century ago it was regarded as laughable for women to vote; now it's laughable to realize they once didn't. In 1980, the Berlin

Wall, the Soviet Union, and apartheid all appeared to be immutable; a few short years later, they were all gone. At the height of the Cold War, the two superpowers were in a race to build nuclear arms; now we're decommissioning them. And the Supreme Court itself, given enough time, has reversed itself on such issues as affirmative action, right to counsel, poll taxes, and health and safety regulations.

"History is like waves lapping at a cliff," wrote French historian Henry See. "For centuries nothing happens. Then the cliff collapses."

Surely campaign finance reform will not prove harder to achieve than the end of apartheid and the Cold War. Only apologists for the status quo could possibly believe that it's OK for a powerful 0.1 percent of the population to dictate policy to the other 99.9 percent; for only the rich or the kept to win office; for candidates to spend three quarters of their time raising money so that the toll takers known as broadcasters who control the publicly owned airwaves will allow public candidates to speak to the public.

Indeed, on the day this book went to the printer, the U.S. Court of Appeals for the Second Circuit in Manhattan upheld a Vermont law challenging *Buckley*'s core conclusion that spending limits were unconstitutional. In striking language, the majority in *Landell v. Sorrell* said, "Absent expenditure limitations…the race for campaign funds has compelled public officials to give preferred access to contributors, selling their time in order to raise campaign funds.…Quid pro quo corruption is troubling not because certain citizens are victorious in the legislative process but because they achieve the victory by paying public officials for it."

The evil of access.

Either democracy will trump plutocracy, or plutocracy will trump democracy. It is a contest as old as the country. Exactly 210 years ago, in a May 1792 letter, Thomas Jefferson wrote George Washington about the political alignments taking shape—of yeomen versus Tory financiers. Jefferson urged Washington to rally the people into a party that "would defend democracy against the corrupt ambitions of monied interests." The descent of democracy will end when an outraged, organized public tells Congress to tell the Enrons and WorldComs, the Norquists and Keatings that America means majority rule, not money rule.

THE HISTORY OF MONEY IN POLITICS
Scandal, Reform, Scandal...

"An honest politician is one who, when he is bought, stays bought."
—Nineteenth-century senator Simon Cameron, 1862

"Follow the money."
—Deep Throat, 1973

Since its creation, the United States has thought of itself as a society based on the principle of political equality. Despite our lofty aspirations, political power in America has often been a function of wealth rather than citizenship. We talk about one person, one vote, but in practice the vote of a wealthy donor has always mattered more than the vote of the average citizen.

At the founding of the republic, only white male property owners were enfranchised. As a result, of the 4 million citizens living in America at the time of the Revolution, only 800,000 were eligible to vote. The U.S. Constitution's original method for apportioning representation in the House of Representatives treated blacks as only three fifths of a full person. In Maryland in 1776, a person was required to own at least £5000 worth of property to run for governor, and £1000 worth to run for state senator. Even as Thomas Jefferson declared that all men are created equal, African slaves worked his fields, Native Americans were exploited, and all of the country's white women and the majority of its white men were forced to watch their new democracy from the sidelines. A small, wealthy, landed aristocracy ruled early America.

The United States has obviously made huge advances since then toward human freedom and democratic rights. But we still have a government largely of the few, the rich, and the privileged. To understand why money and political power are still so closely linked, it is necessary to look at the history of money in American politics. It is a story filled with corruption, greed, scandal, and reform. Then the cycle repeats itself in different forms. Is the cycle inevitable, or is a different kind of politics possible? In a country where capitalism and democracy exist side by side, will private wealth always control public policy? Before discussing what is and what can be, let's look at what was.

"Swilling the Planters with Bumbo"

Elections in early America were nothing like the media spectacles we witness today. Indeed, outright campaigning was frowned upon as ungentlemanly, if not corrupt. But that didn't keep candidates from devising creative ways to win favor with voters. Since the eligible voting populace was relatively small, candidates focused most of their energy on meeting and swaying voters face-to-face. One of their favorite methods was to ply voters with alcohol. Known as "swilling the planters with bumbo," this practice involved throwing lavish parties called "treats" to which local property owners would be invited and thus convinced of a candidate's qualifications through his hospitality. The landed gentry of colonial America probably inherited the practice from the English aristocrats they emulated, who in turn could trace treating back to fifteenth-century England and before that to ancient Athens and Rome.

One candidate known for his hospitality was none other than George Washington. In 1758 Washington ran for the Virginia House of Burgesses. Since he was away on duty with the British army, Washington asked his friends to serve as his campaign managers, instructing them to spare no expense in their efforts to win votes. Hosting numerous treats in Washington's honor prior to the election, his managers provided 160 gallons of alcohol to 391 voters on election day, more than 1.5 quarts per voter. Of course, all this entertaining cost money, and Washington's managers promptly sent him the receipts for their expenditures. One bill included charges for 50 gallons of rum punch, 28 gallons of rum, 46 gallons of beer, 34 gallons of wine, and 2 gallons of hard cider. Washington's hospitality paid off. He was elected "by a number of votes more than any other candidate," 78 percent of the total.

Treating is not as much a part of the Founding Father's folklore as felling the cherry tree or crossing the Delaware, perhaps because technically this kind of campaigning was illegal. Virginia law at the time prohibited candidates from "directly or indirectly" providing voters with "money, meat, drink, present, gift, reward, or entertainment . . . in order to be elected." For the most part, the law was either ignored or interpreted creatively. Since it banned treating only "in order to be elected," candidates exploited this loophole by throwing parties year-round and by inviting both friends and enemies.

Consequently, it was relatively expensive to run for political office in 1758. But since most candidates were wealthy aristocrats like Washington, they didn't seem to mind much. After winning the election and receiving the large bill for the rum his managers provided to voters, for example, Washington wrote to one of them: "I am extremely thankful to you and my other friends for entertaining the Freeholders in my name. I hope that no exceptions were taken to any that voted against me but that all were alike treated and all had enough; it is what I much desired. My only fear is that you spent with too sparing a hand."

Then as now, however, there were those who objected to the idea of buying and liquoring one's way into office. James Madison was an ardent critic of the practice of treating. In 1777 he lost a bid for the Virginia legislature because, according to his own account, he refused to provide voters with alcohol. In his autobiography, he explained that it was "the usage for the Candidates to recommend themselves to the voters, not only by personal solicitation, but by the corrupting influence of spirituous liquors, and other treats having like tendency." Madison refused to participate in the practice. His supporters filed a protest charging his opponent with "bribery and corruption," but probably due to the widespread practice of treating, the elections committee refused to view gifts of liquor as improper.

Another way money played a role in early elections was through the practice of helping citizens buy land, thus helping them become eligible to vote. In the 1790s, Aaron Burr, the leader of New York's nascent Tammany Hall political machine, recruited wealthy Democrats to loan money to selected workingmen so that they could buy land and become Democratic voters. Eventually Burr found this practice prohibitively expensive, so he persuaded the state assembly to create an anti-Federalist state bank that would do the lending instead.

Money was also used to sway public opinion through the press. Not content with just buying advertisements, candidates came up with the idea of using campaign funds to create their own newspapers to promote their particular candidacy. Anti-Federalists in Philadelphia consolidated their wealth in order to support the *National Gazette* as a party mouthpiece, and Federalists did the same for the *Gazette of the United States*. In fact, in order to get the *National Gazette* off the ground in 1791, Thomas Jefferson hired a poet, Philip Freneau, as a clerk in the State Department and at the same time installed him as the newspaper's editor. Throughout his career Jefferson used his own money to publish his campaign literature; successors such as James Buchanan and Abraham Lincoln continued the practice, with the former spending $10,000 in personal funds to establish a newspaper dedicated to supporting his candidacy.

The Emergence of Professional Politics

Despite the practice of treating, loaning for land, and literally buying publicity, campaign costs in early America remained relatively low. The election of Andrew Jackson in 1828, however, marked a turning point for campaign finance. Since then, money has been the grease that more than anything else makes the wheels of American democracy turn.

The 1828 election was the first in American history in which the popular vote played an important role. By that year, twenty-two of the twenty-four states in the Union had begun to choose their presidential electors through a popular vote, rather than through the state legislatures. Most states had also abandoned the property requirement for voting, and the vote of the everyday (white) man became decisive. Active campaigning became a necessity. Door-to-door electioneering boomed, and so, therefore, did campaign costs.

Although no definite figures are available, it is estimated that a congressional campaign in this period could cost as much as $4000. Gubernatorial races cost closer to $10,000, and a presidential race $50,000. Even as the importance of the common man was on the rise, political office was still restricted to the very wealthy, or at least to those who could find wealthy supporters.

Jackson's opponent in 1828, the incumbent John Quincy Adams, was of the old school when it came to campaigning. For Adams electioneering was still a dirty word, and he refused to take part in any organizational aspects of his campaign. "To pay money for securing [the presidency] directly or indirectly," he wrote, "was . . . incorrect in principle."

Jackson, on the other hand, was eager to avenge what he called the "corrupt bargain" between Adams and Henry Clay, which he believed robbed him of the presidency in 1824, and he began his 1828 campaign as early as 1825. Jackson's supporters established a reelection committee, and started a nationwide effort to solidify support. They also established a network of partisan newspapers spanning the country to support their candidate and to spread venom about Adams.

As president, Jackson is credited with establishing the practice of patronage when he replaced 40 percent of the federal bureaucracy with his own party's operatives. This move would have a huge impact on future campaigning; his appointees would eventually become the backbone of party politics for years to come. It is estimated that by the middle of the nineteenth century as many as 50,000 patronage positions were available in the federal government, with countless more available at the state and local levels.

As participation in the political process became more widespread, a new class of political technicians emerged. These political operatives were paid for their campaign skills, and if their candidate won, they were awarded a patronage position, which then obliged them to contribute to the party again in the next election. This started a practice where appointees were required to contribute a portion of their paycheck back to the political machine that appointed them. In New York City, for example, city employees were required to contribute 6 percent of their weekly pay to the Tammany Hall campaign fund.

The expansion of the electorate also produced the first truly national campaigns, driven by the need to reach more voters than ever before. To manage these campaigns, political strategists needed much more disciplined political parties to shape public opinion and to get out the vote. The development of more organized political parties also led to the emergence of party conventions as the favored method for selecting party candidates, at both the state and national levels. These campaign developments made money more important than ever. No longer was a little liquor enough to do the trick.

The Jacksonian era also marked the first attempts by corporations to influence the political process. In an effort to secure its recharter, for one prominent example, the Second Bank of the United States undertook a massive publicity campaign. Between 1830 and 1832 the bank spent $42,000 to publish pamphlets aimed at swaying public opinion. According to an early biographer, Jackson saw the recharter issue as "one of the greatest struggles between democracy and the money power." In his fifth State of the Union address, President Jackson said that the recharter issue was about "whether the people of the United States are to govern through representatives chosen by their unbiased suffrages, or whether the power and money of a great corporation are to be secretly exerted to influence their judgment and control their decisions."

Mass participation in the electoral process, increasingly expensive campaigns, and electoral high stakes meant that politicians became willing to buy votes outright. In New York City in 1823, the price of a vote was $5, which was then a few days' pay for the average worker. In 1838, both parties in New York imported repeat voters from Philadelphia and paid them as much as $30 each. And this was just the beginning.

Money Starts to Talk

The political rise of Abraham Lincoln was emblematic of the new marriage of money and politics that formed in the 1850s and 1860s. Lincoln, who began his political career as a stump speaker for other candidates, was initially able to finance his own campaign efforts, but his expenses soon became too high. For his unsuccessful U.S. Senate race against Stephen Douglas in 1858, Lincoln arranged expense accounts paid for by wealthy supporters, on which he was able to draw as much as $500 per donor. Nonetheless the campaign bankrupted him, and he wrote at its end that he was "absolutely without money now for even household purposes." Lincoln was forced to go back to his successful law practice to rebuild his finances.

Lincoln soon was able to gather enough money to run for the presidency in 1860, including paying the expenses of a loyal delegate to the Republican National Convention in Chicago. To build popular support for his candidacy, Lincoln secretly purchased a small Illinois newspaper for $400 and persuaded the editor to use the paper as a Republican propaganda mouthpiece. A national presidential campaign required big money, though, and for this he was forced to turn to the leading businessmen of New York City and Philadelphia. The campaign cost the Republican Party more than $100,000, four times what Buchanan's race had cost the Democrats only four years earlier.

In contrast, the divided Democratic Party could not raise the money necessary for a strong campaign. August Belmont, a wealthy Democrat serving as a chief fund-raiser in New York, wrote nominee Stephen Douglas that "if we could demonstrate to all those lukewarm and selfish moneybags that we have a strong possibility of [victory], we might be able to get from them the necessary sinews of war." But the money didn't come through for "the little giant," and neither did the votes: in 1860, Lincoln famously reversed the results of 1858.

After the Civil War, campaign costs continued their constant rise, as both parties began to rely more and more on wealthy individuals for the "sinews of war." In the presidential campaign of 1868, one man, Jay Cooke, a wealthy banker from Ohio who had been key in arranging financial support of the Union war effort, contributed $20,000 of the total $200,000 raised by Republicans to support General Ulysses S. Grant's candidacy. Cooke saw his contribution as an insurance policy for his continued banking success; as he wrote to William Chandler, a longtime secretary of the Republican National Committee, if "it is necessary for you to have more money, of course, you shall have it." Large contributions were also made by the Vanderbilts, the Astors, and several others who had all grown rich from the war and hoped to cash in their wealth for political influence.

Apparently these men thought their investment well worth it; they continued to contribute large sums throughout their lives. In the campaign of 1872, Cooke contributed an unprecedented $50,000 to the Republicans—a quarter of the total they raised that year. One historian of the time wrote, "never before was a candidate placed under such a great obligation to men of wealth as was Grant."

Not to be outflanked, a group of eight wealthy New York Democrats tried to recruit Grant to run on their party's ticket. But when they realized he was going Republican they had to pool their resources to avoid either a Republican presidency or a Democratic one contrary to their business interests. To ensure the necessary funds, the men signed a contract with the chairman of the Democratic National Executive Committee, pledging to raise or contribute $10,000 each "to defray the just and lawful expenses of circulating documents and newspapers, perfecting organizations etc., to promote the election" of their preferred candidate. Economic issues divided the party, and the battle for the nomination was hotly contested and expensive.

Political commentators, journalists, and public officials during this period began to publicly denounce the strengthening grip of money on politics. It came to be called the Gilded Age for its extravagance. Its paradigmatic moment was the Crédit Mobilier scandal—the Watergate of its era—when the Union Pacific Railroad was caught dispensing many millions in bribes throughout Washington. While each party accused the other of shady deal-making and outright bribery, newspaper editorialists and cartoonists had a field day. Joseph Keppler's classic cartoon "Bosses of the Senate" depicted corpulent bosses named "Sugar Trust" and "Standard Oil Trust" towering over tiny senators. In 1873 Edward Ryan, chief justice of the Wisconsin Supreme Court, declared to the graduating class of the University of Wisconsin, "There is looming up a new and dark power. . . . The enterprises of the country are aggregating vast corporate combinations of unexampled capital, boldly marching, not for economic conquests only, but for political power. For the first time really in our politics, money is taking the field as an organized power." He continued his jeremiad: "The question will arise, and arise in your day, though perhaps not fully in mine, 'which shall rule—wealth or man, which shall lead—money or intellect; who shall fill public stations—educated and patriotic free men, or the feudal serfs of corporate capital?'" Subsequent events of the era vindicated Justice Ryan's anxiety.

The Age of Bribery

The period following the Civil War was the most politically corrupt time in American history. This era of bribery and scandal began in the 1860s, with Boss William Marcy Tweed of Tammany Hall. As a state senator, Tweed led a group of New York legislators called the Black Horse Cavalry who openly sold their votes for cash. During the battle over whether Jay Gould or Commodore Vanderbilt would control the Erie Railroad, votes sold for as much as $5,000. Gould later reflected, "I was a Republican in Republican districts, a Democrat in Democratic districts."

From the 1850s through the 1870s, a Pennsylvania Republican Party operative and politician named Simon Cameron perfected the practice of buying off legislators, and served as a mentor for later political extortionists. Cameron repeatedly bribed members of the state legislature, once paying $20,000 for a single needed vote. Cameron invented the "Pennsylvania Idea," which held that it was just and proper for corporations to use their wealth to help the Republican Party maintain its control over the legislature—even if such support was used for buying votes. Cameron described his political machine as "a regularly constituted agency for purchasing votes and the other vehicles of political power."

Since U.S. senators were at the time elected by state legislatures rather than by popular vote, it was possible, even easy, for someone to buy himself a seat. Blatant bribery occurred in Kansas, Colorado,

Montana, and West Virginia—and those are just the ones we know about. In Montana the bribery was so open that William A. Clark was forced to resign his Senate seat after an investigation revealed that he had bought it. Paying for one's Senate seat either through direct or indirect means was so widespread that the Senate was known as a millionaire's club; a popular aphorism said "It is harder for a poor man to enter the United States Senate than for a rich man to enter Heaven." The methods may have changed since then, but the bottom line apparently hasn't: today, almost half of all U.S. senators are millionaires.

Another popular practice was to extract payoffs from corporations through the use of "squeeze bills" or "strike bills." Used by Tammany Hall as well as other political machines across the country, squeeze bills were those introduced purely with the intent of scaring a particular corporate interest into paying for the measure's defeat. This practice became so commonplace and profitable that it supplanted outright bribery; as Mark Twain sarcastically commented, "I think I can say, and say with pride, that we have legislatures that bring higher prices than any in the world."

Vote buying and voter coercion at election time was also practiced on a scale never seen before. In cities like New York and Philadelphia, tightly controlled political machines such as Tammany Hall ran neighborhoods as small fiefdoms, each devoted to a particular political party and monitored by a powerful citywide political boss. The machine would dole out favors and provide protection to neighborhood residents in exchange for their votes. Before standardized ballots were introduced, the different political machines made their own ballots and employed watchers to ensure that no voters forgot who owned them. In a process as efficient as it was immoral, voters were paid for their support directly after casting their ballot.

Once standard ballots were introduced, political machines simply invented more creative ways to guarantee that their candidate prevailed. In Atlantic City, for example, Boss Kuehnle provided voters with carbon ballots to be placed under the real ballot. After voting for the machine candidate, the voter would take the carbon copy as proof to the ward boss in charge of vote buying and receive his pay. And it wasn't purely an urban problem either: one political analyst in 1892 estimated that 16 percent of voters in Connecticut were for sale.

A less obvious form of corruption was the practice of political assessment, a financial stepchild of the patronage system. Under political assessment, both elected and appointed officeholders were assessed a fee to be paid to their political party. For most of the nineteenth century, the majority of a party's campaign expenses were raised this way. The idea was that the officeholders owed their jobs to their party, and it was only natural that they should be expected to help replenish the party coffers to retain their job after the next election. Boss Kelly of Tammany Hall turned assessment into a science by establishing a standardized system based on the level of the office sought. A candidate for mayor was required to contribute up to $30,000, a comptroller $10,000, and a district attorney $5000.

In 1883 this system of political assessment provoked one of the earliest efforts to reform the political money system. The Pendleton Act of 1883 outlawed, among other things, contributions from federal employees; this drove political fund-raisers to find alternative sources of cash. By removing this primary source of campaign revenue, the act instead increased reliance on funding from wealthy businessmen and corporations.

One fund-raiser who mastered the post–Pendleton Act shift to corporate funding was Republican senator Boies Penrose. Described as a man who "fought his way down rather than up in the world," Penrose was a fund-raiser of mythic proportions. At six feet six inches and weighing in at over 300 pounds, he was famous for his enormous appetite for food and prostitutes alike. Penrose wielded enormous power over both corporations and fellow politicians. In order to replace the money lost from political assessments, he developed a process called "frying the fat," whereby corporations were pressured through squeeze bills and other extortionist tactics until the heat was so unbearable that they handed over whatever contribution the senator demanded.

Penrose was so adept at using his power to pressure businessmen and corporations into "giving" that in one forty-eight-hour period he

was able to raise $250,000 for his successful 1896 U.S. Senate cam-
paign, which he then used to bribe the Pennsylvania legislature. Penrose was also not embarrassed by his tactics. "I believe in the division
of labor," he once candidly told a group of supporters. "You send us to
Congress; we pass laws under which you make money . . . and out of
your profits, you further contribute to our campaign funds to send us
back again to pass more laws to enable you to make more money."

Even more than Cameron or Penrose, however, it was another
Republican, Mark Hanna, who was responsible for turning the practice of collecting corporate campaign cash into a science. A wealthy
Ohio industrialist and shipper, Hanna was the first political operative
to develop an organized and systematic approach to extracting corporate contributions. He realized that he could exploit the economic anxieties of banks and corporations as leverage for political contributions.
Under Hanna's system, banks were assessed at 0.25 percent of their
capital and corporations were assessed according to their "stake in the
general prosperity of the country." The system was so precise that
$50,000 was *returned* to Standard Oil, one of the largest and most
powerful corporations in the country, because its correct assessment
was $250,000 and it had overpaid.

Hanna's money-raising prowess made him a star in the Republican
galaxy. And after spending $100,000 of his own money to secure the
presidential nomination of William McKinley in 1896, he became the
chairman of the Republican National Committee. Beyond just raising
money, though, Hanna also knew how to spend it: McKinley's run for
the presidency that year is regarded as the prototype for the modern
campaign, in which vast sums of money are spent to advertise the candidate like a soft drink. The industrialist spent millions of dollars to
put McKinley's face on thousands of posters, buttons, billboards, and
pamphlets. Thanks to Hanna's fund-raising and advertising efforts,
McKinley's campaign was the most expensive in history, a title
retained until after World War I.

Hanna took pains to avoid the appearance of a quid pro quo, even
going so far as to return $10,000 to a group of Wall Street bankers
whose demands were too specific. But there was still an "explicit recognition" by supporters that by contributing to the Republican Party they

were "paying for a definite service." According to Hanna biographer Herbert Croly, corporations knew that by contributing to the Republicans they were helping their own cause—for if the Republicans won, "the politics of the country would be managed in the interests of business," as Hanna himself openly acknowledged. While Cameron, Penrose, and Hanna—whose political skills have been praised by Karl Rove, President Bush's top political adviser—may not have been ashamed of selling their political soul and vote to special interests, many Americans were beginning to recognize that government of the corporation, by the corporation, and for the corporation was nowhere to be found in the U.S. Constitution. The system was no doubt logical and beneficial to those who gave and got, but it abandoned the millions of taxpayers who weren't rich enough to buy an influential ear, leaving them to watch their government from the sidelines.

Progressive Reform?

As the nineteenth century became the twentieth, public outrage over backroom payoffs, outright vote buying, and corporate corruption of the political process began to build. The rise of the Progressives was partly a backlash against what many Americans saw as the excessive influence of money in politics. Recognizing the need to regulate corporate power, Progressives advocated such economic and political reforms as antitrust laws, fair labor standards, women's suffrage, and greater citizen participation in and control of politics. Muckraking journalists, political satirists, and Progressive advocates exposed the destructive power of unrestrained monopolies and the corrupting influence of political money. At the local and state levels, Progressives attempted to reform the political process through secret and standardized ballots, stricter voter registration procedures, restrictions on corporate lobbying and campaign contributions, the use of the referendum, and direct primaries.

Then occurred an event that shifted the battle lines between corruption and reform: the assassination of President McKinley in September 1901, only a few months into his second term, which elevated

Theodore Roosevelt, his war-hero vice president, to the Oval Office. Roosevelt had been added to the McKinley ticket partly because Republican political bosses like Matthew Quay of Pennsylvania wanted him politically "out of the way." On the McKinley funeral train from Buffalo to Washington, Mark Hanna, now a U.S. senator, was heard cursing the day McKinley chose him.

Roosevelt was exactly the kind of president Hanna feared he would be. The Rough Rider's distaste for corporate influence in politics in general, and his vigorous trust-busting activities in particular, persuaded the usual corporate contributors that Roosevelt would not faithfully represent their interests. Hanna, still a Republican Party kingmaker, led the business opposition to Roosevelt's reelection, and for a while hinted that he himself might be their candidate. But Hanna died before the 1904 election, and eventually corporate financiers realized that Roosevelt was their only choice.

Any Progressive hopes for less corporate influence in the 1904 campaign were also quickly shattered. Fearing defeat, Roosevelt rejected pleas by Progressives to rely on small individual contributions and turned instead for financial support to the very bankers and industrialists who had only recently supported Hanna as the most acceptable Republican candidate. Roosevelt especially worried about losing in his native New York, but his campaign operatives assured him victory could be had as long as "the funds were furnished." Some of the country's richest men—Cornelius Bliss, J. P. Morgan, and Andrew Carnegie among them—contributed hundreds of thousands of dollars, and once it was known that the President was accepting corporate money, other financiers flooded the campaign with contributions, many of which were never publicized. Roosevelt won the presidency by a landslide.

Roosevelt's reliance on corporate money to finance his campaign was a topic of bitter controversy, and eventually led to the first real attempts at comprehensive campaign finance reform. In the final days of the race, Democratic nominee Alton Parker charged that the Republican Party was whoring itself to the corporations. At the same time, it was alleged that E. H. Harriman had raised $250,000 for the Republican Party, of which $50,000 came from his own pocket, in exchange for a promise by Roosevelt to appoint New York senator Chauncey Depew ambassador to France. "They are in a hole," Harriman bragged to an aide, "and the President wants me to help them out." Roosevelt vigorously denied the charge and Depew wasn't appointed, but the President was never able to shake the presumption that a quid pro quo had indeed been involved. Like Watergate seven decades later, the general stink of corruption led to a national call for reform.

Roosevelt himself was embarrassed by his reliance on corporate money. "Sooner or later, unless there is a readjustment," he complained to a reporter during the campaign, "there will come a riotous, wicked, murderous day of atonement." Nevertheless, Roosevelt was too calculating, or too enamored of the presidency, to acknowledge the full corrupting potential of big money in politics. "It is entirely legitimate to accept contributions, no matter how large they are, from individuals and corporations," he wrote in defense of his fund-raising efforts, as long as funds were raised with an "explicit understanding that they were given and received with no thought of any more obligation."

On the defensive, Roosevelt's first message to Congress after his election included a call for the publication of spending records by both political committees and candidates. There was already a movement for legislation requiring the disclosure of campaign expenditures by the National Publicity Law Association, a citizens' lobbying group. New York adopted such a disclosure law for state elections, but despite the President's endorsement of the association's goal for a national law, Congress delayed adopting any federal disclosure requirements for a decade.

At the local level, corruption continued without pause. In 1905, as many as 170,000 votes were bought in one district in Ohio. In New York City, an investigation revealed that 26 percent of voters had sold their vote for cash. In fact, vote buying was still so widespread that one Ohio woman defended her husband's decision to sell her vote by saying "we thought it was the law to pay us for our votes."

Public opinion was increasingly critical of the pervasiveness of corporate funding of campaigns. The discovery by New York State's Armstrong Committee of widespread attempts by insurance companies to influence state politics with campaign contributions caused a public outcry. When Charles Evans, counsel for the committee, asked Republican State Senator Thomas Platt if he felt morally obliged to work for the corporations that funded his campaign, he replied, "That is naturally what is involved."

In 1907 Congress finally responded with the first really significant campaign finance reform law, the Tillman Act. It outlawed campaign contributions and expenditures by banks and corporations—something that a century later many states, including New York, Illinois, and Florida, have still failed to do. The same year Congress also strengthened the Pendleton Act by prohibiting campaign participation by civil servants. Also in 1907, Teddy Roosevelt became the first president to propose caps on individual contributions, full disclosure of campaign funding and expenditures, and public financing of campaigns. "The need for collecting large campaign funds," Roosevelt said, "would vanish if Congress provided for an appropriation for the proper and legitimate expenses of each of the two great national parties."

Reform continued, and so did scandal. In 1908, for the first time in the nation's history, both presidential candidates volunteered to disclose their campaign funding sources and expenditures. This disclosure revealed that the Republicans spent $1.7 million and the Democrats spent $629,000. The same year two U.S. senators were charged with buying their seats from their respective state legislatures.

With Progressive legislators pushing continually for reform, the movement to require public disclosure of campaign funding and expenditures finally succeeded in 1910 with passage of the Publicity Act. Then, in 1911, Congress took the extraordinary step of limiting campaign contributions and expenditures for Senate and House campaigns to $10,000 and $5000, respectively; although the First Amendment had been around for more than a century, no commentators thought to claim that such restrictions on money violated the free speech of the rich. And finally, due to widespread public disgust over the buying of Senate seats through state legislatures, in 1913 the states ratified the Seventeenth Amendment, requiring that Senate elections be decided by popular vote.

Despite these essential reforms, money continued to pervade politics. Why? First, as the mass-advertising style of political campaigning invented by Mark Hanna became the predominant way to run for office, media costs and hence campaign costs continued to climb. Second, both the direct election of senators and the concurrent move to a direct primary as the prevalent method for choosing party candidates increased campaign costs. The passage in 1920 of the overdue Nineteenth Amendment granting suffrage to women also raised costs of reaching these new voters. It was the price of democracy, but it didn't come cheap.

After the 1907 prohibition on campaign contributions by banks and corporations, both parties simply relied more heavily on contributions from the heads of corporations. In fact, so much money was being spent on just the nomination of the GOP presidential candidate in 1920 that a special Senate committee was formed to investigate whether there was a plot to buy the nomination. Even though the committee found no such plot, the scandal undermined the Republican front-runner, Leonard Wood, and led to the nomination of Warren Harding instead. When all was said and over, it was revealed that the Republicans spent $6 million and the Democrats $1.4 million on the 1920 campaign.

In 1921, the Supreme Court ruled in *Newberry v. United States* that Congress had no constitutional authority to regulate spending in the primary process. (This overly restrictive view of federalism remained the law of the land until 1941, when in *United States v. Classic* the Court reversed *Newberry* and ruled that Congress did have the authority to regulate primaries wherever a state's election law influenced the general election. Congress did not assert its newly confirmed authority until three decades later.) Under *Newberry,* money was so pervasive and corruption such a fear that Calvin Coolidge felt compelled to declare in his speech accepting the 1924 Republican presidential nomination that "no individuals may expect any governmental favors in return for party assistance." Apparently, this had not been previously made clear.

The next year saw the passage of the Federal Corrupt Practices Act, the most ambitious attempt at reform to date. The act—provoked by the Teapot Dome Scandal where the company leasing the oil reserve bribed a leasing official and contributed huge amounts to retire the Republican Party's 1920 campaign debt—required candidates to report all receipts and expenditures in federal congressional campaigns but exempted presidential races. The law also imposed caps on federal campaign expenditures. As with previous attempts at reform, however, the act was full of loopholes and provisions without teeth. For one thing, the limits on expenditures were easily avoided by the claim that any excessive expenses were incurred without the candidate's "knowledge or consent." Moreover, by limiting expenditures by candidates themselves or by their political party only, the act later encouraged the creation of the first political action committees, through which campaign funds could be legally laundered. Not only was no auditing of campaign funding or expenditures required, but campaign financial statements filed with the clerk of the House of Representatives were virtually inaccessible, unintelligible, and very rarely made public. By almost all accounts, the act was essentially meaningless.

The weakness of federal law governing campaigns was vividly demonstrated in a 1926 Illinois Senate campaign by Republican candidate Frank M. Smith. He defeated the incumbent Republican by engaging him in a spending war in which each candidate illegally spent over half a million dollars. It was revealed that half of Smith's contributions came from public utilities executives who had cases pending before the Illinois Commerce Commission, of which Smith was the chairman. The Senate eventually refused to seat Smith or his Democratic opponent.

Also, in 1926, William Vare, a Republican congressman from Pennsylvania, seized on *Newberry* to start a spending war to defeat the incumbent in his party's Senate primary, and then went on to win the seat while flagrantly accepting illegal postprimary contributions. A formal investigation by the Senate Committee on Privileges and Elections revealed contributions by industrialists more than half a million dollars over the $10,000 limit set by the Corrupt Practices Act (and complied with by Vare's Democratic opponent). In response, the Senate refused to allow Vare to occupy the office. But corruption won out when the governor appointed Joseph Grundy, an industrialist who had himself illegally contributed more than half a million dollars to Vare's campaign. Vare was never prosecuted under the act's enforcement provisions. In fact, no one ever was.

The ineffectual Corrupt Practices Act would serve as the nation's only federal campaign finance regulation for the next forty-six years.

FDR vs. "Economic Royalists"

While the period before the Great Depression was marked by open and often tolerated corruption, after 1928 both parties' platforms gave lip service to the need to remove the taint of money from politics. But neither party did much to achieve that goal. The Republicans declared "the improper use of money in governmental and political affairs is a great national evil," and the Democrats condemned "the improper and excessive use of money in elections [as] a danger threatening the very existence of democratic institutions." Where candidates and parties had once openly flaunted the law, they now used loopholes and creative legal interpretations to shroud their money raising and spending in legitimacy. Money did not become less important, only less obvious—and corruption harder to detect.

In large measure due to the Depression, expenditures for the 1932 presidential campaign were relatively low. The financial advantage historically enjoyed by the Republican Party narrowed (when the campaign was over, the Republican National Committee spent $3 million, the Democratic National Committee $2.2 million). Franklin Roosevelt was chosen partly for his own personal wealth and his ability to obtain contributions from his wealthy friends. While the Depression soured public opinion against incumbent president Herbert Hoover, the Democrats still worried about being outspent. During the campaign, Democratic senator Huey Long commented half jokingly, "The problem with the Democrats is that we have all the votes and no money . . . the best thing we could do is to sell President Hoover a million votes for half what he is going to pay to try to get them. We can spare the votes and we could use the money." Though Roosevelt benefited from a group of wealthy benefactors—and was derided as a "traitor to his class," for doing so, FDR still became the first presidential candidate and president to explicitly attack wealthy contributors—as would subsequent political aspirants from John Anderson in 1980 to Gary Hart in 1984 to John McCain in 2000. Such attacks, not unexpectedly, produced more votes and fewer dollars.

Four years later Roosevelt's New Deal policies helped to again fill Republican coffers with financial support from outraged bankers and industrialists, and they built a strong opposition to FDR's reelection. Roosevelt rose to the challenge, famously declaring war on the "economic royalists" in no uncertain terms: "I welcome their hatred. . . . I should like to have it said of my first Administration that in it the forces of selfishness . . . have met their match . . . [and] I should like to have it said of my second Administration that in it these forces met their master."

As always happens, when the stakes are raised, so is spending. For the 1936 presidential election both parties returned to their old spending patterns, with the Republicans spending $8.9 million and the Democrats $5.2 million. That year also marked the first time labor unions contributed significantly to the political process, as the Democrats extracted half a million dollars from labor with almost complete secrecy. The Democrats also developed a creative way to circumvent the federal ban on corporate contributions. Printing up a "Book of the Democratic Convention of 1936," they made $250,000 selling advertising space. This practice caught on and became commonplace in the years that followed; by 1964 a one-page ad cost as much as $15,000.

The Hatch Act of 1940—both a GOP effort to curb unions and another attempt at political reform—limited the amount an individual could contribute to a federal candidate to $5000, but again the effort was largely cosmetic. First, it failed to prevent a large contribution from being divided among family members, allowing a large family to circumvent the $5000 limit easily. Second, the law failed to close a loophole, left open in earlier reform efforts, that enabled an individual to give an otherwise illegal contribution by dividing it up among various political committees all working to promote the same candidate.

In 1947 Congress extended the 1907 federal ban on corporate donations to include labor union contributions as well. But rather than reducing the influence of labor on politics by reducing the amount it could contribute, it actually strengthened labor's influence by provoking unions to become more strategic in their campaign activities. To circumvent the new law, the Congress of Industrial Organizations (CIO) coined the term "PAC" by creating the CIO-Political Action Committee, allowing it to work actively for candidates it felt were supportive of its interests without contributing directly to the candidates' campaigns. This idea revolutionized campaign finance and evolved into the independent expenditures that saturate the system today.

This period also saw the development of what has become perhaps the most standard method of collecting campaign checks: the pay-to-play fund-raising dinner. Invented by Democratic fund-raiser Matthew McCloskey to support FDR's inauguration, the practice quickly caught on as a fast, relatively easy way to raise large amounts of cash. The events began by charging $100 per plate, and in the years since 1936 the cost has skyrocketed: today a seat at a fund-raising dinner with a federal candidate routinely costs the $1000 legal limit (now raised to $2000 under the new McCain-Feingold law). Richard Nixon's presidential campaign in 1968 took the innovation one step further by linking twenty-two dinners together by closed-circuit television; the campaign was able to raise $4.6 million with one speech and a few thousand plates of stuffed chicken breast.

The New Media Age

The most significant development of the past century affecting campaign costs was the advent of radio and television. Radio, introduced in 1924, and then TV revolutionized the way campaigns are run; more than any other factor, they are responsible for the exponential growth of campaign costs over the past eighty years. In 1924 the Republican Party operated its own radio stations and broadcast for three straight weeks before the November election, an experiment that cost $120,000, or one third of their total publicity expenditures. And they won. Its effectiveness proven, spending on radio mushroomed four years later as the Democrats spent $650,000 and the Republicans $435,000.

More than radio, though, television has been the single most expensive campaign innovation in history. In 1946, it is estimated, there were only 8000 privately owned televisions in the United States, but by 1974, 97 percent of all American homes had a TV. Between 1952 and 1980, spending on radio and television political advertising went from less than $4 million to more than $30 million. In 2000, the parties spent a total of $200 million on political television advertising alone, and the Annenberg Public Policy Center tracked more than $500 million in TV spending on issue advocacy—ads that purported to push or attack a cause rather than a candidate.

The 1952 presidential campaign marks the beginning of a new era for campaign design and finance. From then on, campaigns would be dominated by highly organized polling of the electorate, costly media blitzes, professional political consultants, and nationally coordinated publicity and get-out-the-vote efforts. During the second half of the twentieth century, political campaigning in America became a massive industry unto itself. The total cost of all campaigns in the United States went from $200 million in 1964 to $1 billion in 1980 and over $4 billion in 2000—a 2000 percent increase in thirty-six years.

While some idealistic candidates tried to finance their campaigns by soliciting as many small contributions as possible, as campaign costs rose, the political parties' reliance on "fat cat" contributors increased exponentially. It was a whole lot easier to raise $100,000 from one financial angel than $1000 from each of 100 supporters. In 1948, 69 percent of the Democratic Party's revenue came from individuals who gave $500 or more. In 1956, 74 percent of the Republican Party's revenue came from such donors. By 1968 over 400 people gave more than $10,000 each to the parties. That same year Clement Stone, CEO of Combined Insurance Company, gave almost $3 million to pay for the prenomination expenses of Richard Nixon. To avoid contribution limits, Hubert Humphrey's campaign established more than ninety-five separate PACs, which enabled a contributor to give $5000 to each one. Organized labor was also a large contributor, giving almost $7 million in 1968.

The financial pressures of campaigning naturally led to the rise of the self-financed multimillionaire candidate. For it was even easier for a hugely wealthy candidate to write himself a $100,000 check than to persuade 100 people at $1000 each—or even one fat cat to give the same amount. In 1964 Nelson Rockefeller used his family fortune to mount an unsuccessful but expensive bid for the presidency. All told he spent about $3 million of his own money—an astonishing figure at the time—trying to win the Republican nomination. Rockefeller's example—combined with the Supreme Court's *Buckley* decision a decade later (see next chapter)—really launched the trend of self-financed candidates.

So much money entered the political process in the early days of the new media age that campaigns, not required to disclose contributions or expenditures during the prenomination period, couldn't or wouldn't keep track. According to one report from the 1968 campaign, the Democrats often paid bills in cash. One night after that year's Wisconsin primary, just before Lyndon Johnson withdrew from the race, a Democratic operative approached the man responsible for campaign funds and asked for payment for a large advertising bill. The two men then went to the men's room where the moneyman began to count out $100 bills on the toilet seat. "My God," the operative said to himself, "this is to renominate the President of the United States!"

More Reform and More Scandal

John F. Kennedy was the first modern president to recognize and to move against the dangers of too close a relationship between money and politics. Sensitive to accusations that his family's wealth was responsible for his political success, Kennedy made light of the issue at a campaign dinner in 1960, joking that after he announced that he "would not consider campaign contributions as a substitute for experience in appointing ambassadors," he suddenly stopped receiving contributions from his father. The candidate went on to make fun of the Nixon campaign's fixation on raising money. Noting Nixon's pledge not to use profanity on the stump, he said, "I am told that a prominent Republican said to him yesterday in Jacksonville, Florida, 'Mr.

President, that was a damn fine speech' [*Laughter*]. And the Vice President said, 'I appreciate the compliment but not the language.' And the Republican went on, 'Yes sir, I liked it so much that I contributed a thousand dollars to your campaign.' And Mr. Nixon replied, 'The hell you say.' [*Laughter and applause.*]"

In 1961, President Kennedy appointed a bipartisan Commission on Campaign Costs "to prepare and present to the President recommendations with respect to improved ways of financing expenditures required of nominees for the offices of President and Vice President." Formed even before the inauguration, the commission included Alexander Heard and Herbert Alexander, both giants in the study of campaign finance and eager reformers. The commission released its report less than a year later, detailing the ways in which money played an excessive role in the political process and outlining a plan for comprehensive reform. The report proposed:

- a tax credit for contributions up to $1000;

- the removal of the limit on expenditures by interstate political committees;

- full disclosure of all federal campaign spending by candidates and PACs;

- the creation of a registry of campaign finance data for enforcement and research purposes;

- government financing of a president-elect's transition costs.

In 1962 President Kennedy presented Congress with draft bills for each of the commission's proposals. Capitol Hill received the report without much interest, and there was no public demand for action. After Kennedy's assassination, the matter was dropped.

Over the next decade, however, so much more money entered the political system, and the use of loopholes became so flagrant, that the public resumed its clamor for reform. In 1964, four senators used the "knowledge or consent" loophole—they didn't know what their aides didn't tell them—to report *zero* campaign expenditures. Representative Jim Wright (D–TX), in 1966 congressional testimony, admitted that "there is not a member of Congress, myself included, who had not knowingly evaded its purpose in one way or another."

Embarrassed by media attention on the excesses of political money in the 1968 and 1970 campaign cycles, and spurred by newly formed citizens' lobbying groups like Common Cause and Public Citizen, Congress finally decided to act. In 1971, in a period of two months, it attempted to regulate campaign finance in a systemic way for the first time since the Federal Corrupt Practices Act of 1925. The landmark Federal Election Campaign Act (FECA) and the Revenue Act revolutionized campaign finance—at least on paper.

First, the FECA required far more disclosure than any previous reform effort, by compelling candidates and political committees to make detailed, periodic reports of contributions and expenditures and by making the information more accessible to the public. Every contribution of $100 or more had to be reported. (Needless to say, campaign coffers were filled with checks for $99.99.)

Second, it limited the amount a candidate could contribute to his or her own campaign. Presidential candidates were limited to $50,000 in personal and family contributions, senators to $35,000, and representatives to $25,000.

Third, the act limited the expenditures candidates could make for media purposes during any stage of the campaign process. House candidates were limited to $50,000, or 10 cents for every eligible voter in the district, whichever was greater. Senate candidates were limited to $50,000, or 10 cents for every eligible voter in the state. Limits on media expenditures by presidential campaigns were also calculated at 10 cents per eligible voter.

The Revenue Act gave taxpayers a choice to receive either a tax deduction or a tax credit for political contributions made to a campaign at any of the three levels of government. It also created a system allowing taxpayers to help subsidize a presidential campaign by checking off a box on their tax form indicating that they wished to participate.

One immediate effect of this reform effort was to start an all-out race to fill party war chests with as much unregulated cash as possible before the FECA went into effect on April 7, 1972. Between January and April, President Nixon's reelection campaign engaged in a concerted program to raise $10 million in unregulated and unreported contributions. In an effort eerily similar to Mark Hanna's corporate assessment scheme almost a century earlier, Nixon's campaign managers established a "conduit system" that assessed corporations 0.5 percent of their net worth. As one fund-raising letter put it, "The standard of giving is ½%, more or less of net worth . . . [and] we have a deadline of April 7th . . . because this is the effective date of the new Federal Campaign Finance Law [*sic*] which will require reporting and public disclosure of all subsequent campaign contributions in excess of $100, which we all naturally want to avoid."

The April 7 deadline also played a role in the Watergate scandal, which exploded in the summer of 1972. In fact, without campaign money and without the ability to maintain unaudited accounts before the FECA took effect, Watergate would not have been possible. "Watergate is not primarily a story of political espionage," wrote John Gardner, the founder of Common Cause, in April 1973, "nor even of White House intrigue. It is a particularly malodorous chapter in the annals of campaign financing. The money paid to the Watergate conspirators before the break-in—and the money passed to them later—was money from campaign gifts."

When Nixon's henchmen were arrested breaking into the headquarters of the Democratic National Committee at the Watergate Hotel on June 17, they were carrying $100 bills that had been laundered partly by utilizing the pre–April 7 disclosure grace period. A $25,000 cashier's check from Ken Dahlberg, the President's campaign finance chair for the Midwest, was discovered in one of the burglars' bank accounts. Also found in the account was $89,000 from Manuel Ogarrio Daguerre, a prominent lawyer from Mexico, which was later traced to $750,000 in campaign cash from Texas fat cats that was contributed via a suitcase flown from Texas, which arrived just prior to the April 7 deadline.

As reporters Bob Woodward and Carl Bernstein disclosed only a month before Nixon's landslide reelection, the FBI investigation revealed that "virtually all the acts against the Democrats were financed by a secret, fluctuating $350,000–$700,000 campaign fund." Numerous other cash accounts were held in safes by campaign operatives. Millions of dollars were laundered through Mexico and Luxembourg, and hundreds of thousands more deposited into the accounts of political committees that didn't exist. And as the tape recordings of the President demonstrated just four days before his resignation, Nixon knew that campaign funds were being used to finance the Watergate break-in, and had even agreed to help in a cover-up. Never before had the need for spending caps and disclosure requirements been more forcefully demonstrated.

The ensuing scandal, and the attendant revelation of massive contributions made during the 1972 campaign, blew new wind into the sails of campaign finance reform. In 1974 Congress enacted a series of amendments to the FECA. These "Watergate reforms" did the following:

- ◄o► limited the amount an individual could contribute to a federal candidate in an election cycle to $1000;

- ◄o► limited the total amount an individual could give to all federal candidates in a year to $25,000;

- ◄o► limited PAC contributions to a candidate to $5000 per election, with no aggregation cap;

- ◄o► limited the amount a candidate or his or her family could contribute to $50,000;

- ◄o► limited spending per House seat to $140,000 and a sliding scale for Senate campaigns based on the number of votes per state;

- ◄o► established the Federal Election Commission to monitor and enforce the new law.

For the first time in American history, between 1971 and 1974 Congress had made a real effort to reduce the influence of money in politics. Unfortunately, however, this time the Supreme Court stepped in to defend the status quo and to reinforce the marriage of money and democracy by declaring several key provisions unconstitutional. *Buck-ley v. Valeo* set the ground rules for the big-money game we still play today, and it ensured that yet another generation of Americans would be forced to watch their pay-to-play democracy from the sidelines.

Reading this history reminds one of the Spice Girls' lament, "Will this déjà vu never end?" Reforms to keep corrupt money out of politics have been infrequent, inadequate, and evaded. Scandal leads to reform that fails because of designed-in loopholes. Ergo, nothing works.

But it's also important to recall that, unlike a century ago, we have little if any vote buying. Contributions that were once made in secret are now made public on-line, and limits on hard and soft money have dammed up a lot of corrupt influence. Progress has occurred— glacially perhaps, but it has occurred.

But as the volume and targeting of so-called legislatively interested money increases—and corporate governance and accounting scandals continue—so will the public clamor for change more enduring than the laughable 1925 Federal Corrupt Practices Act and even the laud-able 1971 Federal Election Campaign Act. When will the cycle of scandal and reform finally cease? When members of Congress fear angry voters more than they fear overturning the system that got them into Congress?

RULES AND LAWS
How Money Shouts

"Politics has got so expensive that it takes a lot of money to even get beat with."
—Will Rogers, 1931

"[Buckley is] one of the most weakly reasoned, poorly written, initially contradictory court opinions I've ever read."
—Senator and former federal district court judge George Mitchell (D–ME), 1990

"You're more likely to see Elvis again than to see [McCain-Feingold] pass the Senate."
—Senator Mitch McConnell (R–KY), 1999

Buckley Rules

Along with the essential regulations on contributions, expenditures, and disclosure, the 1974 FECA amendments included a provision, written by Conservative New York senator James L. Buckley, that gave private citizens the right to challenge the constitutionality of the law in court. On January 2, 1975, the first business day after the 1974 amendments went into effect, a bizarre coalition of plaintiffs including Buckley, former Senator Eugene McCarthy, and liberal philanthropist Stewart Mott raced to the federal courthouse in Washington to file what would be called *Buckley v. Valeo,* the decision that defined campaign finance rules in the last quarter of the twentieth century.

James L. Buckley is the younger brother of famous conservative

William, who founded the magazine *National Review*. In 1970, James ran on the Conservative Party ticket in New York and was elected to the Senate by a plurality of the vote, outflanking Republican incumbent Charles Goodell and Democratic Representative Richard Ottinger. Buckley, who is now a federal judge, said he "depended on a few people" to finance his senatorial bid; had two creditors of $50,000 and $15,000; and received a $100,000 contribution on the condition that he would repay his benefactor if he won. Without the support of these few individuals, Buckley asserted, a third-party candidate like himself would have lacked the "initial credibility that gets the attention of the public, the voters and the press that leads to contributions."

In contrast to the high-profile lead plaintiff, Frank Valeo—the defendant of record only by virtue of his title as secretary of the Senate—played no role in actually arguing the case. In fact, when the Supreme Court handed down its ruling in 1976, Valeo was at first not even allowed into the courtroom. "When the case came up for decision I wanted to go to the Supreme Court to hear it, and I found out you couldn't get in, that they were so crowded with lawyers," he recalled. "I said, 'You mean I can't get in to hear this case even though it's got my name on it?' " (Chief Justice Warren Burger later found a seat for him.)

When faced with a decision of such far-reaching consequences, a court normally engages in an extensive, deliberate process to gather and assess the relevant facts before rendering its decision. But in *Buckley*, with the 1976 campaign season fast approaching, the judiciary felt pressured to resolve the case as soon as possible. So the lower courts short-circuited the traditional fact-finding processes; the parties simply made assertions on matters of fact called "offers of proof," which were then negotiated out among the parties and adopted by the court.

And precisely because the Court was trying to give what Justice Benjamin Cardozo called in another situation "an omnibus answer to an omnibus question to adjudge the rights of all," the resulting decision was among the longest in history: the Opinion of the Court itself spanned 143 pages and included 178 footnotes; the decision included a 92-page appendix containing the text of the relevant sections of the law; and 59 additional pages were devoted to separate opinions by individual justices concurring with and dissenting from specific points of the opinion. The sheer volume of the *Buckley* decision led one legal scholar to lament, "It takes the better part of two days simply to read, diagram, and note the Court's conclusions."

In order to defray the burden of writing such a sweeping opinion in a short time, the Court took the extraordinary step of writing the opinion by committee. The result of this piecemeal effort was an opinion that lacked a coherent, unifying vision; the statement varies in both style and substance from section to section.

The Court began its analysis of the law with what proved to be a decisive presumption: it took as its premise that restricting the flow of money into campaigns was tantamount to restricting speech because "virtually every means of communicating ideas in today's mass society requires the expenditure of money." The justices rejected out of hand the government's argument that it had a compelling interest in maintaining parity in the electoral influence of individuals, asserting that "the concept that government may restrict the speech of some elements of our society in order to enhance the relative voice of others is wholly foreign to the First Amendment." The majority opinion did recognize, however, a compelling governmental interest in preventing actual or apparent corruption.

It went on to make a critical distinction between contributions and expenditures: contributions did not deserve the same level of constitutional protection as expenditures because contributions had no direct communicative value beyond "a general expression of support for the candidate and his views." Also, contributions created the possibility of quid pro quo arrangements between donors and candidates, while expenditures raised no such dangers. Based on these distinctions, the Court upheld the law's limits on contributions by a 6–2 vote but struck down the restrictions on campaign expenditures.

The Supreme Court upheld the act's rigorous disclosure requirements because they deterred corruption and helped to detect illegal contributions. It also recognized an interest in informing the electorate about where campaigns received their money, thereby "help[ing] voters to define more of the candidates' constituencies"; significantly, the justices ruled that this informational interest justified the disclosure of independent expenditures, even though they supposedly raised no danger of corruption.

And the Court also sustained FECA's public financing system for presidential campaigns, finding that the public subsidies "further[ed] First Amendment values," including "eliminating the improper influence of large private contributions."

The majority coalition shifted from issue to issue; only Justices William Brennan, Potter Stewart, and Lewis Powell agreed with the opinion of the court in its entirety (see figure 3.1).

The divergent treatment of expenditures and contributions has turned out to be *Buckley's* single most important and most damaging legacy. As Chief Justice Burger warned presciently in his dissent, striking down the FECA's spending caps while sustaining the rest of its regime would have devastating effects for our democracy:

> The Court's piecemeal approach fails to give adequate consideration to the integrated nature of this legislation. A serious question is raised, which the Court does not consider: when central segments, key operative provisions, of this Act are stricken, can what remains function in anything like the way Congress intended? The incongruities are obvious. . . . All candidates can now spend freely; affluent candidates, after today, can spend their own money without limit; yet, contributions for the ordinary candidate are severely restricted in amount. . . . I cannot believe that Congress would have enacted a statutory scheme containing such incongruous and inequitable provisions.

Quite simply, in the real world money *isn't* speech—as Justice John Paul Stevens recently concluded, "it is property." In the vernacular it's true that "money talks," but isn't that the problem, not the solution? If money really is equivalent to speech, why are there antibribery laws making it a crime to say the sentence "I'll give you $5000 if you vote for this bill"?

Of course laws can prohibit or regulate speech: there are various, necessary "time, place, and manner" restrictions that regulate not the

FIGURE 3.1

THE SHIFTING MAJORITY IN *BUCKLEY V. VALEO*

Justice	Caps on Contribution	Caps on Expenditure	Disclosure	Public Financing
BURGER	Strike	Strike	Partially uphold	Strike
BRENNAN	Uphold	Strike	Uphold	Uphold
STEWART	Uphold	Strike	Uphold	Uphold
WHITE	Uphold	Uphold	Uphold	Uphold
MARSHALL	Uphold	Partially uphold	Uphold	Uphold
BLACKMUN	Strike	Strike	Uphold	Uphold
POWELL	Uphold	Strike	Uphold	Uphold
REHNQUIST	Uphold	Strike	Uphold	Strike

content of speech but rather its volume or location—one can't use electioneering speech within 100 feet of a polling place. In the words of legal scholar John Hart Ely:

> Suppose I buy a bullhorn and aim it at your bedroom window at three in the morning (or smarter still my opponent does): "Ely for Congress—I know you're in there—Ely for Congress!" That can't be a constitutional right, protected as the *message* obviously has to be. . . . The "absolutely protected" character of the message cannot insulate these forms of expres-

sion from regulation: *context*—the threat the particular expressive event poses—obviously is relevant and sometimes will be dispositive.

If the government may bar the use of a 100-decibel amplifier at midnight in a residential community, or the use of a bullhorn to accost one's neighbors at 3:00 A.M., why can't Congress also regulate the volume of 1000-decibel expenditures? It's an odd interpretation of the First Amendment that allows the loudest voices to drown out the softest, that guarantees the free speech of the powerful but not that of the average citizens who can't afford million-dollar ad campaigns.

For something with such far-reaching consequences, the crucial distinction between expenditures and contributions makes precious little sense. After all, if spending money is a precondition for expression, as *Buckley* says, isn't it just as necessary for a campaign to have received contributions before it can make campaign expenditures? By *Buckley's* own suggestion, both are to some degree antecedents of expression, and ought to be treated similarly.

And what about self-financed candidates? *Buckley* invalidated restrictions on self-financing as an impermissible limit on expenditures. But Justice Thurgood Marshall, who at the time accepted the contribution-expenditure distinction (he later changed his mind), thought that self-financing should be treated as a contribution to one's own campaign.

History has proven Chief Justice Burger and Justice Marshall right. Congress never anticipated that the Court would render a split decision that limited what regular candidates could raise but not self-financed ones. So, inevitably, wealthier candidates increasingly ran and won. But if there were campaign rules that disproportionately excluded, say, women, blacks, or blue-eyed people from office, people would rebel. How could we trust a government of only white, brown-eyed men to treat everyone fairly? Why then is it acceptable that average-income people are being increasingly pushed out of public office by the wealthy?

By encouraging a tenfold increase in campaign spending and discouraging qualified, non-multimillionaire candidates, *Buckley* has been as disastrous to democratic elections as *Dred Scott* was to race relations.

Someday it too will be reversed, but for now it remains the law of the land.

The First Wave After Buckley: PACs and Boren

It was the combination of the 1974 law, the *Buckley* decision, and the FEC's *Sun Oil* decision—which allowed corporations to solicit contributions from shareholders and employees—that launched PACs as the dominant players of campaign finance in the 1980s.

PACs are voluntary associations of like-minded people—steel executives, tech executives, dentists, trial lawyers, environmentalists, Jews for Israel, and so on—who pool their resources to maximize their political clout. Since 1974, PACs have been able to give five times as much as individuals, donating up to $5000 per candidate per election; more important, there is no legal limit to the *total* amount of money PACs can contribute. PACs also serve as a vital conduit for money from corporations and labor unions; although both are barred from direct contributions from corporate or union treasuries, the law allows them to make contributions through "a separate segregated fund to be utilized for political purposes." A now forgotten amendment to an otherwise good law created this money source that currently accounts for a third of all monies raised by members of the House of Representatives.

Ever since 1940, Section 611 of the Federal Corrupt Practices Act had prohibited corporations with government contracts from creating PACs; and since most large corporations had important federal contracts, most didn't have a PAC. But labor worried that its PAC could be considered "government contracts." So labor and business put aside their other differences to team up to end this restriction.

It was an unusual alignment. On one side were Senator William Proxmire (D–WI), Common Cause, and most editorial opinion (the *Washington Post* called the amendment "another loophole to more corruption in American politics"). On the other side, the U.S. Chamber of Commerce, the National Association of Manufacturers, the AFL-CIO, and liberal Senators Edward Kennedy, Walter Mondale, and Alan Cranston. On July 27, 1973, the Senate agreed with the House, 51–38, to eliminate Section 611. Then, three years later, when *Buckley* eliminated the expenditure ceilings of the FECA, the era of PACs began: labor PACs in the next ten years grew 75 percent— and business PACs 1750 percent. If the labor movement has suffered a worse self-inflicted political wound, it does not come readily to mind.

But it was the *Buckley* decision that—by blowing the lids off campaign spending—made PACs a central source of political money. The number of PACs ballooned from 608 in 1974 to 4009 just ten years later; PAC contributions to congressional candidates increased from $22.6 million in 1976 to $111.6 million in 1984, accounting for 27 percent of all campaign receipts. And with increased participation came greater notoriety; PACs made the cover of the October 25, 1982, issue of *Time* magazine and became, in the words of political scientist Frank J. Sorauf, "the public's whipping boys for the excesses of campaign finance."

And not without reason. PAC advocates love to claim that PAC money doesn't buy votes. "No one has ever shown me one body—not one—who has sold his vote for a contribution," said Bernadette Budde, a lobbyist for fourteen years with the Business Industry PAC. But candid candidates would disagree—among them, Representative Jim Leach (R–IA). "Members indignantly say, 'Money doesn't affect my vote,'" he has commented, "but that defies human nature. If you take money, there's absolutely an implication that you'll listen to them. . . . I don't know a member who doesn't believe that."

In 1983, first-term Senator David Boren (D–OK) attended a seminar organized by the Democratic Senatorial Campaign Committee to help senators run successful (read: well-financed) campaigns in the coming elections. Boren was struck by the seminar's unabashedly Machiavellian attitude toward PAC money: the message was to play industries off each other and sell access to the highest bidder. The experience disgusted Boren and, in a reference anticipating a colleague's previously quoted comments years later to Senator Feingold, he recalled, "I wanted to go home and take a bath."

After winning reelection in 1984 (refusing all PAC contributions),

Boren made campaign finance reform his top priority. In 1985, he recruited retiring senator and maverick conservative Barry Goldwater to cosponsor a bill that would limit the total amount of PAC money— because it was "legislatively interested money"—that any congressional candidate could accept. Determined to get his bill to the floor, Boren offered his proposal as an amendment to a bill the Senate would have to pass, the Low-Level Radioactive Waste Compact, which renewed a lapsed agreement between the United States and the Marshall Islands regarding missile testing and nuclear waste. The Senate approved Boren's amendment by a vote of 69–30. But the following year, after Majority Leader Bob Dole (R–KS) arranged to transfer the main provisions of the nuclear-waste measure out from the amended bill and attach them to other legislation, the rump bill died without a final up-or-down vote when the 99th Congress adjourned.

Any parliamentary antics on the Boren-Goldwater bill would pale in comparison to the tactics used by the 100th Congress to thwart efforts at campaign finance reform. Boren, now allied with new Senate Majority Leader Robert Byrd (D–WV), introduced the Senatorial Election Campaign Act, S. 2. It called for a system of public subsidies and voluntary spending limits for congressional elections (permitted by *Buckley* because candidates could choose to limit spending in exchange for public monies) and capped PAC receipts at 30 percent of the spending limit.

The resulting fight over S. 2 was reminiscent of Frank Capra's classic film *Mr. Smith Goes to Washington,* in which freshman senator Jefferson Smith (played by Jimmy Stewart) launched into a climactic filibuster to block the passage of a bill riddled with graft. To be sure, the bizarre spectacle in the U.S. Senate in late February 1988 was Capraesque, but with the wrong ending.

Knowing that the bill had the support of 52 senators, the Republican opposition—led by Minority Leader Dole and Mitch McConnell—resorted to a filibuster to kill the proposal. Byrd then made a record seven unsuccessful attempts to cut off the filibuster—which required 60 votes—and move the bill forward. After the failure of his seventh such "cloture" motion, Byrd decided, as Cokie Roberts reported on PBS, "to force the Republicans to filibuster the old-fashioned way—to stay on the floor all day and all night talking the bill to death."

Senate Republicans left the floor in an effort to force the Senate to adjourn for the lack of a quorum present; Byrd retaliated by ordering the absent senators back to the floor through a seldom-used provision of the Senate's procedural rules. Senate Republicans defied the order to return. Byrd invoked another procedural rule, calling on the sergeant-at-arms, a former police officer named Henry Guigni, to arrest the truant senators and compel their attendance. Shortly before midnight on February 24, Guigni and a posse of Capitol policemen began looking for the holdouts, and the night took a turn toward the truly absurd:

◄o► Senator Steven D. Symms (R–ID) managed to escape from the Capitol police by literally running away. Authorities were unable to chase him down.

◄o► Senator Lowell P. Weicker Jr. (R–CT), "a man of formidable size and temper," simply refused to cooperate when authorities found him.

◄o► Senator Bob G. Packwood (R–OR) fled to his office, barricading one of the doors with a chair and locking the other. When Guigni, who had been tipped off to Packwood's hideaway by a cleaning woman and armed with a skeleton key, began to enter through the locked door, Packwood attempted to force the door shut by throwing his shoulder against it, in the process reinjuring a broken finger. While being escorted back to the chamber, a still defiant Packwood informed Guigni that he would not walk into the Senate chamber under his own power; two of the officers had to physically carry him back onto the floor.

After a marathon fifty-hour session, Byrd lost an eighth vote, 53–41, and the sponsors shelved the legislation; money had talked and talked—and talked the bill to death.

Undaunted, Boren carried on the fight into the 102nd Congress in 1992, where he joined with a small cadre of senior Democrats—

Majority Leader George Mitchell; Wendell Ford of Kentucky, chair of the Rules Committee; Byrd, now chair of the Appropriations Committee; and Carl Levin—to sponsor S. 3, the Senate Election Ethics Act. Going further than its predecessors, S. 3 included voluntary spending limits, public financing for congressional elections, limits on total PAC contributions, and restrictions on soft money (see page 70 on this emerging force of soft money). It passed both chambers easily that spring and went to President Bush (the father) in April.

Despite public statements to the contrary, legislators on both sides of the aisle knew from the beginning that the bill would be dead on arrival at 1600 Pennsylvania Avenue. Bush had made numerous statements indicating his intent to veto any bill including public financing. And this was not a man loath to use his veto power; by the time S. 3 landed on his desk, Bush had vetoed 27 bills without a single override.

Dole decried the bill as nothing more than election-year posturing: "We have known exactly what will happen. We have known that the Democrats . . . came here looking for an election-year fight with President Bush." Dole wasn't entirely wrong. The certainty of a veto undoubtedly allowed secret opponents of reform to vote for the bill and score points with their constituents. Still, it was an extraordinary, comprehensive bill that, if enacted into law, would have avoided most of the money excesses and scandals of the next decade.

But Bush did veto the bill, declaring his apparent opposition to public financing, despite having accepted over $200 million in public subsidies over four presidential campaigns. And sure enough, the Senate failed to override the veto, 57–42. And for all the public protestations from Democrats and Republicans about the need for reform, legislators made no credible efforts to reach a compromise.

The Second Wave: More Scandal—S&Ls and Keating

In the 1980s, a scandal erupted that showed just how intimately connected money and power had become in the post-*Buckley* era.

Early in the decade, the savings-and-loan industry—banks established primarily to provide home loans—wanted to be deregulated. To prevail, S&L PACs and lobbyists legally pumped millions of dollars into the campaign coffers of hundreds of members of Congress. To avoid the $1000 contribution limit, one S&L owner, Carl Lindner, got each member of his large family to contribute; altogether they were able to give almost $1 million over several election cycles. Common Cause estimates that S&L-related PACs and individuals contributed almost $12 million to federal candidates in the 1980s. That's not even counting the millions contributed by other industries that stood to benefit from S&L deregulation—for example, the insurance industry gave $9.3 million and the real estate industry $8.9 million. Even as the S&Ls themselves were going under, they were still giving millions of dollars to the people they needed to bail them out.

The infusion of money paid off. Throughout the decade, congressmen, beholden to their S&L contributors and spurred by the Reagan administration, passed the Gramm–St. Germain deregulation bill allowing the industry to become a vast banker playground where S&L executives recklessly gambled away billions of dollars of other people's money. Even as the façade crumbled around them, members of Congress continued to bail out their contributors. In the end, the American taxpayer got stuck paying the $500 billion bill for their bad judgment.

ౝ౨ ౬౸

The events that led to the downfall of Charles H. Keating Jr., an eccentric and flamboyant Arizona real estate developer and antiporn crusader, are emblematic of how *Buckley* allowed influence peddlers to thrive.

In 1987, Keating, director of the Lincoln Savings and Loan, was worried that the federal government was getting too interested in the affairs of his bank. A heavy contributor to his state's congressmen, the banker decided it was time to call in his favors. So first he contacted his most loyal friend in Congress, Democratic senator Dennis DeConcini. Keating had given thousands of dollars to the senator's campaigns, and he figured he could use that support as leverage for a special favor.

DeConcini agreed to set up a meeting with the federal banking regulators to tell them to end their investigation of Lincoln.

DeConcini was able to recruit four other senators, Republican John McCain, also of Arizona, Alan Cranston (D–CA), John Glenn (D–OH), and Don Riegle (D–MI), all recipients of Keating's contributions and all members with influence over banking regulation. Together the senators met with the regulators. Not once but twice, they intervened on Keating's behalf and urged the regulators to end their investigation of Lincoln. Despite direct evidence of its ongoing illegal deals and its impending insolvency, the senators were briefly successful in stalling the investigation and Keating was able to keep Lincoln afloat for a few more months.

Those five senators—the Keating Five—along with the California Democratic Party received $1.4 million in campaign contributions from Keating, his family, and his associates. Not only did the Arizonan throw numerous fund-raisers for the senators, but also DeConcini's campaign manager got $30 million in loans from Keating and the first man to orbit the earth, Senator Glenn, accepted a $200,000 undisclosed gift from Keating to his personal PAC. It was at this point, when asked if he thought his campaign contributions had secured the senator's assistance, that Keating uttered his famous retort: "I want to say in the most forceful way I can: I certainly hope so."

Within months Lincoln Savings and Loan collapsed, with losses estimated at $3.4 billion, the biggest loss of any of the failed S&Ls. News of the meeting between the senators and the regulators leaked, and the Keating Five became a symbol of the danger of allowing private money to sway public policy. In 1989, only two years after the Keating Five had urged regulators to leave him alone, Keating was arrested. He was ultimately convicted of seventy-three counts of wire and bankruptcy fraud and sentenced to twelve years, only to have his sentence overturned on a technicality four years later.

The Third Wave: The Clinton Roller Coaster and Soft Money Explosion

"To renew America," said President Bill Clinton dramatically at his first inaugural, "we must revitalize our democracy. Let us resolve to reform our politics so that power and privilege no longer shout down the voice of the people."

The Clinton presidency began with new hope for campaign reform. In his first press conference, President Clinton said that reforming the political system would be one of his administration's top priorities, and one of its crowning achievements.

But the grip of money on politics proved too strong for even the new, reform-minded president.

The possibility for reform first began to slip away at a meeting in the Cabinet Room at the White House in February 1993, as recounted in Michael Waldman's *POTUS Speaks*. The President convened a formal meeting of the Democratic congressional leadership to discuss campaign finance reform. Among them were Speaker of the House Tom Foley (D–WA), House Majority Leader Richard Gephardt (D–MO), and Senate Majority Leader George Mitchell. "It was the high-water mark for the issue, though nobody knew it at the time," said White House policy aide Waldman, who attended the meeting.

Speaker Foley warned the President not to push too hard for reform, and not to set a deadline for action by Congress. Publicly, Foley spoke of the need to move ahead quickly: "We are under the close scrutiny of the American people," he said after the 1992 election. "They have signaled their impatience with the pace of reform." But behind the closed doors of the Cabinet Room, Foley was anything but enthusiastic. In his most recent reelection effort, Foley had outspent his opponent 2 to 1 and had received more than 70 percent of his funding from PACs. Now the Speaker didn't want to jeopardize the Democrats' majority status by altering the rules that had created it; and he reminded the room that any strong-arming to win campaign finance votes might derail other presidential priorities, like health care reform. Clinton agreed not to set a deadline.

In the months that followed, the momentum toward change sputtered out. The administration tried to rally congressional Democrats with a unified plan for reform, but no one could agree on the details. The White House delayed four times, before finally releasing its reform proposal three months late. The year before, while Bush was still president, the Democratic majority in Congress had passed a strong bill knowing Bush would veto it. Now that Clinton was in office and had pledged to support reform, Democrats in Congress hypocritically balked.

Most Republicans were outright opposed to reform. Bob Dole, the Republican leader in the Senate, announced his opposition to the Clinton plan before it had even been released. Democrats were torn between a desire for reform and a fear of being outspent in the next election. It was estimated that the Democratic National Committee (DNC) would lose 40 percent of its funding if a ban on soft money was enacted. Proposed limits on PAC contributions were particularly controversial, since many members owed their seat to PAC money. In the 1991–1992 election cycle, Democrats had received $30 million more than Republicans in PAC contributions; now they were being asked by the White House to forgo political advantage.

While Senate Democrats pushed through most of the President's proposals (though not public financing), Foley and his Democratic colleagues in the House continued to procrastinate. Poll numbers showed that the public wanted change, but Congress preferred the status quo. "I talk to these members," said a frustrated Clinton at a meeting with aides to discuss reform strategy later in 1993. "But they wouldn't listen. They think they win or lose elections on their money." Congressional Democrats would talk about reform out of one side of their mouths, while asking for contributions out of the other side.

By the time Democrats in Congress finally brought a bill to a vote in October 1994, it was too late. The Republicans had used the year of delays to generate enough support to mount a strong filibuster, and the measure died on the Senate floor. A disgusted Fred Wertheimer said in a 2002 interview, "So we passed bills in both houses for three Congresses but never changed one word of law for all that. We had a campaign finance bill on the Senate floor for fifteen of eighteen years and got every piece of a good bill at one time or another." But never all together with a presidential signature.

Foley's dilatory approach succeeded in derailing the bill . . . and himself and his party. For in November he lost his seat and the Democrats their majority.

ᴄᴏ ᴏᴗ

If the 1980s was the era of PACs, the 1990s saw the ascendance of soft money—money going to parties that was not subject to contribution limits or disclosure—as a major force in campaign finance.

Soft money first appeared on the scene in the 1970s, as a result of a complication arising out of federalism: many federal and state elections campaigns, though governed by different rules, take place simultaneously. So if Arizona's Republican Party airs an ad promoting the GOP, ostensibly benefiting candidates for both federal and nonfederal office, should federal and/or nonfederal candidates pay for the ad? And to what extent should federal law or Arizona state law govern?

In 1976, the Illinois Republican Party sought advice from the Federal Election Commission (FEC) regarding the apportionment of funds for general party-building activities. The commission decided that one third of the costs should be borne by federal candidates, and the remaining two thirds should fall on the local and state candidates; however, the FEC added that such activities could be financed only with FECA-compliant contributions—that is, only hard money, not soft money, could fund these party expenditures.

But two years later the FEC changed its mind, and allowed the Kansas Republican Party to use corporate and union contributions (permitted under Kansas law) to pay for the nonfederal portion of the party-building activities. In 1979, the FEC decided to allow the national parties to establish nonfederal accounts and accept contributions that would otherwise be barred under federal law "for the exclusive and limited purpose of influencing the nomination or election of candidates for nonfederal office."

In effect, the FEC overturned the 1907 and 1947 laws banning unlimited contributions from corporate and labor treasuries to help federal candidates. Soft money supposedly going for local "party building" was usually coordinated to help Senate and House nominees. The FEC had officially opened the floodgates of money.

Because soft money was not subject to disclosure until 1991, estimates on the size and rise of soft money in the decade after the 1979 ruling are somewhat speculative. But the figures suggest that in the 1980 elections, the Democratic and Republican Parties combined spent $19.1 million in soft money; by 1988, the figure had ballooned to $45 million.

As early as 1984, Common Cause and other groups were pleading with the FEC to implement tighter regulations. In 1987, Common Cause sued the agency in federal court and obtained a court order requiring the FEC to develop rules on how to allocate the federal-nonfederal mix. After years of dragging its feet, the commission finally promulgated new guidelines in 1991 requiring parties to disclose soft money activities. But rules specifying the allocation of burdens between the state and federal parties for shared expenses had the counterintuitive effect of increasing the role of soft money by "giv[ing] party organizations a clearer sense of how to spend soft money legally, and in at least some instances . . . permit[ting] them by regulation to pay a greater share of their costs with soft money than they had been before."

Soft money then increased astronomically. For the 1992 elections, the national parties spent $79.1 million, almost double the prior presidential cycle; four years later, soft money expenditures reached $271.5 million; in the 2000 elections, the national parties spent almost half a billion dollars in soft money, compared with $692 million in hard money. This increase in soft money vastly outstripped inflation; if expenditures had simply kept pace with the consumer price index between 1992 and 2000, total party spending for the 2000 elections would have been $95.2 million, not $497.6 million.

So what caused this meteoric rise?

First, large contributors jumped in number, tracking the stock market's creation of new wealth. In the 1994 elections, 96 corporations gave more than $100,000; by 1998, 218 corporations did so. This period also saw a concomitant increase in large individual donations; in the 1998 elections, 114 households gave $100,000 or more.

Second, the parties and their presidential nominees in 1996 became much more aggressive about soliciting soft money donations. After twenty years, political operatives, lobbyists, and election lawyers had mastered the loopholes in the Watergate reforms. Corporations, individuals, and labor unions were able to thwart contribution limits by giving millions for party-building activities, the definition of which had been distorted to include sham "issue ads"—ads that technically promoted an issue but operated as a de facto candidate endorsement or attack. In 1996 corporate soft money contributions accounted for 62 percent of the total raised by both parties. Contributions from labor accounted for 6 percent.

All told, candidates, PACs, individuals, and other organizations spent $4.2 billion during the 1995–1996 election cycle, a 32 percent increase from 1991–1992. Between 1992 and 1996, state party spending on media went from $2 million to $65 million. The 1996 election cycle set new records for spending but produced the lowest voter turnout since 1924.

At the presidential level, the fund-raising race began even before the reelection campaign.

As the sitting president, Clinton was able to raise millions of dollars for the DNC early in the two-year electoral cycle. In mid-1995, the Clinton campaign pumped $44 million in soft money into a media blitz of "issue ads" aimed at bolstering the President's image. Clinton also had no problem raising hard money, and his campaign eventually raised a new record of $25 million.

Republicans also began fund-raising early. The race for the Republican presidential nomination dissolved into a media spending war between Bob Dole and Steve Forbes, compelling the Senate majority leader to spend nearly all the federal law allowed well before the convention. Dole was relegated to largely replaying old campaign ads exclusively on cable TV in order to stay within the spending limits.

Yet Republicans, while attacking Clinton's soft money excesses and Al Gore's Buddhist Temple embarrassments as symptoms of the political money disease, continued to ignore a cure. They couldn't abandon their deep-seated, antidemocratic idea that wealthy special interests should have more political power than average citizens. In early 1997, even as he was calling for investigations into Democratic fund-raising practices, Trent Lott, Dole's successor as Senate majority leader, declared that unregulated soft money giving was "the American way."

That spring Lott chose Fred Thompson to conduct a Senate investigation into alleged campaign funding abuses by the Democrats in 1996. Thompson, an authentic believer in campaign finance reform, wanted to broaden the investigation's mandate to cover all possible funding improprieties by both parties. Thompson proposed an investigation into the massive proliferation of soft money in the 1996 campaign, as well as charges of illegal foreign money into the Clinton campaign. He wanted to look into the system itself, at not just what might be technically against the law but also what might be legal yet inconsistent with democracy. Thompson's Republican colleagues weren't pleased. As Elizabeth Drew notes in *The Corruption of American Politics,* by urging an extension of the mandate to cover both "illegal acts" *and* "improper acts," Thompson was bucking Republican orthodoxy by focusing attention on the corrupting power of too much *legal* money in the system.

Thompson's hearings failed to fulfill the high expectations excited by early claims of rooting out foreign money. But they did reveal story after story of how money buys political access and power, which in turn gave needed ammunition to the early McCain-Feingold legislation in Congress. Senator McCain, sensitive to the system after his scrape with Keating, used those stories. "If you want to build a pipeline through Central Asia—pay up, you'll get an audience with government purchasing agents," he complained. "But if all you pay is your taxes, and you want your elected representative to seek redress for some wrong, send us a letter. We'll send you one back."

As 1997 came to a close, so did the Thompson hearings. Congress continued to refuse to pass comprehensive campaign finance reform, and the battle to reduce the control of money over politics continued into the next century.

The Fourth Wave: McCain-Feingold

James Buckley and Stewart Mott aren't the only odd couple associated with campaign finance. Though their names have become inextricably linked over the past seven years, Senators John McCain and Russ Feingold didn't have too much in common. McCain is a war hero with a famous temper; Feingold is a mild-mannered Rhodes Scholar with a degree from Harvard Law School. The duo's first encounter came on the floor of the Senate, while Feingold was pushing to cut funding for an aircraft carrier. McCain indignantly asked Feingold if he had ever been on a carrier. Feingold admitted he hadn't. McCain's response: "Then learn about it."

But it was, as Humphrey Bogart said in *Casablanca,* "the beginning of a beautiful friendship." Following this confrontation, Feingold recalls, "out of the blue, a while later he called and suggested we work together on bipartisan reforms." The two men successfully collaborated in 1995 on restricting gifts to senators, then set their sights on campaign finance reform.

Together with Fred Thompson, McCain and Feingold proposed S. 1219, which provided for a package of reform measures, including bans on PACs and soft money, a requirement that senatorial candidates raise 60 percent of funds from their home states, and a system of voluntary spending limits in exchange for free TV and discounted mail rates. Interestingly, when the bill's sponsors listed their priorities, the soft money ban was ranked last out of eight. When the Senate failed to end a Republican-led filibuster in June 1996, McCain declared, "We will have campaign finance reform—if not this year, then next."

In the following year, the Senate gradually whittled away some of McCain-Feingold's more ambitious proposals. In September, the National Association of Broadcasters successfully lobbied to drop the bill's system of free airtime and subsidized mailings in exchange for voluntary spending caps. The bill's requirement that candidates raise 60 percent of funds inside their home states was also removed at the request of Senate Democrats from small states, including Minority Leader Tom Daschle (D–SD).

The PAC ban was another early casualty. After Daschle announced on September 11, 1997, that the forty-five Senate Democrats were united in their support of McCain-Feingold, Democratic senators soon found that they were having a harder time raising funds for their campaigns. Upon the suggestion of Steve Stockmeyer, a lobbyist for the National Association of Business PACs, when a Senate Democrat asked for a contribution from a corporate or trade association PAC, the group would answer, "You've put us in a very hard position because our board has said don't give to people who support the PAC ban or reduction, and you signed a statement that endorses a bill that limits PAC contributions." Two weeks later, the limits on PAC contributions disappeared from the bill.

While the bill's sponsors were still modifying the proposal in order to gain more votes, Majority Leader Trent Lott, hoping to catch the sponsors off guard, announced on September 25 that he would bring McCain-Feingold up for consideration the next day. Lott then offered an amendment, cosponsored by Senator Don Nickles (R–OK), that prohibited unions from using union dues for political activity without getting each member's written permission—an administrative impossibility. This "paycheck protection" amendment was a poison pill aimed at making the bill unpalatable to Democrats and thus forcing them to filibuster the amended bill.

On October 7, McCain-Feingold was scheduled to come up for a vote. Yet by this time there were dueling filibusters on the Senate floor, one by Senate Democrats against the Lott-Nickles amendment and another by Republicans against McCain-Feingold itself. Lott's strategy had succeeded. The cloture motions to cut off debate failed, 52–48.

Following the vote, in a remark mirroring the syntax and the hubris of Governor George Wallace's famous 1963 declaration on segregation, a triumphant Mitch McConnell said, "This effort to put the government in charge of political discussion is not going to pass now, is not going to pass tomorrow, is not going to pass ever."

When the bill again was pulled in early 1998 after another failed cloture vote, the irrepressible McCain—sounding like a wait-till-next-year Brooklyn Dodger—vowed to keep fighting for reform: "I believe there will be more scandals, there will be more indictments and more people going to jail. There are probably scandals happening while we speak. The system is badly broken. We'll continue to try."

Meanwhile, in the House of Representatives, reformers had succeeded in forcing Newt Gingrich to put campaign finance on the agenda; Gingrich agreed to consider campaign finance in March 1998 and promised "a fair, bipartisan process."

Only he didn't mean it. In late March, Shays-Meehan, the House version named for its sponsors, Christopher Shays (R–CT) and Martin Meehan (D–MA), had still not come up for a vote. In fact, Gingrich told Shays that "there couldn't be a vote on his bill, because it would pass." Instead, Gingrich proposed allowing a vote on the "suspension" calendar—usually reserved for pushing through uncontroversial measures—which did not allow any amendments, limited debate to twenty minutes per side, and required a two-thirds majority for passage. On the evening of March 30, between a funeral for one of the members and the usual assortment of fund-raisers later that night, the House considered several campaign finance bills, but Shays-Meehan was not permitted to go to the floor for consideration. The resulting debate was a farce. The Republican leadership's bill failed 337–74; all 196 Democrats and 140 of the 214 Republicans voted against the bill.

While Gingrich's overtly obstructionist tactics succeeded in burying Shays-Meehan, they ultimately served the cause of reform by alienating moderates and energizing the constituencies of groups such as the AFL-CIO, Sierra Club, Public Citizen, and Common Cause. During the Easter recess, advocates pushed congresspeople to sign a "discharge petition" begun by the "Blue Dog" Democrats (more conservative Democrats). With signatures from a majority of the chamber, the petition would go over the Speaker's head and force the House to consider the bill. By late April, with the discharge petition inexorably closing in on the magic number—218—the House leadership relented and agreed to a real debate on Shays-Meehan and the other campaign finance bills.

No longer able to suppress the calls for an open and fair debate, the Republican leadership then tried to bury Shays-Meehan under a mountain of amendments, deviating from House rules to allow debate on an unlimited number of amendments, no matter how irrelevant. The objective was "to sow legislative chaos and run out the clock," in the words of the *New York Times,* by delaying action long enough that it would be impossible for the bill to pass both houses of Congress by the October recess.

Included among the 258 proposed amendments were several intentional poison pills. The first serious test of the reformers came on June 19 in the form of an amendment offered by Representative Bill

Thomas (R–CA) to nullify Shays-Meehan in its entirety if any part of it was invalidated by the courts. Somewhat surprisingly, the amendment was handily defeated, 254–155, with 65 Republicans breaking ranks with the leadership.

But an amendment sponsored by Representative Vito Fossella (R–NY) barring federal candidates from taking contributions from permanent residents—lawful immigrants who were not yet citizens—complicated matters for the reformers. Shays urged members to vote against the amendment: "One of the things I find extraordinarily ironic is I hear a member say there is agreement this amendment has to be part of Meehan-Shays [*sic*]. Yet the people who are saying it are not going to be voting for Meehan-Shays. So this is not particularly a friendly amendment. . . . I encourage my colleagues to realize that we cannot allow this amendment, if it passes, to be a killer amendment because [if we do] they will have won." But despite Shays's protests and similar warnings from other Democrats, the House adopted the amendment, 282–126.

The Fossella amendment alienated members of the Hispanic Caucus, whose votes were considered crucial to the reformists' cause. As the House neared a final vote on Shays-Meehan, the American Civil Liberties Union sent a letter to members, signed by sixty-five immigrants' rights groups, calling for the bill's defeat because of the Fossella amendment. But when the vote on Shays-Meehan was taken that August, the reform coalition held together and the soft money ban passed 252–179, with the support of 61 Republicans.

It was after the passage of Shays-Meehan in the House that McConnell said, "You're more likely to see Elvis again than to see this bill pass the Senate." Notwithstanding McConnell's mockery, a very determined McCain decided to give his bill another shot. Sure enough, on September 10, the Senate voted 52–48—the same margin as in February—to sustain the filibuster.

After the vote, Feingold warned that the 2000 elections would be more abusive than ever. "There will be a disgusting display," he said.

By 1999 the House had a new Speaker, Illinois's Dennis Hastert. Hastert's comparatively fair treatment of Shays-Meehan sparked some concern on the part of the sponsors, who worried that the GOP's new strategy, in Shays's words, "was killing us with kindness." Not only did this round of debate lack the rancor of the previous year, but the reform coalition held together, rebuffing killer amendments and passing Shays-Meehan by basically the same margin as before, 252–177. But yet again, it died by filibuster in the Senate.

The 2000 elections, however, brought new allies to the cause. The Democrats had picked up four seats in the Senate. Others had simply grown weary of the status quo. Senator Thad Cochran, a conservative Republican from Mississippi, called McCain and Feingold to join the reformers. "I've had it. The system stinks," he said. With these new pro-reform votes, McCain finally had enough votes to break a filibuster. In early 2001, McCain-Feingold came back for yet another round of debate.

Meanwhile, the sponsors of McCain-Feingold made further alterations to broaden the bill's appeal. The Senate passed the so-called millionaire's amendment, raising contribution limits for candidates with self-funding opponents. Not everyone was happy with this change; Daschle, echoing the concerns of several Democrats, observed, "With each change I think you lessen the opportunity for us to keep Democrats together." Some Democrats were further irked by an amendment— negotiated with the sponsors by Senators Feinstein and Thompson— raising the contribution limits to $2000. This idea had financial logic (since inflation had eroded a $1000 gift to about $300 in 1974 dollars) but risked giving contributors more power.

McCain-Feingold faced one final hurdle in the Senate. Senators Bill Frist (R–TN) and John Breaux (D–LA) proposed a "non-severability" amendment under which the whole bill would be thrown out if one section was later deemed unconstitutional. Supporters expressed concern over what would happen with only a ban on soft money without restrictions on issue ads, but McCain considered the proposal to be sabotage. "Severability is French for 'kill campaign finance reform,'" he said. In part due to the efforts of Daschle—who talked to undecided Democrats and, according to colleagues, persuaded at least a half dozen to vote no—the Senate rejected the measure. In the final vote to approve McCain-Feingold, the Senate passed the bill on April 2, 59–41.

Over the August recess, reformers went to work gathering signatures for a discharge petition to force a vote on Shays-Meehan, once again started by more conservative Blue Dogs. Slowly the discharge petition gained support; by the new year, reformers needed just four signatures to bring Shays-Meehan back. Then came the Enron scandal, which gave the cause the final push it needed. It was fitting that the final four signatures—from Republicans Tom Petri of Wisconsin and Charles Bass of New Hampshire and Democrats Corrine Brown of Florida and Richard Neal of Massachusetts—came on the day Congress began hearings on the Enron collapse.

In February 2002, Shays-Meehan came back up for consideration. Republican opponents were as determined as ever to derail the bill—Hastert spoke of the impending vote as an "Armageddon" for the GOP—and threw up the usual obstacles. But just before the House was set to debate, Ari Fleischer, President Bush's press secretary, remarked that Bush thought the bill would "improve the system." The President's apparent support devastated the obstructionists. One staffer lamented, "It was an uphill climb to begin with. When Ari made that comment that morning, that was the equivalent of shoving a boulder down the side of that mountain you are climbing." This time—for the third time in three years—Shays-Meehan won final passage, 240–189; 41 Republicans crossed the floor to approve the bill.*

In the Senate, Daschle—now the majority leader after the defection of Senator James Jeffords (Ind.–VT)—pledged to move the bill through the Senate by Easter. With Bush continuing to express tepid support, the reformers picked up the votes necessary to invoke cloture. The bill passed, 60–40, on March 20.

President Bush signed the bill in the morning on March 27, 2002, quietly. There was no press on hand and only Vice President Cheney and National Security Adviser Condoleezza Rice witnessed the signing.

---

*As scholar and campaign finance expert Norman Ornstein enjoyed pointing out, the three most prominent Republican representatives who led the opposition were named Ney, Doolittle, and DeLay ("you couldn't make this up").

The bill's sponsors were not present for the nonceremony; McCain received a call from a White House staffer informing him the bill had been signed. Adding to the passive-aggressive display, the same day Bush embarked on a fund-raising tour to help Republicans raise millions.

Also the same day, the NRA and McConnell rushed to the courthouse to challenge the law's constitutionality. In April, the three-judge panel hearing the consolidated complaints announced the timetable to govern the case. Stressing the need to develop "an accurate factual record," the court rejected the extremely rushed schedule proposed by the plaintiffs. Instead, the court's timetable includes five months for the parties to cull evidence through discovery. The parties must submit briefs by November 4; oral arguments are scheduled for December 4, 2002, in the D.C. Circuit Court of Appeals, with a likely Supreme Court resolution by the spring or fall of 2003.

ॐ ॐ

Why were the reformers successful this time around when they had been stalled so many times before? First, Enron refocused national attention on the power of money in politics and underscored the need for reform; it also made it very difficult for President Bush to publicly oppose reform without looking like a tool of the special interests. "We would have gotten over the goal line eventually," says Feingold of the scandal. "But Enron enabled us to score on first down."

Of course, McCain's presidential bid and his national popularity also helped the reformists' cause in its critical moments. During the 2000 general election, the Republican Party had capitalized on McCain's appeal by trotting the senator out to many key races to stump for Republican candidates. In the process, twenty-five House Republicans whom McCain had helped elect had publicly announced their support for campaign finance reform. The GOP leadership had a hard time thereafter getting Republican members to bolt from the reformist camp because, in the words of a source close to Bush, "almost every one of them was on videotape pledging allegiance to reform."

The passage of McCain-Feingold ends seven years of legislative gridlock and enacts the most significant reform since 1974. Taking effect on November 6, 2002, it has these major provisions:

◄○► Soft money donations to the national parties are banned; state and local parties may collect contributions as large as $10,000, but these funds may not be used for broadcast ads for federal candidates.

◄○► Outside groups (corporations, unions, and nonprofits) are barred from using soft money to air ads that clearly identify a candidate within thirty days of a primary or within sixty days of the general election. Anyone or any group may still air such ads before these deadlines but (a) can't coordinate the ads with candidates, (b) must use only hard money, and (c) must comply with reporting and disclosure rules.

◄○► The limits on hard money contributions from individuals are increased to $2000 per election (or a total of $4000 for primary and general elections combined). Individuals may make up to $95,000 in total contributions per two-year election cycle. These limits are indexed for inflation. As noted, the statute provides for increased contribution limits for candidates who face wealthy, self-financed opponents.

◄○► A court may strike down one section without nullifying the entire law.

Certainly, McCain-Feingold represents a huge improvement over a system dominated by soft money and sham issue advocacy. But simply banning soft money and curbing these ads really turns back the clock only about ten years, before the rise of these abusive practices of the 1990s. The more ambitious provisions of the bill's prior versions— which would have gone a long way to curb the influence of special interests—were stripped away over the years to forge a coalition. In order for the new rules to have their full effect, they will have to be vigorously enforced by the FEC, a body crippled by its very structure and renowned for its inefficacy (on which more later). The FEC will have to be especially vigilant regarding independent expenditures, which are sure to increase dramatically now that soft money is no longer an option. As Peter Beinart of *The New Republic* warns, "If the FEC doesn't aggressively check whether coordination is taking place, the loophole will undermine the bill."

Moreover, the final version of McCain-Feingold may have some unintended, perverse consequences that actually make the system worse in some respects:

◄o► Ellen Miller observes that the higher hard money maximum "helps elite donors, the 0.1 percent who give $1000 [and now can give twice that sum] and disproportionately influence Congress."

◄o► Meanwhile, the soft money ban coupled with the increase in hard money is a double whammy for many Democrats: while they had reached near parity with Republicans on soft money, they continue to lag behind on hard money, which is now even more important. As Michael Crowley writes, "Many Democrats feel like they've just woken up after a one-night stand. Campaign finance reform may have felt good last night, but the question this morning is: What have we done?"

◄o► And it's a blow to presidential public financing. Under the current rules, the federal government matches up to $250 of each contribution in the primaries to presidential candidates who opt in to the public matching process. Because the maximum contribution has doubled, abiding by the voluntary limits is less attractive—the added value of matching funds is now just one eighth of the maximum contribution, not one quarter as before. Former FEC Commissioner Trevor Potter speculates that public funds will constitute only 15 percent of a typical presidential campaign budget, which may undermine a candidate's incentive to seek public money and abide by spending limits.

◄o► If the restrictions on issue ads are struck down in courts, the ban on soft money, in the words of Senator Bill Frist, may merely "follow the course of least resistance" and end up in the coffers of outside issue groups to run waves of independent negative ads. In such a situation, Senator Robert Torricelli (D–NJ) worries, "the real battle will be fought by surrogates, and candidates will be nothing but spectators."

As Scott Harshbarger, president of Common Cause, observes of a law his organization struggled nearly three decades to enact, "this is only an incremental step. If this becomes the final step, we have failed."

Current Rules of Engagement

What's behind the spiraling cost of campaigning?

Campaign finance is a classic example of what is known in international relations jargon as the security dilemma. Consider the arms race. Neither the United States nor the Soviet Union wanted to pour billions of dollars into nuclear arms that would never be used, but each superpower's worst fear was to be rendered defenseless by a crippling first strike. So Washington and Moscow built up their stockpiles, each time upping the ante and forcing the other to call. And so it goes with campaign finance. Nobody *likes* having to spend every day raising money, but without any way of being sure the other guy or gal isn't going to do exactly that, the fear of being outspent and outadvertised in the crucial final two weeks is enough to get you on the phone one more time, as the next chapter describes.

Before the FECA, if the person on the other end of that additional phone call was wealthy enough and liked you enough, he could solve all your funding woes (for a while, at least) by simply writing you a huge check. In recent years, Mr. Big was once again able to use a huge sum of money to help you out; he just had to funnel that money through several different pipelines.

Indeed, as Chief Justice Burger feared, by restricting the supply of election money while doing nothing to combat the spiraling demand for money, *Buckley* had the perverse consequence of creating a black market for funds: candidates became ever more dependent on the very special-interest groups whose influence the law was intended to curb.

As shown in figure 3.2, the FECA establishes a regulatory framework and a matrix of rules that vary depending on who is giving to whom.

The Federal Election Commission: A Comb Without Teeth

After Watergate, the public correctly understood that politicians required adult supervision. Although many on Capitol Hill got the message and set out to hire a "tough cop," self-interest interfered and the job ultimately went to a "dithering nanny," according to Brooks Jackson, author of *Broken Promise: Why the Federal Election Commission Failed.* When Congress created the FEC in 1974 it was intended to enforce the nation's federal campaign finance laws. Fearing independent oversight, though, Congress designed it to be weak, ineffective, and deferential. It succeeded on all counts. Throughout its life, the FEC has routinely been called the "Failure to Enforce Commission"; it's also been dubbed "a toothless tiger," "a watchdog without a bite," "a pussycat agency," "FECkless," and "the little agency that can't."

The Securities and Exchange Commission, which oversees America's financial markets, has until now been historically everything that the FEC is not: well respected, nonpartisan, independent. The FEC is bipartisan, which means that it is governed by partisan considerations. While the nomination is formally made by the president, in effect Democratic and Republican party leaders each choose three commissioners, and any action the FEC takes requires majority approval. The result is an agency frequently paralyzed by politics and deadlocked along 3–3 party line votes. As noted in the *Washington Post,* "Intense partisanship envelops almost every major decision the FEC's six commissioners make. . . . Time and again partisan standoffs have prevented the Commission from pursuing enforcement actions against

FIGURE 3.2

CONTRIBUTION LIMITS EFFECTIVE NOVEMBER 6, 2002

	Candidates	National Parties	State and Local Parties	PACs	Aggregate Limits
INDIVIDUALS	$2000 per election	$25,000 per year	$10,000 per year	$5000 per year	$95,000 per election cycle
MULTICANDIDATE COMMITTEES	$5000	$15,000	$5000	$5000	No limit
OTHER POLITICAL COMMITTEES	$1000	$20,000	$5000	$5000	No limit

major politicians and powerful interest groups, even when the FEC's general counsel recommends going forward."

In 1999, to take one example, the FEC's general counsel recommended that the commissioners find probable cause to investigate whether the Republican National Committee (RNC) illegally accepted $1.6 million in foreign contributions through an "independent" organization, the National Policy Forum (NPF), which the RNC staffed and financed and whose chairman, Haley Barbour, was also the RNC chairman. At issue was whether NPF used foreign contributions to repay a "loan" from the RNC. The commission deadlocked—the three Democrats voting for and three Republicans voting against—and the issue died. The Democratic commissioners called the scheme a "charade," adding, "the Federal Election Campaign Act means very little if it can be so easily evaded. . . . By approving of such trickery, our colleagues' decisions in the matter are plainly contrary to both the plain language of the statute and the Commission's regulation."

Both parties can be blamed for nominating commissioners whose first loyalty is to the party rather than to the law. Of the twenty individuals who have served on the FEC, only two have had strong experience in administrative oversight and law enforcement. Most have been former members of Congress, congressional or White House staffers, or party or political operatives. The most recent commissioner to be appointed, Michael Toner, had previously served as chief counsel to the RNC and general counsel to the Bush-Cheney presidential campaign. Another current commissioner, David Mason, served on the staff of then Representative Trent Lott (R–MS) and as a senior fellow at the Heritage Foundation.

Congress's partisan appointments to the FEC are in step with its other efforts to shield itself from scrutiny. Republican leaders recently attempted to fire the FEC's widely respected general counsel for his persistent efforts to enforce the law. In addition, congressional leaders, particularly since the Republican takeover in 1995, have repeatedly attempted to slash the FEC's already underfunded budget, prompting columnist David Broder to write, "The easiest way to gut regulation is to hobble the regulator."

In fact, Congress had already taken the FEC out by the knees in 1979 when it revoked its power to conduct random audits of candidates' campaign finances. "In effect," wrote Brooks Jackson, "Congress put itself on the honor system," and the results have been as predictable as those of a speeder controlling his own radar gun. Candidates routinely act with impunity, knowing that any penalty, however unlikely, will come long after the election. Former senator Bob Kerrey (D–NE) summarized the prevailing opinion in Washington: "If I win an election by accepting illegal campaign contributions, the FEC might levy a $50,000 fine on me three years after the fact. You know, I can raise that in a single night in a campaign event. So that's hardly what I would call a deterrent against illegal behavior."

In fact, $50,000 fines are few and far between; most violations go undetected or uninvestigated, and many open cases get dismissed because of a severe lack of resources. In 1997, after several years of budget cuts and freezes, the FEC dismissed 55 percent of its cases. Compounding the budget problem, the FEC is saddled with cumbersome bureaucratic procedures that, in the words of Commissioner Scott

Thomas, "make it difficult—if not impossible—for the Commission to resolve a complaint in the same election cycle in which it is brought."

The FEC is flawed not only in process but in policy. As noted earlier, it was the FEC itself, not Congress or the courts, that created the soft money monster.

Following the soft money abuses in the 1996 election, the FEC's staff recommended pursuing penalties against both the Clinton and Dole campaigns for illegal use of soft money. In a series of 3–3 votes, however, the commission declined to take any action. After the deadlocked votes, Thomas remarked, "You can put a tag on the toe of the Federal Election Commission."

Despite the presidential public financing provision, the FEC's creation of soft money revived the incessant pressure to fund-raise, with disastrous results. A myriad of soft money fund-raising scandals became national embarrassments, as the price of a White House coffee made even Starbucks blush. Charlie Trie, John Huang, and Johnny Chung, foreign nationals who understood how American democracy works, became household names. "The White House," said Johnny Chung, who contributed more than $350,000 in soft money to the Democratic National Committee, "is like a subway: you have to put in coins to open the gates."

When the House of Representatives was considering the Shays-Meehan bill to ban soft money in 2002, two FEC commissioners, David Mason and Bradley A. Smith, apparently acting at the behest of House Republican Whip Tom DeLay, injected themselves into the debate, decried the "intellectual bankruptcy" of the bill's supporters, and declared the bill "flatly unconstitutional" and unenforceable. "Anyone intent on circumventing the law," said Mason, "runs little risk of detection."

And now that the law has passed, are we to trust them to enforce it? *Wall Street Journal* columnist Al Hunt noted that Smith and Mason "acted for all practical purposes as appendages of the House Republican leaders," and that their actions were "an inexcusable partisan intervention by regulatory officials whose task it would be to implement any law." It was an unprecedented episode that sunk the FEC's reputation, if possible, to a new low.

The creation of soft money is only the most egregious example of the FEC's prowess in opening loopholes. Another is its sabotage of the FECA's prohibition on private funds for party conventions.

Support for public financing of party conventions gained strength after International Telephone and Telegraph (ITT), which was then being investigated for an illegal merger by the Nixon Justice Department, made a $400,000 contribution to the 1972 Republican Convention. When ITT shortly thereafter reached a favorable settlement with the Antitrust Division, it appeared to be a quid pro quo, particularly after a newspaper columnist turned up a memo by ITT's Washington lobbyist indicating that a deal had been struck.

The FECA included a provision mandating publicly financed conventions for parties that agree to forgo private fund-raising. But in 2000, although the Democratic and Republican Parties each received more than $13 million in public funds to finance their conventions, the FEC's rules also allowed the parties to raise additional unlimited amounts. The Republicans, who spent more than $60 million on their convention, received an $8 million contribution from Motorola, as well as million-dollar contributions from AT&T, General Motors, Microsoft, Verizon, and others; the Democrats had big corporate donors too, and spent just under $50 million.

The best efforts of Mason and Smith failed to defeat Shays-Meehan, but the fight didn't end on the House floor. Instead, it moved inside the commission's chambers, where the FEC drafted proposed rules interpreting McCain-Feingold that would have eviscerated the soft money ban. Only after sharp editorial rebuke from newspapers across the country, and a full-court press from the bill's sponsors, did the commission amend some—but not all—of its proposed rules.

For instance, the FEC adopted rules that allow elected officials, with a wink and a nod, to solicit soft money so long as they don't "directly ask" for it, despite the law's clear intent to prohibit involvement by federal candidates in soft money fund-raising. Before the FEC adopted the rule on a 4–2 vote, its own general counsel, Lawrence Norton, warned that "this definition has the potential for great mischief."

The FEC created other loopholes as well, including broadening the purposes for which soft money can be used. The *New York Times,* in a lead editorial entitled "Election Law Coup d'Etat," called it a "mugging of the statute . . . by unelected bureaucrats pushing a corrupt agenda of favoring special-interest money over the voices and votes of citizens." And the *Washington Post,* in an editorial entitled "Stop Opening Loopholes," was left to hope only that the FEC "does no further damage." Following the FEC's decisions, McCain and company called on Congress to roll back the agency's attempt to rewrite the law. Whether the effort succeeds, the ban on federal soft money is still mostly intact—for now. The same cannot be said, however, of the FEC's credibility.

Bundling: The Sum of All Your Friends

As zealous contributors soon discovered, it was child's play—literally—to circumvent the limit on individual contributions:

➤◦► *Father knows best:* Skye Stolnitz (age ten) contributed $1000 to 1996 Republican presidential hopeful Lamar Alexander on the same day her parents made $1000 payments. Skye's father, Scott Stolnitz, who funded Skye's checking account, later remarked that his daughter's contribution "was my decision based on what I thought was in her best interest."

➤◦► *With fiduciaries like these . . . :* Andrea Harris gave $36,500 to Republican candidates between 1991 and 1993 while she was a student. She and her sister subsequently sued to have their father, Harold Simmons, removed as trustee of the family fortune, alleging that he had made contributions from their accounts without their permission. Simmons has since reached an out-of-court settlement with his daughters.

➤◦► *But how did he sign the check?* The precocious Bradford Bainum gave $4000 to Democratic candidates before his second birthday, making his first political contribution when he was just eighteen months old.

Between 1991 and 1998, students gave 8876 federal contributions of at least $200 (the reporting threshold) for a total of $7.5 million; there were 163 contributions of $5000 or more. Between the 1992 and 1996 presidential elections, student donations increased by 45 percent to $2.6 million. Since 1975, the FEC has investigated and closed just four cases involving alleged illegal donations by minors. The only person to be subjected to punitive action was Stewart Bainum Jr., Bradford's father, who was fined $4000. In McCain-Feingold, lawmakers finally responded to this glaring loophole; the law bars children aged seventeen and under from making political contributions, period.

Family giving represents one variant of the widespread fund-raising tactic known as bundling, "in which people or organizations collect checks written by others, present them in a 'bundle' to a candidate, and gain political credit from the candidate for the full package." For instance, after a corporation determines which candidates to support, it will make "suggestions"—it is barred by law from outright coercion—to employees about where and when to send money. Some corporations also make illegal de facto contributions by providing strong incentives for their employees to make political contributions, such as giving bonuses to reimburse employees for their political contributions and matching employees' political contributions with donations to the employees' favorite charities. Under federal law, if bundled money is not coerced by a superior and actually comes from the employee's bank account, it's legal; however, the boss may not order or pay for the donation.

Bundling is a preferred method of fund-raising because like-minded individuals can maximize their political influence: a candidate might not remember the names of all the people who give him $1000, but he will not soon forget the person who delivers $25,000 from twenty-five people in his/her law firm or corporation. The problem is that bundling greatly facilitates special-interest influence, since candidates understandably regard XYZ Realty Corporation as a $25,000 donor—or a $100,000 donor—the law's $1000 maximum notwithstanding.

Still, bundling is and should be legal. The essence of private fund-raising is when supporters in turn persuade their friends and colleagues to contribute to their candidate. It would be neither possible nor desirable to force separate, solicited donors to each mail in their checks rather than allowing them to hand them to the person making the (publicly disclosed) solicitation. Still, bundlers can convey large amounts and get large credit.

In the 1994 election cycle, credit card and banking giant MBNA organized over $900,000 in bundled contributions to federal candidates; approximately $500,000 of that money went to four senators, including Alfonse D'Amato, then chair of the Banking Committee, who wasn't even up for reelection that year. In the 2000 elections, MBNA bundled $2.3 million in contributions to candidates and parties, with $240,700 going to George W. Bush. By giving through bundled donations instead of through a PAC (in which case it would have been limited to $10,000 per election), MBNA was able to increase its perceived donation to the Bush campaign by 2300 percent.

In the 2000 elections, EMILY's List (the group promotes pro-choice women candidates; EMILY is an acronym for "Early Money Is Like Yeast") topped the list of PAC bundlers, raising $21 million in lawfully bundled donations to support female Democratic candidates in the 2000 elections. Each of the 50,000 members of EMILY's List contributes $100 directly to the organization and promises to make $100 contributions to at least two candidates. The success of EMILY's List has inspired imitators and persuaded candidates to both solicit EMILY's List and be solicitous of their agenda.

What MBNA and EMILY's List do is lawful bundling. Then there's the illegal version: for example, when Simon Fireman, finance vice chairman to the 1996 Dole presidential campaign, gave $69,000 in bogus bundled contributions from employees at his own company, Aqua-Leisure Industries. Fireman's secretary, Carol Nichols, reportedly instructed employees to donate to the Dole campaign; when one employee balked at the instruction, Nichols actually gave the employee $2000 in cash to be used for the contribution. The cash was Fireman's, laundered through a shell corporation in Hong Kong and a Boston-area bank. Fireman was fined $60,000 and sentenced to six months' jail time.

In 1986, the National Republican Senatorial Committee (NRSC) launched a direct-mail campaign soliciting donations for vulnerable GOP candidates by listing four candidates in need of help. To avoid the contributions counting against its own limits, the NRSC reported the donations as individual contributions, claiming that the funds had been earmarked for particular candidates. In fact, the solicitation letter had instructed donors to make checks payable to the NRSC and without any indication of which candidate to support; the committee then rerouted the funds as it saw fit, often without even consulting the original donors. For instance, E. W. Dixon of Tulsa, Oklahoma, who had allegedly donated to Senator Mack Mattingly (R–GA), is quoted in Phil Stern's *Still the Best Congress Money Can Buy,* saying, "I don't know Mattingly from Adam's old fox." Similarly, Katherine Eberhard of Grand Rapids, Michigan, declared, "No way I would have sent money to Louisiana to Senator Moore or whoever he is." The NRSC funneled over $6.6 million in these contributions to Senate candidates by October 1986. Though the FEC recommended the maximum possible fine of $4.6 million, the sanctions were reduced to only $24,000 because the judge deciding the case felt that the NRSC "did not deliberately violate the law."

But the "reigning champion" of bundling is without a doubt President George W. Bush, who amassed $117 million in hard money contributions for the 2000 elections. Bush took bundling to unprecedented heights through a network of 212 so-called "Pioneers." Each Pioneer earned the title by bundling together over $100,000 in individual donations to the Bush campaign. In the 2004 elections, Dubya may be able to raise several hundred million dollars in hard money alone, in which case he may reject public financing for both the primary and the general elections.

"Independent" Expenditures

Instead of making monetary contributions *to* a candidate's campaign, would-be donors may decide to make what is commonly called an "independent expenditure" *for* a candidate. For example, an individual can purchase airtime and produce a television ad expressly supporting the candidate(s) of his choosing, so long as he does not coordinate these activities with the campaign. As far as *Buckley* is concerned, even unlimited expenditures of this kind raised no danger of corruption, since the campaign had no control over them.

This again displays the political naïveté of the *Buckley* court, a court where none of the eight ruling justices had ever run for political office (although Justice Byron White had experience in the Kennedy presidential campaign—and dissented from the majority opinion). First of all, an "independent" spender can read the newspaper and easily spend funds in ways beneficial to the campaign, or even speak to third parties—without any fear of detection, since there's no one watching or investigating—who in turn chat with campaign strategists. Second, the big donor may—and almost certainly will—discuss his activities with a winning campaign after the fact in the hopes of winning recognition and reaping rewards. As a result, what are theoretically independent expenditures often resemble in-kind contributions in practice.

In the twenty years after *Buckley,* the Supreme Court, in two landmark cases, set the stage for a dramatic increase in independent expenditures. In *FEC v. National Conservative Political Action Committee* (1985), the Court struck down a section of the law limiting PACs to $1000 in independent expenditures supporting federally subsidized presidential candidates. Eleven years later, in *Colorado Republican Federal Campaign Committee v. FEC,* the Court widened the loophole even further, ruling that the Colorado Republican Party's attack ads on the presumptive Democratic nominee were an independent expenditure and therefore did not count against the party's spending limits. In *Colorado Republican,* the Supreme Court ignored its previously stated conclusion that "party committees are considered incapable of making 'independent' expenditures in connection with the campaigns of their party's candidates."

It is likely that the 1976 *Buckley* Court simply did not appreciate the potential importance and growth of independent expenditures. In the 1972 elections, only 21 people made independent expenditures on the presidential race, spending a total of $98,060. By the 1980 elections, however, 105 PACs and 33 individuals spent a total of $16.1 million in independent expenditures, the bulk of it ($10.6 million) going to support Ronald Reagan. Some commentators have pointed out that because the circumstances of *Colorado Republican* are fairly uncommon—that is, parties generally don't spend a lot of money attacking opponents before choosing a nominee—the decision should be read narrowly. But in the six months between the *Colorado Republican* decision and the end of the 1996 election cycle, the Republican Party spent $10 million in independent expenditures, and the Democrats spent $1.5 million. In the 2000 elections, due to the growth of soft money, the Republicans made only $1.6 million in independent expenditures; Democrats spent $2.3 million.

But given the ban on soft money after November 2002, it's likely that a river of money will now flow to permissible "independent" committees instead. Already, economic, ideological, and partisan groups are organizing to recapture as much as they can of the $500 million in soft money that went to party committees in 2000. While there will likely be less such money, the mediating and moderating influence of a party organization may now be replaced by groups with specific legislative or ideological objectives. So watch for less money overall, but even more narrow, special appeals (the right to bear arms; *Roe v. Wade*; drilling in Alaska), paid for by the money that stays in the system.

At the same time, some of the most effective examples of independent expenditures have strained the meaning of "independent" beyond recognition. In the 1980 elections, for example, the National Conservative Political Action Committee (NCPAC) spent $3.3 million, with $1.4 million going to attack ads targeting six Democratic senators; one such ad asserted that because of liberals, "crime continues to rise . . . our nation's moral fiber is weakened by the growing homosexual movement, by the fanatical ERA pushers (many of whom publicly brag they are lesbians), by leftist-produced movies and television programs that are often indecent and full of sex." In South Dakota, NCPAC chairman John Terry Dolan encouraged Jim Abdnor to run against Senator George McGovern and supplied him with favorable polling data.

How independent was NCPAC? Senator Jesse Helms—dubbed by one reporter "the patron saint of NCPAC"—noted that federal law "forbids me to consult with him [Reagan on political issues]. I've had to, sort of, talk indirectly with [Senator] Paul Laxalt [Reagan's national campaign chairman]. . . . I hope that he would pass along, uh, and I think the messages have gotten through all right." Several senior NCPAC personnel had substantial links with the Reagan campaign; Dolan himself owned property with longtime Reagan aide Lyn Nofziger; Paul Russo, a member of the 1980 Reagan campaign; and former NCPAC treasurer Roger Stone, Reagan's northeast coordinator for the primary season. These links prompted Democrats to file complaints with the FEC, but to no avail.

The next year, emboldened by the defeat of the four targeted liberal senators, Dolan wrote a letter to Representative Stephen L. Neal (D–NC), urging him to support President Reagan's tax cut. In exchange for Neal's publicly supporting the measure, Dolan offered to "withdraw all radio and television ads planned in your district" and "to run radio and newspaper ads applauding your vote to lower taxes."

And in 1982, NCPAC spent $73,755 attacking Senator Daniel Patrick Moynihan (D–NY). The language used in NCPAC's ads bore a telling resemblance to official campaign commercials aired by Republican challenger Bruce Caputo: Moynihan "voted to give away the Panama Canal" and was responsible for the "runaway welfare system." In fact, both ad campaigns were coordinated by GOP consultant Arthur Finkelstein. It was not until 1986, four years after the election and three years after Caputo himself had admitted to coordinating the spending, that the FEC obtained a judgment against NCPAC.

The diary of Senator Bob Packwood, infamous for reasons having nothing to do with campaign finance, sheds light on his 1992 campaign against Democrat Les AuCoin. On October 6, Packwood writes of his meeting with a representative from the National Rifle Association: "He showed me the piece the [NRA] is going to send out hitting [AuCoin]. God, is it tough. . . . He said if he has enough money he's going to send it out to 100,000 Oregon gun owners, something like that. Now the question is: Are they going to do a second mailing just before the postcard about 'get out the vote'?" Packwood also benefited from $65,539 in independent expenditures by the Auto Dealers for Free Trade, about whom Packwood said, "Elaine [Franklin, Packwood's chief of staff] has been talking to me privately about independent expenditures. . . . Of course, we can't know anything about it. . . . We've got to destroy any evidence we've ever had of [blank] so that we have no connection with any independent expenditures."

The Supreme Court got it right the first time. While it's conceivable that a party could spend money for its candidate independently, it's desirable that a party and its candidate, who share a very common electoral goal, would collaborate and coordinate. *Colorado Republican* creates the unnatural situation of forcing party chairs to stop communicating with their own nominees, which is like Tinkers trying to turn a double play without Evers and Chance.

Issue Advocacy: Four Letters, Starts with a V, Sounds like "Note"

In order to justify subjecting campaign finance to federal regulation, *Buckley* distinguished election-related speech from general political speech, the latter being constitutionally protected from government interference. In a famous footnote, the Court suggested that the distinction could be drawn based on whether the communication included "magic words" such as "vote for," "elect," "support," "cast your ballot for," "Smith for Congress," "vote against," "defeat," or "reject." If those words were used, the funds used to pay for such electioneering communication were clearly subject to campaign finance limits; if they were not, the funds could not be regulated.

Distinguishing between "issue advocacy" and "express advocacy" makes a good deal of sense in principle. The paradigmatic case of express advocacy, as one thoughtful lawyer and scholar has put it, "(1) names one or more individual candidates for public office, (2) attributes one or more actions or beliefs to the candidate, (3) appears in close proximity to an election, and (4) explicitly urges the viewer to vote either for or against the candidate." Issue advocacy, on the other hand, "(1) addresses an issue of national or local political importance, (2) discusses only the issue and not the actions of particular political actors in regard to that issue, and (3) is broadcast at a time when legislative or executive action on the issue may be pending or contemplated, but no election is imminent."

The problem is that the "magic words" test does a terrible job of actually diagnosing what is and is not electioneering in reality. Con-

sider the following advertisement, aired in 2000 during the run-up to
the Ohio presidential primary:

> Last year, John McCain voted against solar and renewable
> energy. That means more use of coal-burning plants that pol-
> lute our air. Ohio Republicans care about clean air. So does
> Governor Bush. He led one of the first states in America to
> clamp down on old coal-burning electric power plants. Bush's
> clean air laws will reduce air pollution more than a quarter mil-
> lion tons a year. That's like taking five million cars off the
> road. Governor Bush, leading, for each day dawns brighter.

Or consider the following ad aired in Montana toward the end of the
1996 election season:

> Who is Bill Yellowtail? He preaches family values, but he took
> a swing at his wife. Yellowtail's explanation? He "only slapped
> her," but her nose was broken. He talks law and order, but is
> himself a convicted criminal. And though he talks about pro-
> tecting children, Yellowtail failed to make his own child sup-
> port payments, then voted against child support enforcement.
> Call Bill Yellowtail and tell him we don't approve of his wrong-
> ful behavior. Call (406) 443-3620.

Under the "magic words" test, neither advertisement is considered electioneering—despite their clear electioneering message.

As it turns out, whether a political advertisement contains "magic
words" bears virtually no relationship to the actual content or function
of the message. In a survey by political scientist David B. Magleby, individuals were shown two advertisements classified as issue advocacy and
were asked their impression of each ad's "primary purpose or objective."
Eighty-nine percent of the respondents said they thought the primary
purpose was to get them to vote either for or against a particular candidate; only 6 to 8 percent thought the primary purpose of the ad was to
present an issue. In fact, among the advertisements produced by the candidates themselves in 2000, only 10 percent used the so-called magic

words; in 1998, only 4 percent of candidate ads themselves would have been classified as express advocacy under the "magic words" standard.

The gross and obvious failure of this standard has allowed outside players—parties and interest groups—to take over the airwaves during elections. In the 2000 elections, $509 million was spent on purchasing television and radio spots for so-called issue advocacy. The two major parties accounted for almost one third ($162 million) of these expenditures. The top six nonparty spenders accounted for another third of spending, as given in figure 3.3. All told, nonparty groups purchased 142,421 television advertisements in 2000; in the 1998 elections, nonparty groups purchased only 21,712 advertisements.

An analysis by the Brennan Center for Justice at the New York University School of Law reveals that 83 percent of the ads aired by these outside players were really aimed at electing candidates. All of the ads sponsored by political parties also fell into the category of electioneering issue ads. In the crucial final sixty days before the 2000 election, a staggering 99.4 percent of the group-sponsored ads were electioneering ads; only three different ads, airing a total of 331 times (out of 142,421), were genuine issue ads.

FIGURE 3.3
NONPARTY SPENDING ON ISSUE ADVOCACY

Group	Expenditures ($ in millions)
CITIZENS FOR BETTER MEDICARE	$65
COALITION TO PROTECT AMERICA'S HEALTH CARE	$30
U.S. CHAMBER OF COMMERCE	$25.5
AFL-CIO	$21
NATIONAL RIFLE ASSOCIATION	$20
U.S. TERM LIMITS	$20

If that doesn't prove the Supreme Court made a monumental mistake in *Buckley* by allowing such spending to go unregulated, what would?

Many of these sham issue ads are funded by nonprofit groups organized under Section 527 of the Internal Revenue Code. Until recently, these so-called 527s were exempt from even disclosing contributions or expenditures; their lack of accountability earned them the nickname "stealth PACs." On July 1, 2000, President Clinton signed a bill authored by Senators John McCain and Joseph Lieberman (D–CT) requiring 527s to notify the FEC of their existence and make regular reports of contributions and expenditures. In April 2002, the House defeated a measure sponsored by Representatives Bill Thomas and Kevin Brady (R–TX) that would have rolled back some the disclosure provisions of the McCain-Lieberman bill.

Self-Financed Ballot Proposals

In addition to self-financing campaigns for office—which will be discussed in greater detail in chapter 5—powerful people are increasingly using their financial advantage to enact laws by paying for initiatives and referendums. Now permitted in twenty-four states, initiatives allow citizens to draft and vote on laws directly by putting them on the ballot, while referendums give citizens the right to repeal state laws by popular vote.

Originally seen as a democratizing reform that would allow citizens to bypass corrupt or paralyzed legislatures, the initiative today, as Michael Nelson writes in the *American Prospect,* "is a device used mostly by a dark trinity of wealthy individuals, special interests, and professional initiative activists to force their pet causes to the top of the political agenda."

Here's how it works. First, a well-endowed interest—sometimes a person, sometimes an industry group—drafts a ballot question it favors for financial or ideological reasons. It may involve monetary incentives, like rolling back property taxes, or social issues, like school vouchers on the ballot. Whatever the question, the less organized and funded the potential opposition, the better its chance of passage. Also important to a ballot question's success, writes George Pillsbury of *Dollars and Sense* magazine, is that it "poses an issue on which the public is ambivalent or lacks basic knowledge." In other words, the less of an opinion the public already has on the matter, the more easily influenced by expensive advertising it will be.

Once these conditions are in place, the self-financer can hire lobbying firms to manage the campaign, outside companies to gather signatures to get the proposal on the ballot, polling groups to target voters, high-priced media gurus to run ad campaigns, and lawyers to defend the question's legality.

The process of citizens bypassing legislatures and sponsoring laws is growing rapidly. While there were fewer than 100 ballot questions in the 1960s, there were nearly 250 in the 1980s, around 400 in the 1990s, and 76 in the year 2000 alone. Some of the effects of ballot questions financed by big interests have been pronounced: landlords and realtors spent $1.5 million to pass (by 54,000 out of 2 million votes) a 1994 initiative banning rent control in Massachusetts, and the gambling industry used a 1998 measure to bring riverboat gambling to Missouri.

Wealthy *individuals*—on the left and the right—have exerted considerable influence, too. Billionaire cosmetics heir Ronald Lauder recovered from a landslide defeat for the New York City mayoralty in 1989 to single-handedly finance a successful campaign to institute term limits. He spent $2 million for it, next to nothing was spent against it—and it passed with 59 percent of the vote. Reed Hastings, a former software executive worth $750 million, spent more than $4 million in California in 1999 to allow local schools to finance new classrooms with taxes approved by a majority of voters. Billionaires George Soros, Peter B. Lewis, and John Sperling sponsored a $2 million 1998 campaign to legalize medical marijuana in six states and Washington, D.C. Only after the initiative passed with little opposition in Arizona did Representative Mike Gardner, a Republican, realize that the measure covered not just marijuana but 116 other drugs, including LSD, heroin, and PCP.

What can be done to curb the influence of wealthy individuals nearly single-handedly writing our laws? Author and professor Richard Ellis has voted no on each of the seventy-four statewide initiatives he's seen in twelve years as an Oregon resident—out of principle. Arguing that initiatives eliminate the deliberative process of committee hearings and floor debates refining legislative language, Ellis suggests that a decent start would be Illinois's system, in which initiatives amending the state constitution require three-fifths majorities, or Nevada's model where initiatives need to be passed in two straight elections.

Ultimately, though, the answer may be a system of public financing that helps fund underrepresented viewpoints opposing a torrent of special-interest or individual treasuries. Now, elected officials who persistently promote unpopular causes can be voted out of office. But not so self-financers. Unless there are either constitutionally permissible spending limits or public funding to level the playing field, or both, unaccountable and unelected multimillionaires will be able to supplant elected legislatures to enact their pet grievances or causes.

Other Loopholes

In addition to shelling out large sums of money for political campaigns, special interests can also curry favor with politicians through a variety of other loopholes in the law.

In the past, one particularly effective way to gain favor with a representative was to invite him or her to give a speech, and then pay a speaking fee—or to have lunch with a member, call it a "speech," and pay an honorarium. In fact, because such money went directly to the legislator as personal income, these "dishonoraria" could be even more potent than a campaign contribution. In 1990, House Ways and Means Committee chairman Dan Rostenkowski (D–IL) collected $310,000; the House's second most prolific speaker, Pat Schroeder (D–CO), earned $160,000. In the Senate, Ernest "Fritz" Hollings (D–SC) and Bob Dole led the way, with $82,200 and $78,100, respectively. All told, the U.S. Congress pulled in almost $8.4 million in honoraria that year, down from the high-water mark of almost $10 million set in 1987. Starting in 1991, however, the House of Representatives barred members from collecting honoraria; the Senate then passed a similar ban.

Another favorite device was for interest groups to provide members of Congress with expense-paid trips, often to popular vacation spots.

As a 1991 report by Public Citizen's Congress Watch puts it, these junkets "provide special interest groups with the unique opportunity to meet privately with powerful lawmakers in a manner not typically enjoyed by the average constituent." Members of the House accepted a total of 3984 privately funded trips in 1989 and 1990, two thirds of which were paid for by corporate interests. In 1995, Congress banned purely recreational junkets.

This rule change, however, has not stopped determined interest groups and members from, respectively, offering and accepting junkets; now they have to go through the pretense of having official business. For instance, in February 1996, Senator Trent Lott spent three days in Aspen thanks to the largesse of Domino's Pizza Team Washington. Given that the officially stated purpose of the trip was to speak to D.C.-area franchisees, it's hard not to wonder if the Domino's headquarters in Alexandria, Virginia—a short cab ride from the Capitol—might have been a more convenient location than flying Lott out to Colorado.

Politicians can also consolidate their power by setting up independent nonprofit organizations and so-called leadership PACs. Because campaign finance laws "do not effectively regulate money that goes to ostensibly independent bodies," these organizations serve as a useful back channel for money. Bob Dole was especially adroit at exploiting this loophole, raising millions of dollars through Campaign America (his leadership PAC), the Dole Foundation for People with Disabilities (a charitable organization), and the Better America Foundation (a social welfare organization). Of these, the Dole Foundation was officially apolitical; however, a survey of contributors to the foundation revealed that 65 percent of donors also gave to Dole's campaigns. And the Better America Foundation disbanded in 1995 under criticism that it was nothing more than a front for Dole's political activities, but not before spending $1 million during the 1994 elections on television ads featuring Dole.

Leadership PACs not only act as an alternate means of fundraising; they also create political debts by helping candidates make campaign contributions to their own right-wing colleagues. Democratic presidential hopefuls are already aggressively raising money through leadership PACs for the 2004 election season. The leadership PAC of Senator John Edwards (D-NC), created in late 2001, has a balance of $2.4 million as of July 2002, including $1.7 million in soft money. And potential presidential candidates Tom Daschle, Richard Gephardt, Joe Lieberman, and John Kerry all had between $500,000 and $1.5 million each.

In the first year of the 2002 election cycle, contributions from leadership PACs to candidates increased by 68 percent from two years before. Don Nickles, whom some believe may challenge Lott for the top Republican post in the Senate, gave $350,000 to favored colleagues. Senator Hillary Rodham Clinton (D–NY) gave $290,000, and in the House Tom DeLay gave $377,000. Giving money to other members is a perfectly legal way to enhance one's power within Congress, which in turn can multiply fund-raising later. Power attracts money; money entrenches power.

And the lack of money risks forfeiting power. I myself was called by a member of Congress and a friend seeking a leadership post in 2002. Here was the pitch: "My opponent is raising a million bucks to give to incumbents. And if he gives them $10,000 and I give $2000, I don't have to tell you, Mark, what that means."

CAMPAIGNING FOR MONEY
30,000 Phone Calls Later . . .

"I get elected by voters; I get financed by contributors.
Voters don't care about this; contributors do."
—A Democratic congressman to the *Washington Post,* 1989

"Today's political campaigns function as collection
agencies for broadcasters. You simply transfer money
from contributors to television stations."
—Former Senator Bill Bradley, 2000

"I'm not calling to ask for your vote. It'd be a waste
of time to make a phone call for a single vote. My purpose is
far more humiliating. It's the chemotherapy of a political
campaign. It's painful. Wouldya give me some money?"
—Senate candidate Alex Sander, 2002

Like the designation "cc" (for "carbon copy") on an e-mail screen, "running for office" is an outdated term. Thanks to today's high-cost races, candidates spend very little time *running,* in the traditional sense of the word—mobilizing voters, communicating ideas, debating opponents, attending public meetings. Instead, candidates *fund-raise for office.* Their time is dominated by the incessant chore of pleading, cajoling, schmoozing for campaign cash. "It's this incredible, almost evil process, of me sitting on the phone for hours at a time, begging people for money," grumbled one local candidate from Missouri. Senator Carl Levin, reminiscing how he spent $950,000 to win his Michigan seat in 1978 and $6 million to hold it in 1996, said in a phone interview on a fund-raising trip, "If you don't like raising money—and I don't—you've got to grit your teeth and do it." The real running that occurs in modern American politics is the sprint for the gold.

Over the last thirty years, campaign costs have been growing at stratospheric rates, faster than even baseball and movie star salaries. Because television is by far the most effective means of reaching potential voters, the candidate who wins the battle of the airwaves usually wins the war at the polls. The only way to assure airwave victory is to outspend—and therefore outraise—your opponent.

As the money chase ensues, candidates naturally turn to donors who have deep enough pockets (specifically, PACs and wealthy individuals) to fund their expensive campaign tabs. The golden triangle of politics—campaign costs, the dash for cash, and interested money— may bend, as when an outspent challenger occasionally defeats an established incumbent. However, it is tough to break: 94 percent of congressional races end in victory for the candidate who outspends his or her opponent.

The Arms Race and the Ads Race

The Cold War may have ended more than a decade ago, but an arms race to scare off potential threats is alive and well in American politics. Consider New Jersey's Bob Torricelli, a skilled fund-raiser weakened by a Senate Ethics Committee that "severely admonished" him for accepting gifts from a big donor. The senator hoped to thin the field in his 2002 reelection bid by announcing that he'd raise $20 million. Did the strategy work? He was uncontested in the primary, and his Republican opponent in the general was not Tom Kean, the very popular former governor, but rather businessman Doug Forrester, a political neophyte who spent enough money in a low-profile primary to defeat two New Jersey state senators.

True, unlike nuclear weapons, which exist in order never to be used, the political arms race creates an insatiable competition to raise money for attack ads that certainly will be used. The effect is not merely psychological but also functional: money pays for everything, from campaign staff salaries to public opinion polls to advertisements.

To get an idea of the scope of this political arms race, consider that in 1972, the year the Federal Election Campaign Act became law, total campaign expenditures by House and Senate candidates was $77 million. Twenty-eight years later, in the 2000 elections, total hard money spending by congressional candidates reported to the Federal Election Commission reached $999 million, an increase of nearly 1200 percent. At this rate of inflation, moviegoers who paid $2.50 in 1972 to see Robert Redford win a Senate seat in *The Candidate* would have paid $32.50 to see "Senator" Joan Allen survive as a vice presidential nominee in the 2000 film *The Contender*.

Table 4.1 displays campaign expenditures from the last six congressional election cycles. While the overall annual average rate of increase for total expenditures was almost 18 percent, a definite pattern appears to be taking shape: a sharp increase in one year, followed by several years of level spending, then another meteoric single-year jump. In the 1992 presidential election year, congressional campaign expenditures jumped more than $200 million from 1990. Expenditures held the line at the $700 million range until the 2000 elections, when they increased about another $250 million to settle at $1 billion. Reported expenditures so far in the 2002 election cycle seem to support this pattern, with spending likely to remain in the $1 billion range.

Beyond the arms race psychology, why the ever higher spending pattern? Because costs are rising far faster than inflation, especially one cost: television advertising, which is, without question, the single largest expense item on the typical campaign balance sheet. Especially for statewide races, candidates harness TV's unmatched ability of reaching the greatest number of potential voters. As media consultant Hank Sheinkopf bluntly stated, "Television is dominant, it is overbearing, it is overreaching, and it gets into people's homes." His professional advice to candidates in statewide races is to dedicate as much as 70 percent of their campaign budget to television. If the TV budget falls much below 50 percent of all spending, a campaign is regarded as wasteful, incompetent, and likely unsuccessful.

TABLE 4.1

CONGRESSIONAL CAMPAIGN EXPENDITURES, 1990–2000

$ in Millions in real (after-inflation) dollars   *Change (%)*

	1990	1992	1994	1996	1998	2000	1990– 2000	1998– 2000	Annual Rate
SENATE EXPENDITURES	$180.4	$270.8	$316.9	$286.6	$287.5	$431.9	139.4	50.2	19.1
HOUSE EXPENDITURES	$264.7	$404.3	$404.4	$472.5	$448.3	$566.6	114.0	26.4	16.4
TOTAL EXPENDITURES	$445.2	$675.1	$721.2	$759.1	$735.8	$998.5	124.3	35.7	17.5

Source: Federal Election Commission.

Note: Because of rounding, totals may not add up.

Even as broadcasters receive free licenses to operate the public airwaves, they do their best to exploit candidates desperately seeking voters, particularly in the latter weeks of a race. A recent Bear Stearns study revealed that "in even-numbered election years, political advertising is now the third biggest category of ads sold on local broadcast television—behind automotive and retail stores, but ahead of movies and fast foods."

According to an analysis of the top seventy-five media markets during the 2000 election by the Alliance for Better Campaigns, political ad sales accounted for $771 million; when the nation's remaining smaller markets are included, that figure would likely cross the $1 billion mark. These figures represent the sales revenues of broadcast television only, not cable, and include hard-money expenditures by candidates as well as soft money expenditures by parties and interest groups. Table 4.2 reveals the biggest hard money spenders on broadcast television advertising in 2000 Senate races. Not surprisingly, the three biggest spenders, Jon Corzine, Rick Lazio, and Hillary Rodham Clinton (the last two running against each other), ran in the country's number one media market. Several candidates adhered to Sheinkopf's advice, dedicating about 70 percent of their budget to television, led by two southern senators, Zell Miller (D–GA) and Bill Nelson (D–FL); see table 4.3.

TABLE 4.2

TOP CAMPAIGN SPENDING ON BROADCAST ADS BY U.S. SENATE CANDIDATES, 2000

Candidate	State	Total Spent	Spent on Broadcast Ads	Percentage Spent on Broadcast Ads
Jon Corzine (D)	NJ	$63,202,492	$39,999,560	63
Rick Lazio (R)	NY	$43,038,453	$20,935,067	49
Hillary Clinton (D)	NY	$29,595,761	$16,530,095	56
Spencer Abraham (R)	MI	$14,415,920	$ 7,961,319	55
Mark Dayton (D)	MN	$11,957,115	$ 7,722,091	65
Maria Cantwell (D)	WA	$11,538,133	$ 7,007,000	61
Rick Santorum (R)	PA	$12,826,761	$ 6,290,145	49
George Allen (R)	VA	$ 9,894,904	$ 5,650,709	57
John Ashcroft (R)	MO	$ 9,742,579	$ 5,568,434	57
Dianne Feinstein (D)	CA	$11,604,749	$ 5,126,440	44

Source: Alliance for Better Campaigns.

TABLE 4.3

TOP CAMPAIGN SPENDING ON BROADCAST ADS AS PERCENTAGE OF TOTAL SPENDING BY U.S. SENATE CANDIDATES, 2000

Candidate	State	Total Spent	Spent on Broadcast Ads	Percentage Spent on Broadcast Ads
Zell Miller (D)	GA	$ 2,517,702	$ 1,910,144	76
Bill Nelson (D)	FL	$ 6,674,656	$ 5,043,704	76
Charles Robb (D)	VA	$ 6,778,099	$ 4,539,343	67
Mack Mattingly (R)	GA	$ 1,019,524	$ 662,653	65
Mark Dayton (D)	MN	$11,957,115	$ 7,722,091	65
Ed Bernstein (D)	NV	$ 2,446,048	$ 1,570,727	64
Jon Corzine (D)	NJ	$63,202,492	$39,999,560	63
David Johnson (D)	IN	$ 1,173,299	$ 736,649	63
Herb Kohl (D)	WI	$ 5,535,630	$ 3,385,991	61
Maria Cantwell (D)	WA	$11,538,133	$ 7,007,000	61

Source: Alliance for Better Campaigns.

The chips are stacked against political campaigns when it comes to purchasing television ads. Thrust into a highly competitive, free-market system that rewards the highest bidder, candidates not only square off against their opponents for optimum time slots but also must contend with giant corporations like General Motors, which alone spends close to $2 billion a year on TV advertising. In the fight for airspace, it's as if candidates are trying to wage an air battle in a hang glider, jousting against the corporations' F-16 piloted by Tom Cruise's Maverick.

The anatomy of the TV advertising market is based on a unit of measurement called the gross rating point. Stations charge advertisers on a per point basis, and only the market regulates the cost per point. The cost of a spot varies based on the time when the commercial airs (known as the *slot*), with primetime ads—when most viewers are tuned to their sets—costing the most. Slot classifications are not as simple as primetime and daytime. Within primetime, there exist numerous slots, such as the 9:45–9:59 P.M. slot, which has a completely different cost-per-point value than the 10:00–10:15 P.M. slot. The fourth quarter, from October through December, happens to be the most expensive time of year to purchase an ad, thanks to the holidays, when advertisers of all kinds are jockeying for airtime.

In any given television market, 100 gross rating points is the equivalent of 100 percent of a target audience (e.g., adults ages 25 to 49) seeing a spot one time. A 500-point buy means the target sees the commercial five times; 1000 points, ten times. Because it usually requires ten viewings for a spot to be recognized and remembered, candidates usually purchase ads in the range of 800 to 1200 points per spot.

Complicating matters even more is that the price per point depends not only on the commercial's slot and season but also on its *class*—that is, the nature of the package you buy from the media outlet. The most expensive class is "fixed rate," where an advertiser pays a premium price, ensuring the commercial will air at the desired time. "Current selling level" is the next class, representing the current market rate for an ad. "Preemptible with notice" is available at a cost below market rate, but if another advertiser is willing to pay the fixed rate or current selling level, the station will notify the original advertiser that the ad has been bumped. Finally, "preemptible without notice" is the cheapest class and means that a station will not even warn an advertiser that a higher bidder has bumped them. For really hot slots during the primetime hours, stations might cram as many as ten classes into a slot, then sit back and watch—like an eBay entrepreneur auctioning off a vintage Jackie Robinson bobble-head doll—as advertisers bid the price through the roof.

"It's a clever thing the stations have done," says Steve McMahon, a Washington, D.C.–based political consultant and experienced buyer of political advertising. "If you throw the dice and win by purchasing at the cheapest time class, you're doing great, especially in races where there are spending caps. But if you purchase "preemptible without notice" time and get pushed off from a 9:37 P.M. slot to 10:37 P.M., your candidate's not going to be very happy." As a result, most political ad buyers concede that it's too risky to purchase in the preemptible classes, and are forced to pay more money to secure the desired slot.

In addition to slot and class, the cost per point varies according to TV market. The price in statewide markets, which relates to Senate and gubernatorial races, can range from $35 per point in a state like South Dakota to $2400 per point in a state like California. During the 2001 mayoral race in New York City, the most expensive local market in the nation, the cost per point in the "current selling level" class for a primetime September slot was roughly $860. At 1000 points, this brings the cost for one thirty-second ad to $860,000.

The only safeguard protecting candidates from price-gouging television stations is a flimsy thirty-year-old law known as the Lowest Unit Charge (LUC), which requires television stations to offer candidates most-favored-advertiser status. A favored advertiser is one that buys a lot of "up-front" time, purchasing ads as much as a year before they're actually aired. Because they buy ad time in bulk and early, up-front buyers are given huge discounts at the non-preemptible, fixed-rate class. Under LUC protection, political advertisers are supposed to receive these same discounts without having to buy early and in bulk.

But LUC has several loopholes, through which broadcasters have managed to punch a fistful of dollars. For example, many ads sold at the LUC aren't in the fixed-rate class. They can be bumped, without notice, if another advertiser offers more money. So a campaign can go along with the LUC and pay the preferred rate, but they'll have to accept that their ad may be buried in a 2:00 A.M. slot. Candidates usually opt for the more expensive guarantee that viewer-voters will actually see the spot. "One of the big, dark secrets of politics is the industry standard," said one East Coast media consultant. "If a campaign's willing to bite on a $1 million TV buy and the station charges the [LUC] industry standard, that station manager's a shmuck."

Also, stations routinely change rates from week to week, sometimes dramatically, and it's no coincidence to see a crescendo in these rates as campaigns enter the final weeks with candidates vying for precious airtime. In my 2001 mayoral race, the $860 per point that was spent toward the end of the summer grew to $1400 per point for the Democratic runoff in early October, to $2400 per point in the early weeks of the general election, finally settling at $3000 per point in the last couple of weeks before the November 6 election.* That's about $3 million for one 1000-point ad. So a $16.2 million war chest may sound like a lot, but not when it costs $3 million to finance one ad. And stations know they have the candidates right where they want them; it's not as if any of us can call up and say, "No thanks, I prefer carrier pigeon."

New York City isn't the only place where stations squeeze candidates. In a review of more than 16,000 candidate ad sales logs at ten television stations in medium-size and large markets, the Alliance for Better Campaigns found that candidates paid, on average, 65 percent more for their ads in the closing months of the 2000 campaign than the base candidates' rate published on the station's own rate card. "The stations are flimflam artists running a great big shell game," concludes McMahon, who compares the political advertising market—with all its slots and classes—to the airline ticket market, where you can pay $1000 and find yourself next to a passenger who paid $250 for the same flight.

An amendment to the McCain-Feingold bill proposed by Senator Torricelli was intended to keep stations from inflating ad rates in the

*Stations claimed that they had to increase rates by so much because they lost substantial revenue as a result of the uninterrupted news coverage after September 11.

stretch run of campaigns by enforcing the discount law. Candidates would have been assured fixed-rate, non-preemptible status by purchasing ads at the lower, preemptible rates. The amendment easily passed the Senate 70–30, but after the National Association of Broadcasters (NAB) emphasized that "candidates must operate in this supply and demand market," the amendment died in the House.

Why? Largely because of the broadcast television industry itself, which John McCain has called "the most powerful industry in Washington." Representative Louise Slaughter (D–NY) was even more candid in an interview: "Obviously the broadcasting industry bought off members of the House. . . . Members said they had to vote against it because their little radio or TV station back home begged them. Come on. Who owns the stations? Show me one not owned by a conglomerate or media giant."

Not coincidentally, NAB lobbying efforts included donations to both the Democratic and Republican Congressional Campaign Committees—monies that go to House members' own campaign war chests, which conveniently are then spent for expensive airtime.

And there's another factor at play here. Candidates are under increasing pressure to buy "paid media" because of the gradual decline of "free media." Television news programs are covering political campaigns less, as they themselves compete with cable news by airing more "sexy" stories that appeal to hard-to-please viewers. After if-it-bleeds-it-leads coverage of crime, terrorism, and war, plus local features and weather, there's rarely time left for local campaigns*—not to mention that television stations have a market incentive to create a demand for candidate ads by undercovering elections.

Compounding this problem is the fact that most of the debates from the 2000 election were not even televised. A report by the Committee for the Study of the American Electorate found that only 37 percent of debates in ten states were actually aired, with a paltry 18 percent

---

*In the fall of 2000, local stations averaged just 45 seconds per night of election campaign coverage, while national networks devoted 64 seconds a night. And today's ever precious sound bite averages about 7 seconds, compared with some 40 seconds in the early 1970s.

broadcast on a major network affiliate. "For the vast majority of citizens in these states and districts, it was as if these debates never happened," said Curtis Gans, director of the group. "These debates are the only means to cut through the demagogic advertising that dominates campaigns, the dearth of coverage, and the interpretations of journalists."

The costs of producing a television commercial are also on the rise, in part because of more expensive, technologically advanced equipment and also because of the need to create ever flashier spots that will stand out amid the visual clutter and grab the wandering attention of merciless remote-control- or TIVO-wielding viewers. "In the MTV age, candidates are more interested in sizzle than steak," laments Sheinkopf, who himself has no choice but to give the candidates what they want.

Finally, the Telecommunications Act of 1996, along with the deregulation fervor of the Federal Communications Commission, has encouraged a concentration of powerful conglomerates in broadcast and newspaper markets, including Disney, AOL Time Warner, News Corporation, General Electric, and the New York Times Company. From the early 1980s to 2000, the number of owners of major media outlets in the United States dropped from about fifty to just six. Less competition produces higher ad rates.

To Paul Taylor, executive director of the Alliance for Better Campaigns and a national advocate for keeping political ad rates low or free, there is a certain irony in the increased spending and reliance on broadcast ads. "Political advertising as a form of persuasion is less effective than it used to be," says Taylor, sitting in front of the cluttered desk in his M Street office, loaded with reports, articles, and notes on the broadcast industry, "in part because there's more saturation, in part because the audience is fragmented. It used to be, a generation ago, if you hit the network-affiliated stations you were hitting a much larger slice of your target audience than you are today. You're no longer quite the captive couch potato you were a generation ago, with clickers and replay TV; not only do you have more choices, but you have greater ability, once the ad appears, to get rid of it.

"Product advertising has responded to this new, more difficult reality by making the advertising a lot better than it used to be. Product advertising is some of the most creative, gorgeous, funny stuff on television. Political advertising is the same damn ads we've been watching for thirty years. Candidate advertising is by its nature straightforward meat and potatoes. It seems out of place, of a different era. Consultants know that the click-off rate for a political spot is extremely high.

"The conundrum is that these ads are less and less effective than they've ever been, [yet] the response of the political community is to run more and more of them. 'My ads aren't working; double the volume.' Candidates are not rational economic thinkers; they are candidates. Even in a world where smart candidates understand that other methods may be more efficient, there is a validation that [comes from] being on TV that makes all of those other activities more efficient. It's the closest thing we have to a public square."

To compensate for the dry nature of political ads, and to make a lasting impression on the viewer-voter, candidates are relying more on attack ads, especially in close races. Tony Schwartz's famous "daisy" spot for Lyndon Johnson in the 1964 presidential race—where a little girl counts down the petals of a daisy, and at "one" a huge mushroom cloud appears, presumably because opponent Barry Goldwater's election risked nuclear war—established the gold standard of the power of negative advertising, paving the way for the scathing attacks that are now commonplace in politics.

Today, most competitive races have nasty attack ads. The Brennan Center for Justice found that in the 1998 congressional elections 27 percent of all political ads could be classified as attack ads, versus 48 percent that promoted a candidate or issue and 20 percent that contrasted them. The author is no exception. Wanting to run only positive ads in the general election, I began with an endorsement spot with former governor Mario Cuomo and one with me speaking about education. Then Michael Bloomberg began spending $30 million in three weeks on well-crafted ads essentially saying that I was anti-police and anti-minority.

In 2000, Hillary Rodham Clinton and then Representative Rick Lazio engaged in a high-profile battle, blasting each other on the airwaves with numerous attacks and counterattacks in their fight for an open New York Senate seat. One ad—produced and paid for by the Christian Action Coalition, not Lazio—luridly discussed Hillary and Bill Clinton's private sex lives and marriage. It crossed the line, and most

New York stations actually refused to run it. Still, Clinton answered with her own attacks, accusing Lazio of missing important votes in the House, and linking him with the unpopular Newt Gingrich.

In the 2002 primary election cycle, Artur Davis forced a runoff with—and then defeated—eighteen-year incumbent Representative Earl Hilliard in Alabama's Seventh Congressional District; Davis's campaign featured negative ads showing Hilliard, who had proposed a bill in Congress to lift sanctions against terrorist-sponsoring nations, smiling and clapping opposite images of Osama bin Laden and Saddam Hussein.

"People don't like them, but they work," believes media consultant McMahon of negative ads. "Repetition is what it takes to make the message stick, and positive ads need a lot more repetition than negative ones. If you show ten advertisements to a focus group—nine positive, one negative—then ask them their impressions, almost without fail they will prefer the positive ads. But in a blind callback two or three days later, they will invariably be able to recite the negative ad and have forgotten the positive ones."

Although television is by far the most significant campaign cost, other communication media are contributing to swelling budgets.

Radio, like television, is a largely unregulated market, where political ads compete for slots against an open field of time buyers.

Direct mail is a proven method of informing particular voters of a candidate's assets and arguments. Unlike broadcasting, where all viewers in an electronic market see the same television ad, direct mail allows candidates to *narrow*cast, sending a "black" piece to African American communities, a "woman's" piece to women's lists, and a "law and order" piece to white ethnic zip codes. This is especially effective in local assembly and council races, where television costs can be prohibitive, since the media market is far larger than the voting market. Costs have escalated, of course, as postage has risen. Since 1991, the price of first-class postage has increased 48 percent, a cost that gets passed forward to campaigns. Yes, even the federal government is guilty of making campaigns more expensive.

Voice broadcasting is a new, popular campaigning technique, especially in the last few days of a race. Through the technologies of automated telephony, candidates themselves—or other luminaries—can leave personalized pitches on voters' home answering machines, urging them to vote for a particular candidate. It leaves a strong impression on a voter's mind when he or she gets home from work, hits the play button on the machine, and hears, "Hello, this is Bill Clinton. I'm calling to let you know that I support Jim Smith for U.S. House of Representatives . . ." After the 2001 mayor's race, our consultant for voice broadcasting was proudly describing to a Bloomberg consultant how we used the voices of Bill Clinton, David Dinkins, Gloria Steinem, and Martin Sheen in several hundred thousand calls. The Bloomberg consultant responded that they had bought 11 million *live* calls during the campaign—this in a city of 5 million eligible voters.

Companies providing this kind of automated voice broadcasting service claim that it's cheaper than direct mail and has better results. Target Marketing USA, Inc., offers price comparisons in its marketing literature, advertising 100,000 automated calls at 6 cents a call, or $6000. This is a bargain compared with direct mail, where postage alone costs 37 cents an item, making the cost of 100,000 items at least $37,000—not to mention that it's much more likely for a piece of junk mail to be thrown away than for someone to hang up on a twenty-five-second call from a celebrity.

The *Internet* is the newest medium for capturing voters' attention, as well as soliciting contributions. It's cheaper and can be more targeted than television or radio, though well-designed, interactive Web sites can be costly to build and update.

The Professionalization of Politics

As campaigns have become more strategic and intricate, an industry of professional political consultants has emerged. A typical candidate for the Senate or House might hire five to ten different firms to handle the various facets of a campaign, including media, polling, direct mail, negative research, telemarketing, voter lists, and, of course, fund-raising. In turn, these firms often hire additional support specialists. This web of firms, contractors, and subcontractors forms a vast political-industrial complex that has proven indispensable to winning political races, but has also tacked hundreds of thousands of dollars onto House races and millions of dollars onto Senate campaign budgets.

It should come as no surprise that the roots of professional political consulting sprang up in Hollywood's backyard, with the advertising agency team of Clem Whitaker and Leone Baxter. They played a critical role in the 1934 smear campaign against Upton Sinclair's bid for the California governor's mansion. After winning the Democratic primary on a platform nicknamed EPIC (End Poverty in California), the populist-minded Sinclair put a real scare into the state's political establishment. Enter Whitaker and Baxter, hired by the interests behind Republican nominee, Governor Frank F. Merriam, to malign the upstart Democrat. The ad men hired Hollywood filmmakers to produce the very first candidate commercials, in the form of newsreels that painted Sinclair as an immigrant-loving Communist. In one reel, a bearded comrade sporting an unmistakable Russian accent is asked why he supports Sinclair. "Vell, his system worked vell in Russia," he muses. "Vy can't it work here?" After receiving the most votes of any candidate in either primary, Sinclair lost the general election, managing only 38 percent of the vote.

The business of political consulting has come a long way since this inauspicious start. Not all consultants play the game as ruthlessly as Whitaker and Baxter, although most are as strategic as the pioneering ad men. The tactics of today's consultants range from shocking negative ads, to creative approaches to fund-raising, to what the late Lee Atwater once described as any "stunt you can pull that will give you fourteen seconds of news hole."

One area where the professionalization of politics has really taken off in contemporary campaigns is the extensive gauging of public opinion. Taking a cue from corporations, which have long relied on focus groups and surveys to test and develop products, politicians use these same practices to package and "sell" their campaigns. Expert pollsters have been referred to as "the central nervous system of modern political campaigns."

When done properly and effectively, a poll can be a very complicated, costly task. The foremost determinant of cost is the size of the sample involved in a poll. The larger the sample, the more expensive the poll. The typical sample size is 600, which, depending on several additional factors, can cost more than $40,000. Two other factors that affect the price of a poll are the length of the interview and the experience of the firm performing the research and analysis. In terms of a campaign's budget, consultants advise candidates to dedicate between 5 and 10 percent of their expenses to polling. The difference between a candidate who can afford just $2000 for a poll and a candidate who can spend $200,000 is vast. "If you can only afford to poll to determine if you're ahead or behind in a race," says veteran pollster Mark Mellman, "you're at a great disadvantage to someone who can poll voters' reaction to three different messages."

Mellman, who has polled for a dozen sitting senators, adds, "Polling is at its best when it is testing the relative merits of competing ideas, hypothesis, and theories. Some of the members of the campaign team may think the best message is talking about the future of the district; others may think focusing on the candidate's record as a tough crime fighter will be more effective. Polling can determine which approach will, in fact, be more fruitful. Some members of the campaign team will argue that Ward Three voters should be the campaign's prime targets while others say Hispanic voters, wherever they may live, ought to be top priority. Again, polling can help resolve these conflicting theories."

Several types of polls are performed throughout the course of a political race. One of the first actions of a campaign is the benchmark poll. The most extensively researched survey, it is used to lay the campaign's strategy and identify the most important issues and ideas. Trend and tracking polls are taken during the campaign to measure reactions to the candidate's campaign, as well as to identify any updates or changes in public opinion from the benchmark poll. Finally, focus groups are periodically conducted to test-market everything from the content of commercials to the selection of prepared lines in debates. The Gore campaign was known for planting an inspirational guest in the audience and leveraging her experience to expound on a particular issue. The "plant" was one of several choices focus-grouped by the Gore campaign and selected based on its value of vote capital.

Beyond the costs for ads, consultants, and polls is the fuel that makes all campaigns go or stall—fund-raising. The focus is not the gross amount a candidate raises, but the net income value after accounting for the high cost of fund-raising itself. When Oliver North ran for the Senate in Virginia in 1994, he managed to raise $17 million, yet his fund-raising expenses were $11 million, netting the campaign only $6 million. Striving for fund-raising efficiency by maximizing the net yield is the fund-raiser's priority. If a gala dinner costs, say, $200,000 to run but only grosses $210,000, it's more a fun-raising than a fund-raising event, and barely worth the effort. So how do candidates raise the millions necessary to pay their entry ticket, even their winning ticket?

Dialing for Dollars

In the past three congressional election cycles, only 88 winners out of 1399 races were outspent, or barely 6 percent. With those odds, an underfunded candidate has as good a shot at lasting a couple rounds in the boxing ring with Lennox Lewis as he does at winning an election. No matter your record, skills, or integrity, odds are you lose if you can't reach the voters.

Consequently, raising money is the number one activity by far of American politics. Professional fund-raisers have developed a multitude of methods that provide candidates the necessary jabs and left hooks to go toe-to-toe against political heavyweights, ranging from carefree hobnobbing to scientific formulating. Ultimately, what counts is repeated direct contact with proven large donors so that they feel a personal stake in the election of the soliciting candidate. The era of candidates like former New York Governor Mario Cuomo, who *never* made a telephone call for money on his own behalf, is over. We've entered the era of candidates like California Governor Gray Davis, who makes tens of thousands—and who has said that he's personal "friends" with all his big donors.

Because it's unlawful for members of Congress to use government offices to make fund-raising calls, "you go to the Democratic National Committee headquarters into what they call a clean room," Georgia Senator Zell Miller, an outspoken critic of the process, recalled last year. "You have an aide who's getting somebody on the line and handing you a card or sheet of paper that tells you who this person is, what their main interests are, what their spouse's name is, and what you might be able to extract from them. Then you call them up and act like you're their best buddy and ask, 'How's Mary and the kids?' and 'By the way, how about donating $1000 to my campaign?' I always left that room feeling like a cheap prostitute who'd had a busy day."

So, in midafternoon of an election year, one can see streams of members leaving their government work for the political work of dialing for dollars. West Coast members have it worse: since their constituents are three hours behind Washington, D.C., they feel pressured into using the evenings for phoning. Said the wife of one aspirant, "If his constituents knew how much time he spent away from the office and the work they sent him to Washington for, they'd impeach him."

Few ever pull back the curtain, but Bill Bradbury, a 2002 Senate candidate from Oregon, allowed a reporter to glimpse his call room one day in early June. Here's the script of one of his pitches to a local lawyer:

"Kathy! Hi! How are you doing? Cold? On the first weekend of Rose Festival? No! Listen, I wanted to thank you for your support in the primary, and I wanted to ask you for some more support. I wanted to see if you could contribute $1000 to the general election campaign. We're in a real knockdown, drag-out with Senator [Gordon] Smith. He's already up on the air with negative ads."

This kind of exchange transpires thousands of times a day in an election season. The process is so debilitating it can drive politicians right out of public service—like former New Jersey Democratic senator Frank Lautenberg, who announced to reporters in 1999 that he would not seek a fourth term: "A powerful factor in my decision was the searing reality that I would have to spend half of every day between now and the next election fund-raising. . . . I would have to ask literally thousands of people for money. I would have had to raise $125,000 a week, or $25,000 every working day. That's about $3000 an hour."

⟨⟨☙   ❧⟩⟩

Scott Gale is the Ichiro Suzuki of fund-raising. Suzuki, the eight-time batting champ (seven times in Japan, once in the States), doesn't simply step up to the plate and swing blindly for the fences. Instead, he takes a very calculated and methodical approach to hitting, striving for average and on-base percentage rather than home runs.

Gale is the same way when it comes to fund-raising. He doesn't believe in grouping all of the campaign's fund-raisers into one big event; rather he gets the candidate to encourage each of his major supporters to do individual events. He has designed an assembly-line approach to fund-raising, transforming the practice the same way Henry Ford's production of the Model T and Frederick Taylor's "scientific method [of] time-and-motion studies" revolutionized manufacturing. It wasn't exciting, but it sure was effective.

A Connecticut native, Gale got his start as a political fund-raiser in 1983 on the U.S. Senate campaign of now Congressman Lloyd Doggett (D-TX). After chasing Doggett's ornery campaign manager for a fund-raising post for weeks, only to hear the same response—"You've got the job but I have to work out the details"—Gale finally left a message with the Doggett campaign from a pay phone at D.C.'s National Airport, explaining that he'd moved out of his apartment and had just $100 and an airplane ticket left to his name. He hung an out-of-order sign on the pay phone and kept an eye on it. Several hours later, that very same campaign manager finally returned the call, and in his now famous Cajun drawl James Carville told Scott, "Wail, wuh brungun uh Yankuh down to Texas."

Carville set Gale up with the Doggett deputy campaign manager, Paul Begala. Realizing that the campaign had no fund-raising staff outside Austin, Gale persuaded Begala to send him to Dallas to work the candidate's contacts there. As Gale relays the story, "Here I was, a twenty-two-year-old kid, working my first real campaign ever. I hitched a ride to Dallas and tracked down a lawyer, forty years old, who was helping to raise money for the campaign. I told him we weren't raising enough money in Dallas, we needed to do a better job, and how could I help? To which he responded, 'Son, you are not from Dallas. You are not from Texas. Who the hell are you to come into my office and tell me what we ought to be doing in Dallas, Texas?' I paused for a moment, looked at his Rolodex and said, 'You're right, I don't know what I'm talking about, but I see that Rolodex sitting on your desk and I have Doggett's donor list here in my briefcase. Why don't we go through your Rolodex and see who ought to be on this list that isn't.'" As it turned out, the lawyer had called only a few people on his Rolodex. So the two compiled a list that the lawyer and his candidate plowed through.

After the Doggett campaign, Gale honed his fund-raising craft on a couple of more races in the South, for Howell Heflin for Senate in Alabama and Ann Richards for governor in Texas. By 1991, when he was hired by Harris Wofford—a Senate candidate from Pennsylvania, far behind five months before election day—Gale was prepared for his biggest test.

Gale's fund-raising system follows a two-part model. He calls part one "outlining the life story," and part two "the hourly wage rate approach." Outlining the life story involves sitting down with the candidate anywhere between eight and twenty hours and listing every individual he has ever known. It is an exhaustive search, going through junior high, high school, college, and graduate school yearbooks; members of his church, synagogue, country club; lists of any organizations he has belonged to, clubs, groups, neighborhood associations; the parents of his kids' soccer teammates; wedding invitation lists; even the yellow pages from the town he grew up in.

Once this list is complete, the next step is to add the "usual suspects": wealthy and frequent donors who contribute to causes the candidate supports, or to comparable candidates. Finally, the most important step, and the one that Gale cites as the linchpin of the process, is to reach out to everyone on the candidate's list and—if they're supportive and willing—get similar (if shorter) life-story lists from him or her. Gale calls these the second, third, and fourth generations of the Rolodex, or "Rolodexing the Rolodexes."

During a recent campaign he worked on for a western candidate, Gale's candidate received a $250 contribution from a supporter. Per standard practice, a staffer from Gale's team sat down with this donor to extract her life story, discovering that one of her friends had recently hit it big on information technology stock options. The candidate had breakfast the next week with this friend of the $250 donor—who had never donated a single dollar to a political campaign—and walked away with a $100,000 check, the single largest political donation in the state's history. This alone allowed the candidate to hit the television airwaves two weeks early.

Since the candidate is both salesperson and product, it's reasonable to wonder who's going to have time to make all these calls. That's where the hourly wage rate approach, designed to maximize efficiency in fund-raising, comes in. The wage rate is determined by dividing the candidate's fund-raising receipts by her time. The more people a candidate talks to and raises money from, the higher her hourly wage rate. If a candidate sits down with the phone for an hour, she can probably get through to three or four people. But if staff coordinates the candidate's call time, then makes preliminary contact with the secretary of a prospective donor and asks when Mr. Smith will be available without leaving a message, the candidate can inexpensively reach six or seven people an hour. It's a rather simple procedure, but one that increases the wage rate 50 percent. The staff plays an integral role in Gale's system. He seeks young, low-paid, energetic workers who not only provide support to candidates but also staff the candidates' friends and donors. Each staffer is like an account representative with thirty to forty clients. It is their job to obtain the clients' life stories and assist them in soliciting contributions.

Back to Pennsylvania in 1991. With five months to go in the race, the Wofford campaign, running 40 points behind former U.S. Attorney General and Pennsylvania governor Dick Thornburgh, had no real fund-raising base. Gale's first move was to hire five young people and place them in Philadelphia, Pittsburgh, and Harrisburg. Their mission: identify Wofford supporters and help them contact friends and acquaintances, asking if they would donate $X and raise $Y. Next, he sat down with the candidate—and learned there was no Rolodex. Wofford had lived a fascinating life (member of the Kennedy administration, author of one of the first English-language books on Gandhi, president of Bryn Mawr College) but had never recorded his contacts. But the candidate's son had just been married, and the invitation list was all Gale had. Wofford called everyone on the list, asked them to donate $X and raise $Y. Then, working with the staff, he reached out to the second generation of people—friends of the wedding guests, then their friends, or the third generation. Wofford ended up winning that special election in 1991, and by the end of the 1994 election he had raised $10.5 million.

Another example of the model's success occurred during one southern governor's race. A staffer was debriefing a friend of the candidate and noticed the friend had many contacts out of state. Mentioning that the candidate was heading to New York, the staffer asked the friend if she knew anyone in the area. As it turned out, her husband was Earl Graves's cardiologist. A few weeks later, Gale was seated beside his candidate in Graves's office, waiting to see the famous businessman who founded and publishes *Black Enterprise* magazine. "I worked for every African American U.S. Senate Democratic nominee since Reconstruction," Gale reflected, "and the only candidate I worked with who met with Earl Graves did it through some thirty-six-year-old cracker from the South. The one person Earl Graves couldn't say no to was his cardiologist."

❦

A journey past the door of campaign headquarters and into the inner sanctum of fund-raising operations is not the prettiest site to behold. Fund-raising, as Bismarck said of sausage making, produces an enjoyable product, but you don't want to watch the process. "Call time" is a daily ritual where the candidate, flanked by two or three people putting out calls, bunkers down with a telephone at a large conference table littered with printouts from the potential donor database. For every hundred calls put out to good lists, perhaps twenty people will agree to talk. "John Smith on line number one," yells caller number two, and the candidate obliges by picking up Smith on line one—and makes a pitch he'll remake dozens of times a day, hundreds of times a month, thousands of times a campaign. As a candidate who made an estimated 30,000 such calls in 2000–2001, the closest analogy I can come up with is eating sawdust.

Fund-raisers generally suggest that their candidates make up to seven hours' worth of calls, from 9:00 A.M. to noon and 2:00 to 6:00 P.M. during crunch time. Noon to two o'clock is reserved for public appearances or money lunches; evenings are reserved for public appearances or fund-raisers. In fact, call time is never over now that a candidate can glue a cell phone to his/her ear. The candidate must be willing to make calls on the street, in the car, on a train, in a plane.

It's no secret that most candidates detest call time. "One day I walk into campaign headquarters, and I was being badgered, by my campaign manager and my fund-raising consultant," reminisced a pacing Bob Abrams, the former New York Attorney General who lost the 1992 Senate race by one point to incumbent Al D'Amato. "They said, 'Come on, you gotta raise the money. Even if you're a great guy, even if you have a great record, even if you are a person of integrity, you're not going to be able to win this race unless you raise the money. We gotta deliver the message. The only way to deliver the message is to put the ads on television and radio. You've gotta raise the money!'

"So this one day, I allocated six or seven hours to fund-raising. I'm making these phone calls for hours on end, and I'm losing my voice. I am hoarse. I've got four cough drops in my mouth just trying to keep some moisture so I can speak and make the next phone call." As soon as he takes a break, "my campaign finance manager pokes his head in and yells, 'Why aren't you on the phone! We have to make 6.2 completed phone calls per hour! You're falling behind!' So I took the phone right from the wall," said Abrams, universally regarded as amiable and even tempered, "and I physically threw it at him."

Some of the ugliest moments inside campaign headquarters are the daily battles fought between the political and fund-raising staffs, beyond the view of the candidate. It's a fight for votes versus dollars, endorsements versus ads. With a finite amount of time to be allocated as election day approaches, the two sides of the campaign staff are pitted against each other, competing for precious minutes with the candidate. Since most groups hold any fund-raising events on Tuesdays, Wednesdays, and Thursdays, fund-raising generally owns the middle days of the week. "It is the yin and the yang, political and fund-raising," explained one campaign finance director, Tara Ochman, as she sat at the headquarters of her most recent candidate. "It'd probably be better if the two sides were not in the same office. It's the number one internal tension in almost any campaign."

Unfortunately for the fund-raisers, the political side is the romanticized half of the campaign—the part that finds its way into movies and TV series. To make matters worse, nearly all candidates would prefer to chat about politics rather than money. Who ever entered politics because they enjoyed begging for money? At best, fund-raising is pedestrian and boring, a matter of managing the minutiae of finance, budgets, and relationships. But keeping up with these details is extremely important. Overlook one little task, like a simple thank-you note, and it can rupture a relationship and cost the campaign thousands of dollars.

One Senate candidate in the Northeast believes a major reason he lost was a minor, innocent fund-raising mix-up that escalated into a major scandal overnight. The candidate, a statewide officeholder seeking higher office, made a cold call to a longtime contributor in his state. He asked for a contribution, received a check, and sent the requisite thank-you note. The media soon discovered and exposed that the contributor had a business relationship with the candidate's office. The media portrayed the contribution as nothing short of a dirty bribe, his lead quickly withered, and he eventually lost the race. The candidate wasn't corrupt or guilty of doing the wrong thing—he didn't even know that the contributor had pending business with his office, in part because he properly separated his fund-raising office from his government office. The process, and the pressure to raise money by making voluminous calls, put the candidate in this compromising position.

The most successful candidates don't only just put in the time, they're shameless about it. Bernard Nussbaum, President Clinton's White House lawyer, tells a story about a major political aspirant who called him asking for money. The candidate asked Nussbaum to donate and raise $5000; instead Nussbaum promised that if the candidate won the primary, he'd send $1000. The candidate won and Nussbaum sent the check. A week later the candidate called, thanked Nussbaum for the money, but reminded him that he wanted $5000; Nussbaum reminded him that he agreed to give only $1000, not give or raise $5000. A week later the candidate called again with the same request, and again Nussbaum's response was no. The candidate then called a third consecutive week, asking for $5000. At last, Nussbaum caved and agreed to raise the rest "just to get him off my back." A good candidate never met a "no" that didn't sound like "probably."

The nonstop begging doesn't always pay off, especially with respect to a candidate's relationship with his friends and relatives. "You become a pariah of your own social circle," groaned Charlie King, a candidate running for the Democratic nomination for lieutenant governor in New York against a self-funded opponent. Shaking his head, King continued, "Friends will disguise their voice when I call, and hide from me if they spot me in public. I can't always get my mom on the phone because she thinks I'm just calling to hit her up for another fifty bucks."

And consider this: all the time and energy that go into "dialing for dollars," and managing the conflicts between the fund-raising and political needs of the campaign, vanish for the self-financed candidate. He can spend all his time learning issues, plotting strategy, meeting voters, and wooing political support—without ever having to worry when the next round of calls is slated to begin.

Incumbent Protection Program

The single greatest advantage a candidate can have over an opponent is being the incumbent. The difference between fund-raising as the incumbent and fund-raising as the challenger is the difference between sailing with the wind at your back or in your face.

For example, any controversial legislation can be adroitly milked so that a chin-rubbing incumbent can leverage each side's anxieties to raise money from the other. Recall that these used to be aptly called "squeeze bills" in the nineteenth century. "I hated to see the telecommunication bill pass in 1996 because it was such a gold mine," Representative Bill Paxon (R-NY) privately told a colleague. A former aide to the Senate Commerce Committee said of one "tort reform" bill, "Everyone knew from the outset that it wouldn't become law. It was kept alive for fund-raising purposes. Its virtue was that only the trial lawyers were against it."

As elected officials, incumbents have a campaign infrastructure already intact—including free mailing privileges, professional staff, voter lists, and, of course, a direct line to political action committees and wealthy donors. They also have a steady salary, a luxury most nonincumbents must do without. Exploiting these resources, current officeholders stockpile cash in anticipation of their reelection campaigns.

Senator Charles Schumer (D–NY) has the biggest head start of them all. In 2001, he raised $4.9 million, according to the FEC, and had $8.8 million in cash on hand at the start of 2002—and he's not up for reelection until 2004. Two other senators not up for reelection in 2002, Richard Shelby (R–AL) and Kay Bailey Hutchinson (R–TX), had $6.2 million and $4.7 million cash on hand, respectively, in the beginning of 2002.

The overwhelming majority of incumbents in Washington seeking another term are reelected (see figure 4.1). While well-funded Senate incumbents have an obvious advantage, states are too large for almost anyone other than a Kennedy in Massachusetts or Thurmond in South Carolina to dominate. But, since a representative can just about meet and repeatedly mail to all his or her 650,000 constituents over the years, money-entrenching incumbency is even more of a predictor of success in House campaigns.

Consider the three-state analysis in table 4.4. In California, incumbent House candidates for the 2002 elections had already raised, on average, $459,416 by January 2002; their opponents had raised an average of $38,691. In Texas, incumbents had an average of $454,155 in their war chest, compared with challengers' $43,815. Finally, in New York, House incumbents had $458,697 by the beginning of 2002, compared with challengers' $23,264.

TABLE 4.4

EARLY MONEY, AVERAGE AMOUNT RAISED IN HOUSE RACES BY JANUARY 2002 CALIFORNIA, NEW YORK, TEXAS

State	No. Incumbents	Avg. Raised	No. Challengers	Avg. Raised
CA	50	$459,416	26	$39,681
TX	29	$454,155	16	$43,815
NY	29	$458,697	6	$23,264

Source: Federal Elections Commission.

The greatest advantage for incumbents, simply put, is more money—not just at the start of the election year but especially at the end. Competitive campaigns are like short-track speed skating, where competitors coast bunched together until the final, furious sprint. In these last days, commercials hold the key to winning. And candidates

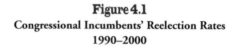

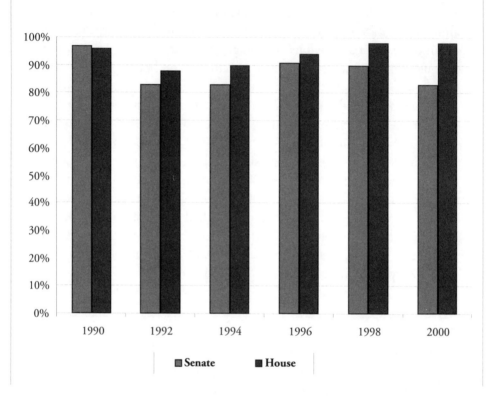

Figure 4.1
Congressional Incumbents' Reelection Rates
1990–2000

who run out of money are, well, out of the money. If they can't pay the broadcasting toll, they're left behind at the booth, while incumbents zoom across the bridge en route to another term.

There are tricks to the incumbency trade other than money. In 1985, Senator Rudy Boschwitz (R–MN) circulated a fourteen-page confidential memo to twenty-two GOP senators up for reelection the next year, revealing his secrets for winning as an incumbent. The memo was leaked to the *Wall Street Journal,* which published several excerpts. In addition to noting the perfunctory tasks of raising money early and buying tons of TV time, "à la Budweiser," Boschwitz warned incumbents to avoid speeches and debates with challengers, especially debates sponsored by "such hostile groups as the League of Women Voters." He continued: "I wouldn't release my tax returns (I gave them percentages, assured them I paid taxes every year, etc.). . . . You'll be attacked, and if you're a businessman, conflict of interest will be alleged due to some of your votes; and if you hold any stock, your votes and PAC money will be tied to that ownership (one of the reasons I didn't make my tax returns public). It's just plain unpleasant, and the press loves it. It is vital that attacks not go unanswered. That's when your paid consultants really earn their fees."

Since incumbents are constantly in the public spotlight, they benefit from name recognition with voters and can adopt the game plan of simply running out the clock. That's good for incumbents, but not for democracy. Candidates can mask their true identities from voters by refusing to participate in debates and then benefiting from the dearth of "free" news coverage, all the while relying on paid consultants to position them under a media-friendly, though not too bright, spotlight. When election day comes around, voters find themselves basing their decisions on who has the familiar name, not the better platform or policy suggestions. And that's just the way incumbents like it.

The Challenger's Paradox

From the perspective of a challenger, however, fund-raising is a Sisyphean task. In the controlled environment of today's political races, voters encounter the candidate's message through poll-tested sound bites. Challengers wind up competing less against the actual incumbent and more against the millions of bits of information people are exposed to on a daily basis. To break through, challengers need ample money to get their message across effectively.

But considering how difficult it is to unseat an incumbent, donors on average are less likely to donate to challengers, who just don't stand a strong chance of winning. It's a severe condition in American politics known as the "challenger's paradox": you can't win without spending money, but you can't raise money if people don't think you're going to win. "I don't give my people's money to those I think are going to lose," says George Gould, a PAC manager for the letter carriers union, "so you have to convince me you're going to win." The convincing can be difficult when the numbers state that only 2 percent of House challengers actually win.

On the congressional level, the few challengers who pull off a victory are most often those who outspent the incumbent. Table 4.5 shows comparisons of challenger and incumbent spending for those 2000 races won by the challenger. In the Senate, three of five winning challengers outspent the incumbent, averaging about $1.5 million more in expenditures. In the House, three of six winning challengers outspent incumbents.

Representative Adam Schiff (D–CA) was one of the few challengers who has bucked the odds and defeated a bigger-spending incumbent. Schiff's Republican opponent, Jim Rogan, was celebrated within his party for playing a prominent role as a House impeachment manager in 1998. Rogan's name and stature in the party helped him raise almost $7 million. Schiff, meanwhile, had already lost two previous elections to Rogan in the California State Assembly, by a combined 38-point margin. Since those losses, though, he had made a name for himself in California politics, becoming the youngest member of the state senate in 1996 at thirty-six.

"Early money is the most difficult," says the soft-spoken Schiff, reminiscing on his race from the confines of his fourth-floor Cannon House Office Building suite. "My opponent had a higher profile, so the burden of persuasion was on me [to prove] that it was not just likely, but [even] possible, for me to win." From his time in the state senate, Schiff had built up a constituency and has a knack for persuasion, proven by his ability to ultimately spend more than $4 million in the race against Rogan. That is huge money for a challenger, but in this race it was still $2.5 million behind the incumbent. Rogan and Schiff were second and third in total money raised by House candidates in 2000; between them the two candidates raised $11.2 million, a record for a House campaign.

"As a challenger, you can never expect to outraise your opponent," warns Schiff. "Institutional stakeholders support the incum-

TABLE 4.5

SPENDING BY CHALLENGERS WHO WON 2000
CONGRESSIONAL RACES

Race	Challenger	Incumbent	Difference
Senate			
Delaware	$ 2,608,942	$ 4,366,884	($1,757,942)
Michigan	$ 7,892,518	$13,028,636	($5,136,118)
Minnesota	$11,957,114	$ 6,024,866	$ 5,932,248
Virginia	$ 9,995,980	$ 6,610,252	$ 3,385,728
Washington	$11,553,295	$ 6,402,488	$ 5,150,807
Average	$ 8,801,570	$ 7,286,625	$ 1,514,945
House			
Arkansas CD4	$1,626,164	$1,786,307	($ 160,143)
California CD27	$4,351,025	$6,889,947	($2,538,922)
California CD36	$1,998,739	$1,988,938	$ 9,801
California CD49	$1,926,497	$1,846,574	$ 79,923
Connecticut CD2	$1,060,197	$1,616,863	($ 556,666)
Minnesota CD2	$ 886,650	$ 848,795	$ 37,855
Average	$1,974,879	$2,496,237	($ 521,359)

Source: *Almanac of American Politics*, 2002, National Journal.

bent, and they have a large network of contributors, depending on how long they've been in office. [My goal was] not to outspend [Rogan] but to communicate in each medium he was in: mail, cable, and broadcast."

Schiff believes he surprised his opponent by being the first to broadcast television ads. Although broadcast is the least cost-effective method of campaigning—especially in a market like Los Angeles, where an ad goes out to 8 million people but only 650,000 of them actually live in the district—Schiff feels that the tactic established him as a formidable contender.

While Schiff acknowledges the difficulty of raising money early, it doesn't get much easier later in the race. "We had raised so much it was hard to raise more. For every dollar we raised, my opponent raised two. The challenge was no longer to prove I was a viable candidate, but that I still needed more money."

Schiff showed that while a challenger doesn't have to necessarily spend more than an incumbent to win, he does have to reach a certain threshold of funding to become viable. In the 1998 House races, about half of the challengers raised only $100,000. In 2000, the average House incumbent raised $817,000 to the average challenger's $146,000. A study by the Committee for Economic Development found a correlation between a challenger's campaign expenditures and his/her percentage of votes. The study found that once challengers hit a spending threshold of $300,000, they consistently garnered at least 40 percent of the vote. Any challenger expenditure amounts below $300,000 resulted in a lopsided victory for the incumbent.

Beyond the challenger's paradox, there's another reason donors hesitate giving to a challenger: the fear factor. Even when a donor believes in a challenger's message, supports her platform, and believes she has a shot to win, there still exists the potential wrath of the incumbent standing in the way. Should the incumbent win the election, which is always at least a possibility, he may look unfavorably upon a donor who contributed to the campaign that sought to end his public life—a considerable risk if the defeated candidate should ever again be elected to public office. To avoid such ill feelings, many donors don't give to challengers, give through a spouse, or give to both the incumbent and challenger, usually giving the incumbent more.

The 1997 mayoral race in New York City exemplifies this plight of the challenger. Ruth Messinger, then the Manhattan borough president, chose to run against the aggressive Republican incumbent, Rudy Giuliani. Messinger recalls working twenty hours a day, putting in a full day as borough president before walking across City Hall Park to her campaign headquarters for fund-raising calls. "Even when I was spending every minute on the phone that anybody could expect, I ran into a lot of [double giving]. And a lot of money that wasn't the maximum. I'd call someone, pleading, 'I know he's likely to win, but you're a Democrat and I'm raising a lot of important issues and you never can tell, certain things might work in my favor.' So, then I'd convince them and they'd give me $1000 [out of a maximum of $7700]."

Carolyn Maloney was a Democratic challenger who overcame tremendous obstacles to beat Republican Bill Green in 1992. Not only did Green, a fourteen-year incumbent, outspend Maloney 5 to 1, he was also the only New York City representative from either party on the powerful House Appropriations Committee. Maloney remembers sending just one mailing, while Green, who "claimed to be an environmentalist, must have chopped down a forest with all his mailings."

Like many talented but below-the-radar challengers, Maloney lacked the institutional financial support of the Democratic Party and allied interest groups. The Democratic Congressional Campaign Committee forced Maloney to test the waters with a poll before they would contribute to her campaign, the results of which demonstrated that she could win. Still, the DCCC refused to give her money. So did EMILY's List, a PAC that by any measure she should have been able to count on. But trends helped Maloney when funds couldn't.* In the end, she won the race, having raised only $250,000. Running for reelection in 1994, incumbent Maloney raised more than $1 million. "After I became an incumbent, a miracle happened. I no longer had both hands tied behind my back."

Supply Side Warriors

It is only half correct to blame the skyrocketing cost of campaign spending over the last generation on the increased costs for television ads. The supply side—of traditional donors, wealthy individuals, and PACs—is equally culpable for driving spending to its current levels.

Table 4.6 presents an overview of the supply side. In the 2000 con-

---

*First, the 1992 election was the so-called Year of the Woman, when many female candidates prevailed. Second, Bill Clinton led the Democrats back into the White House after a twelve-year hiatus, extending his coattails to a number of congressional candidates on the ticket. Maloney also benefited from her prominence as a New York City councilwoman for ten years.

TABLE 4.6

CONGRESSIONAL CAMPAIGN RECEIPTS, 1990–2000
($ IN MILLIONS)

	1990		1992	
	Amount	Percent	Amount	Percent
Congress				
Total Receipts	$471	100	$654	100
Individuals	$249	53	$352	54
PACs	$150	32	$178	27
Candidate	$ 38	8	$ 87	13
Other	$ 34	7	$ 36	6
No. Candidates	1,521		2,290	
Senate				
Total Receipts	$186	100	$262	100
Individuals	$120	64	$162	62
PACs	$ 41	22	$ 51	19
Candidate	$ 12	7	$ 34	13
Other	$ 13	7	$ 15	6
No. Candidates	151		249	
House				
Total Receipts	$284	100	$392	100
Individuals	$129	45	$190	49
PACs	$108	38	$127	32
Candidate	$ 25	9	$ 53	14
Other	$ 21	7	$ 22	5
No. Candidates	1,370		2,041	

Source: Federal Election Commission.
Note: Candidate receipts include candidate contributions and candidate loans,
as reported to the FEC.

	1994		1996		1998		2000	
	Amount	Percent	Amount	Percent	Amount	Percent	Amount	Percent
	$736	100	$784	100	$776	100	$1,039	100
	$400	54	$440	56	$420	54	$563	54
	$179	24	$201	26	$207	27	$245	24
	$121	16	$105	13	$106	14	$173	17
	$ 35	5	$ 38	5	$ 44	6	$ 58	6
	1,928		1,890		1,552		1,589	
	$317	100	$284	100	$287	100	$434	100
	$185	58	$167	59	$166	58	$250	58
	$ 47	15	$ 46	16	$ 48	17	$ 52	12
	$ 68	21	$ 56	20	$ 54	19	$107	25
	$ 17	5	$ 15	5	$ 19	7	$ 25	6
	225		210		188		198	
	$418	100	$500	100	$489	100	$604	100
	$215	51	$273	55	$253	52	$313	52
	$132	32	$155	31	$159	32	$193	32
	$ 53	13	$ 49	10	$ 52	11	$ 66	11
	$ 19	4	$ 23	5	$ 25	5	$ 33	5
	1,703		1,680		1,364		1,391	

gressional election cycle, total candidate receipts surpassed $1 billion for the first time in history, which was more than a 100 percent increase from 1990 receipts. Individuals, who contributed $249 million in 1990, increased their ante to $563 million in 2000. PACs increased their candidate contributions from $150 million in 1990 to $245 million in 2000. Meanwhile, self-financed donations, including both self-contributions and self-loans, jumped from $38 million in 1990 to $173 million in 2000. Political parties contributed the remaining funds, totaling $53 million in 2000.

Individuals

Contributions from individual donors have historically represented the lion's share of donations to political campaigns. In 1976, individual donations accounted for 75 percent of all receipts for Senate and House candidates. Throughout the last decade, while total receipts have grown tremendously, contributions from individuals have held steady around 55 percent, growing from $249 million in 1990 (or 53 percent of all contributions) to $563 million in 2000 (54 percent of all contributions).

In the 2000 election cycle, House candidates received $313 million from individuals, and Senate candidates received $250 million. Republicans are more likely to get donations from individuals than Democrats: in 2000, Senate Republicans received $54 million more in contributions from individuals than did Democrats; House Republican candidates received $20 million more than their Democratic counterparts.

So who are these individuals, and why are they giving candidates so much money anyway? Of course, to Scott Gale and other fundraising gurus, these individuals are people in the candidates' Rolodexes, and the individuals in their Rolodexes, and so on. Essentially, the first level of individual contributors is the social network of family, friends, colleagues, and acquaintances surrounding any bona fide candidate. It is not rare in these donation circles to find a Republican contributing to a Democrat, a liberal to a conservative, simply because they went to the same college or once worked together at an investment banking firm. As one $250 contributor to the 2002 Senate campaign of Oregon's Bill Bradbury explained, "One of the primary reasons I contributed, frankly, was that I went to law school with his wife."

In addition to personal contacts, the other type of individual contributor is the "usual suspect"—traditional donors who give to certain types of candidates, such as environmentalists or prolifers, activist Hollywood actors or oil executives. But they are by no means the only ones: local businessmen, union members, and doctors are all usual suspects (however, the wealthier these individuals are, the more likely they are to donate more money, more often). Enron and big business interests might get all of the media attention in coverage of political contributions, but the reason today's candidates are glorified telemarketers is that most candidate donations come from individuals who contribute less than $1000 per election.

For the 2000 congressional election cycle, the FEC classified individual donors into four size categories: amounts less than $200, amounts between $200 and $499, amounts between $500 and $749, and amounts $750 and over. Nearly three quarters of individual contributions fell at the high and low ends of the spectrum. Small contributions, below $200, equaled $168 million, or 30 percent of all individual contributions. Meanwhile, large contributions of $750 or more totaled $249 million, 44 percent of all individual contributions.

Beyond personal or ideological affinity, another motivation to donate is ego. Some people just like to be part of such a thrilling experience as a campaign and to have their name known to the next senator or governor.

Finally, of course, money tries to buy access. Legislatively interested money is more invested than given, in an unspoken contract both sides understand. This is not a sin unique to politicians; in the favor bank of life, nearly everyone is nicer to people who are generous to them. "I own a $25,000 Ford Explorer. When someone hands me a $25,000 contribution, they're not buying access, they are giving me the equivalent of a car," one candidate explained. "They've got my attention, and in the future I feel it's rude of me not to take their call immediately the next time they call." The largest lodestones of such access money are bundlers, described earlier, and of course political action committees. If Willie Sutton were a Senate candidate, he'd say that's where the money is.

Political Action Committees

In 1974, about 600 PACs donated $12.5 million to congressional candidates; in 2000, nearly 4500 PACs donated $248 million.

Although the novelty and notoriety of PACs has worn off, their influence in Washington and beyond is more prominent than ever. "The sad thing about Enron is that people expressed shock and dismay like this was an isolated incident," said one PAC manager. "Enron was just another example of the same basic formula that the corporate community has been using for the last twenty-plus years. They knew where they played ball, they set the rules, they drew the ball field, they decided what ball was going to get used, and they did all of it with dollars."

The rise in PAC spending has been ushered in by the multiplication of PAC organizations. In the 2000 election, 4499 PACs participated, including 1725 corporate, 350 labor, 1362 independent, 900 trade/health/membership, and 162 other PACs. While labor PACs dominated the field when PACs first became prominent in the 1970s and 1980s, corporate PACs now rule by a 5-to-1 ratio. PAC contributions by party reflect this change: in 1988, Democrats received $92 million in PAC funds compared with $56 million for Republicans; by 2000, the tides had turned, with Republicans now on top, receiving $134 million from PACs to the Democrats' $123 million. For the Republicans the big shift occurred between 1994 and 1996, when PAC contributions jumped 60 percent, from $67 million to $107 million. Most observers credit Newt Gingrich and Tom DeLay for "advising" the business community that a small investment to the right side of the aisle—now that the Republicans controlled both chambers—would result in widespread industry deregulation and big payoffs for properly positioned firms.

Despite the rise of corporate and independent PACs, labor PACs that give predominantly to Democrats still rank among the largest-contributing PACs. In 2000, six of the ten biggest PAC donors were labor groups, including IBEW (International Brotherhood of Electrical Workers), AFSCME (American Federation of State, County, and Municipal Employees), and the Teamsters, which combined gave approximately $2.6 million, at least 93 percent of which went to Democrats.

To a fund-raising candidate, PAC money can be a savior, since PACs can give as much as $5000 per election, versus an individual's $1000. Moreover, PACs are not limited by an overall spending cap, while individuals can't donate more than $25,000 per election year (these amounts will change when the McCain-Feingold law takes effect). Funds permitting, a wealthy PAC could donate the limit to every candidate running for federal office in any particular year—certainly to every preferred candidate in competitive races. Finally, as we've seen, PACs are permitted to make independent expenditures on behalf of a candidate as long as the spending is not coordinated with the candidate. This soft money freedom enables the reach of PACs to extend well beyond the amounts reported to the FEC.

But unlike contributions from individuals, which are made for a variety of reasons, PAC donations are made clearly and simply for the purpose of furthering the interests of the sponsoring organization(s). Of course, PAC managers and (sitting) politicians will deny that PAC money explicitly buys votes—that would be a felony. And that's no doubt true . . . again, because it's no doubt unnecessary.

The numbers make it clear that the majority of PACs are in the business of investing in not good government but in a government good for them. Donors want to give to winners and leaders whose decisions matter. Here's how one utility executive explained the rationale behind his company's PAC decisions: "When people help you get a tax abatement or someone goes out of their way to make certain that rights of way are more easily procured or certain bureaucratic obstacles are removed, you tend to want them to be there if you ever need to come back again. So you will make those contributions in that situation."

The most meaningful analysis of PAC giving looks not at donations by political party but at contributions by type of candidate: incumbent, challenger, or open seat. When PACs first emerged on the scene in the 1970s, there was a certain ideological theme to their giving, with most corporate PACs, albeit small in number, backing Republican challengers. But over the last ten to fifteen years, PACs have followed a strict routine of contributing to incumbents. Between the 1988 and 2000 elections, PACs made out an amazing 74 percent of their donations to incumbents; only 11 percent went to challengers and 15 percent to open-seat candidates.

"After the 1982 election, Tony Coelho, then head of the Democratic Congressional Campaign Committee, met with groups of corporate PAC directors and explained that access to Democratic lawmakers required contributions to Democrat House members, not to Republican challengers," wrote Paul Herrnson in his book, *Risky Business: PAC Decisionmaking in Congressional Elections*. "As a result, by the 1990 election cycle, more than half of the contributions of corporate PACs went to Democratic incumbents, and only 8 percent were given to Republican nonincumbent candidates."

The biggest advantage for today's incumbents is their prime position for receiving PAC dollars. In the 2000 congressional elections, the average House incumbent raised $864,000, $367,000 of which came from PACs. Senate incumbents facing reelection that year raised $3.9 million on average, $1 million of which was underwritten by PACs.

Beyond incumbents, PACs go straight for the most prominent and influential politicians—those who sit on powerful committees. In 2000, top House leaders were among the largest PAC recipients, including Speaker Dennis Hastert and E. Clay Shaw (R–FL), chair of the Social Security subcommittee of the influential Ways and Means Committee. Both representatives received $1.3 million from PACs.

This trend has contributed to the growing influence of "outside money" in political campaigns. The incumbent who sits on the right committee or is perceived to vote consistently on certain issues might receive donations from national PACs, even if they have no particular involvement or presence in the candidate's district. "PACs nationalize elections in a way the Founders, who wanted each member to represent the interests of his district, never intended," says Representative Jim Leach in an interview. "Big PACs like Big Oil have nothing to do with our small-business state, yet we're now a playpen for PACs because Iowa congressmen vote on their issues."

Perhaps the most telling indicator of PACs' true goals is their habit of giving to both candidates in a race—or turning around and donating to a winner after supporting the loser throughout the campaign. According to a 1987 study by Common Cause, in the 1986 North Dakota Senate race, thirty-nine PACs that had contributed to the unsuccessful reelection campaign of Republican Mark Andrews did an about-face and gave to the newly elected Democrat, Kent Conrad, after the election. These PACs included the American Bankers Association, which donated $10,000 to Andrews before the election and $10,000 to Conrad afterward; the Marine Engineers Beneficial Association, which gave $6500 to Andrews before the election and $5000 to Conrad afterward; and the National Association of Letter Carriers, which sent $5000 to Andrews before the election and $10,000 to Conrad afterward.

"These PACs obviously weren't contributing because of the candidate's philosophy, ideology, or political party," said then Common Cause president Fred Wertheimer. "They wanted first and foremost to assure that they had bought influence with a United States senator. PACs often argue that PAC giving represents citizen participation. Citizens, however, don't vote for both candidates, once before the election and a second time after the winner has been chosen."

The original concept of PACs was to enable like-minded people to pool their resources in support of a candidate or candidates. How this plays out in practice is not quite the collective experience it appears to be on paper. PACs are governed by committees and boards, which are responsible for determining the PAC's strategies and budget. How PACs solicit their members' input varies—from strictly financial input through a check-off box on paychecks or union dues, encouraging members to funnel a percentage of wages to the PAC; to more substantive input, such as candidate questionnaires and candidate focus groups. The PACs that represent activist organizations, such as unions or issue-oriented groups like NARAL, are more likely to engage their members' input, as well as organize events to involve members in the political process. Rarely will a corporate PAC do much more than write a check. "I doubt Enron held voter registration initiatives in Houston," deadpans one labor union PAC manager.

In the past few decades, the number and variety of entities that play a role in the industrial complex that is political campaigns have become staggering. Take, as just one example, the world of retail. The National Association of Convenience Stores alone contributed $379,000 to federal candidates in the 2000 election cycle ($296,500 to Republicans and $82,500 to Democrats). And individual retailers were right there with them. Wal-Mart's PAC distributed $461,000 in 2000 to federal candidates; Sears gave $62,800; even Home Depot and Radio Shack disbursed funds—$27,000 and $10,600, respectively. For a candidate, the stamp of approval of an influential PAC can mean a windfall, because PACs often run in packs. If one oil firm likes Joe Slick, ten others may as well—and the payday can run into six figures or more.

Of course, the more PACs that enter the game, the more money that gets invested in campaigns. PACs don't cancel one another out, as their proponents often suggest; rather they compete with one another, driving the money involved in campaigns through the roof. The result is that fewer people run for office, the bank accounts of incumbents bulge, races are less competitive—and we're left with a permanent Congress.

૮૯ ૭ﾌ

It takes a certain kind of candidate to raise millions successfully by phone: he or she ideally combines (a) an ego sufficient to make the "ask"—and also to cope with a high percentage of rejections, with (b) the character not to say whatever the donor wants to hear.

Put yourself in an *honest* candidate's shoes: what do you do when a known big donor says "So where do you stand on X?," X being something that hugely helps or hurts his economic interests? You realize not only that your answer could immediately affect a large contribution—and perhaps even marginally your prospects of winning—but also that the cost of paying for the policy of X will fall on taxpayers who are not listening on the phone, and who of course won't know to blame you if years later their taxes slightly rise.

Or suppose you're going to fund-raiser after fund-raiser hosted by business supporters, since line workers don't have discretionary income, and since businesspeople have commercial networks to raise money. "The dependence on Wall Street money really suppresses argument," Michael McCurry, an ex–Clinton White House press secretary said of that one sector. "If you . . . schlep up and down Wall Street with your tin cup, then you listen to these guys making their arguments about the efficiency of financial deregulation and so forth, you begin to say, yeah, they've got a point."

Or suppose you're in government, and you believe the right policy will infuriate someone who has been financially loyal and generous. Once, as the New York City consumer affairs commissioner, I was considering filing a legal action that, if successful, could cost a major Democrat and businessman millions of dollars. I still sued, and after we won he didn't speak to me for a decade. But this outcome *had* crossed my mind as I weighed my prosecutorial decision—given the current political money process, how could it not?

Put into such inevitably compromising situations, a fair number of candidates and officials understand what Oscar Wilde meant when he said that he could "resist anything except temptation."

Welcome to the smoking gun, which is not criminal but commonplace. Do you lose the sale or your integrity? An awful lot of otherwise good people might find themselves bending on a debatable issue—and when you multiply this situation by the tens of thousands of times it directly or implicitly occurs during the fund-raising season (that is, all the time), what you end up with is a democracy for sale.

THE COST OF MONEY
Democracy Under Attack

"The day may come when we'll reject the money of the rich as tainted, but it hadn't come when I left Tammany Hall at 11:25 today."
—George Washington Plunkitt, 1905

"I don't think we buy votes. What we do is we buy a candidate's stance on issues."
—Allen Pross, executive director of the California Medical Association's PAC, 1989

"I got $3500 over 10 years [from Enron]. Heck, I'm the chairman of the committee. That wasn't a contribution. That was an insult."
—Senator Ernest F. Hollings (D–SC), 2002

In April 2002, when President George W. Bush's approval rating—bolstered by post–September 11 patriotism—stood at 74 percent, six out of ten Americans surveyed by Greenberg Quinlan Rosner Research agreed with the following statement: "When it comes to domestic policies, the Bush administration always seems to do what the big corporations want." President Bush wasn't alone. In other polls commissioned around the same time, large majorities believed that "special-interest groups own Congress" and have too much influence over elected officials. And while 29 percent of those polled by the University of Michigan's National Election Studies in 1964 felt the government was "run by a few big interests looking out for themselves," that number rose to 76 percent in 1994.

This growing belief that big interests run Washington parallels the growing donations that big interests have sent to Washington—and the perception that money gets results.

In a study conducted by Ellen Miller for the Center for Responsive Politics, 20 percent of the members of Congress *admitted* that campaign contributions affected their voting; only half claimed contributions had no effect, and 30 percent said they weren't sure. "Let's be clear," writes Fred Wertheimer, former president of Common Cause. "Though for many years it has been taboo in most Washington circles to use the word 'corruption' to portray the political money system in action, that is precisely what's going on."

Put yourself in the shoes of a candidate. If elections cost millions of dollars to win—and given the ego and the high stakes involved, you'd sure like to win—you'll need to get the money from somewhere. Support from friends and family is a good start, but if you're like most people, it wouldn't be nearly enough to make you competitive. So whom do you count on when your personal network is exhausted? (Hint: It's not working people and advocacy groups.)

There's a huge cost involved when candidates engage in the primordial task of hunting and gathering monetary gifts from the 1 percent of wealthy Americans who do the vast majority of the contributing. And a huge cost when a Congress becomes in effect a pay-per-use system utilized only by those wealthy enough to afford the membership dues.

Most *current* incumbents try to explain away the inevitable reality that when Joe Citizen calls on line 1 and Marty the Millionaire on line 2, Marty's line is going to get picked up first. But most *former* elected officials complain about the wear and tear of the money chase on their time and their integrity.

The pay-to-play mentality has so seeped into our system that there now exist two classes of citizens. There are those for whom tax breaks, bailouts, and subsidies are granted; for whom running for and winning office is plausible; and with whom elected officials take time to meet. And then there are the rest of us—the non-donors for whom taxes go up, consumer prices rise, and influence evaporates.

In *The Godfather,* Marlon Brando's Don Corleone tells a man named Bonasera in the opening scene: "Someday, and that day may never come, I'll call upon you to do a service for me. But until that day, accept this justice as a gift on my daughter's wedding day." The only difference between Bonasera and a member of Congress is that, for the latter, that day will *surely* come.

Some lobbyists, and even some elected officials, will argue that industry campaign contributions reward a member's *past* performance, and have no implication for how he or she should behave in the *future*. But the past-future analysis is a distinction without a difference. For candidates and contributors aren't just mineral matter, with no sense of the future. Bribes are unnecessary when everyone involved in the money chase knows implicitly that gifts will keep coming if a candidate keeps supporting the industry.

Lobbyists themselves can be part of the problem. Of course, lobbyists—named for those in the 1800s who huddled in the lobbies off the floor of Congress waiting to pounce—are exercising their right to "petition government" and "redress grievances" under the First Amendment. And since members of Congress and their staffs can't know everything about everything, or even something about everything, they look to interested parties (discounting for bias) to bring key information to their attention. The problem occurs when an army of lobbyists for one interest—say, a lower capital gains rate, or bigger gas-guzzling cars—combines with big contributions from that interest to overwhelm a less vocal or invisible opposition. And 17,000 lobbyists in Washington overall—or more than 30 per member of Congress—is quite an army.

"Every day there's a cadre of special-interest lobbyists lined up outside the House chamber on the sidewalk," reports Matt Keller, legislative director of Common Cause, who's spent years lobbying on Capitol Hill. "It's like a caricature. You've got Mr. Oil Man, Mr. Gas Man, Mr. Tobacco Man. It's like something out of *The Simpsons*. These guys spend their days trying to defeat something so obviously in the best interests of the country and the planet, and they can't possibly believe in what they're doing—but money talks. It's bizarre and frightening to watch up close."

In the introduction, I mentioned that in *Federalist* #10 James Madison envisioned factions that would compete with other factions, but he never imagined financial Goliaths that would invariably outtalk weaponless Davids. When lobbying becomes as one-sided as the Yankees versus the Rockford Peaches (Tom Hanks's woeful team in *A League of Their Own*), it produces flawed laws. Lobbyists should be a weight on the scale of decision—but not the scale itself.

In this chapter, we'll examine the costs to democracy of a Congress daily engaged in a political game show that might as well be called *The Price Is Right*.

The Money Chase Discourages Voting and Civic Participation

As special-interest dollars in elections go up by the millions, voter participation goes down. While Israel reliably achieves over 80 percent turnout in its elections for prime minister, and France and the United Kingdom typically turn out about three quarters of their voting-age populations, the United States has not broken *60* percent since 1968 (see table 5.1). The turnout for American elections is no higher today than it was in the 1930s—with roughly half of eligible voters staying home in presidential elections, and nearly two thirds in congressional elections.

The 1988 presidential race between George Bush and Michael Dukakis had the worst turnout (50.1 percent) in 64 years, but that dubious honor was not held long: two cycles later, 1996's Clinton-Dole contest yielded a limp 49.1 percent. And four years after that, not even the tightness of 2000's Bush-Gore fight could inspire many more than half of registered voters to turn out. On the local level, the trends are similar: In a May 2002 Nebraska primary, a microscopic 20 percent of registered voters went to the polls, shattering the previous low mark of 36 percent.

When right-wing extremist Jean-Marie Le Pen took second place in France's 2002 presidential race, legions of press attributed the accused racist's surprise finish to the large number of so-called absent voters. Soberingly, the 72 percent turnout for that race—France's lowest in nearly four decades—is higher than any U.S. turnout in the twentieth century. "The nation that prides itself on being the best example of government of, for, and by the people," notes Curtis Gans, director of the nonpartisan Committee for the Study of the American

TABLE 5.1

TURNOUT OF ELIGIBLE VOTERS IN PRESIDENTIAL ELECTIONS SINCE **1960**

Year	Percent	Year	Percent
1960	63.1	1984	53.1
1964	61.9	1988	50.1
1968	60.8	1992	55.1
1972	55.2	1996	49.1
1976	53.6	2000	51.2
1980	52.6		

Source: Federal Election Commission.

Electorate, "is rapidly becoming a nation whose participation is limited to the interested or zealous few."

Consider these regressive trends, as reflected in Robert Putnam's much discussed *Bowling Alone: The Collapse and Revival of American Community:*

◄○► Just 11 percent of eighteen- and nineteen-year-olds eligible to vote for the first time in 1998 actually did so.

◄○► Beyond a 25 percent decline in voting, there has been a 50 percent dip in political involvement (measured by campaign activities) over the last forty years. In 1973, a majority of Americans wrote an article, signed a petition, made a speech, or sent a letter to an elected official; twenty-one years later, most Americans did none of these.

◄○► In 1973, two-thirds of Americans attended at least one organization or club meeting a year; in 1994, the reverse was true. Over the same time span, membership in social and civic organizations fell 16 percent, while active participation in these same groups dropped by 50 percent.

◄○► Volunteering has diminished among nearly every age
group, churchgoing has gone down 10 percent, and
active involvement in church activities has plummeted
by 25 to 50 percent.

"There is now a lower level of trust toward our government than at
any time perhaps since the 1920s, perhaps ever," explains Gans. One
reason, he says, is "the media's increasingly cynical portrayal of politics,
aided by thousands of deaths in Vietnam, the Iran-Contra affair,
George [H. W.] Bush's 'Read My Lips, No New Taxes' vow, and
impeachment."

Gans believes that citizens watching six hours a day of TV are left
with little time to do much else but work, eat, and sleep; their civic
information base is unvaried and limited because it's filtered nearly
exclusively through the TV screen. He points also to the increasingly
stressful lives people lead today: more Americans are single, divorced,
commuting, generally anxious, and therefore less likely to participate
in civic affairs—including voting—when faced with a crude cost-
benefit decision. Also, Gans notes, although "leaders" like Newt Gingrich and Tom DeLay call government the enemy, demagoguing
against the government isn't likely to encourage participation in government.

Beyond the campaign finance arena, however, in recent years a
number of plausible and promising ideas have been proposed to
boost voting. One idea is the nationwide adoption of election day
registration (EDR). Currently practiced by six states, EDR reduces
barriers to participation by enabling voters who mistakenly think
they are already registered to do so on election day. This would also
solve the additional problems of voters being turned away because
their registration hasn't been processed in a timely manner, or
because they've been wrongly purged from voter lists. According to
a report by the nonpartisan research group Demos, states using
EDR in the 2000 presidential election had turnout rates nearly 12
percent higher than the national average—63.2 percent versus 51.3
percent.

Another pro-turnout initiative is 1993's "Motor Voter" Act, or the National Voter Registration Act. This historic bill, aimed at increasing participation, enabled voters to register at their department of motor vehicles, public assistance offices, or other state agencies while applying for driver's licenses or government assistance. The legislation also provided for mail-in voter registration. The results have been modest but encouraging: from 1992 to 2000, registration went up 5.2 percent.

In Oregon, voting by mail has proven to boost participation. In addition to being cost-effective (between 1995 and 1997, Oregon counties saved over $1 million in three voting-by-mail special elections), the system is obviously more convenient for voters than driving to the polls. In the 1996 Republican and Democratic presidential primaries, Oregon led the nation in turnout, with over 53.7 percent of voters mailing in their ballots. New Hampshire ranked second, with a 45 percent turnout.

Despite these signs of improvement, turnout and registration remain low among many demographic groups, including persons of low income (less than half of those making under $50,000 annually are registered, compared with 77 percent of those making $75,000 or more), communities of color (Latinos, for instance, register at approximately half the rate whites do), and young people (only 44 percent of citizens eighteen to twenty-four were registered in 1998, compared with a rate of over three fourths among senior citizens).

While from 1992 to 2000 soft money contributions increased five-fold, hard money nearly doubled, and party fund-raising tripled, voting in federal elections went *down* four percentage points overall. Obviously nothing can be done to change the statistical fact that one person's vote is highly unlikely to sway an election (although the tightness of Bush-Gore should make voters think twice). But with the combination of incumbency and money apparently predetermining election results, many voters rationally assume their vote can't really matter.

This problem is of concern not just to liberals but to all small-d democrats. "We're perilously close to not having democracy," said Paul Weyrich, a prominent conservative who heads the Free Congress Foundation. "Non-voters are voting against the system, and if we get a bit more than that, the system won't work."

The Money Chase Discourages Competitive Elections

In an age when incumbency and money are mutually reinforcing and "redistricting" is little more than a synonym for "incumbent protecting," the realistic number of potentially competitive seats in this fall's general elections can be counted on one's fingers and toes. In fact, getting reelected has become so automatic that a member of Congress is almost more likely to vacate his or her seat by *dying* than by losing.

In both 1998 and 2000, more than 98 percent of House incumbents who sought reelection won their races. (Senate challengers fared slightly better, winning 10 percent and 18 percent, respectively.) In 1996, every single one of the 113 Congress members first elected in the 1980s won his or her race for reelection. All but 4 won by 10 percent or more, and 75 won by a whopping 30 percent or more. While 142 incumbents were defeated in the 1960s, that number fell to just 97 in the 1970s, to 88 in the 1980s, and to 102 in the 1990s.

As chapter 4 discussed in the context of fund-raising, the incumbent's advantage is largely predicated on money. Of course, the fact that incumbents can gerrymander districts once a decade also helps their bids for reelection but is marginal when compared with the potent mixture of money and incumbency. In 1988, incumbents ended up with twice as much in *leftover* funds as their challengers *spent*. In 2000, House incumbents outspent their challengers by better than 4 to 1 ($408.5 million to $89 million), enjoyed an 8-to-1 edge in PAC money, and by the end of October had a 13-to-1 advantage in cash on hand. Senate incumbents in 2000 raised $155.9 million, compared with $63 million by their challengers, and held a 6-to-1 edge in both PAC funds and cash on hand.

With both Speaker Dennis Hastert and Representative Martin Frost (D–TX) bemoaning how terrible McCain-Feingold will be for their respective parties, one can't help but conclude that the two distinct political parties in Washington have given way to one monolithic alternative: the incumbent party.

Carrying over war chests is one of the great time-honored traditions of the incumbency protection program. Amass as much cash as you possibly can—even if you have no known opponent—and then use it to intimidate potential challengers, who will drop out or never even run to begin with. Once reelection is achieved, the member of Congress carries over the war chest into the next campaign and the next and the next. In a very real sense rolling over such treasuries violates the spirit of the campaign finance contribution limits, since a John Donor may give Challenger X only $2000 for a particular campaign in a particular year but may have given Congressman Z a total of $8000 for a campaign against Challenger X ($2000 in each of four election cycles).

In Public Citizen's Congress Watch study *House Insurance: How the Permanent Congress Hoards Campaign Cash,* members of the 101st Congress were found to have over $67 million stowed away in campaign war chests *the month they took office,* "virtually assur[ing] reelection [and] certainly discourag[ing] qualified candidates from challenging the financially stronger representatives." According to the same Congress Watch report, 89 percent of House incumbents faced financially noncompetitive races in 2000, meaning they faced either no opposition or challengers with less than half their campaign resources.

The only ways to crack open this continuing "unfair advantage" are serious campaign finance reform or congressional term limits. And we'll get reform only when members of Congress start fearing limits on their terms more than they fear limits on their money.

The Money Chase Creates "Part-Time Legislators, Full-Time Fund-Raisers"

On any given workday, you can see streams of Congress members leaving their Capitol Hill offices to go to small campaign cubicles in order to dial for dollars. "The problem is much worse than portrayed," says Senator Ron Wyden (D–OR). "The money chase is so time-consuming that people should wonder how we have time to get anything done. Yes, the day after an election, people sleep in on Wednesday. But then the money chase starts in again, day after day, year in and year out.

"In an election year," he continued, "members have cards or Blackberrys that say '8–9 Grange; 9–10 Hearing on Technology; 10–4 money calls at DCCC.' For that much of the day, a significant number of public officials are sitting in a dank office away from their public office with their tin cup out instead of thinking about how to help their constituents."

Ask anyone involved in the game, and, if they're honest, the refrain will be the same. In his autobiography, Bill Bradley wrote that, despite his fame and popularity, he had to spend 40 percent of his freshman Senate term fund-raising for reelection. One New York congressman, well known for raising tons of special-interest money, confided at a fund-raiser in early 2002, "I spend almost half my time raising money." When asked if his job performance would change if he didn't have to fund-raise incessantly, the representative didn't hesitate. "Oh yes, I'd be much more independent and effective."

Even Senator Dick Durbin (D–IL), among the hardest working of the new senators, is candid enough to admit in an interview, "Of course I won't miss votes, but after that, fund-raising has to take precedence. We'll schedule fund-raisers and then build around them." Representative Sherrod Brown (D–OH) confides that he has three full-time jobs: "Congressman, campaigner, fund-raiser."

Senator Robert C. Byrd, the longest-serving member of either chamber, put it best, calling his colleagues "part-time legislators and full-time fund-raisers." Senator Byrd told Mark Shields that during his tenure as Senate majority leader he often had to delay votes because of fund-raising conflicts. He mocked the parade of requests he endured for years: "Please, no votes Monday . . . no votes after four on Thursday . . . I've got a fund-raiser scheduled in Los Angeles . . . in New York . . . in my home state." Senator John Kerry, who refuses to take PAC money and has 55,000 donors averaging $36 each, said in the early 1990s, "A few months ago, I was out in Columbus, Ohio. And the same day I was there, across the hall was Tom Harkin of Iowa, and the next morning there was a room reserved downstairs for Bill Bradley of New Jersey. Now, that is Columbus, Ohio. That is ridiculous."

Stanley Sheinbaum, a prominent Democratic donor and activist in California, grew so frustrated with members of Congress calling to ask for money that he told a high-ranking senator he would accept his request for a meeting only "on the proviso that money not be discussed." But given the rules of engagement, is it really a surprise that incumbents regard donors more as ATMs than as people, and that donors come to resent it?

The Money Chase Deters Talent from Seeking Office

Challengers know they must make it through a "money primary" first if they ever want to reach the "voters' primary"—and the polling place of donors can turn away anyone without secure financing, which of course deters potential contenders who have more talent than funds. "At some point," argues Joshua Rosenkranz of the Brennan Center for Justice, "the spending of money is less an exercise in speech, and more an exercise in raw power—the power to dominate the conversation and to scare away all potential challengers." Of course it's impossible to calculate how many good women and men decide not to seek office because of the prohibitive costs, but most astute observers assume that it's many. As Senator Paul Wellstone (D–MN) laments, "People are giving up and not running for senator or governor because the money chase is too much."

When Elizabeth Dole aborted her run for president in October 1999, money was the single reason she cited. She pointed to the 80-to-1 fund-raising edge George W. Bush held over her. "I hoped to compensate by attracting new people to the political process, by emphasizing experience and advocating substantive issues," she told a roomful of tearful supporters. "But as important as these things may be, the bottom line remains money."

Perhaps most alarming is the case of Reubin Askew. So vast and disquieting were the demands for money in Askew's 1988 Florida Senate race that the former governor abruptly dropped out—despite opinion polls showing him with a 4-to-1 lead in the primary and a 2-to-1 advantage in the general election. "Something is seriously wrong with our system," Askew explained, "when many candidates for the Senate need to spend 75 percent of their time raising money." As Askew's issues director for the campaign, Dexter Filkins, wrote, "The need to raise so much cash so fast limited Askew's contact with the average voter—that is, one who did not donate money. We simply didn't have time for them." If Askew, a popular elected official, couldn't handle the incessant demands of fund-raising, how do you suppose an unwealthy, unfamous, and unsubsidized workingman or -woman might make out?

Of course, there's no formal "money primary" in the law or Constitution. All potential candidates are allowed to raise up to $1000 a donor per election or give themselves as much of their personal wealth as they can. "The law, in its majestic equality, permits the rich as well as the poor to sleep under bridges, to beg in the streets and steal bread," wrote Anatole France, which inspired this extrapolation from the late U.S. Appellate Court Judge J. Skelly Wright: "The law, in its majestic equality, allows the poor as well as the rich to form political action committees, to purchase the most sophisticated polling, media and direct mail techniques and to drown out each other's voices by overwhelming expenditures in political campaigns. Financial inequities . . . undermine the political proposition to which this nation is dedicated—that all men are created equal."

These financial disparities account in part for why there are so few blue-collar workers in Congress. "Do you honestly think that a butcher could get elected to the Senate today?" Senator Byrd rhetorically asked. "A garbage collector? A small grocery man? A welder?"

The Money Chase Favors Multimillionaires

When soliciting funds from individuals and PACs turns out to be inadequate to cover the costs of campaigning, candidates will often supply the requisite funds by drawing from their personal finances. In 2000, twenty-seven House and Senate candidates spent at least $500,000 of their own money on their own campaigns. Self-financing is especially pronounced for challengers and for candidates in open-seat races. Challengers in the 1996 House elections spent an average of over $40,000 of their own money, one sixth of their total campaign costs; candidates in open-seat races spent over $90,000. The average Senate challenger that year spent $645,000—one quarter of his/her total campaign costs—out of his/her own pocket.

Already, more than a third of Senate members are millionaires—and the number keeps growing. At least 50 members of the two houses are multimillionaires, among them the following senators: John Kerry, with a net worth of $675 million; Jon Corzine, $400 million; Herbert Kohl (D–WI), $300 million; Jay Rockefeller IV (D–WV), $200 million; Peter Fitzgerald (R–IL), $50 million; Mark Dayton (D–MN), $20 million; and Bill Frist (R–TN), $20 million.

Asked why so many of the deep-pocketed senators are, surprisingly, Democrats, Senator Carl Levin laughs. "It's a growing solution to Republican money. Since we can't raise as much special-interest money, we look more for candidates who can spend their own." Corzine, a former Goldman Sachs CEO, agrees. "Democratic leaders more eagerly recruited [wealthy self-financers] to relieve financial pressure on the party and because more such Democrats [than Republicans] run believing that government does good things," New Jersey's junior senator explains. "There's a tradition from FDR to JFK of Democrats who do it to fix the world and level the playing field of society."

Indeed, party leaders acknowledge that they explicitly try to recruit self-financing candidates, not necessarily the best candidates, to run. But since *Buckley v. Valeo* permits the wealthy to contribute as much to their own campaigns as they like—because the Court reasoned a person can't corrupt *himself*, never considering how such spending could corrupt the *process*—the strategy is legal, and often a winning one. Think about the thousands of hours of fund-raising that can be used for other things, like wooing party officials and opinion leaders, reaching out to voters, studying up on issues, and making news. Or the bottomless budget for television advertising that enables the candidate to flood the airwaves with her message.

Those who counter that advertisements don't force voters to vote for their candidates are correct, at least in a narrow sense. There's probably no amount of money that could persuade a majority to vote for Pat Buchanan, or to buy an Edsel. But advertising is a $600-billion-a-year industry for a reason—and the reason is that, overall, the more advertising a candidate does, the more likely he is to make the sale. Or to raise doubts about an opponent who can't afford to rebut. Put it another way: Suppose the New York Yankees are the best team in baseball; who would you bet on if the Yankees could bat in only two innings while their opponent, the worst major-league team, could bat in nine?

That said, being a multimillionaire certainly doesn't guarantee victory. Sometimes a candidate does something so self-immolating, or is found so untenable, that not even money can glide him into office. Jay Rockefeller and Jon Corzine—and even publishing magnate William Randolph Hearst, whose newspaper empire helped fund winning campaigns for Congress in 1902 and 1904—may have been successful, but Michael Huffington and Al Checchi are two examples of wealthy self-financing candidates in California who lost. Huffington, in his $30 million campaign for U.S. Senate in 1994, lost the election after attacking the immigrants flooding the state while, it was revealed, he himself had hired an illegal alien in his household. Checchi, the past head of American Airlines, lost his $40 million Democratic gubernatorial primary in 1998 after he ran a barrage of ads so brutally harsh that people began to resent *him*. Both candidates also faced opponents who were well financed and able to spend at least half their amounts—incumbent Senator Dianne Feinstein against Huffington, and now-Governor Gray Davis against Checchi.

But self-financers are starting to win major races now, which encourages other very wealthy people to try to do the same. As I mentioned earlier, multimillionaires Tony Sanchez in Texas and Douglas Forrester in New Jersey won competitive primaries in 2002. Following the success of Michael Bloomberg in New York City, five multimillionaires ran in statewide races in New York in 2002: Jane S. Hoffman (who later dropped out due to health) and Dennis Mehiel for lieutenant governor, William Mulrow for comptroller, and Tom Golisano for governor. Eliot Spitzer, the incumbent Attorney General, also significantly self-financed his initial victory in 1998.

Mark Schmitt of the Open Society Institute wrote, "The self-financed Democrats of most recent vintage . . . have all shown themselves to be as capable, liberal, and brave as their older counterparts like Jay Rockefeller. But there is no getting around the fact that the advantage of self-financed candidates has created a political plutocracy that looks less like America, economically, than at any time since before the direct election of senators."

If something doesn't change soon, there will be only three types of people running for and holding office in the future: super-fund-raisers, celebrities, and multimillionaires.

The Money Chase Corrupts Legislation— "Buying Sharp's Silence"

Of course, much of the $3 billion contributed to candidates in 2000 came because donors knew the candidate, believed in the candidate's philosophy, liked his/her personality, looks, religion, or race. The problem, however, is that the system is also flooded with a Niagara of contributions from economic interests seeking a return. And getting one.

A dozen years ago, the Democracy Project, a policy institute I founded, published a study attempting to analyze the costs of the private financing of elections. *Public Funding vs. Private Funding: Two Case Studies of the Benefits of Campaign Finance Reform* was an early attempt to quantify a significant and largely immeasurable problem. We started by examining how special-interest-inspired legislation can increase a product's cost to consumers, how tax breaks due to PACs increase the burden to taxpayers generally, and how legislation needed but forestalled by PACs can impose additional health and other costs on taxpayers.

The results, similar to estimates conducted more recently by groups like Public Citizen, were staggering. In *taxpayer* costs alone, the bailout of failed S&Ls cost $25 billion a year, the deregulation of tobacco (plus a farm bill authorizing manufacturers to buy stored tobacco at 90 percent discounts) cost Americans $2.1 billion a year, and loopholes won by Chicago's commodities traders hit taxpayers with a $300 million tab.

Then add new *consumer* costs. Sugar price supports (delivered to repay seventeen major sugar PACs who doled out $3.3 million to Senate and House members) cost consumers $3 billion a year. Similarly, dairy and milk price supports milked consumers by tacking an additional $9 billion onto the $45 billion shoppers already were spending on dairy.* Add to that an additional $2 billion a year on utilities, $10 billion a year on beer and wine, and $4.3 billion on health costs stemming from the passage of a much weaker version of the Clean Air Act, and the impact of PACs on American families is, in effect, a political corruption tax.

In all, the rough cost to Americans of the *private* system of financing elections was $50 billion annually. By contrast, the costs of *public* financing are modest and transparent (as chapter 8 details); no serious proposals for public funding of elections have exceeded $500 million to $1 billion.

"I think most people assume—I do, certainly—that someone making an extraordinarily large contribution is going to get some kind of an extraordinary return for it," said Supreme Court Justice David H. Souter. "I think that is a pervasive assumption. And . . . there is certainly an appearance of, call it an attenuated corruption, if you will, that large contributors are simply going to get better service, whatever that service may be, from a politician than the average contributor, let alone no contributor."

What follows is an industry-by-industry update on how legislatively interested money yields dividends in the favor bank of politics.

The Airline Industry

For the airline industry, 1999 was not a great year. Over 5000 complaints were processed with the Department of Transportation (more than double that of the previous year), canceled and delayed flights were up, and newspaper headlines augured financial and legal setbacks.

In response to the onslaught of passenger complaints, members in both chambers of Congress introduced passenger-rights bills and held hearings assessing the treatment of airline passengers. Under the main proposal, the Airline Passenger Fairness Act introduced by Senators John McCain and Ron Wyden, the Department of Transportation would be authorized to hold the airlines responsible for better cus-

---

*To put this in perspective, the market wholesale price of a gallon of milk at the time was 61 cents worldwide versus 87 cents in the United States.

tomer service. The hearings held in the House and Senate revealed a history of consumer mistreatment, including the proliferation of no-refund policies, overbooking, and reticence about lower fares. As disgruntled airline passengers joined consumer groups in the fight for passenger-rights legislation, the case against the airlines seemed strong, and passage of some kind of legislation inevitable.

For its part, the airline industry argued that the legislation was not necessary and could even wind up hurting the consumer. Carol Hallet, of the industry group Air Transport Association (ATA), defended the industry's record, saying it was "closer to perfection" than that of any other mode of transportation, and argued that the bill's passage would result in higher fares, fewer available seats, and "less rather than more disclosure of useful information to passengers."

The airlines had one additional tool of persuasion. Faced with a bill that would force the industry to drastically reform its procedures, the airlines strongly increased their campaign contributions during the two months that the legislation was being introduced, donating more than $200,000 in soft money to the political parties during February and March alone. Three months later, as the committee vote approached, more soft money arrived: more than $225,000 in the week leading up to the vote.

These donations, Common Cause would later say, "seem[ed] to have been well spent." The Senate Commerce Committee voted on June 23 to relax several of the strictest provisions of the McCain-Wyden bill, taking the ATA's word that it would voluntarily step up passenger treatment. In the end, the bill stipulated that the airlines do only what was previously required; the original legislation was essentially dead. Every senator, with the exception of cosponsor Ron Wyden, agreed to pass the weaker bill.

"The industry is solely driven by the bottom line, and the regulatory agencies for safety have been so captured and subsumed by the industry that they don't act independently anymore," laments Paul Hudson, executive director of the Aviation Consumer Action Project (ACAP). "Congress has not taken up the slack and is captured by campaign contributions and lobbying."

In addition to the passenger-rights legislation, which was killed two years later as well, a concern of ACAP's has been safety. According to the 1996 presidential study known as the Gore Commission, airline safety has not improved since 1980. In response to a panoply of security recommendations issued by the Gore Commission, the ATA has used extensive lobbying and contributing to delay Congress from enacting the suggested requirements. In 2000, it lobbied to weaken legislation that would have mandated background checks for all airport screeners. That year, the top nine airlines plus the ATA spent $16.6 million on lobbyists, ten of them former members of Congress, two of them former secretaries of the Department of Transportation (which oversees the FAA), and another three former senior officers at the FAA. There were 210 lobbyists in all, and with their help the industry was successful in curbing new regulations.

Con Hitchcock, a longtime airline consumer advocate now employed by the for-profit company Orbitz, defends the airlines against charges that they take too long to implement security changes, noting that limitations in personnel and equipment can make it hard to achieve rapid change. But "that having been said," Hitchcock adds, "airlines are resisting on the basis of costs."

ACAP's Hudson notes that while each decade prior to 1980 saw measurable improvements in safety and lower fatality rates, the reverse has been true over the last two decades. Technology has improved, but safety hasn't. He attributes this primarily to the tremendous power of the airline lobby to block increased safety demands by Congress. "In the aviation debate, the public is outspent 100 to 1 by the industry. They spend over $20 million a year on lobbying expenses and campaign contributions," he says, seated in his tiny two-person office with two computers and a fax. "If the public were only outspent by 10 to 1 or 20 to 1, there would still be a possibility of getting just decisions made. But we don't have a prayer [when we get outspent] 100 to 1."

Indeed, while the airlines contributed more than $8 million to federal candidates and political parties from 1999 to 2002, ACAP, the preeminent advocacy group representing airline consumers, could not afford to fund a $100,000 study that would evaluate and rank the airlines on safety and service. Between 1997 and 2000, the top nine airlines and the ATA spent over $60 million lobbying Congress and federal officials. During the first half of 1999 alone, American Airlines sent $228,056 in soft money to Republican national party committees, and $120,000 to Democratic committees.

Recently, the airline industry garnered attention for its role in the events and aftermath of September 11, 2001. While some critics of the airlines have questioned the $15 billion bailout the industry received from Congress, Hudson is sympathetic. He just wishes the government would first have passed the Aviation and Transportation Security Act—to show that passengers, not just the airlines, are a priority. (The security bill was eventually enacted—airlines, consumers, and victims were all on the same side on the issue, with polls showing 80 percent of Americans wanted heightened security and government takeover—but the industry's bailout was passed first, and legislation shielding airlines from lawsuits passed next, before the security bill was finally enacted.)

When the security bill was signed into law on November 19, 2001, a safety clause calling for all bags to be matched with all passengers was deleted, despite protest from the Association of Flight Attendants. The industry's rationale for its multimillion-dollar lobbying effort to defeat bag matching was that the safety measure would take too much time and cost too much money. But an FAA-funded study conducted by an MIT professor showed the average delay would be seven minutes, and would affect only 14 percent of the flights, while the added cost would be 25 to 52 cents a passenger. It's hard to imagine that an industry that charges $2 for a pair of earphones would expect their consumers to deem exorbitant a quarter or two for increased security.

The Auto Industry

Americans make up only 5 percent of the world's population but use 26 percent of the world's oil. Over the last decade or so, events in the Middle East have reminded us that unlimited use, a disinclination toward conservation, and dependence on foreign oil could pose dire consequences. In 1991, as we headed to war in the Persian Gulf to prevent Saddam Hussein from controlling the world's oil supply, the need for us to conserve our own resources could not have been more clear. At the time, the United States was receiving 290 million barrels a year from Iraq and Kuwait—roughly 9.6 percent of our total oil imports.

Just one year before, Senator Richard Bryan (D–NV) had introduced a bill to require increased fuel efficiency by 20 percent in 1995 and 40 percent by 2001. "The fuel economy law passed in 1975 has been one of the most effective conservation measures ever undertaken," Bryan said. "[But] larger, gas-guzzling cars are again being built, and the United States has increased its reliance on imported oil. We are moving backward, not forward." Cosponsored by thirty-three other Democrats and Republicans, the bill sought to expand the 1975 law that established the CAFE (corporate average fuel economy) standards, rates that hadn't been changed since 1985. Upping the auto mileage by 40 percent would have saved 2.8 million barrels of oil a day and significantly reduced emissions of carbon dioxide. Despite its importance and urgency, Bryan's bill was stalled, with the promise that it would receive Senate consideration later in the year.

"After yet another sudden, painful lesson about dependence on Mideast oil, the United States is still addicted to the stuff and still paying the price," wrote Jeffrey Denny for *Common Cause* magazine. "But when it comes to curbing oil consumption to ward off the next crisis, nobody wants to bite the bullet."

By September 1991, the auto industry had crafted a multilayered, multimillion-dollar lobbying and advertising strategy aimed at crashing the legislation. At first, the high-pressure effort (including a filibuster) was enough to prevent the Senate from putting the legislation to a vote. When the Senate voted to end the filibuster (by a 68–28 margin), the bill was reintroduced for debate to the delight of the Sierra Club, Public Citizen, and other advocacy and public interest groups. But when a business coalition joined with the auto industry and the first Bush administration, a second filibuster was mounted. This time, despite the antifilibuster vote of just a few days earlier, the second filibuster killed the legislation.

What accounted for eleven senators changing their antifilibuster votes in the short time between the votes? As Phil Stern notes in *Still the Best Congress Money Can Buy*, 64 percent of those senators who had received $20,000 or more from the auto industry in the previous five years ended up voting for the filibuster and against the legislation; of those given between $12,000 and $19,999, 42 percent sided with the industry; of those given $0 to $11,999, just 15 percent supported the industry. In the end, the facts that consumers would have saved $38 billion annually, that our need for foreign oil would have decreased, and that carbon dioxide emissions would have diminished greatly were not persuasive enough to overcome the political strength of the auto lobby.

About a decade later, lightning struck again in the same place. After Senators John McCain and John Kerry sponsored a proposal to raise CAFE standards from 24 to 36 miles per gallon by 2015, Senators Carl Levin and Christopher Bond (R–MO), the recipients of the fourth and eighteenth greatest amounts of auto industry contributions in U.S. history, introduced amendment S. 2997. Favored by the industry, the amendment called for the elimination of such fuel-economy requirements, leaving the executive branch free to issue its own standard. The efficiency-minded Kerry-McCain bill could have saved the United States up to 1 million barrels of oil per day by 2016. Instead, sixty-two senators opposed Kerry-McCain in April 2002 and supported Levin-Bond, even though, as Public Citizen reports, "They know that global warming is real; they know that our dependence on foreign oil cripples us at home and abroad; they know that Americans want safer vehicles to go farther on a tank of gas."

How did the auto industry do it again? John McCain was indignant and explicit in an interview: "In 1985, Congress voted for higher fuel efficiency standards; yet in 2002 we lost 62–38 on the same issue—and I was naïve enough to believe we had easily more than 50 votes and might have gotten 60 for cloture. What changed and what happened? Soft money, for chrissake!"

Adding insult to injury, a multimillion-dollar ad campaign was launched in the states of undecided senators. "Farming's tough enough with healthy-size pickups," bemoans a small farmer leaning on his pickup in one Detroit print ad. "Imagine hauling feed barrels around in a subcompact." Of course no one was calling for the extinction of pickups, but no matter; the ad was effective. As Public Citizen reports, "During the floor debate, senators displayed total ignorance of the laws of physics and modern vehicle technology, making ridiculous statements about how new fuel economy requirements would force Americans to farm with subcompact vehicles."

Amendment cosponsor Christopher "Kit" Bond went so far as to warn his colleagues that higher CAFE standards would actually force soccer moms out of their minivans. "They would have to have a string of golf carts," he said with a straight face on the Senate floor. "You can see the golf carts going down the highway to soccer practice, maybe two kids in each golf cart."

According to Ellen Miller, the auto industry spent nearly $4 million in soft money, PACs, and individual contributions to national candidates and parties in 2001, of which nearly four fifths went to Republicans. Of the 62 senators who voted with the industry against raising fuel efficiency standards, the average senator received more than $18,800 from auto companies. Those who voted against the industry received an average of only $6000. (See table 5.2.)

The lobbying element of the industry's strategy was an effective tag-team approach that involved sending the auto unions to visit liberal Democrats and auto executives to lobby Republicans. "The current administration did a very good job of pitting labor against the environmentalists," laments Deanna White, deputy political director of the Sierra Club. "Unfortunately, with the CAFE issue, some Democratic senators bought the corporate line that fuel efficiency would cost jobs. We actually conducted a poll that oversampled UAW [United Auto Workers] members, and it turns out they not only favored increased CAFE standards, but they favored it more than even the average voter!"

In an interview the week after the vote, one senator insisting on anonymity concurred with White's depiction of the industry's lobbying success: "That vote was one of the most politically cowardly things I ever saw in the Senate. We know how to be energy efficient and it starts with cars. Detroit used the same arguments today against CAFE they used in the 1970s—the technology is impossible; it'll make cars less safe; consumers won't buy cars; it'll kill jobs. In 1975 Congress said security was more important and devised a ten-year plan to double fuel efficiency. It worked. Yet now the new CAFE was defeated 62–38. It's shameful," he said, raising his voice and shaking his head.

TABLE 5.2

TOP SENATE RECIPIENTS OF AUTO INDUSTRY CONTRIBUTIONS (1995–2000) AND THEIR VOTES ON S. 2977

Recipient	Total	Vote
Phil Gramm (R–TX)	$230,980	Yes
George V. Voinovich (R–OH)	$203,424	Yes
John McCain (R–AZ)	$167,026	No
Richard Lugar (R–IN)	$136,750	Yes
Christopher Bond (R–MO)	$126,169	Yes
Bill Frist (R–TN)	$116,850	Yes
Mike DeWine (R–OH)	$ 83,525	Yes
John W. Warner (R–VA)	$ 82,960	Yes
Sam Brownback (R–KS)	$ 80,050	Yes
Jeff Sessions (R–AL)	$ 80,000	Yes
Mitch McConnell (R–KY)	$ 75,875	Yes
Ron Wyden (D–OR)	$ 74,900	No
Kay Bailey Hutchinson (R–TX)	$ 74,050	Yes
Richard C. Shelby (R–AL)	$ 74,013	Yes
Gordon Smith (R–OR)	$ 72,516	No
Fred Thompson (R–TN)	$ 70,800	Yes
Rick Santorum (R–PA)	$ 70,200	Yes
Arlen Specter (R–PA)	$ 68,350	Yes

Source: Public Citizen.

Tax Laws

When the idea of a minimum wage increase was raised in 1996, House Majority Leader Dick Armey (R–TX) vowed to oppose it "with every fiber of my being." With momentum and a mandate to push their Contract with America through the 104th Congress, Armey, Speaker Newt Gingrich, and the Republicans seemed nearly omnipotent. How, then, did the 1997 minimum wage bill get passed? The answer is another illustration of money impacting politics.

Gingrich ultimately came to believe that opposing a minimum

wage increase could be fatal in an election year. So he passed a minimum wage bill in name but stuffed it with so many benefits for friendly business interests that in the end it was less about minimum wages and more about $21 billion in corporate tax breaks.

The bill, H.R. 3448, did lift the lowest hourly wage from $4.25 to $5.15. But, as Eric Pianin of the *Washington Post* noted, "Congressional benevolence extended far beyond blue-collar beneficiaries. Buried in the bill's fine print were a raft of benefits custom-designed not for the working class but for well-heeled business interests." With special-interest corporations and PACs breathing down their necks, Congress transformed the bill for "the little guy" into a treasure chest of tax breaks for everyone in corporate America from Coca-Cola to General Electric.*

Their magnanimity is understandable. As the 1996 elections approached, the House Ways and Means Committee and the Senate Finance Committee were deluged with campaign contributions from corporate sources. The members who supported the corporate tax breaks tacked onto the minimum wage bill received more than $36 million in that election cycle. "Special interests have long used campaign contributions to push their legislative agendas," Pianin wrote. "But the link between campaign cash and HR 3448 . . . was bold [and] the magnitude of money impressive."

More than half of the $21 billion in new tax breaks went directly to members of the powerful National Federation of Independent Business, which was mobilizing to protect vulnerable Republican incumbents in the upcoming election cycle (the group's PAC contributed $1.2 million to key GOP congressional candidates during the 1996 campaign). Also protected in the tax bill were large corporations whose PACs had given $2.1 million in 1995–1996 to members of the tax-

---

*One provision allowed small businesses to deduct $25,000 (up from the previous mark of $17,500) on purchases of major equipment, like computer systems. Another loosened requirements for forming corporations under "subchapter S," a part of the tax code under which small businesses and family-owned firms receive lighter tax burdens. Still another provision written in by the Ways and Means Committee enlarged a special restaurant tip credit, granting restaurant owners (including corporate chains like Pizza Hut, Inc.) relief on social security taxes paid on tips for workers delivering food off premises.

writing committees; a hotly contested $18 billion contentious tax credit they received remained untouched.

Commenting on the so-called minimum wage bill and its protection of the corporate interest, former Representative Sam Gibbons (D–FL), once the Ways and Means chairman, observed: "Members are only human. You can't entirely dissociate yourself from something like a campaign contribution. How much it impacts on you and how far you're willing to move from your own principles is something each member has to decide for himself."

Just two years later, corporations received an even nicer present. While House Speaker Dennis Hastert was crowing about returning tax money to taxpayers, he was funneling the overwhelming majority of tax breaks in the 1999 tax bill to the staunchest contributors of GOP campaigns—$60 billion worth.

"Republicans have great discipline," says Robert McIntyre, director of Citizens for Tax Justice. "They keep their troops in line. They care about taxes more than anything. It's what defines them; it has since time immemorial. I don't know how they got the 'balanced budget' reputation. The liberals within their party are allowed to defect on any other issue they want, like trade, but not on taxes. It's all they care about."

Taking advantage of loopholes in the tax law, scores of corporations had for years avoided paying taxes. To avert this, Congress in 1986 had instituted the Alternative Minimum Tax (AMT). The AMT prevents profitable corporations from escaping tax liability by mandating that they compute the taxes they owe under regular tax rules and under special, stricter AMT rules. Companies must then use whichever calculation requires them to pay more.

In response, the nation's most powerful companies formed the AMT Coalition to fight the tax, often succeeding in weakening its rules. One such success came in 1997, when the AMT's depreciation rules were rewritten to greatly reduce the tax liability of companies investing in new equipment. Another example was the AMT foreign tax credit; while previously it could only eliminate up to 90 percent of a company's minimum tax bill, the 1999 tax bill allowed a company to use the clause to wipe out its entire liability in any one year. This provision was estimated to cost taxpayers $7.9 billion, with cumulative changes to the AMT from 1997 to 1999 costing $26 billion.

Companies belonging to the affected trade associations gave the political parties $22.2 million in soft money from 1991 to 1997. "When candidates are forced to spend so much time listening to the problems of the wealthy," wrote Mary H. Cooper in *The CQ Researcher*, "they don't hear about how hard it is to get decent health coverage or child care. Instead they get an earful about taxes or government regulations. That the wealthy keep the president on a leash is [made] obvious by what gets done in Washington—and what doesn't."

Another benefit in the 1999 tax bill concerned multinational corporations. Section 901 of the bill used obscure language to grant some of the nation's most profitable multinational corporations tax breaks costing taxpayers nearly $24 billion over ten years. Before the 1999 tax bill, a foreign company needed to be 80 percent U.S.-owned for its debt to be counted against the U.S. corporation's foreign income. When this new provision extended the privilege to companies that were only 50 percent U.S.-owned, one corporate lobbyist called it "the vein of gold." From 1995 to 1998, board members and lobbying companies of the National Foreign Trade Council donated $23.1 million to the political parties.

"What's so often misunderstood about the way we finance campaigns is [that] it doesn't affect big decisions, such as how to fix social security," explains one former Democratic member of Congress. "It's the smaller things, which don't get reported—on spending bills, on tax bills, on authorization bills."

Three years later, little has changed regarding the parties' philosophies on tax law. After the terrorist attack on the World Trade Center, President Bush and congressional leaders quickly agreed in concept to a $50–75 billion, one-year plan to stimulate economic growth and provide aid to those most hurt by the disaster. But much like the minimum wage bill of 1997, this so-called economic stimulus plan was a Trojan horse full of corporate lobbyists who again infiltrated Congress looking for corporate tax breaks.

"This administration is the worst," McIntyre says, shaking his head. "You could embarrass Reagan. You can't embarrass Bush, Armey, and DeLay. They can cover their behavior up and they don't care."

Under the stimulus legislation proposed by House Republican leaders in December 2001, two thirds of the tax cuts would go to corporations; the bill would cost $202 billion in revenues over the next three fiscal years. In addition to corporations, wealthy individuals also benefited: capital gains taxes dropped 10 percent and three quarters of the total tax reductions were granted to the top tenth of all taxpayers.

The early House proposal also called for the corporate AMT to be repealed permanently. Not only would this enable companies to bypass the AMT rules, but those that had paid the minimum tax over the *previous* fifteen years would get an immediate refund. That would have amounted to $25 billion in corporate rebates, and $6.3 billion of it would have gone to fourteen tax-avoiding Fortune 500 companies, averaging $450 million each. IBM would have received $1.4 billion, General Motors $671 million, Texas Utilities $608 million, Daimler-Chrysler $600 million, and ChevronTexaco $572 million.

The House bill ran into trouble in early 2002, as questions about Enron provoked skepticism about corporate welfare. Senate Budget Committee Chairman Kent Conrad said the bill didn't "pass the laugh test." And even Senator Pete Domenici (R–NM), ranking Republican on the Budget Committee, and Treasury Secretary Paul O'Neill considered the House bill inconsistent with the originally agreed upon contours of the stimulus bill.

But the compromise bill that was enacted was only slightly better. While the AMT repeal was dropped, the same $114 billion in corporate tax cuts over three years remained. Also included was a 30 percent increase in corporate depreciation write-offs over the next three years, at a cost of $97 billion. And like the failed December legislation, the bill enacted in March 2002 provides $9 billion in tax relief to multinationals sheltering their U.S. profits from taxes.

Moreover, in a bill initially intended to help those struggling and/ or out of work, only 7 percent will go to helping the unemployed, with eight dollars going to corporate tax cuts for every dollar allocated to the unemployed. The new bill dropped the plan to extend tax rebates to low-income workers and eliminated efforts to help pay for health insurance for laid-off workers. "The corporate guys backed them huge," McIntyre says, explaining Congress's motives in turning an economic stimulus bill into another corporate tax break bonanza. "They promised they'd pay them back, and so they seized on an airplane crash [as a cover to get it done]. The public thought the bill was funding unemployment and health insurance benefits. Amazingly, focus groups show that when you explain to people how little is actually going toward unemployment benefits, they don't believe it. They literally won't believe it, even when you tell them." Why? "The President's a congenial guy," he explains. "No one wants to believe he's a corporate tool. He's leading us in a war; no one wants to criticize him. I don't."

Speaking of the September 11 impetus for this bill, the $55 billion that large companies avoided paying in taxes is the equivalent of hiring 960,000 teachers, firefighters, or police officers, at the annual salary of $50,000 a year—or of the annual health insurance costs of 12 million Americans.

Big Tobacco

"Once again, we see that dollars speak louder than sense on Capitol Hill," said Public Voice executive director Ellen Haas in 1987. Her consumer group's study had just found that representatives voting to continue the federal tobacco support program in 1985 had received more than double the tobacco PAC contributions that opponents of the program received. Tobacco PACs' gifts had risen by 27 percent in the 1985–1986 election cycle, when the amendment and other anti-smoking initiatives were being considered. "On the one hand, Congress is warning the public of the health dangers of smoking," Haas noted. "On the other hand, it is actively promoting the use of tobacco through a price support program that costs the taxpayers more money."

Her allegation that the tobacco industry was using money to influence policy was later corroborated—by the industry itself. Internal Philip Morris memos labeled "sensitive" eventually fell into the hands of the health advocacy group called Doctors Ought to Care. The interoffice documents used stunningly candid language to detail the company's plans to spend $600,000 in seven states in 1989 on campaign contributions, speaking fees, and donations to legislators' pet projects in an effort to "convince" policymakers to support the industry. One such memo, "Defensive and Offensive Strategies/Review of Tools to Accomplish Strategies," contained the following plans and admissions:

- ◄o► "Last year, we gave out about $11,000 to Kansas legislators. It may not sound like much, but that's the most we could give without sticking out like a sore thumb."

- ◄o► "We already help sponsor a [Louisiana] legislative dove hunt, but I think our own fishing trip would be of benefit. We give these members so much money in campaign contributions and I think that knocks out the need for an honorarium unless they requested it coupled as a trip."

- ◄o► "This [Missouri] group really loves to hunt. The same guys I took to the racetrack in [Oklahoma] and hunting last year were the very ones that helped us hold the leadership firm on no cigarette taxes. We will be doing some racetrack trips in 1990."

- ◄o► "Our new [Texas] comptroller . . . will be John Sharp. The plan is to give early and large campaign contributions to Sharp, thereby jumping on the bandwagon early and at the very least buying Sharp's silence when it comes to locating new revenues."

Perhaps the most notorious example of the tobacco lobby's strength was the $50 billion "mystery amendment" of 1997. In a case of what Senator Susan Collins (R–ME) later called "backroom politics at its worst," a one-sentence, forty-six-word provision granting $50 billion in tax breaks for cigarette makers was snuck through a House bill in the dead of night, and rushed to a vote the next day with members of Congress unaware of its existence. Worse yet, the amendment, which granted the industry the right to use tax revenues as credit against a $368 billion smoking-related illnesses settlement, was apparently embarrassing enough that no one in Congress was willing to take credit for inserting it. This led Senator Dick Durbin to call the provision "a legislative orphan" that "shines and stinks like rotten mackerel by moonlight."

How did the "Joe Camel Tobacco Loophole," as Senator Edward Kennedy (D–MA) called it, get through and pass the House? In addition to having no apparent author and being inserted at the last minute, it was appended to a must-pass balanced budget bill that no one had time to read. After Collins and Durbin shined the light on the tobacco tax break—revealed later by *Time*'s Margaret Carlson to have been written by former RNC chair Haley Barbour, a wealthy tobacco lobbyist—the Senate eventually rejected it 95–3. While House Minority Leader Richard Gephardt called the anonymous, eleventh-hour tactic "an absolute outrage," Representative Wayne Edward Whitfield (R–KY) was not quite as horrified. "When you consider how politically incorrect it is to defend the industry and how everybody is after it," he boasted, "we did extremely well."

Whitfield had a point. Although the amendment failed to get past the Senate, the industry had managed to save a federal crop insurance program despite strong opposition, and to defeat proposals to provide to the Food and Drug Administration (FDA) $34 million earmarked for enforcing underage smoking laws.

Few, if any, policy makers (among those who don't represent tobacco districts anyway) are eager to publicly embrace an industry responsible for one in six deaths over the health interests of their constituents. But tobacco executives and lobbyists have been successful in overcoming the reluctance by coaxing them with money. The flow of campaign contributions from major tobacco companies reached $9.9 million during the 1995–1996 cycle. In the months leading up to these victories, the industry pumped hundreds of thousands into both the Republican and Democratic party organizations (with much more going to the GOP), and PACs associated with the industry raised $740,000 from tobacco employees alone. (For contribution figures per firm, see table 5.3.)

According to Public Citizen, the industry's $35.5 million overall lobbying effort in 1997 was unprecedented. With more than $66,600 spent for every member of Congress, Big Tobacco bought the services of dozens of prominent law firms and political insiders to join its cause. Former representatives joined former governors and party heads in a field of lobbyists totaling over 200. Philip Morris spent $15.8 million, followed by RJR Nabisco's $5.4 million, providing the tobacco industry with the means to employ one lobbyist for every 2.5 members of Congress.

In 1999, President Clinton filed legal action against the industry to win back $20 billion in federal health care costs to veterans, federal employees, and Medicare patients, declaring the civil suit a top priority for the Justice Department. When the House voted in June 2000 on whether to fund the suit, the 207 members voting against it received an average of five times more tobacco money ($9712) than did those voting to fund the suit ($1750). When they voted a second time, the 183 dissenting members received seven times more money than their pro-health opponents ($10,715 versus $1539).

By the following year, President Clinton had been replaced by George W. Bush. Since Bush's party had accepted $6.5 million in soft and PAC money from Big Tobacco during his campaign, it was no surprise when the new president took steps to settle the suit against the industry. "The administration is seeking yet another way to let the tobacco industry off the hook for decades of deception and wrongdoing," Matthew L. Myers, the president of the Campaign for Tobacco-Free Kids, said. The President offered a wan defense of his decision: "I . . . worry about a litigious society. At some point, you know, enough is enough."

The annals of the tobacco lobby's participation in politics are loaded with example after example of the industry using its financial prowess to craft, influence, pass, or kill legislation, depending on its needs. Here are some additional instances:

◄o► When the 104th Congress took office riding the wave of the Gingrich revolution, Representative Thomas Bliley (R–VA) was named new chair of the House Commerce Committee. Bliley had received more PAC contributions from the industry—$22,900 in the 1994 election cycle, and $53,025 in 1996—than any other member of Congress. Not surprisingly, the new chair publicly promised that his committee would not investigate any charges against the tobacco industry or consider any legislation regulating it. That's money well spent.

◄o► Around the same time, House Speaker Gingrich—who had received nearly $100,000 in tobacco contributions to his campaign, personal PAC, and college course and who occasionally traveled around in an RJR Nabisco jet—called tobacco critic and FDA Commissioner David Kessler "a bully and a thug."

◄o► Tobacco companies often hire former Congress members to be lobbyists, paying the ex-legislators to use their friendships to persuade current policy makers to support the industry. Among those who shifted from the persuaded to the persuaders are former Representatives Ed Jenkins (D–GA) and James Stanton (D–OH), both now employed by Philip Morris.

◄o► A major victory for the tobacco industry was the June 1998 defeat of Senator John McCain's proposed comprehensive tobacco legislation. With only 57 senators voting to end debate and bring the bill to a final vote, the legislation fell to a filibuster. The average amount in tobacco money taken by the 42 who opposed the McCain bill was $17,902, versus $4810 for the 57 who supported it.

◄o► According to *The Nation,* 25 percent of exported cigarettes are smuggled, which has enabled multinational tobacco companies to evade local tariffs and compete head to head with domestic producers overseas—increasing sales significantly. Foreign governments (e.g., Canada, Colombia) have sued Philip Morris and Brown & Williamson's British parent company for violating the Racketeer Influenced and Corrupt Organizations Act (RICO) by engaging in smuggling and money-laundering schemes. They are charged with "defrauding governments of hundreds of millions in tax revenues and of hiding and ultimately taking the illicit profits back to the United States." The U.S. government's response: with the support of the White House, the tobacco industry secured in Congress changes in the USA Patriot Act, which could shield the companies from liability.

◄○► National Republican Congressional Committee head Representative Tom Davis has introduced, with the support of Philip Morris, a bill called the National Youth Smoking Reduction Act (HR 2180). The bill enacts loopholes undercutting FDA authority, and fails to adequately address tobacco exports. Its major effect is actually to reduce and relax numerous FDA powers—but in an effort to fool the

TABLE 5.3

BIG TOBACCO'S CONTRIBUTIONS TO FEDERAL CANDIDATES AND NATIONAL PARTY COMMITTEES, 1995–2000

Company	Total
Philip Morris	$10,291,208
RJR Nabisco	$ 4,704,427
US Tobacco	$ 3,355,017
Brown & Williamson	$ 2,886,521
The Tobacco Institute	$ 1,186,862
Lorillard Tobacco	$ 606,050
Smokeless Tobacco Council	$ 588,253
Swisher International	$ 356,025
Conwood Co LP	$ 297,427
Pinkerton Tobacco	$ 157,000
TOTAL	$24,428,790

Source: "Buying Influence, Selling Death," by Common Cause, the Campaign for Tobacco-Free Kids, the American Heart Association, and the American Lung Association.

public, its name implies a more benign purpose. Davis, the GOP's chief fund-raiser, received $11,800 in tobacco PAC money from 1995 to 2000.

The Energy Industry

The energy industry had few friends more loyal during the 1980s than Senator Bennett Johnston (D–LA), chair of the Senate Energy and Natural Resources Committee. Johnston carefully passed a bill through his committee in March 1989 opening the coastal plain of the Arctic National Wildlife Refuge in Alaska to oil and gas drilling. After years of trying, he finally squeezed the bill out of committee by an 11–8 vote. Then, nine days later, a ship called the Exxon *Valdez* dumped 10 million gallons of crude oil into the Prince William Sound. This case of colossal bad timing led Johnston to withdraw the proposal, because, he said, it would be "politically foolish" to push it at the time.

That setback notwithstanding, Johnston has had his fair share of success stories on behalf of the industry. In 1986, he succeeded in enacting legislation that favored privately owned utilities over public utilities in federal licensing of hydroelectric power. In 1988, he fought back legislation making contractors at nuclear facilities owned by the Department of Energy (DOE) liable for accidents caused by their own gross negligence.

Looking at a 1954 law that required the DOE to price its enrichment services so that it recovers program costs, the General Accounting Office reported in 1987 that the DOE had not recovered $8.8 billion in the prior year. Two years later, at the behest of the commercial nuclear power industry, Senator Johnston helped propose an initiative to restructure the uranium industry by setting the amount of unrecovered costs at roughly $364 million, a figure approved by the utilities and a break of over $8.4 billion.

Johnston's friendship with energy was not one-sided. While up for reelection in 1984, he received more than $121,000 from energy PACs and at least $84,000 from individuals who worked in the business. In 1988 he earned $8000 in honoraria from General Electric, Chevron, and electric utilities. The year before, he set up his own Pelican PAC, and had it managed by former aides who had become big-energy lobbyists. Funds for the PAC came in large part from individuals working for energy companies. Those helping him raise money for Pelican included Robert Szabo, a electric utilities lobbyist, and Charles McBride, a nuclear utilities lobbyist. Questioned about the propriety of such an arrangement, Johnson answered, "I'm very much playing by the rules."

Johnston was right: for the energy industry, money was and is the heart of the matter. From 1990 through early 2002, the industry invested $140 million in the political system, including $40.6 million in PAC money and $49.1 million in soft money. One instance in which the industry's benevolence paid off was the $5.5 billion Shoreham Nuclear Power Station built by the Long Island Lighting Company (LILCO). Viewed as a safe and economical way to provide 500,000 homes with electricity, the Shoreham plant was originally expected to cost $75 million, but accidents, increased costs, community opposition, and licensing issues ran the total cost to more than 70 times the expected figure. When Shoreham was unable to recoup the billions in added costs, state regulators allowed LILCO to raise its electric rates, and Long Island residents became the highest-paying electricity consumers in the United States—through no fault of their own.

"The industry in large part has been spared by its customers," wrote Deborah Lutterbeck of *Common Cause* magazine. "Just as LILCO's ratepayers continue to pay for the Shoreham plant, ratepayers across the country are paying for their electric companies' bad investments." Alan Noia, president of New York's Allegheny Power System, estimated in 1995 that consumers had paid $38 billion in excess costs. While the ratepayers paid the price, the electric companies had copped a bargain, giving approximately $1 million or so to congressional candidates in the 1993–1994 election cycle and $1.5 million in soft money from 1988 to 1995.

The return on its investment that the energy industry was seeking in the mid-1990s was deregulation, through which the industry hoped to be freed from government requirements that had been forcing them to buy alternative forms of energy or cap the prices they charged. The proponents of deregulation promised smaller bills to consumers, strong stock returns, and stability and reliability. But, as California would later show, consumers don't often benefit from energy laissez-faire. Industry giants do.

When California decided to deregulate its electric utilities in 1996, proponents of the move promised that market competition would drive consumer electric bills down by at least 20 percent. But they have been proven wrong. Because just a few corporations controlled the power plants sold by the California utilities, in the deregulation deal these companies suddenly had an opening to grossly increase electricity rates without fearing the competition—and they did. By charging three times more in 2000 than the year before, the top ten sellers boosted their profits by 54 percent.

In early 2001, eight western governors (half of them Republicans) asked the federal government to put a temporary cap on the region's wholesale electricity prices, citing ballooning costs and low supplies. They were joined by two of the Congress's most conservative Republicans, who sponsored a bill urging the installment of caps. Yet President Bush ignored their calls, despite a manufactured crisis that was exploiting taxpayers and consumers. Why?

One explanation is that ten of Bush's largest contributors in 2000, whose gifts totaled $4.1 million, were energy suppliers who were poised to benefit from such a hands-off policy. Three of the corporations making large profits in California were Texas-based companies that gave $1.5 million to the President's campaign. Another was Reliant, whose board includes James A. Baker III, the former secretary of state who oversaw Team Bush's recount struggle in Florida. Baker's law firm, Baker Botts LLP, which contributed $113,621 to Bush-Cheney in 2000, received $14.5 million for services provided to Reliant in 1999. Electric utilities, which donated $825,000 to the President's inaugural committee, and Reliant, whose CEO, Steve Ledbetter, gave $47,000 to Bush's gubernatorial campaigns in 1994 and 1998, gained enormously by this hands-off policy.

Energy companies did not restrict their influential donations only to federal officials. The 2000 election cycle saw the industry spend over $17 million in contributions and lobbying to state and local energy policy makers in California. Nearly $1 million alone was given to the three state elected officials with the greatest influence over policy: Governor Gray Davis got over $600,000 (though he wasn't even on the ballot that year), while State Senate President Pro Tempore John Burton received over $250,000, and Assembly Speaker Robert Hertzberg $220,000. To cover their bases, investor-owned utilities (IOUs) contributed to every single state legislator but one. "Nobody in the legislature is standing up for what's right because they don't want to give up campaign contributions," complained Harry Snyder, spokesperson for Consumers Union.

While the IOUs had pushed the failed deregulation policies of 1996, they nevertheless were able to influence new policy because of their $4 million in contributions to those in power.* In the words of Laura Tyson, dean of the Haas School of Business at UC–Berkeley, "The solution to the policy problem is moving agonizingly slowly because there are several powerful political groups that can block any piece of legislation."

Beyond Enron, the power of corporate contributors to influence energy policy has begun to garner national attention. Vice President Cheney's refusal to release the list of participants on his energy task force and Energy Secretary Spencer Abraham's private meetings with energy executives have already been noted. The Center for Responsive Politics estimates that six of the individuals and groups Abraham met with accounted for nearly $3.3 million in political contributions to Republicans over the prior three years—almost triple what the same group gave Democrats.

One group that *was* consulted in crafting the energy plan was Exelon, the nation's largest nuclear energy company, whose wish was granted when the administration endorsed its new nuclear reactor. In supporting the so-called pebble-bed reactors, which environmentalists have questioned as vulnerable to terrorist attack, Vice President

---

*By contrast, the "green" energy industry learned the hard way how important contributions can be. After it gave only 0.3 percent of what IOUs did in campaign contributions, the deregulation plan provided *disincentives* for customers to use "green energy" retailers.

Cheney explained, "The industry has an interest in this." According to the *New York Times,* only Exelon, which provided hundreds of thousands of dollars to Republican (and Democratic) campaigns in recent years, has an interest in the reactor. As is typical with these kinds of money-for-favors transfers, Exelon's name is not mentioned in the energy report (the corporation itself conceded its identity to the *Times*), and the task force's endorsement of the reactor takes up just one small paragraph in the report. But that doesn't make the endorsement less important—just harder for journalists and the public to discover. In 2001, the year preceding the task force's recommendation, Exelon had upped its contributions to the Republican Party to $347,514.

As these revelations were appearing in newspapers across the country, the nuclear energy industry won another massive victory in February 2002. Over the protests of environmental groups, scientists, and the state of Nevada, President Bush approved Secretary Abraham's recommendation to store 77,000 tons of nuclear waste permanently in the Yucca Mountains. The Nuclear Energy Institute—self-described on its Web site as "the policy organization of the nuclear energy and technologies industry"—had donated over $18 million to Republicans in soft money from 1991 to 2001.

Drugs and Health Care

In an effort to widen their wallets, the health care industry has often resisted measures that would make medicine and health care cheaper and safer for patients. To do so, it has spent millions on campaign contributions, lobbyists, front groups, soft money, and issue ads. One result: the lack of a prescription drug plan for elderly Americans and a health care economy in which our seniors pay more than double what others pay abroad.

Drug companies profit from their patents. If a company has a monopoly patent on a drug, other companies cannot market it. So cheaper competitors or generic alternatives are not available. For example, many drug companies are capable of manufacturing the antibiotic known as Cipro, which became well known during the anthrax scare in the fall of 2001. But by law only Bayer can sell it, because the giant firm holds the monopoly patent on the drug.

But after September 11, Bayer pushed for legislation (S. 838) that would reauthorize a 1997 law that extended by six months the patents of many of the most expensive drugs on the market, including Cipro. All drug companies would have to do to get their monopoly patents lengthened was to test the drugs for safety (and effectiveness) in children. But pediatric testing is something that many groups, such as Public Citizen and the Elizabeth Glaser Pediatric AIDS Foundation, feel should be required as a condition of FDA drug approval anyway.

The pediatric patent extension has long been a sticking point in drug industry legislative negotiations. Companies have often refused to test their products for safety and efficacy in children, because the children's market for prescription drugs is smaller and therefore less lucrative than the adult market. "Because of the small market for pediatric formulations, a pharmaceutical manufacturer has no incentive to invest resources in such trials," admitted the drug industry's trade association, the Pharmaceutical Research and Manufacturers of America. This would explain why some children's advocacy and health groups agreed to what was essentially a bribe—they needed to give the drug companies the incentive to perform the pediatric tests. "This is an incentive that has become such a windfall for blockbuster drugs," said Paul Glaser, chairman of the Elizabeth Glaser Pediatric AIDS Foundation. "However, as I see it, that is all part and parcel of buying into our system that stresses money and power and where there is very little room for mandating a moral imperative. There is no choice."

Why is pediatric testing so important? Children react differently to medicines than adults do, and without information on how children will respond to a given medication, pediatricians have to guess when prescribing drugs how a child might react.

According to a study by the Tufts Center for the Study of Drug Development, pediatric tests cost an average of $3.87 million per drug. Since the FDA has requested tests on 188 drugs, the total cost to the industry would be about $700 million. By contrast, the FDA estimates that patent extensions on the drugs are worth at least forty times that number, or $29.6 billion, in added sales for the companies holding the patents. Beyond $592 million in additional profits each year for drug companies, the added costs to consumers will be over twenty times that, or $14 billion, because consumers will lack access to cheaper generic alternatives.

Presumably, convincing members of Congress to support a plan that drives drug prices up would be a tough sell. Consequently, drug companies are very prolific donors to assure that their access to policy makers can make them more susceptible to industry arguments.

In all, the drug industry spent $262 million on lobbying, campaign contributions, and issue ads in 1999–2000, more than any other industry. The Democratic sponsor of the Cipro bill, Representative Anna Eshoo (D–CA), received $131,544 in drug industry campaign contributions from the time she was elected in 1992 until she sponsored the bill. All this generosity worked to yield the desired result: subcommittee members who supported the patent extension received 250 percent more in campaign contributions from the industry ($64,691 on average since 1990) than did those voting to reduce it ($25,492). After initially standing by Bayer—even though it would take the company twenty months to meet the government's demand for the drug, while generics could jointly reach the goal in three—Health and Human Services Secretary Tommy Thompson eventually succumbed to public criticism and forced the company to reduce its price for Cipro.

Claritin is another example of what Public Citizen's Frank Clemente calls the industry's "uncontrolled drive for monopoly patent extensions and sky-high profits." Drug manufacturer Schering-Plough's legislative vehicles, S. 1172 and H.R. 1598, would allow three-year patent extensions for this multibillion-dollar allergy drug and six other "pipeline" drugs (so named because they were in the FDA review process as the 1984 Hatch-Waxman Act, which made it easier for generic manufacturers to market copies of brand-name drugs, became law). This extension would cost Claritin consumers an extra $7.3 billion, and extensions for all seven drugs would cost a cumulative $11 billion. After Schering-Plough began its drive in 1996 to persuade Congress to extend the company's patent on Claritin, it significantly increased its soft money contributions and lobbying expenditures, giving nearly $1 million in soft money to Democratic and Republican party committees. The company gave 4.5 times more in 1999 than it did during the previous two election cycles.

New Jersey Senator Robert Torricelli, who received the greatest amount of contributions from the corporation's PAC and executives ($31,050), became a major supporter of the Claritin patent extension bill. Orrin Hatch (R–UT), then the Senate Judiciary Committee chairman and its second-highest recipient of Schering-Plough PAC and executive contributions ($16,000), was treated to the company's corporate jet on multiple occasions in July and August of 1999, within days of speaking in support of the legislation at a committee hearing.

One legislative director for a midwestern congressman explained how drug industry lobbyists try to capture legislators. "What happens on a day-to-day scale is [that] lobbyist organizations hold fund-raisers, get the ear of the Congress member, and the member is beholden to them. And then, when there's legislation that affects the lobbying group, they call and make their opinions known." She acknowledges that "a good member is open to hearing but not accepting verbatim. But members not in leadership positions—and thus not guaranteed to continue getting industry money—have ethically difficult decisions to make."

One "ethically difficult decision" was keeping Medicare from providing coverage for prescription drugs, leaving 13 million Americans under Medicare to pay top retail prices for their prescriptions. Studies show that consumers without prescription drug coverage are charged retail prices double the amount manufacturers charge their most favored customers. To maintain this lucrative status quo, the industry spent approximately $230 million in the 2000 election cycle on lobbying, campaign contributions, and issue ads to block Democratic-backed legislation that would provide such coverage.

The industry's spending included $170 million for lobbying, almost $15 million in direct campaign contributions, at least $35 million in campaign ads (produced by a front group benignly called Citizens for Better Medicare, which is really run by the industry), and $10 million funneled to the U.S. Chamber of Commerce for pro–drug industry issue ads. Such spending was required, industry lobbyists believed, because polls showed expensive prescription drugs to be an issue paramount to voters.

TABLE 5.4

**ADDED REVENUES AND CONSUMER COSTS OF TOP 10 DRUGS
HEADED FOR PEDIATRIC PATENT EXTENSIONS**

Drugs	Manufacturer	Added Revenue	Consumer Cost
Prilosec	AstraZeneca	$1,435,768,250	$676,862,175
Lipitor	Pfizer	$1,292,429,950	$609,288,405
Prevacid	TAP	$ 991,410,700	$467,379,330
Prozac	Eli Lilly	$ 898,487,450	$423,572,655
Zocor	Merck	$ 772,464,700	$364,161,930
Celebrex	Pharmacia	$ 705,427,800	$332,558,820
Zoloft	Pfizer	$ 661,645,600	$311,918,640
Paxil	GlaxoSmithKline	$ 632,784,250	$298,312,575
Claritin	Schering-Plough	$ 583,571,450	$275,112,255
Glucophage	Bristol-Myers Squibb	$ 421,215,900	$198,573,210

Source: Public Citizen.

So far the investment has paid a healthy dividend, for the industry but not seniors: the industry's push has kept Congress from providing prescription drug coverage through Medicare. And it keeps coming: the constituency that gave the most $250,000 donations to President Bush's record-setting $30 million fund-raiser in June 2002 was the drug industry.

※

In the early 1980s, Bernadette Budde, then the longtime PAC director of the Business Industry PAC, said heatedly, "No one has even shown me one body—not one—who has sold his vote for a contribution."

Apparently Ms. Budde never had a conversation with the former senator Rudy Boschwitz (R–MN). At one time, Boschwitz actually had his staff give donors different-colored stamps for them to put on the mail they sent to his office to indicate their donation levels in order to facilitate preferential treatment. Boschwitz's gaffe—again in the words of Michael Kinsley—was not that he told a lie but that he told the truth. Every candidate in American history would privately confirm that they sold access to big donors, and this fact became the crux of the majority's opinion in the 2002 Vermont campaign finance decision.

Since it's a felony, punishable by up to two years in prison, to accept "anything of value" for or because of a public act, admissions of bribery are as unusual as cherry blossoms in Washington in November. Bribery is also rare because it's not necessary.

It exists, of course. President Eisenhower vetoed national gas rate deregulation that he favored in 1956 because of an apparent $2500 bribe to a New Jersey senator by an industry lawyer. Former Representative Tony Coelho told author Brooks Jackson how a lobbyist offered him a $500 cash bribe on his second day as a congressional administrative assistant in 1970; when Coelho refused, "he absolutely resented it [and] tried to get me fired." In 1979, of eight members offered bribes by supposed Arab interests in the ABSCAM sting, seven went along (and were prosecuted). And as this is written, a New York State senator and a New York City council member are under indictment for bribery.

If envelopes stuffed with $100 bills were common thirty years ago, however, today they're not. Why commit a crime when you can make a contribution? Here's the difference: if a lobbyist says "I'll give $10,000 *if* you support x," that's a crime; but if a lobbyist says "I'm giving $10,000 and I hope you look at x, our top priority," that's customary. And elected officials, not being dumb people, understand what's then implicitly expected of him/her. Which explains why Bernadette Budde was technically right, and why Senator Russell Long was also correct in his oft-cited observation that "there's a hairbreadth difference between a bribe and a contribution."

Since Ms. Budde's declaration, I've asked members of Congress over the past twenty years what lobbyists and their colleagues *privately* say about the influence of big contributors:

◄o► When Representative Jim Leach (R–IA) once suggested to an urban Democrat with no dairy constituency that he should oppose a dairy price support, the Democrat said, "Their PAC gave me money. I have to support them."

◄○► When former Representative Claudine Schneider (R–CT) asked a colleague to oppose more funding for a nuclear reactor, he declined, explaining, "Yes, but Westinghouse is a big contributor of mine."

◄○► Former Representative Al Swift (D–WA) recalled how "one PAC director told me that he heard colleagues saying that they wanted to deliver a check just before a vote but also that members were calling *expediting* checks before a vote."

◄○► Former Representative Dan Glickman (D–KS) asked a colleague to oppose a bill to prohibit the Federal Trade Commission from regulating auto dealers. "I'm committed," answered the colleague. "I got a $10,000 check from the National Automobile Dealers' Association. I can't change my vote now."

◄○► Former Representative Leon Panetta (D–CA) described how a $1500 contributor asked him to support a trade protectionist bill; when Panetta asked about the substance, he was told, "I don't have to tell you anything substantively—we gave you money and we expect you to." Panetta kicked the man out of his office and voted no.

◄○► Senator Paul Wellstone observed that "colleagues are not so crass as to actually say money made them do it. What they do say is 'My people back home just won't let me do it'—and what's insidious is that it's understood he favors the measure but moneyed interests won't let him."

◄○► One Northeast Democrat representative, who asked to remain anonymous, said with some indignation: "It shows exactly how corrupt Congress is when every single Republican and 46 percent of Democrats vote to help credit-card companies squeeze money out of low- and middle-income families in bankruptcy because of financial distress. Member after member said the same thing to me: they had previously voted against these companies and the banks on X, Y, or Z issue and they had to throw them one vote. 'I can't vote against them *all* the time,' they'd say, implicitly referring to campaign donations."

Since, as mentioned, 20 percent of members actually confessed to a private survey that money affects their vote—and who knows how many others agreed but wouldn't admit it—we now know that quid pro quo contributions are as frequent as cherry blossoms in Washington in April.

THE PLAYERS
Profiles from the Money Game

> *"Talking to politicians is fine, but with a little money they hear you better."*
> —Justin Dart, chairman, Port Industries, 1982

> *"In public policy, it matters less who has the best arguments and more who gets heard—and by whom."*
> —Ralph Reed, head of Christian Coalition, in memo to Enron executives, 2000

The Company

Gone—$66 billion of shareholder investment and some $1.5 billion in the retirement accounts of its own workers alone. Fraudulent practices and accounting scams had brought about the biggest bankruptcy in U.S. history. So when the Bush White House sought to portray Enron as purely a business scandal and not a political scandal, it seemed natural to focus solely on the financial aspects of the debacle.

But in fact it was both.

In the case of Enron, giving millions to coddled politicians and regulators—has become Exhibit #1, proving the intimate relationship between money and politics.

Treasury Secretary Paul O'Neill and Commerce Secretary Don Evans both acknowledge speaking with Enron executives in late 2001 who had asked them to orchestrate a government bailout, but claim that they didn't lift a finger to help. Of course, neither did O'Neill or Evans lift their voices to call for an immediate investigation of what was fast becoming a historic financial meltdown involving likely criminal misconduct.

O'Neill went so far as to proclaim that it wasn't the government's responsibility to protect people from such failures. "Companies come and go," declared O'Neill, referring to Enron's dramatic rise and fall as a "triumph of capitalism."

Enron was founded in 1985, when Houston Natural Gas merged with Nebraska-based InterNorth, another natural gas company. The new corporation bought and sold infrastructure commodities, including wholesale electricity contracts, natural gas pipelines, wastewater-management facilities, and power plants, from and to wholesale suppliers and retail customers worldwide. The next February, Kenneth Lay became its CEO.

By 2000, Enron had expanded far beyond the reach of a traditional energy company—trading energy and telecommunication commodities online, providing risk-management consulting services, and supplying broadband services for the Internet. That same year Enron jumped from the eighteenth to the seventh largest company in the United States in the Fortune 500, with profits of over $101 billion. At its height, Enron employed 21,000 people in Europe, Asia, and South America, owned 25,000 miles of natural gas pipeline, and produced more than 9000 megawatts of electricity in its power plants worldwide.

Ken Lay, CEO for most of Enron's life, got a doctorate in economics at the University of Houston before joining Exxon in 1965. After a stint as a federal energy regulator, Lay returned to the private sector to take charge of Houston Natural Gas during the deregulation-friendly Reagan administration and oversaw the merger that created Enron.

During the next fifteen years, Enron grew ever larger under Lay's stewardship, becoming a Wall Street phenomenon. But by 1998 the company was padding its quarterly reports, and creating so many off-shore (and off-the-books) partnerships that it became impossible to figure out the true financial state of the firm. In January 2001, Lay turned over the position of CEO to Harvard MBA Jeff Skilling. By the time Skilling resigned that August, claiming he wanted to spend more time with his family, Enron had already begun its downward spiral. When Lay finally left in January 2002, he was a national disgrace. But along the way he'd earned himself a famous nickname.

When George W. Bush gives you a nickname, that means you're "in" with the president. And then, quicker than you can say "accounting fraud," Lay went from being "Kenny Boy" to "Kenny Who?" Although Bush would like us all to forget that he and Lay were ever friends, dozens of handwritten pieces of correspondence between the two suggest otherwise. Indeed, for the better part of a decade, Kenneth Lay has had the ear of the Bush family. Their relationship began no later than 1992, when Lay was serving as cochair for the Republican National Convention's Houston host committee. At the time, Bush Sr. was running for reelection as president; George W. was gearing up for his run for Texas governor.

Lay was initially closer to W.'s parents, who belonged to the same Houston country club as he. But once George W. announced his run for governor, Lay became his very first donor, letting Texan businessmen know that they finally had a viable alternative to the incumbent Democrat, Ann Richards. Lay wasn't just Bush's first donor, he turned out to be his most valuable one as well: for the 1994 gubernatorial race, Enron's PAC and executives donated $146,500 to Bush—seven times more than they gave Richards. Does this really jibe with the January 10, 2002, statement by President Bush that Lay was "a supporter of Ann Richards in my run in 1994?"

After Enron donated $50,000 to Bush's inaugural committee, Lay apparently felt close enough to begin a barrage of correspondence with the governor-elect, sending him suggestions on energy policy, taxes, and tort reform, and recommending people for jobs in the new administration—people like Patrick H. Wood III, whom Bush named as chairman of the Texas Public Utility Commission.

In 1994, Lay asked Bush to make tort reform his "highest priority during the early months of your administration." Bush then declared the issue a state emergency, putting it on the Texas legislature's short list; the bill passed in 1997, limiting awards in civil suits and restricting the definition of what constitutes liable parties.

Bush and Lay worked so closely in Texas that one Enron lobbyist from the era recalls that, whenever the company needed a little extra grease in the legislature or the executive branch, Enron's crew in the capital would use the phrase "go to Plan B"—as in Bush. "We knew he would take Ken Lay's call," said George Strong, another Enron lobbyist in the 1990s. So at Enron's urging and Bush's acquiescence, Texas passed a bill creating what many consider to be the most extensive deregulated energy market in the United States. No less an expert than Lay called it the "best deregulation bill in the country."

When Bush announced his candidacy for president in 1999, Lay ensured that Enron would remain the Bush campaign's largest donor. Lay cochaired what was—at the time—a record-breaking $21 million fund-raiser for Bush, was one of the very first to become a Bush "Pioneer" by raising $100,000, arranged for Bush aides and family members to use Enron jets, and helped to underwrite the 2000 GOP convention, the Florida recount, and the inauguration. With all that was accomplished in Texas, what was possible if the act went national?

A lot.

Under Bush's presidency, former Enron employees and consultants stepped into several top administrative positions: Lawrence Lindsey was named the White House chief economic adviser, Robert Zoellick became the U.S. Trade Representative, and outside counsel Harvey Pitt became chairman of the Securities and Exchange Commission. Lindsey received $100,000 as an Enron consultant—and although his responsibilities included assigning staff to monitor energy markets, Lindsey has claimed that Enron's deteriorating situation never warranted a response. Zoellick was a paid consultant on the Enron advisory board before joining the administration; he also owned Enron shares worth between $15,000 and $50,000, which he sold after joining the administration. Pitt represented not only Enron but also Tyco, Global Crossings, and the entire accounting industry. So when the "corporate responsibility" crisis mushroomed in the summer of 2002, Pitt became a political liability for a president loyal to a fault.

Another Enron veteran, Thomas E. White, the former head of key subsidiary Enron Energy Services, was named secretary of the Army. Upon taking the job, White announced that he would apply his Enron experience to privatizing utility services on military bases. How this experience has helped the United States Army in Afghanistan is unclear.

What is clear is that White, a senior executive at Enron for more than a decade, with over $25 million in company stock, was rebuked by the Senate Armed Services Committee for failing to divest that stock in a timely manner, as is required. It wasn't until October 2001, just before Enron tanked, that White finally unloaded the last of his stock. Strangely, though, White is documented as having spoken to his former Enron colleagues more than a dozen times by telephone, although he has insisted that they weren't talking about the impending disintegration of the company in which he had retained such a major financial interest.

But the most problematic appointment emerging from the Bush-Lay relationship involved the chairman of the Federal Energy Regulatory Commission (FERC), Curtis Hebert Jr. In a phone call made during the late spring of 2001, Lay told Hebert that Enron would support him in his job only if he backed a national push for more retail competition in the energy business and did a better (read: faster) job opening up access to the power grid to companies like Enron. Hebert said that the CEO told him that "he and Enron would like to support me as chairman, but we would have to agree on principles" before Lay could consider him worthy of his support. Even though Hebert said that he was "offended" by these comments, he knew that refusing to do as Lay asked could cost him his job.

"Everything they espoused to Congress and to state leaders was always what's in the best interests of Enron, never what's in the best interests of American energy companies," said Hebert, insisting that Enron was actively trying to manipulate energy policy from behind the scenes of the administration. "When I told [Lay] that I didn't think it was the right thing to do and also that there was no legal basis for it under the federal power act, he told me that he and his company, Enron, could no longer support me as chairman."

Apparently, in Enronese, "lack of support" means "you're fired." That August, only a couple of months after Lay's call, Hebert wound up resigning as FERC chairman. Lay wasn't sad to see him go, though; the President helpfully replaced Hebert with old buddy Patrick Wood, Bush's former Texas Public Utility Commission chair, now recommended by Lay to head the FERC.

Enron's money and friendships yielded not only desired personnel in the Bush government but also desired policy. Energy Secretary Spencer Abraham—who received Enron contributions while a U.S. senator—met with several dozen representatives of the energy industry to produce the administration's national energy report, but never met with a single environmental group, citing his "busy schedule." He was certainly busy in late February 2001, when he met with six oil executives, a railroad executive, and the head of a coal-producing company—all in the two days following his rejection of the environmentalists' meeting request. In that same week, Abraham also met with top executives from American Coal, UtiliCorps United, Exxon-Mobil, BP/Amoco, Shell, ChevronTexaco, Anadarko Petroleum, and Ashland Inc., as well as a dozen representatives from utility and nuclear power companies.

As noted in chapter 1, it turned out that the veep held no less than six secret meetings with Lay and other Enron officials as he developed the energy plan; one of those meetings took place on October 10, 2001, only six days before Enron admitted that they had overstated profits by some $586 million since 1997. Cheney now says that he doesn't specifically recall what they talked about in October, only that it didn't have to do with Enron's rapidly deteriorating financial status.

Sierra Club executive director Carl Pope, however, remembers a meeting he had with Cheney quite vividly. He and leaders from other environmental activist groups saw the vice president soon *after* Cheney had released his energy policy, which caused them to wonder: why meet at all? It soon became clear, as they left the White House and were instantly surrounded by reporters in an impromptu press conference. Pope recalls thinking it strange that the Bush people seemed so eager to be seen in the company of environmentalists out in front of the cameras (and after the energy policy was already decided) but were loath to meet with them to discuss substantive policy issues while the plan was actually being formulated. Where was the press conference with Lay and his representatives after any one of their six secret meetings with Cheney?

That didn't stop Cheney from bragging to the cameras that he had actually adopted eleven of twelve environmental recommendations into his energy plan. But as Pope recalls, "It was more like one . . . Arthur Andersen must be doing their counting."

The Bush-Cheney energy blueprint looks like it was written on Enron letterhead. So was the energy bill they introduced in 2001. Passed by the House as of this writing, the bill provides some $3.5 billion in tax breaks for natural gas gathering and distribution lines. Based on Cheney's task force recommendations, the bill would also allow utilities to buy stock in or sell transmission properties under the guise of electricity-restructuring programs, without having to pay taxes. This would cost the government another $2.4 billion over the next ten years.

Since he has taken office, President Bush has halved the funds for renewable energy sources, such as solar, thermal, biomass, and wind. He has delayed regulations to reduce arsenic levels in drinking water, repealed forest service regulations in roadless wilderness areas, and rejected the international global warming treaty. His energy policy is committed to an increase in supplies of traditional fossil fuels like coal, the deregulation of the electric utility industry, the development of new nuclear power plants, and a proposal to begin drilling for oil in the Arctic National Wildlife Refuge.

With Bush in the White House, Lay had a powerful ally to help him extend his company's influence, not only beyond the confines of Texas but also far away from American shores. President Clinton—who received $11,000 from Enron, less than either Bob Dole or Al Gore got as candidates—first helped Enron with their dealings in 1996, after India delayed approval of a $3 billion power plant project in Dobhol, near Mumbai (Bombay). Clinton counselor Mack McLarty ordered the U.S. ambassador in New Delhi to keep abreast of the situation and file regular reports directly to Lay.

The Clinton administration assisted in smoothing over the dispute for a while, but after Bush took office Enron's help in India received an upgrade: direct assistance from the National Security Council. Amid mounting local protest from Mumbai residents and Indian nationalists, Enron decided it had had enough of the Dobhol debacle. Hoping to bail out on the project and recoup the bulk of their losses, Lay was able to persuade the Bush administration to have both Cheney and

Secretary of State Colin Powell speak personally to high government officials in India on behalf of Enron. Powell even threatened his counterpart, Foreign Minister Jaswant Singh, telling him that the "failure to resolve this matter could have a serious deterrent effect on other investors." (Powell's statement must especially have worried Singh four months later, when Lay told the *Financial Times* that "there are U.S. laws that could prevent the U.S. government from providing any aid or assistance or other things to India going forward, if, in fact, they expropriate the property of U.S. companies.")

Even after September 11, when it became crucial to secure India's help in the war on terrorism and to alleviate its smoldering border dispute with Pakistan, the Bush administration continued to pressure India to acquiesce to Enron's demands. It wasn't until November 8, 2001—when the SEC delivered subpoenas to Enron about its accounting practices— that the administration finally let up on India concerning Dobhol.

｟ ｠

Congress too fell under Enron's spell. It only makes sense that the top recipients of Enron's cash should be home-state favorites like Senator Kay Bailey Hutchison, who has received $99,500 since 1989; Senator Phil Gramm, $97,350; Representative Ken Bentsen, $42,750; Representative Sheila Jackson Lee, $38,000; Representative Joe Barton, $28,909; Representative Tom DeLay, $28,900; and Representative Martin Frost, $24,250.

Among these recipients, however, there is one standout. No one in Congress is as close to Enron as Phil Gramm and his wife, Dr. Wendy Gramm.

Dr. Gramm accompanied her husband to Washington when he was elected to the Congress in 1978. In the capital, Dr. Gramm made a career for herself in a succession of federal appointee positions with different regulatory agencies. She was head of the economics bureau of the Federal Trade Commission's Division of Consumer Protection and served as administrator of information and deregulatory affairs in the Office of Management and Budget.

During the 1980s, President Reagan referred to her as "my favorite economist," and named her to chair the Commodity Futures Trading Commission (CFTC), the agency that oversees the nation's commodities and futures exchanges. After Bill Clinton was elected in 1992, Dr. Gramm knew that her time in Washington as one of the Reagan era's most prominent deregulators was coming to an end. Only six days before resigning her position at the CFTC, Dr. Gramm responded favorably to an earlier request by Enron that she exempt the company's trading of futures contracts from federal oversight. Only five weeks after stepping down from the CFTC, Dr. Gramm was appointed to Enron's board of directors. By 2000, Dr. Gramm's initial Enron stock options of $15,000 had grown to more than $500,000.

Then there's her helpful husband, whose now famous observation that "ready money is the most reliable friend you can have in American politics" can be especially understood in the Enron context. In December 2000, Senator Gramm helped ram a bill through Congress—without any committee hearing—that deregulated all energy commodity trading. The Commodity Futures Modernization Act enabled Enron to operate an energy-trading subsidiary free of any federal oversight or price controls. As a direct and immediate result, the company's annualized revenues exploded within a month of the act's passing, increasing from $12 billion to almost $50 billion in January 2001.

Interestingly, this was about the same time that California was suffering through a wave of "rolling blackout" emergencies. There were thirty-eight such emergencies from December 2000 until June 2001, when federal regulators helped end the crisis by reimposing price controls (in the same period the year before, there had been only one). Subsequent federal and state investigations have proven that Enron—among other big power companies—intentionally withheld power, creating artificial shortages to increase the price and milking Californians for tens of billions of dollars.

An internal memo circulated among Enron energy traders in December 2000, for example, describes Enron trading schemes with names like "Death Star," "Load Shift," and "Fat Boy." The Death Star strategy was created to make sure Enron got paid "for moving energy to relieve congestion without actually moving any energy or relieving any congestion." The Load Shift involved techniques to create "the appearance of congestion through the deliberate overstatement" of power meant to be delivered, now widely recognized as the classic Enron tactic. Yet another plan used California's own price caps against the state, buying power from the state at the maximum capped rate of $250 a megawatt-hour, and selling it out of state for five times the amount.

Lay had denied these very accusations in a March 2001 *Frontline* interview, saying, "Every time there's a shortage or a little bit of a price spike, it's always [suspected of being] collusion or conspiracy or something. I mean, it always makes people feel better that way."

All of this might have been avoided—or at least discovered sooner—if Congress hadn't been so dead set against Levitt's June 2000 proposal to stop accounting firms from consulting and auditing the same company. Levitt's changes would have made it much more difficult for Andersen to "cook the books" and hide Enron's slow unraveling. But with strong opposition from the accountant lobby—and a few dozen lawmakers threatening to cut his budget if he acted—the final version of the legislation did quite the opposite. As Levitt says, Congress's action on the matter "reflects . . . to a great extent [the accounting industry's] concerns."

Now the time has come to pay the piper: thousands with their retirement accounts wiped out, thousands more unemployed, untold billions of dollars in losses to answer for; no less than eleven separate congressional investigations have been launched into Enron—*after* Congress enacted the Gramm-Enron energy law, *after* the accounting scandals at Enron, WorldCom, and others that Levitt had warned about, warnings that a Congress didn't hear because they were listening instead to Enron's money.

Of the 248 senators or members of the House on committees now investigating Enron, 212 of them took campaign contributions from Enron or Arthur Andersen. As a *New York Times* headline succinctly put it: "To Investigators, from the Investigated." Most of the legislators (astonishingly, *only* most of them) redonated the money to a fund to relieve those Enron employees who lost everything.

Not a "political scandal"?

The Hammer

Widely considered to be the de facto leader of the House—even though he is technically the third-ranking member of the Republican leadership—Tom DeLay of Texas has forged one of the most impressive political and financial machines in Washington. Marshall Wittmann, a congressional analyst for the conservative Heritage Foundation, says, "He is the most powerful majority whip in the history of the House of Representatives."

A former Texas exterminator, the ruddy, diminutive DeLay first entered politics in 1978, when he was angry at the government's regulation of pesticides and what those regulations were costing him. DeLay still believes that the pesticide DDT should be in use today, and decries the Environmental Protection Agency as "the Gestapo of government, purely and simply . . . one of the major claw hooks that the government maintains in the backs of our constituents."

Since becoming majority whip in 1994, DeLay has pushed his fellow Republicans ever further to the right. DeLay fights hard—and makes sure House Republicans toe the line—on such issues as holding down the federal minimum wage, weakening environmental controls, loosening restrictions on the energy, tobacco, and auto industries, as well as curbing gun control, abortion rights, and gay rights. The causes of youth violence, argues the Texan, are "day care, the teaching of evolution, and working mothers who take birth control pills."

To keep the party's moderates faithful and in step with his program is no easy task, but DeLay has many weapons at his disposal, not the least of which are the two braided-leather bullwhips he keeps in his Capitol Hill office. They symbolically reinforce his reputation as a man unwilling to tolerate any differences of opinion or dissent about the GOP. "They needed a rottweiler" in the Republican party, says Norm Ornstein of the American Enterprise Institute. "There aren't many members who have that kind of toughness."

DeLay is not merely the brute enforcer of the Republican right wing's agenda in the House; he also runs a savvy full-service operation for his Republican colleagues. If a member needs a plane to race off to yet another fund-raiser, DeLay can secure one. Feeling particularly hungry during a late-night session of the House? DeLay's office is invariably stocked with Texas barbecue, Chinese takeout, or pizza to help keep up the troops' strength.

For the 2000 Republican National Convention in Philadelphia, DeLay ensured that his "friends" would enjoy a grand old party indeed. Republican members were provided with their own car and driver; a concierge service was offered around the clock; an opulent "hospitality lounge" made up of five Union Pacific–donated vintage railway cars helped keep the lawmakers stress-free. DeLay held court over it all from his own double-decker luxury railway car, its side emblazoned with a flamboyant "ARMPAC," for the Americans for a Republican Majority, one of the many PACs that DeLay controls. The smorgasbord of perks and special services would set the GOP back a cool $1 million, all paid for with soft money courtesy of political action committees controlled by DeLay or his chief deputy, Roy Blunt (R–MO).

It was all certainly worth it, considering that DeLay had already raised several million dollars long before any delegates stepped out onto the convention floor at Philadelphia's First Union Center. As the *Washington Post*'s Dana Milbank noted, "Representative J. C. Watts is brought to you by DaimlerChrysler, the New York delegation comes courtesy of Merrill Lynch, House Speaker Denny Hastert is provided by Morgan Stanley, Representative Bill Archer is sponsored by the Spirits Wholesalers of America, and the Commerce Committee is made possible by the American Chemistry Council."

But DeLay's skills go far beyond serving cookies and soda to his fellow lawmakers; his strong-arm tactics to extract hefty donations from corporate donors and votes from balking colleagues have earned him the Hill nickname of "the Hammer." And he's not afraid to live up to it, having helped his fellow Republicans pound out more than $30 million in contributions in just the first quarter of 2002 alone.

"If you want to play in our revolution," says DeLay, bluntly, "you have to live by our rules." The message is clear: you're either in or you're out. But just in case you're not getting the message, DeLay is armed with his two infamous lists of the 400 largest PACs—those who are "friendly" to the cause, and those who are "unfriendly." It seems that the more you give to the Republicans, the higher on DeLay's "friendly" list you can find yourself. DeLay's philosophy is eminently pragmatic: "We're just following the old adage of punish your enemies and reward your friends."

But Democrats believe he's taken his old adage to new heights. In May 2000, the Democratic Congressional Campaign Committee (DCCC)—led by Rhode Island representative Patrick Kennedy—filed suit against DeLay. Using RICO, a law usually associated with breaking up organized crime groups, the suit charged DeLay with using intimidation and extortion to compel lobbyists and PACs to donate money to his universe of political organizations. In April 2001, the DCCC agreed to end the suit, claiming to have achieved its goal of publicizing and weakening the majority of DeLay's "shadow" fundraising operations.

Only three days later, Judicial Watch, a conservative group that made their bones repeatedly suing President Clinton, filed suit against DeLay, charging that he solicited donations by promising meetings with top Bush officials. What got Judicial Watch up in arms was a particular effort to raise money for the Republican ad campaign promoting the President's tax plan. In a recorded phone message that went out to small businesspeople across the country, the answerer was greeted with DeLay saying the following: "I am asking you to serve as an honorary member of our new Business Advisory Council. . . . As an honorary member, you will be invited to meetings with top Bush administration officials where your opinions on issues like tax reform will be heard."

"It is improper and illegal to sell official public office for political campaign contributions," said Larry Klayman, the general counsel for Judicial Watch. "We cannot look the other way when Republicans do the same thing."

In 1998, while debating an amendment that would put the burden of proof on candidates accused of accepting contributions from foreign nationals, DeLay, who was spearheading the effort to kill Shays-Meehan, took the floor. In an attempt to score points off the Clinton finance scandals, DeLay rattled off the names of several individuals implicated in the Clinton case.

If you have a friend by the name of Arief and Soraya, and I can't even pronounce the last name, Wiriadinata, something like that, who donated $450,000 to the DNC and was friends with Johnny Huang, and later returned it because Wiriadinata could not explain where it came from, then probably there is a high probability that it is money from foreign nationals. . . . And I could go on with John Lee and Cheong Am, Yogesh Gandhi, Ng Lap Seng, Supreme Master Suma Ching Hai, and George Psaltis. These are American names, I know, and a lot of them are Americans and American citizens, but many of them did business with foreign nationals and brought money to the DNC and others.

DeLay's remarks prompted Shays to interrupt: "I know the gentleman did not mean it to sound this way, but when I listened to it, it sounded this way: It sounded like if you have a foreign name, there was a high probability they were foreigners." Under fire from Democrats and Asian American groups, DeLay later apologized in a written statement: "I feel terrible about the possibility that my remarks would be misinterpreted. In no way did I mean to suggest that Asian Americans should not participate in our democracy."

That same year, DeLay blasted the Electronic Industries Association for its perceived disloyalty when it hired former congressman Dave McCurdy (D–OK)—a highly regarded, conservative Democrat—to head its operations in the capital, saying that it was an "insult to the majority to hire a partisan Democrat." DeLay then threatened to hold up legislation that the lobby had been interested in, an action that brought much criticism from his colleagues and a rebuke from the House Ethics Committee.

DeLay's "friendly" and "unfriendly" lists also invited scrutiny about whether he might have directly linked campaign contributions to official action, a question that led to an official inquiry in late 1995. Although the Ethics Committee dismissed the complaint, it reminded him how "particularly important" it was for a person in his position not to "discriminate unfairly by the dispensing of special favors or privileges to anyone."

But DeLay is unrepentant. He relishes calling himself "the most investigated man in America." And he told *Congress Daily* that "money is not the root of all evil in politics. In fact, money is the lifeblood of politics."

Home-state powerhouse Enron must have followed this same line of reasoning, as it poured more than $200,000 into DeLay's political network over the last seven years. During 2000–2001, ARMPAC received some $60,000 in soft money from Enron and its employees, and between 1995 and 2000, $47,250 in hard money. Another of DeLay's top fund-raising operations, the Republican Majority Issues Committee, got $50,000 from Kenneth Lay in 2000. Enron provided DeLay with a veritable transfusion of "lifeblood"—until its meltdown.

Yet unlike so many dozens of his colleagues, DeLay refuses to return any of his Enron contributions. He reasons that returning a contribution from a company under investigation for wrongdoing would be to admit that the money was donated in order to secure favors.

In fact, to take one example, according to Public Citizen, no other lawmaker rakes in so much money from Big Tobacco—$131,500 in soft money from June 2001 to June 2002. What did Big Tobacco get from their investment in Tom DeLay? Action, if not always results.

In October 2001, as Congress rushed to pass antiterrorism legislation in the wake of 9/11, the White House and DeLay slipped in a measure—known in legislative parlance as a "rule of construction"—that would have blocked foreign governments from attempting to use U.S. courts to recoup billions of dollars in lost revenue and damages from the largest tobacco conglomerates. Federal civil racketeering suits had already been filed by Canada, the European Union, and Colombia, all of which charge tobacco companies with evading taxes and duties on their products by smuggling cigarettes into the respective nations. Though the measure was not part of the final legislation which President Bush signed (Democratic senators railed against it), wording that would have expanded existing law on money-laundering crimes—specifically including fraud against foreign governments—was eliminated.

The Texan's ethical lapses with public money have also been reflected in his own private dealings. The IRS hit Albo Pest Control, the extermination business that DeLay owned and managed for years in Texas, with tax liens in 1979, 1980, and 1983, because DeLay hadn't been paying his payroll or income taxes. DeLay was also forced twice to pay court settlements to former business associates who claimed that he had cheated them. Both associates were lifelong Republicans who'd voted for DeLay. One of the wronged associates, Bob Blankenship, sued in 1994, asserting that DeLay and another partner were using company funds to pay off their personal debts.

While deposing DeLay, Blankenship's lawyer ran into trouble over the simple matter of DeLay's position in the company. "Are you presently still an officer or director" of Albo? he asked. "I don't think so. No," DeLay answered; he'd left by informal agreement "two, three years ago." And yet even on his most recent financial disclosure forms—and again three months *after* the deposition—the lawyer learned that DeLay listed himself as chairman of Albo's board of directors. The following year DeLay dropped the title on his disclosure report and settled with Blankenship for an undisclosed amount.

As a longtime advocate of business and deregulation, DeLay was nicknamed "Dereg" by his colleagues in the Texas legislature, so perhaps it was no accident that Enron and its executives showered this group with contributions. But it is exceedingly strange that Enron would go out of its way to specifically contract with DeLay's operatives for $750,000 in a "grassroots" effort to push energy deregulation. Or that the meeting that cemented the deal was held at DeLay's home in Sugarland, Texas.

Certainly, DeLay was committed to helping Enron—of all the Republican leadership, it was DeLay who was most responsible for pushing through the 2001 House energy legislation that Enron sought. And when Enron lost out on a contract to a Japanese firm to build a power plant in the Northern Marianas Islands, a U.S. territory in the Pacific, it was Tom DeLay who asked for the bidding to be reopened—bidding the Japanese company lost and Enron won, much to the islanders' chagrin. For now that Enron is gone, the Marianas still suffer from the same power outages they had experienced two years ago.

The Senator from Big Business

In 1997, as President Clinton stood poised to introduce his Patient's Bill of Rights—a proposal that would have given Americans more say in their own health coverage, including the right to sue HMOs—then Senate majority leader Trent Lott told representatives of the health care industry to "get off your butts" and "get off your wallets" if they wanted the Republicans on Capitol Hill to mobilize against the proposal.

The insurers reacted just as Lott hoped they would; money began pouring into GOP coffers from the nation's managed care companies. Then Lott reacted just the way the insurers hoped *he* would: working with several major HMOs and health insurance companies that formed the Health Benefits Coalition (HBC) to fight passage of the bill, Lott instructed Assistant Majority Leader Don Nickles to write a Republican pro-industry version of the legislation.

After the HBC gave $8.9 million to Republicans from 1997 to 1999, over 80 percent of the party's total pro-managed-care contributions, the national PAC coordinator for Blue Cross and Blue Shield explained, "We are giving more to Republicans because they've been carrying our water on a lot of issues." In 1999 Lott continued to carry their water, by breaking his promise to bring the Democrats' version of the Patient's Bill of Rights to the Senate floor and helping pass a watered-down version that denied people the right to sue their HMOs. The Senator from Big Business had come through for his corporate friends once again.

In fact, the majority leader's alliance with corporate America was so mutually beneficial that he jumped through hoops trying to stop McCain-Feingold and its soft money ban from being passed, year after year. Former House speaker Jim Wright commented in a 2001 editorial that for Lott "the backroom tactic is different [each] time, but the goal is identical: kill the bill without appearing to do so." In 1998 and 1999, the House was set to pass Shays-Meehan by wide bipartisan margins, but the GOP leaders delayed scheduling the vote—until it was late enough in the session for Lott to prevent it from getting onto the Senate calendar. This shielded House members hoping to continue taking soft money from having to vote against the populist reform, since they knew they could safely register their public support for the bill by voting for it, all the while knowing it would never see the light of day in Trent Lott's Senate.

In early 2001, anticipating the same games of years past, McCain preempted Lott's "it's too late" refrain by publicly calling for an early Senate vote on McCain-Feingold. After the measure received a bipartisan vote of support in the Senate, Lott let three months pass without formally sending the legislation to the House. Finally the pesky Arizonan took action, publicly calling the majority leader's actions "arbitrary and unfair," persuading the Senate to pass a 61–36 nonbinding resolution reprimanding Lott for stalling, and urging him to send the bill to the House. In self-defense, Lott called the move "uncalled for" and said McCain "could have worked it out without doing this, but John had the bit in his mouth."

"You know, you actually could have some legitimate campaign finance reform that would even affect soft money in a constitutional way," Lott told Fred Barnes of Fox News that July. "But [the Democrats'] attitude is, 'You do it our way or else we're going to ram it through.' If they try to do that," he promised, "all they're going to do is to tie up the Senate in very difficult ways. And in this case it will make life more miserable for Daschle this time, not for me," he said, sharing a laugh with Barnes. Of course, McCain and Daschle had the last laugh when McCain-Feingold was finally passed less than a year later.

Born October 9, 1941, in Grenada, Mississippi, Trent Lott grew up in the town of Pascagoula, the son of a shipyard worker and a teacher. He attended Ole Miss, where he made his name as a cheerleader, honing his skills in rallying troops and defending his team. To put himself through school, Lott ran Ole Miss's alumni affairs office, where he accumulated a catalogue of critical contacts. After his graduation from law school, this thick Rolodex would serve him well: the young Lott worked in the office of Democratic representative William Colmer, and sought his boss's seat in 1974 when the congressman retired. Lott won election to the seat—as a Republican—and would serve there until entering the Senate in 1988.

After shrewdly winning the post of Republican conference secretary in 1992 over Missouri's Kit Bond, Lott challenged Republican Whip Alan Simpson two years later, winning by one vote, despite Majority Leader Bob Dole's support of Simpson. The junior Senator Lott—sporting a mat of thick brown hair plastered so meticulously into a side part that the *Washington Post* observed how people approached him "to touch his Pleistocene strands to see if they're real"—was well groomed, erectly postured, and full of swagger. He had ascended to the number two leadership position in the Senate on the strength of his southern charm, astute political instincts, and appeal to younger conservatives. And he had a penchant for being in the right place at the right time: Just two years after Lott's rise to Whip, Dole surprisingly resigned his seat to focus on beating President Clinton. The former cheerleader Lott ran away with the post, defeating his own state's senior senator, Thad Cochran, 44–8.

Trent Lott would serve as Senate majority leader until June 2001, when Vermont Senator Jim Jeffords's stunning defection from Republican to Independent gave the Democrats a 50–49 advantage, and Tom Daschle the majority leadership. Lott called Jeffords's decision, which demoted him to minority leader, "a coup of one" that "trumped the will of the American people."

It certainly trumped the will of several special-interest groups, perhaps none more so than the gambling industry. The effects of gambling can be devastating: an estimated 2.5 million Americans have developed gambling problems so severe they're labeled "pathological," an additional 3 million Americans are classified as "problem" gamblers, and 15 million are considered "at risk." As a defense, the industry has given large amounts of money to lawmakers, hoping they'll turn the other cheek. Over the years, it has had no safer bet than Trent Lott.

From 1995 to 1998, the casino industry gave $4.23 million to the three national Republican Party committees. A November 1997 fund-raising trip to Las Vegas by Senators Lott and Mitch McConnell, courtesy of the American Gaming Association, netted $951,000. And on top of that jackpot, the Mississippi senator takes in significant amounts of hard money from industry interests in his home state.

What does the industry get in return for its investment? In 1996

Lott played a key role in undermining the authority of the National Gambling Impact Study Commission to subpoena witnesses. While casinos try to maximize earnings by keeping Americans (and their money) in the casino as long as possible, exploiting gambling addicts to the tune of hundreds and sometimes thousands of dollars apiece, Lott acted to curb the power of a watchdog commission trying to protect the public from such strategies. Before the commission was even created, he spearheaded a partnership between Republicans and the industry by helping raise $1.78 million in soft money from casinos, of which 23 percent went directly into the hands of the National Republican Senatorial Committee.

When Republican senator Dan Coats of Indiana led an initiative to fund education programs by prohibiting gamblers from deducting their losses from their winnings when submitting their income taxes, Lott not only opposed the pro-education, antigambling measure but also prevented the Senate from debating and voting on it.

This national leader, known for sermonizing about traditional values, opposed in 1998 the Army–Environmental Protection Agency's decision to study effects on the environment of casino development in his home state of Mississippi. In fighting to keep several environmentally questionable casinos open while the study was under way, Lott single-handedly repudiated the findings of key EPA officials.

That same spring he surreptitiously slipped a provision into the Senate Conference Report on the IRS Reform Bill allowing employers and employees of the casino industry to receive 100 percent tax exemptions for employer-provided meals, whether or not the workers actually needed to eat on the casino premises to properly perform their jobs, as required by IRS regulations.

The Senator from Big Business's provision will save the casinos an estimated $31.6 million a year from 1998 to 2007—a third of a billion dollars. All from an initial investment of only a couple of million dollars—not a bad payoff.

The Hustler

It probably comes as little surprise that California governor Gray Davis's first job in politics was as a fund-raiser for Los Angeles mayor Tom Bradley in the 1970s. From those humble beginnings Davis has become one of the most prominent Democrats in the country *because* he's been about the most relentless and successful fund-raiser in California history.

During testimony given in a July 2000 trial over Proposition 208, a California initiative that had imposed a cap of $1000 per donor in state races, Davis campaign manager Garry South told the court that the governor was not one of those politicians who needed to be urged to raise money. In fact, South testified, Davis enjoyed raising money: "I mean, we're talking some days that would range from eight hours to twelve hours in the office on the phone trying to raise money."

And Davis is very, very successful at raising money, fearless when personally asking for a $100,000-plus donation or working a fund-raiser party, all the while cheerily asking people what he can do for them and diligently making note of their answers in a pad he keeps in his jacket pocket. "I don't think Gray ever rests at fund-raising," a Democratic insider told the *San Francisco Chronicle*. "He has no compunction at calling people up and saying, 'You should give me three times, ten times what you've given before.'" One member of the California congressional delegation confided, "He has a cash register in his head that calculates everything and forgets nothing. He thinks about and raises money morning, noon, and night."

According to a *San Francisco Chronicle* study, the governor has pulled in a stunning $1800 an hour, twenty-four hours a day for the past five years. That's $44,100 a day, some $1.3 million a month, and over $16 million a year. Davis is a cash-making machine, having raised more than $80 million since beginning his first successful campaign for governor in 1997.

Instead of the run-of-the-mill group of elite donors—a $50,000 contribution would customarily suffice to put you in this group— Davis has dozens who have given more than $250,000; over a dozen more pegged at half a million; and at least four $1 million donors, all of them unions.

Because of such stratospheric contributions, along with accusations of a pay-to-play ethic in state politics, California voters approved Proposition 34 in 2000 to limit contributions to $20,000 for gubernatorial elections, $5000 in other statewide contests, and $3000 in contests for the legislature—but not until *after* 2002.

So the new law won't affect how Davis raises money this year, but several well-publicized controversies are. As if he didn't have enough problems already, what with a $24 billion budget deficit, a hangover from last year's energy crisis, painful budget cuts to make, and the abandonment of his vow not to raise taxes, the governor has been forced to cancel some fund-raisers in an effort to stave off ethical questions concerning his moneymaking operations and policy decisions.

For some time, the California Building Standards Commission—most of whose members were appointed by Davis—considered a proposal to allow the state's home builders to use plastic water pipes instead of the traditional copper. That is, right up until the Pipe Trade Council (PTC) disavowed the proposal. Considering the major difference in price between plastic and copper pipes—not to mention the greater ease of installation which plastic has over copper—the PTC was concerned that the deal would force its membership to reduce its rates.

However, the union breathed easier upon learning that the state commission refused to lift the restrictions on plastic piping until an extensive environmental review (expected to take months, if not years) is done. California is now one of only two states that do not allow plastic pipes in homes.

Revelations that the union wrote a check for $260,000 to Davis's campaign only days after the ruling raised eyebrows across the state. The contribution made the Pipe Trade Council Davis's second largest donor, having given more than $1.2 million to the governor's war chest since 1997.

Of all the myriad and agonizing cuts that Davis is going to have to make to shrink California's $24 billion budget shortfall, one of them won't be the 30 percent pay hike awarded state corrections officers in January. The huge increase in pay benefits the California Correctional

Peace Officers Association, which has coughed up $416,000 this year to Davis for Governor, $251,000 of it a single contribution made in March; by the end of the contract, in 2006, officers will be making an average of $65,000 a year before overtime. Pretty good for a job that requires one only to be at least twenty-one and a high school graduate (jailhouse wags like to say the job requires "a GED and no felonies"). The usual California state employee receives a shorter contract, with raises ranging from 1.5 to 2.5 percent annually.

But Davis's biggest headache to date involves a $95 million software contract that California signed with Oracle—only days before an Oracle lobbyist gave a $25,000 campaign contribution to Davis's director of e-government, Arun Baheti. Designed to help the state cut costs by buying software licenses in bulk, the deal was supposed to save California $111 million. But according to a state auditor's report, few state agencies could find any use for the Oracle software; now the state stands to lose up to $41 million more than if it had simply stuck with its previous software arrangements.

Since fired for his part in the debacle—along with three other top Davis aides—Baheti acknowledges that he had broken the governor's rule that bars his aides from accepting contributions directly. Although Davis's administration has assured voters that there was no criminal wrongdoing (accepting donations as a state official is not a crime in California, as it is in many other states), the state Attorney General has opened an investigation.

Of course, when you have this many mouths to feed, somebody's going to have to go hungry. To drum up $80 million in donations in only five years' time is no easy task—few who aren't presidential candidates or self-financing millionaires are up to the challenge—and to accomplish the feat Davis has had to get checks from nearly everybody.

The governor's campaign has cultivated a healthy crop of corporate and organizational donors, running the whole political gamut; one of the few things they all have in common is their desire to coax government to behave the way they need to if they're going to advance their agendas. "With this governor, you know you're not going to get everything you want," says Jim Knox, the chairman of the reform group California Common Cause. "But if you want anything, you know you have to ante up. On every issue he drives right down the center, and that allows him to collect money from both sides. Nobody is out of the picture. Nobody is protected. Everybody has to invest."

Wayne Johnson, president of the California Teachers' Association (CTA), alleged that Davis had pressured him for a $1 million contribution, solicited at least once during a private meeting in the governor's office while discussing an education bill that the union wanted. At the time Davis opposed the CTA's prime legislative interest, A.B. 2160, a controversial bill that would have expanded the rights of teachers to include many public policy and management matters—textbook selection and curriculum planning, for example.

"Davis hit us up two or three times for a $1 million contribution," Johnson said. "About ten to fifteen minutes into the conversation, just out of the blue he said, 'I need a million from you guys.'" According to Johnson, there was absolutely no reaction from him or the other three CTA officials in the meeting ("there was silence in the room," he said). After a pregnant pause, the meeting went on normally, but the CTA refused to ante up and A.B. 2160 died in the state legislature at the end of May. Although the governor has said that he is unable to remember the conversations and is also unable to recollect if he did or didn't request the contributions, Johnson has said that he feels "very strongly" that Davis's opposition to A.B. 2160 had nothing to do with the union's balking at his $1 million request. "He wouldn't have supported it anyhow," Johnson said. "But I think he was trying to get a million out of us before he went public and opposed it."

California state law prohibits lawmakers and officials from accepting campaign contributions within the confines of the Capitol but not from soliciting them, though it is a well-established practice not to ask for them (at least not directly), if only to avoid allegations of impropriety.

The incident with the CTA made such waves in California that it prompted state Republicans to introduce a bill focused specifically on the solicitation of contributions in the Capitol. The bill would prohibit asking for contributions in any face-to-face meeting in any state office or by the use of a state telephone or computer. "This bill is a laser aimed straight at Gray Davis because everyone else understands the content and intent of the original law," said California Secretary of

State Bill Jones, who lost the March Republican primary for the governor's race to Bill Simon Jr.

Davis says that he has no choice but to fund-raise aggressively. After all, he's a career politician of moderate means, not a self-financing multimillionaire candidate like Davis's current opponent, Bill Simon, or Al Checchi, who ran against him unsuccessfully in 1998.

Some plausibly argue that Davis's money has allowed him to choose his opponent come November. Certainly, the Davis campaign put some $10 million into advertising against Richard Riordan, the third candidate in the Republican primary, thereby tipping the scales in Simon's favor and giving candidate Davis the rival he truly wants to face off with on election day, another multimillionaire lacking public surefootedness.

In a sense, Davis is simply acting rationally and intelligently according to the rules of the game. He does need to raise enormous amounts of money to compete with self-financers. And Simon needs to spend his own millions to get known and catch up to the incumbent. So until there's a more systematic change, multimillionaires and special-interest hustlers will blame one another while our political system is priced out of reach of everyone else.

The Wealthy Guy

The *New York Times* editorial board was obviously torn in its October 25, 2000, editorial endorsing Republican Bob Franks for U.S. Senate in New Jersey. The decision posed "a difficult problem for voters," the board wrote, calling Franks "a solid lawmaker [who's] made some disturbing compromises." Still, despite favoring the politics of Franks's Democratic opponent, Jon Corzine, "a commendably compassionate liberal," the *Times* could not support him. Corzine, a former Goldman Sachs CEO worth several hundreds of millions of dollars, had spent a record (at the time) $63 million of his fortune bombarding the airwaves with TV commercials and contributing lavishly to grassroots and clubhouse organizations to curry political favor. The *Times*—by far the leading editorial page against the corrupting influence of money in politics—ultimately regarded the investment banker's contribution to the "outsized role of money in the electoral process" unpalatable and disqualifying.

Corzine, who won the race by 2.5 percent of the vote and now serves as New Jersey's junior senator, was born on January 1, 1947, in the small Illinois town of Taylorville, to a family of politically active Republicans. He worked construction jobs to pay his way through the University of Illinois, where he himself was a Young Republican, before completing an MBA at the University of Chicago. In 1975, with a year's experience as a bond trader in Ohio, he joined Goldman Sachs's fixed-income department. By the time he left Goldman some twenty-four years later, the midwesterner owned—apart from his New Jersey residence—a resort in Telluride, Colorado, a mansion in the Hamptons, an apartment on Park Avenue, and a 2300-acre mesa in Colorado.

Corzine was described by Goldman Sachs co-workers as "a great listener" with a "humble demeanor" and "unfailing politeness." By 1985, the bearded, sweater-vested figure had shot up through the ranks, been named a partner, and been given a seat on the management committee. A year later he became a star when he averted a major crisis for the firm. When Japanese holders of one issue of government securities did not exchange them for a newer issue, prices of older securities didn't fall as they normally would—leaving Goldman Sachs vulnerable to losses of hundreds of millions of dollars for assuming that prices would drop. But Corzine, convinced that the situation would eventually resolve itself, traded around the clock and urged the firm's leadership to hold fast. They did, he was vindicated, and the company actually made huge profits. Throughout it all, Corzine was calm, patient, and friendly, said his old colleagues.

And he was generous. In addition to supporting several charities, Corzine used his wealth to help out needy individuals. When he learned that a Goldman secretary who stayed late every night was having trouble meeting her mortgage payments, Corzine assumed the loan and helped fund her son's college tuition. He also persuaded a Goldman messenger to return to school, paying his tuition too, asking only to see his report cards in return. "Those who are blessed," the senator said with deep sincerity in an interview for this book, "have a responsibility to give back."

In 1994, Corzine rose to become the firm's senior partner, chosen in part for his sanguinity and ability to heal the wounds that had resulted from heavy losses in bond trading. But while popular with subordinates, Corzine irked some partners who believed that at times he acted too autocratically. After losing some support for insisting that Goldman Sachs go public and pare down Goldman's executive committee to just six members, Corzine lost a power struggle when one of his allies retired from the executive committee. Only the second CEO to be ousted in over 130 years at Goldman Sachs, Corzine had $400 million and no concrete plans for the future. Then New Jersey Senator Frank Lautenberg announced his intention to retire.

With the encouragement of Democratic leaders throughout both the state and the nation, Corzine entered the race in 1999, prepared to spend whatever it took to broadcast his name to voters and to establish a serious get-out-the-vote operation. Despite the fact that he had zero political or government experience of any kind—indeed, he hadn't voted in primary elections from 1988 to 1998 or in the 1998 general election—Corzine was welcomed by New Jersey party leaders like Senator Bob Torricelli; his bottomless pockets made him credible, even a favorite.

Republican governor Christie Whitman (now the federal EPA administrator) and Democrats Michael Murphy, Frank Pallone, and B. Thomas Byrne all withdrew from the race, citing Corzine's money. "His use of money was intentionally intimidating," said David P. Rebovich, a professor at Rider University in Lawrenceville. "You spend, you spend, you spend, you're saying to the opposition and to the electorate, 'I'm not going away. I am going to do what it takes to win.'"

In 1999 alone—the year *before* the election—Corzine spent more than $3.6 million on the campaign, paying two campaign managers $20,000 a month, a political director $18,000 a month, and a slew of consultants and pollsters $1.05 million in all (more than double the going rate). Insisting he had to spend heavily to make up for a disadvantage in name recognition, Corzine trailed Democratic primary opponent Jim Florio, the former governor, by a 2-to-1 margin in February 2000.

To his credit, this wealthy guy suplemented with campaign contributions from outside sources. "I raised $3 million early on, to gain credibility with the political establishment," he explained, having raised more than his primary opponent, despite his utter lack of need. Of the $1.4 million Corzine collected in the last six months of 1999, $546,275 came from New York residents, $492,100 from Goldman Sachs employees and Wall Street executives, and $449,825 from residents of New Jersey. Florio, by contrast, had raised just $796,340, leading one of Corzine's campaign managers, Steven Goldstein, to say, "It is utterly incomprehensible how any candidate in the modern media age can run a campaign of even the slightest significance with the embarrassing amount of money Jim Florio is reporting today." Corzine's money shouted, Florio's barely whispered.

But the former congressman and governor was a seasoned veteran who knew how to run a tough race; Corzine was a novice, and it showed. After an eight-week barrage of slick and ubiquitous commercials by Corzine had effectively silenced Florio—who had no money to respond, and was forced to rely on newspaper articles to get his message across—the scrappy veteran took control of the first debate between the candidates, a month before the primary, and put the businessman on the ropes for a full hour. When the unpolished Corzine stuttered about "bold ideas," for example, Florio responded: "Bold is about taking on the gun lobby. Bold is raising the money to finance education for our children. Bold is going out and making sure that we have a clean environment by taking on corporate polluters. Rhetoric is rhetoric, words are words. This is not bold; this is baloney."

When Corzine tried to defend the unprecedented cost of his campaign by saying, "Elections are about a contest of ideas, they're not about money," Florio retorted, "Jon's being a bit disingenuous. Even one of his supporters in the audience said he wouldn't be talking to him if it weren't for his money." Corzine seemed nervous, David M. Halbfinger observed in the *New York Times;* "his syntax frequently derailed, and some of his points were lost on even the most informed people in the audience." Still, despite having been 35 points down in the primary with just ten weeks to go, polls the day after the debate had Corzine within 6 points of the former governor.

In the subsequent debates, Corzine appeared more confident and polished, and levied strong attacks against Florio for the politically damaging $2.8 billion tax hike he had enacted as governor. But while Corzine's performance was encouraging to his campaign, it hardly mattered. With tens of millions of dollars to spend on commercials that transmitted an unfettered prepackaged message, Corzine did not need to rely on debates or free media to get his point across. Florio, on the other hand, had to make waves at the event, hoping that newspapers would pick up a story and broadcast it—for he had only enough money to run minimal ads during the last two weeks of the race, a sorry match for Corzine's fifty weeks. Aware of his opponent's predicament, Corzine agreed to debate only on small radio stations and cable TV outlets. Indeed, the investment banker simply chose not to show up for a debate two weeks before the primary that aired on the networks. Instead, he released three new TV commercials that week.

"No one can tell him what to do," said voter Tommy Akel, five days before the primary, parroting Corzine's "unbought, unbossed" motto. "If he wins, they can't hold nothing over his head." Asked in an interview whether self-financing his campaign made him more independent of special interests and free to consider the public interest, Corzine said he felt the argument was particularly persuasive in New Jersey. "People here like independent candidates like Case, Lautenberg, and Bradley, especially given the history of tainted politicians in my state."

Corzine ran away with the primary by 58 to 42 percent, capping off an incredible two months that saw him make up nearly 50 points in the polls. He had spent $33 million to win the nomination, shattering the previous Senate record of $30 million by Republican Michael Huffington in California, before the general election had even begun.

Representative Bob Franks narrowly won the Republican primary, 36 to 34 percent over State Senator William Gorley. While Corzine carved out a liberal platform supporting universal health care, gun control, and abortion rights, Franks was a cautious moderate espousing limited gun control, limited choice, and controlled spending. Like Florio before him, Franks was a veteran of electoral politics who was unlikely to make damaging campaigning mistakes, but who also had a limited campaign budget. Corzine was the opposite—a mistake-prone novice with a bank account to overcompensate.

He'd need it. In early September he told the Sierra Club he had voted for an open space referendum in 1998, though records show that he hadn't voted at all that year. After refusing to release his tax returns because he claimed it would violate a confidentiality agreement with Goldman Sachs, Corzine disclosed $25 million in charitable dona-tions—much of which was later shown to be money given to groups whose leaders later endorsed his candidacy. In another embarrassing mistake, when he was asked whether he had donated to any of the churches whose ministers endorsed him, he said no; it turned out his *family* foundation had made contributions.

These missteps allowed Franks to stay in the race and capitalize on Corzine's bad press. Aware of the close polls, the self-financer began running millions of dollars' worth of negative ads against Franks, who was unable to respond until the last two and a half weeks. Still, the race remained tight. Leaving nothing to chance, the Corzine camp spent $7.4 million on get-out-the-vote operations aimed primarily at cities, even busing in residents of Philadelphia homeless shelters and halfway houses to work on the campaign.

When all was said and done, Corzine spent around $30 million on the two-month general campaign, and the heavy get-out-the-vote spending proved pivotal. While Franks won most of New Jersey's counties, Corzine took the state's cities by big margins on the strength of a massively advertised, activist message and the assiduous Demo-cratic machine—his 90,000-vote victory in Newark single-handedly accounted for his statewide margin of just 71,000 votes. Having out-spent Bob Franks by 10 to 1, Jon Corzine won his Senate seat by 50.4 to 47.9 percent. In all, he spent $63 million for it.

What Senator Corzine did was legal—and to his credit, he has hewn to the bold progressive agenda he ran on. He's regarded as a very thoughtful senator, whose expertise on financial matters is proving valuable in the post–Enron/WorldCom environment. But he's sensitive to charges that he bought the office and that this is what his legacy will be. "I admit to being thin-skinned about it," he said in his quiet voice. "You see, I'm a real Democrat. I wasn't born close to any money. So it's never been how I defined myself. I guess there will always be a group of people I'll never persuade and who think I had an unfair advantage. But if I work hard and get things done, I'll overcome it."

But over in New York City, businessman Michael Bloomberg— worth ten times more than Corzine—was taking notice of Corzine's well-funded, if narrow, victory.

The Populist

The year Russell Feingold came to Washington seemed full of promise for the idealistic freshman senator from Wisconsin. It was 1993, and a Democrat was in the White House for the first time in a dozen years. Feingold recalls that when President Clinton announced his priorities for the new administration—health care and campaign finance reform—it was the latter that immediately struck a chord with Feingold.

"I was one of ten senators pushing for it, with [Joe] Biden and Kerry in the lead," recalls the still boyishly handsome Feingold in a Manhattan hotel in April 2002—yes, in between fund-raising events. "I thought we were going to win, but Democrats in the House wouldn't go to conference because they liked the system that had kept them in power."

Feingold knows all about running against powerful incumbents. In 1983, his first foray into electoral politics landed him in his state's senate; at age twenty-nine, he had beaten the long-standing incumbent by only 31 votes. Three years later, when Democrat Ed Garvey lost a close contest against Republican Robert Kasten for one of Wisconsin's U.S. Senate seats, Feingold said out loud on election night to the televised image of Kasten celebrating, "I want him."

"People thought I was nuts and everybody told me to wait my turn," says Feingold. A high school debate champion, a Rhodes scholar, and a Harvard Law graduate from a Jewish family of successful professionals, Feingold may appear unpretentious and affable but has never been one to follow protocol. "So I spent five years moving quietly around the state, meeting as many people as I could."

Running in a three-way race in the state's Democratic Senate primary in 1992, Feingold, according to late polls, had somewhere in the low teens while his opponents—a well-known congressman and a wealthy businessman—sat at 43 and 40 percent.

"I knew these two guys hated each other and would do everything possible not to let the other guy win," reminisces Feingold. "They basically creamed each other—and, within a few days, everybody hated these guys."

It wasn't so much that the voters liked Feingold; they didn't know him. Yet their profound distaste for the negative TV campaigns run by the other two contestants astonishingly brought Feingold from 12 percent to more than 70 percent of the vote within three weeks. After winning the primary, Feingold ran a colorful populist campaign, painting his promises to Wisconsinites on his garage door, driving from district to district in his 4x4, and running humorous television ads that purported to show Elvis endorsing Feingold.

But now all of Wisconsin knew who Russ Feingold was, and he was able to coast to victory against incumbent Kasten, the man he had brashly targeted through the television screen six years before.

During his ten years in the Senate, Feingold has earned himself a reputation as a lawmaker who votes his own mind, paying little heed to the party line. Thomas Mann, senior fellow of governmental studies at the Brookings Institute in Washington, says of Feingold, "He comes out of the Wisconsin progressive tradition, with strong feelings of right and wrong. He does march to his own beat."

That he does, often to the chagrin of his fellow Democrats. Time and time again, he has shown a propensity to vote his conscience: he called for an independent counsel to investigate President Clinton's fund-raising scandals in 1997, and during Clinton's impeachment trial he was the only Democrat to vote with Republicans to allow additional witnesses to be heard, before finally voting against conviction. Early in the Bush administration, Feingold broke ranks to be one of the only Democrats to confirm John Ashcroft as attorney general, yet then was the sole dissenting vote in the Senate on the administration's anti-terrorism bill—a bill for which Ashcroft was largely responsible.

But it is perhaps his stand on the influence of political money that makes his senatorial colleagues—on both sides of the aisle—squirm the most.

He doesn't hesitate to blast the "corrupt" politics of special-interest money, even when it involves leaders of his own party. Here's what he told the *Progressive* magazine in May 2002 about the fund-raising policies of the Democratic Leadership Council (DLC):

> The Democratic Party decided that corporatizing was a way to help with fund-raising, especially in an era of soft money. It allowed the Democratic Party, in [the DLC's] view, to blunt some of the issues, like trade, that were causing problems with, frankly, the larger moneyed interests. And the ultimate example of that was the coronation of Gore in Los Angeles. That convention was a corporate trade show. It was nothing like the Democratic conventions of the past. So I see the DLC as, to some extent, taking the soul away from the Democratic Party.

In a fitting tribute to his greatest hero, the early-twentieth-century Progressive Senator Robert "Fighting Bob" LaFollette of Wisconsin, Feingold uses one of LaFollette's props, the "Calling of the Roll"—which Feingold renamed "Calling of the Bankroll"—to indicate the obvious connection between monetary contributions to Senate members and the content of legislation being debated on the floor.

In September 1999, during the floor debate on an amendment sponsored by Republican senator Kay Bailey Hutchison of Texas and designed to allow oil companies to avoid paying some $66 million in royalties to the government, Feingold took to the floor to argue against it. He detailed the amount of both PAC and soft money contributions given by Exxon, Chevron, Atlantic Richfield, and BP Amoco during the 1997–1998 election cycle, noting that it "is more than $2.9 million just from these four corporations in the span of only two years. They want the Hutchison amendment to be part of the Interior appropriations bill. As powerful political donors, I am afraid they are likely to get their way."

Indeed they did, 51–47. But not before Senators Craig Thomas (R–WY) and Mary Landrieu (D–LA) pointedly interrupted Feingold several times during the proceeding, arguing that Feingold's comments were not germane to the debate and that he was out of order.

Does the anger of his colleagues at his maverick ways ever bother him? No, he quickly replies. "As Harry Truman once said, 'If you want a friend in Washington, get a dog.'" It is just this kind of outspokenness that has earned Feingold his reputation on the Hill as a tireless—if to some annoying—proponent of campaign finance reform, the same outspokenness that stirred a kindred soul, a senior senator from across the aisle.

Chapter 3's discussion of the origin of the McCain-Feingold law described how this odd couple first met, disagreeably disagreeing over spending for a nuclear aircraft carrier. Less than a year later, Feingold was in his beat-up 4x4 when he received an unexpected phone call from McCain, suggesting that the two work together on bipartisan reforms. "He told me, 'Hey, you're against the deficit and pork barrel spending,'" recalled Feingold. "'Will you help me fight it?'" Feingold was instantly intrigued by the offer. He asked McCain if he would support a gift ban in the Senate that he was working on and McCain readily agreed.

Feingold had long enforced a strict "no gifts" policy for himself and his staff, his model being Wisconsin's Code of Ethics for Public Officials and Employees. However, when arriving on Capitol Hill in 1993, he saw that many of his colleagues in the Senate had placed no such limitations on themselves. Now they do.

That small victory, as Feingold now puts it, "just whet our appetite."

They started work on large-scale campaign finance reform soon thereafter, jointly introducing the bill in September 1995 that became known simply as McCain-Feingold—a phrase used so often that Feingold half jokes about how many people believe his first name is "McCain."

Most senators and big contributors, however, saw this early version as too strong, too sweeping. Broadcasters bewailed the thirty minutes of free television time the bill offered candidates who voluntarily limited their spending. Labor unions strenuously opposed the ban on PACs, arguing that the contributions of teachers and police officers could hardly be compared to what corporations shelled out. It soon became apparent to the two cosponsors that the only way to save the initiative would be to limit its goals. "Over the years we knew we could never get the fifty votes for free broadcasting, but soft money had grown into a cancer corrupting Congress itself. Eventually, to pass the bill, we stripped it of everything except the soft money provision."

When the bill was first introduced in 1995, the only other Republican who supported it was Tennessee's Fred Thompson, the former Watergate Senate counsel and actor in over a dozen movies. Kentucky's Mitch McConnell mocked the bill as being nearly all-Democrat, with only two Republicans on it. But the 1996 controversies over Clinton's use of the Lincoln Bedroom, Gore's fund-raising visit to a Buddhist temple and the explosion of soft money that year began to convert some Republicans to the McCain-Feingold cause, including Olympia Snowe and Susan Collins, both of Maine.

Feingold felt the tide turning. "Members of Congress eventually became scared of the system. They were afraid of a lot of attack ads against them. And they started believing that soft money—even though legal—looks bad." But did it look bad enough to Congress that they would have to forsake it? Feingold was willing to gamble his career on it.

Although the bill that shared his name was filibustered to death in the Senate in July 1996, and again in February 1998, Feingold committed to living up to the bill's spirit during his own 1998 reelection campaign. So the senator refused many of the natural advantages enjoyed by incumbents, including the big money that can be had from the national PACs, as well as any soft money from the Democratic Party. He also set a lid of 10 percent for PAC contributions, 75 percent of which had to come from within the state, and resolved to limit his spending to $1 a voter, about $3.8 million in Wisconsin.

At first it didn't seem like much of a sacrifice. His Republican rival, Representative Mark Neumann of Wisconsin's First District, was a full 15 to 20 points behind in the polls throughout the summer. But then, in mid-August, everything changed. Neumann—and his national Republican backers—began a withering media attack on Feingold. The National Republican Senatorial Committee, headed by campaign finance reform archenemy Senator McConnell, poured millions into the state, because McConnell knew that a Feingold loss would mean not only a Senate seat but also a major defeat for the movement.

"McConnell wanted to kill McCain-Feingold. He told his buddies that if they could kill it, they could control the Senate for twenty years," recalls Feingold with a smile. "This was one of the most brutal assaults of soft money ever, not only on television but huge mailings and phone banks, all paid for by undisclosed contributions from the big banks, oil companies, and tobacco companies."

By the time Feingold started his own media campaign a month later, the damage was done; by October, Neumann had closed the gap to a dead heat. Democratic leaders in the Senate panicked; after all, if the Republicans could gain five seats, they'd have the votes to break any Democratic filibusters and have the virtual run of the Senate. Angrily, they warned Feingold against risking his seat on what seemed like a quixotic pretense. But Feingold refused to back down and refused to take their money.

In mid-October, Senator Bob Kerrey of Nebraska, chairman of the Democratic Senatorial Campaign Committee, started running independent expenditure ads in Wisconsin supporting Feingold, paid for with national party money. Feingold exploded. "Get the hell out of my state with those things!" he told Kerrey, who immediately complied, though after some negative ads had appeared.

Outspent by more than 2 to 1, Feingold had watched his once comfortable lead over Neumann drop to a 2-point deficit shortly before election day. For the first time, Feingold considered that he might actually lose. But despite the pressures of his party and his inexorable slide in the polls, he didn't flinch and adhered to his self-imposed ban on soft money.

On election night, Feingold held his seat by 2 points. Seen nationally as a referendum-in-miniature on campaign finance reform, the populist's 1998 victory gave his Senate bill a much needed boost. While the measure was defeated again in October 1999 in the Senate, McCain's popularity and high visibility during the 2000 presidential campaign brought the issue back to the forefront.

But it was when Mississippi's conservative Senator Thad Cochran came up to Feingold and told him that he was on board because "the system stinks" that Feingold knew they had the votes to make it. As described earlier, on March 20, 2002, after seven years of struggle, the Senate finally passed McCain-Feingold, which was duly—if reluctantly—signed by President Bush the next week.

Having seen the momentum building on the issue over the years, the intense Feingold is not a man to rest on his laurels. "Now is the time to get aggressive and think big—maybe go after public financing," he says cheerfully. "This victory gives the people the belief that it can be done."

The Refuseniks

Bruce Ratner: From Donor to Reformer

Bruce Ratner was "The Man." That's how Mayor Rudy Giuliani's campaign staffers described the Brooklyn builder in a seating chart for a fund-raising dinner for the mayor's 1997 reelection bid. Why such high praise for a man who had been a top fund-raiser for Mayor David Dinkins's 1993 reelection campaign—against, not incidentally, Rudy Giuliani? The answer, of course, was money. The mayor's grudges could be relaxed for prodigious fund-raisers, and Ratner was one of the best. To this thoughtful Democrat, giving big money was a business decision based not on ideology but on practicality: who would win and enable him to keep building? In 1997, Giuliani looked unbeatable, so Ratner raised more than $100,000 for his reelection campaign.

Ratner—a Cleveland native who attended Columbia Law School—is now the president and CEO of Forest City Ratner Company, one of New York City's largest real estate developers. In a city where real estate is king, Ratner rules over a vast empire that includes MetroTech Center, a sprawling $1 billion commercial, academic, and retail complex that he built a decade and a half ago in downtown Brooklyn. Prior to his rise to real estate magnate, he had climbed to the top of another field: consumer advocacy. As a young lawyer, Ratner had served in the city's Department of Consumer Affairs during the administration of

Mayor John Lindsay. Later, after teaching law for five years at New York University, Ratner was appointed the consumer affairs commissioner by Mayor Ed Koch. In 1982, with a family to support, Ratner left public life and entered the real estate business. He was first solicited for a campaign contribution by his former boss, when Koch was running for a third term in 1985. Ratner gave out of loyalty and friendship, but in doing so, he opened the floodgates.

In an interview at Forest City's headquarters at MetroTech, Ratner described why he became one of New York City's biggest fund-raisers—and why, after a career that included a night in the Lincoln Bedroom, he's no longer in the money game.

"Once it's known that you give," Ratner began, "everybody solicits you. When you do business with the city, you get solicited by everyone from U.S. senators down to members of the City Council." He gave generously to a variety of candidates. "There was an anxiety that, if we didn't give, we might not be able to get a meeting, that it might hurt our development efforts, hurt our access. There was a sense that if you contributed, you were a friend. You knew your competitors were doing it, and so when someone would call, it was hard to say no. For businesses that do a lot of business with the city, it was expected."

To the fifty-seven-year-old developer, raising money was a question not of buying results but of making friends: "Where there was a question, I wanted to be looked at as a friend. For better or worse, politicians divide the world into those who are for them and those who are not. More so than any other business, in politics power is wielded by those people who are friends. And those who are not are not helped and can even be hurt. In my business, you cannot afford to have enemies. . . . I didn't want to be a person on the outs, nor could my business afford to be a person on the outs given how much business we do with government."

So Ratner fund-raised because he felt he had to, but he didn't like it. "It was very unpleasant. I didn't enjoy it. It's very difficult to ask people to give to someone that they may not believe in, and very few people want to contribute the amounts that were being requested. I would much rather ask people to give to a charity that I'm involved with."

While his fund-raising in New York City was business, the Democrat's fund-raising for Bill Clinton was personal. "I met Clinton before the 1992 primaries at a small party," said Ratner, "and he really impressed me. I thought he was terrific when I met him, and I liked his economic ideas. In fund-raising for him, I was trying to support someone that I thought would make a good president. I thought, My God, if a kid from Ohio, the son of an immigrant, could somehow know the president of the United States and be involved in national politics, that would be something. So I decided to go way out for this guy and became one of his first major fund-raisers. I had no agenda. I achieved what I set out to do, and sleeping in the Lincoln Bedroom, in the same room with the Gettysburg Address, was one of the great things that I did in my life."

Ratner's fund-raising gave him entrée into Washington's elite circles, and once there, he was not impressed with what he saw. "I got very disenchanted with the way the DNC was run, the way the money was used. And people were giving money because they wanted jobs and ambassadorships."

Back in New York, Ratner began to grow disenchanted with the local political process as well. By 1997, he says, "the fund-raising got out of control. I found myself giving and raising money for candidates that I didn't necessarily believe in and didn't believe that they would do the best job." In one case, the Brooklynite recalls with distaste giving thousands of dollars to a state legislator, with whom he had little to nothing in common politically, because another politician he supported had asked him to do so. "If you're trying to be on someone's side and you get asked to do something," said Ratner, "if you refuse, it sometimes undermines all your other efforts."

After the 1997 mayoral election, he had had enough. He quit, cold turkey (except for a few favored personal friends). "When I stopped [contributing], people said I was crazy: 'You're going to get yourself killed. It's a mistake. You're going to regret this.'"

Ratner attributed his change of heart to the "huge quantities of money that were being raised," to "the public's loss of faith in government"—and to the connection between the two. He was also worried about his company's public reputation, which he feared was suffering as a result of his high-profile political fund-raising. The issue crystallized for him when he received a call from a U.S. senator from a midwestern state asking him to breakfast. "After talking for an hour [over breakfast]," Ratner said, "he asked me for a couple of thousand dollars, and I thought, 'What kind of system is it that a good, high-quality United States senator has to sit with a real estate developer for an hour of his time to raise $2000? It's a huge amount of time and probably affects how they treat potential donors."

In 1998, Ratner metamorphosed from campaign donor to campaign reformer when he helped bankroll an effort by a New York City advocacy coalition to put an initiative on the ballot for full public financing of elections. The initiative did not make the ballot for technical reasons, but out of the coalition's efforts, the City Council enacted a strong law that year (see chapter 7) improving the city's public financing system.

"He was a huge help," says Richard Kirsch, executive director of New York Citizen Action, the advocacy group that spearheaded the ballot effort. In addition to money, Kirsch believes, "he gave the effort visibility and credibility. He was sick of the whole system, of getting constantly hit up for money, and he was excited about the opportunity to have a system where he could say, 'You don't need my money to run.'"

Calling the new law a "tremendous victory," Ratner said he was "overjoyed" to have supported the effort. In his view, public financing is "seminal to a democracy because you can't have a small group of people with a few agendas dominate the political process. It goes against democracy and it happens all over the country," he concluded. "The average citizen will see it that way and it really gives them a lack of faith in government and democracy. The perception is as important as the reality." And the reality, as few know better than this former fund-raising phenom, is that contributions buy friends in high places.

James C. Callaway: Confessions of a Fat Cat

When soft money came of age in the 1988 election, the first person to come courting was a smitten southern gentleman named James C.

Callaway. Together they went to the big dance, and they caused quite a stir. But before the final song, Callaway left abruptly, feeling pained and wishing he'd never gone. His date became the toast of the town and was constantly and aggressively pursued—but not by Callaway. He never called again.

A wealthy Houston oilman, Callaway first began fund-raising to support a personal friend in Texas politics, but his success soon attracted the attention of Washington's elite. He made a name for himself as a top solicitor for President Jimmy Carter's 1980 reelection campaign, and became an important fund-raiser for the presidential campaigns of John Glenn, Gary Hart, and Walter Mondale. In 1987, he moved to Washington to lead the DNC's Victory Fund, established to raise money for the party's nominee for use in the general election.

"I was the guy who actually started this thing of raising big soft money," says the seventy-one-year-old Callaway in a 2002 interview, "and I feel a little guilty about it." Under his direction, the Victory Fund collected 200 checks for $100,000 and raised over $30 million. It was a wild success, but Callaway wasn't celebrating. In September 1988, in the heat of the presidential battle, he returned to Texas "disgusted with the amount of money in politics." In a 1989 interview with the *New York Times,* Callaway said: "I was a fat cat. Although I hate that term, that's what I was, a fat cat raising money for other fat cats."

Callaway knew that raising soft money for party-building activities, such as voter registration drives, was a ruse. "It's a cover," he now believes. "When it gets to spending money, it all goes to one thing—helping your guy win the election." The courtly Texan offers a frank assessment of his role in the process: "It was wrong and I am ashamed of it. I never promised anything, but I know good and well people do not give $100,000 at a pop without expecting anything." Asked about the claim that money buys access but not influence, he responds: "I don't believe that for a minute." He says that people give to influence candidates, be it on legislative or ambassadorial decisions, or for even more insidious reasons. One of his experiences foreshadowed the foreign money scandals that darkened the 1996 elections.

"In 1988, when Dukakis was leading in the polls, a man no one had ever heard of arrived at the DNC's Washington headquarters and asked to speak to someone in charge of fund-raising. They showed him to my office, and he wrote a check for $100,000. We had a retired FBI man on our research team, and we had him do a background check. It turns out that this man was a registered agent for Libya—he worked for Qaddafi! Well, we returned the check."

After leaving the Dukakis campaign in September 1988, Callaway spent a month alone on his sailboat in Galveston Bay, reflecting on his experience. When only half of the nation's registered voters went to the polls in the November election while 98 percent of members of Congress won reelection, he knew that "too much money washing around Capitol Hill" had led to both results. "These two horrible statistics are connected," Callaway concludes. "The people of this country don't trust the government, mainly because there's so much special-interest money."

After the 1988 election, Callaway decided to stop playing what he calls the "dirty game" of fund-raising. A grandfather of six, now retired and living in Colorado, he still spends a week of every month on his sailboat in Galveston Bay, and no matter who comes soliciting for contributions, he has refused to jump ship. Instead he uses his wealth to sponsor an animal shelter, "a much worthier cause," he says. "I really believe that." He supports any campaign finance reform measure that is constitutionally permissible, including public financing. "I've learned how big money works because I've been there, and I am going to say it has to change no matter whether anyone agrees with me or not."

Jim Leach: He Won't PAC the House

He's a breed apart: an alumnus of Princeton, the London School of Economics, and Johns Hopkins; a moderate Republican in a House dominated by archconservatives from the Southwest; and fiercely independent. As chairman of the House Banking Committee, Jim Leach (R–IA) led the criticism of the Clintons over Whitewater *and* was one of only nine Republicans to oppose reelecting Newt Gingrich Speaker in 1996—Gingrich, he said, "was ethically damaged." And he didn't toe the party line on eliminating estate taxes, saying, "What is credible is an increase in the estate tax exemption to $5 or $10 million. What will be created with elimination of estate taxes on super-sized estates is a moneyed oligarchy."

Leach has a detached, intellectual air—and a loud whisper of a voice that could suggest indecision. He is anything but indecisive, however, when it comes to his signature issue—campaign finance reform—and his courageous act of refusing all PAC money and out-of-state money throughout his fourteen terms in Congress.

"My first race was in 1974, and the overwhelming issue was Watergate," recalls Leach, now sitting comfortably in his huge, high-ceilinged office in the Rayburn House Office Building. "Two of the reasons Watergate occurred [had to do with] money. First, Nixon had so much money he could afford to conduct covert operations; second, the plumbers may have been checking whether Larry O'Brien's files contained anything about the $100,000 Howard Hughes may have given Nixon for his home." Although Leach seemed to be on a successful Republican career path—he had worked for Donald Rumsfeld when the future defense secretary was a congressman and later, when he served as director of the Office of Economic Opportunity—he was disgusted by how Herbert Kalmbach and Maurice Stans "shook down every regulated industry, at how they basically said we want $100,000—and they'd get it.

"Nineteen seventy-two was all about money in politics. Republicans had a well-positioned but unattractive incumbent president. Early on, they were panicked that if Muskie got the nomination, he had a fifty-fifty chance against Nixon. So they went too far."

Leach resigned from the foreign service after the Saturday Night Massacre in 1973. He went into business with his father before his congressional race in 1974, when, in reaction to Watergate and PACs, he refused PAC and non-Iowa contributions.

"I opposed how PACs nationalize elections in a way the Founders, who wanted each member to represent the interest of his district, never intended," Leach explains. "Big PACs, like Big Oil, have nothing to do with our small-business state, yet we're now a playpen for PACs because Iowa congressmen vote on their issues.

"Of course, all my advisers thought I was nuts to refuse PAC money.

They wanted me to buy a lot of TV and generate recognition. So now I raise only about $350,000 per election, largely by direct mail and an annual picnic with a ticket price of $50. For twenty-eight years I've never asked anybody for money. Never. My chairman just sends out a fund-raising letter. My colleagues think I'm nuts."

He lost his first race, won in his second attempt in 1976—and then won his next thirteen elections, even though he was often outspent by 2 to 1 because of his pledge.

But 2002 will be a test, as it was for Feingold, of whether virtue is its own reward. The Iowa state legislature redistricted Leach to the Second District along with the popular Jim Nussle—70 percent of the district's voters were Nussle's. So Leach moved into a different Iowa district and is running against a strong Democrat, Julie Thomas, a Cedar Rapids pediatrician who is significantly outfinancing him. Of the 25 or so campaigns (of 435) regarded as "competitive" by the Republican and Democratic campaign committees, the Leach-Thomas race is one of the most interesting. With his career on the line, Leach is sticking to a pledge that will retain his honor, and perhaps even his office.

REFORMS DON'T WORK?
Visit New York City, Maine, Arizona . . .

"[A] long habit of not thinking a thing wrong, gives it the superficial appearance of being right, and raises at first a formidable cry in defence of custom. But the tumult soon subsides. Time makes more converts than reason."
—Thomas Paine, 1776

"History is the long and tragic story of the fact that privileged groups seldom give up their privileges voluntarily."
—Martin Luther King Jr., "Letter from Birmingham Jail," 1963

"Unless we fundamentally change this system, ultimately campaign finance will consume our democracy."
—Representative Lloyd Doggett (D–TX), 1996

As we've seen, when private money can purchase public policy, voters and consumers pay the price four times over.

First, elections become so prohibitively expensive that women and men of excellence, yet without wealth, are priced out of public service, either never running or leaving office early. Second, the pressure of raising vast sums of money forces nearly all candidates to spend more time fund-raising than meeting voters or legislating—and more time with the top 1 percent than with the "bottom" 99. Third, a pay-to-play political system produces legislation favoring special interests at the expense of average families. And fourth, the ever-increasing sums of big money needed to finance campaigns are discouraging voters from showing up at the polls—once convinced that only the voices of donors will ever count, the public loses its faith in the democratic process.

The Apologists

It's admittedly a challenge for defenders of the status quo to conjure up explanations for a system that so significantly tramples on American democracy and her laws. Indeed, not since some of the same people argued that tobacco wasn't addictive or carcinogenic has there been as big a "stretcher," in Mark Twain's euphemism, as the argument that money doesn't matter. Admitting a preference for a system that is biased toward owners over workers, big corporations over average consumers, and whites over blacks and Latinos would be honest, but it'd also be politically incorrect. So, led by the Four Apologists of big money politics—columnists George Will and Robert Samuelson, Senator Mitch McConnell, and Representative Tom DeLay—defenders have propagated fig leaves that wither under the slightest scrutiny. Here is a rundown of their principal arguments:

THERE ARE OTHER, IMPORTANT VARIABLES THAN MONEY AFFECTING LEGISLATORS. Of course there are. A state's constituent interests and election-year trends—and a Congress member's philosophy, ethnicity, and personality—still weigh heavily on the voter's scale of judgment, as well they should. Charles Rangel and Hillary Rodham Clinton can't trade races. No amount of money would sway a senator's position on a major issue of conscience like abortion. But what about on close, complex—and hugely important—economic questions, like price supports, environmental standards, taxes, tariffs, or technology?

While variables such as constituency, ethnicity, and personality obviously cannot be regulated, money can be—and should be. Some scholars and columnists may maintain that money doesn't matter, but they've never run for office. "I spend this much money, I win," said State Senator Robert Hurtt before a reelection bid in California; referring to a smaller number, he candidly added, "I spend this much, I lose."

PUBLIC FINANCING IS "FOOD STAMPS FOR POLITICIANS." This phrase from Senator McConnell is devastatingly effective rhetoric. Of course, two of the most popular Republicans in this century have accepted such financing; Ronald Reagan accepted more than $90 million in public funds in 1976, 1980, and 1984 combined, and Rudy Giuliani received over $4 million in 1989, 1993, and 1997 combined.

The argument against a federal public financing system of $500 million as "too expensive" reminds one of the immortal couplet: "Do you love your wife?" "Compared to whom?" A $500 million annual price tag for the *public* financing of congressional elections is a bargain compared with the $50 billion annual cost of the current *private* financing of campaigns in special-interest laws, as explained in chapter 5. Or the $150 billion bath taxpayers took with the 1980s S&L scandal because the industry was able to enact a deregulation law allowing it to speculate with depositors' money. Or the percentage of the *two trillion* dollar–plus slide in stock values in the summer of 2002 due to lost investor and consumer confidence because of how Congress had been shut-eyed sentries for years when it came to corporate crime. Or the $3 billion cost of the 2002 Dodd bill to fix voting machines and practices nationally after the Florida debacle. If the public pays for voting machines and inspectors—not to mention newsletters and staff for incumbents in election years—why not other essential costs of a public campaign? If we rightly spend $900 million annually on democracy abroad through the National Endowment for Democracy, why not half that amount for democracy at home?

When I asked Senator McCain about this, he said that he was undecided on public funding because it bothered him that taxpayers would have to fund politicians they didn't support. "So why are you and I paying George Bush's salary?" I asked, to his appreciative laughter.

MEMBERS OF CONGRESS CAN'T BE BOUGHT. But they "can be rented," Senator John Breaux once quipped. Or, as Bob Dole has succinctly put it, "When these political action committees give money, they expect something in return other than good government." These professionals understand, as do their colleagues, that few bite the hand that funds them.

The Four Apologists are forced to argue against the laws of human nature when they conclude that congresspeople accept money from petitioners but don't let it affect them. "We are the only people in the world required by law to take large amounts of money from strangers," Representative Barney Frank (D–MA) explained, "and then act as if it had no effect on our behavior."

Of course the issue isn't the pure bribery or outright vote buying, as just discussed, but the favoritism that money buys at any one of numerous, often hidden legislative contact points. Four-term Senator William Proxmire explained how it works:

> Anyone who has been around the Congress or a state legislature or a city council knows that over time the payoff by public officials for the PAC contributions they receive is as real and sure and certain as the sunrise. Oh, sure sometimes the public action by the elected official may not come immediately. It may not come in a vote. It may come in a speech not delivered. The PAC payoff may come in a colleague not influenced. It may come in a calling off of a meeting that otherwise would result in advancing legislation. It may come in a minor change in one paragraph in a 240-page bill. It may come in laying off or transferring a staff member who is unsympathetic to a PAC. . . . How often can anyone actually prove that any of these actions that advance the interests of a particular PAC flowed from the PAC contributions? In the eyes of both the elected officials and the contributing PACs, this is exactly the beauty of the PAC. The contributions constitute gilded corruption that has no sight, no taste, no smell, no feel, no sound, and of course—no smoking gun or even an empty cartridge to prove the crime. This is one reason why it is so insidious. The other reason is that everybody does it, or almost everybody.

ANY CHANGE WOULD AMOUNT TO AN "INCUMBENT PROTECTION ACT." The argument provokes laughter and invites cynicism. How much higher than a 98 percent reelection rate can we get? And if reform really entrenches incumbents, who doubts that they would have enacted it long ago? Furthermore, why do challengers generally support reform?

It's true there have been a few examples of a wealthy challenger outspending and defeating an incumbent. But the usual situation is that money rewards incumbency and incumbency rewards money—which explains why incumbents and money love this system far more than the taxpayers who pay its cost.

Those who argue that campaign financing reforms are "incumbent protection" schemes might want to ask five presidential and mayoral incumbents affected by them: ex-president Gerald Ford, ex-president Jimmy Carter, ex-president George H. W. Bush, ex-mayor Ed Koch, and ex-mayor David Dinkins. All lost.

Indeed, if there's anything that qualifies as an "incumbent protection act," it's the current system which has reduced the number of competitive House races to perhaps 25 out of 435. Between 1946 and 1952, there were 48 primary reelection losses; only half that many occurred in the six years between 1988 and 1994; in 2000, there were only 2. But as the money-incumbent synergy destroys the likelihood of real elections, what happens to the democratic presumption that competitive elections force incumbents to listen to popular will?

NOTHING WORKS—OR BEWARE THE "LAW OF UNINTENDED CONSEQUENCES." This is one of the few laws that George Will and Senator McConnell favor. Basically, they argue against the concept of human progress by arguing that every campaign reform is flawed, thereby making "the perfect enemy of the good." But should the Edsel mean the end of automobiles? Or the S&L collapse the end of banking? Or Enron the end of energy trading?

Indeed, how then to explain the real-world success stories of campaign finance reforms? If it can work at every other level of government—presidential, gubernatorial, mayoral, state legislative, and city council—it can work at the congressional level.

MONEY IS SPEECH. This is Senator McConnell's ace in the hole, a noble constitutional justification for a sleazy system. Except that even the *Buckley v. Valeo* decision he so often cites never made this pure a declaration, since it did uphold contribution limits. As we've established, if money *were* speech, there could be no laws against saying, "I'll give you $10,000 if you kill this bill in committee"—or "time, place, and manner restrictions"—on loud sound trucks. "Money is not speech," wrote former Senator Bill Bradley. "A rich man's wallet does not merit the same protection as a poor man's soap box." Indeed, no matter how often McConnell tries to elide soft money electioneering and John Peter Zenger, the fact remains that money can't be identical to speech or else Bill Gates has greater First Amendment rights than you or me.

THERE'S MONEY ON BOTH SIDES. Overall, corporate interests out-spend labor interests 12–1 in congressional elections, concludes the Center for Responsive Politics. And the gap is widening. There's a reason that candidates call owners, not line workers.

CHANGE WILL BE "ARMAGEDDON." That's what House Speaker Dennis Hastert predicted for his Republican Party if the Shays-Meehan soft money bill passed. At least Hastert openly admitted his partisan concerns—no fig leaves for him. But while this congressional Cassandra was candid, his prediction proved wrong in two major respects: forty-one House Republicans refused to put party before country and voted with the majority to pass the bill; and the first nonpartisan analysis of the bill's impact concluded in June 2002 that its doubling of the "hard money" limits from $2000 to $4000 per election cycle would significantly help *Republican* candidates. "Expanded givers tend to be wealthy, middle-aged businessmen who are disproportionately conservative Republican," wrote the analysts. Their increased participation "is likely to intensify the existing, upper-status bias of the donor pool and reduce the representation of women."

Reform will be Armageddon only for special interests. For the rest of us—candidates, parties, voters, and taxpayers—it will be salvation. The road to redeeming our democracy from the corruptive influence of big money is a hard one, but, as we shall soon learn, it has been traveled before. And the public is ready for the journey.

Public Sentiments

Catastrophes shock people into action, as Pearl Harbor and 9/11 attest. In contrast, big money's hammerlock on our democracy is a quiet crisis that gets worse and worse by degree. In 2002, the public began to understand that WorldCom and Enron are not the exceptions but the rule. Nonpartisan opinion polls have consistently shown that Americans recognize the costs of the blending of money and politics:

◄○► A 2002 CBS News poll found that 72 percent of Americans think that "many public officials make or change policy decisions as a direct result of money they receive from major campaign contributors"; only 13 percent do not think so.

◄○► A 2001 ABC News/*Washington Post* poll found that 93 percent "think politicians do special favors for people and groups who give them campaign contributions," and 80 percent said that it happens "often." In addition, 87 percent identified this as a problem, and 67 percent said it was "a big problem."

◄○► In a 2000 ABC News/*Washington Post* poll, 70 percent of Americans said that "reforming election campaign finance laws" would be either very important or somewhat important "in deciding how to vote in the 2000 presidential election."

◄○► In a 2000 Harris poll, 80 percent said that "people who give money to political parties and candidates have more influence than voters," versus 12 percent who said voters have more influence.

◄○► In a 2000 *New York Times*/CBS poll, 86 percent said the system for funding campaigns needs either "fundamental changes" or to be "completely rebuilt."

◄○► A 2000 poll by *Business Week* found that 74 percent of Americans say that when it comes to "influencing government policy, politicians, and policy makers in Washington," big companies have "too much influence."

◄○► A 1999 *Newsweek* poll found that 87 percent of Americans believe that "good people being discouraged from running for office by the high cost of campaigns" is a problem for this country's political system, and 63 percent called it a "major problem."

◄○► In a 1997 *New York Times*/CBS News poll, 75 percent believed that "many public officials make or change policy decisions as a result of money they receive from major contributors."

◄○► In a 1996 Gallup poll, 79 percent favored "putting a limit on the amount of money that candidates for the U.S. House and Senate can raise and spend on their political campaigns," and 67 percent favored limiting the amount of money a candidate for federal office, such as the presidency and Congress, can contribute to his or her own political campaign.

Support for reform cuts across every demographic group—race, class, party—except one: incumbency. Included in reform's diverse coalition is a growing organization of business refuseniks who, it turns out, are about as disenchanted with the system as ordinary citizens. A 1998 survey of large donors to congressional campaigns by the Center for Responsive Politics found that 70 percent agree that spending by congressional candidates should be limited, versus 24 percent who disagree; 57 percent agree that donors regularly pressure officeholders for favors, versus 20 percent who disagree; and 55 percent agree that money is the single most important factor in elections, versus 30 percent who disagree. When describing the dozens of pleas for money every day during campaign season, one business lobbyist told the *New York Times*, "I get E-mails. I get faxes. I get phone calls from members of their staff. It's annoying."

In 1999 the Committee for Economic Development (CED), a nonpartisan organization of business and academic leaders, published a report calling for partial public financing of political campaigns and a ban on soft money. CED president Charles Kolb said, "Reform is long overdue. The more CED members looked at the broken system, the more they felt the business community had to weigh in and offer a solution." In the weeks before the 2000 election, a CED-commissioned poll of senior business executives across the country—only 19 percent of whom identified themselves as Democrats—showed that two-thirds supported voluntary spending limits and a ban on soft money, and more than half supported a system of partial public financing based on matching funds.

"More executives are saying they're tired of the 'shakedown,'" added Edward Kangas, a blunt-speaking former chairman of the Big Five accounting firm Deloitte & Touche. "The unrelenting pressure to give ever-increasing amounts—something some say feels like 'extortion.' . . . They increasingly feel trapped in a system that doesn't work for anyone." Kangas concluded that businesses contribute because they fear that "legislative action could happen in the dark of night that could harm us if we do not respond."

When polls reveal a large consensus among voters on an issue of importance to them, elected officials usually respond with legislation. Not so with money in politics. Here there's a disconnect between voters and their representatives, who have a vested interest in the privileges that the status quo affords them. Indeed, the record demonstrates that not only have members of Congress opposed reform of the Federal Election Campaign Act, they have actively sought to undermine its enforcement.

Congress's primary means of stymieing FECA's enforcement is to make appointments to the Federal Election Commission who oppose the very laws they are sworn to uphold. The most egregious example is Bradley Smith, a former professor at Capitol University Law School in Columbus, Ohio, who has been a leading critic of campaign finance laws, calling them "profoundly undemocratic and profoundly at odds with the First Amendment." In a *Wall Street Journal* op-ed piece, Smith wrote: "When a law is in need of continual revision to close a series of ever-changing 'loopholes,' it is probably the law, and not the people, that is in error. The most sensible reform is a simple one: repeal of the

Federal Election Campaign Act." He expanded on his beliefs in a television interview with Bill Moyers: "I think we should deregulate and just let it go. That's how our politics was run for over one hundred years."

Where to begin with such brazen contempt for the integrity of elections and the rights of voters? What planet is he on, Pluto-cracy? What theory of democracy holds that the wealthy should have inordinate influence on public policy? The 1907 Tillman Act, the 1925 Federal Corrupt Practices Act, and the 1971 and 1974 Federal Election Campaign Act all resulted from a national backlash against big money's big role in elections. By Smith's logic—that for a hundred years we survived a prior system—we might as well go ahead and repeal environmental regulations and the federal tax code while we're at it. On planet Pluto-cracy, polluters will go unchecked and public goods—social security, Medicare, public education—will cease to exist. "Putting [Smith] in charge of the FEC," said Senator Chuck Schumer, "is like [appointing] as warden someone who opposes the prison system."

Smith is not only a poor democratic theorist, he's also a bad historian. In the Moyers interview, he stated: "Most of the problems that we've talked about tonight were exacerbated or created by the Federal Election Campaign Act." Actually, most of the problems that have arisen *since* FECA's enactment have been created not by the act itself, but by the FEC's inability to enforce it properly. Nothing better illustrates this than the birth and growth of soft money, as detailed in chapter 3.

Smith's argument is straight from the Four Apologists' playbook: throw up your hands, jabber about "unintended consequences," and predict that nothing will work. This is pessimism, this is defeatism, and—as the evidence clearly shows—this is wrong. Experience at the state and local levels demonstrates that reform programs can be successful if they are comprehensive, adaptive, and vigilantly enforced. Nowhere are the differences between the defeatists and reformers better highlighted than in New York State. The defeatists control the state capitol of Albany, with predictably disastrous results. In the late 1980s, however, they lost control of New York City, where reform has since flourished.

A Tale of Two Cities: Campaign Financing in Albany and New York City

Albany and New York City are obviously different in size and world renown, but one of the starkest differences between the two cities is in how they regulate campaign money.

In February 1988, after a series of municipal corruption scandals involving high-level officials, Mayor Ed Koch and the City Council enacted a comprehensive reform program, which voters strongly supported in a referendum later that year. Candidates who participate in this voluntary program (it can't be mandatory so long as *Buckley* prohibits legislatively enacted expenditure limits) agree to abide by strict contribution and spending limits, full disclosure of their campaign finances, and an audit by an independent and nonpartisan city agency, the Campaign Finance Board (CFB). In return, candidates who demonstrate community support by raising a certain level of "seed money" may qualify for public funds that match private contributions from New York City residents.

Until recently, the matching rate was 1 to 1 up to the first $1000 contributed per resident. On the election night celebrating my reelection as public advocate in November 1997, I announced a drive to rewrite the law because it wasn't achieving its high goals: encouraging small contributions, reducing candidates' dependence on large contributions, and providing qualified candidates with sufficient resources to run competitive campaigns.

A consensus soon emerged among candidates, elected officials, civic groups, and members of the CFB, which led to a new law changing the matching rate to 4 to 1 up to the first $250 contributed (from a city resident) and reducing the top gift from $8500 to $4500. The maximum in public funds per contributor remained $1000, but the new matching rate greatly enhanced the value of small contributions—$10 is now worth $50 ($10 + $40 = $50), and $100 is worth $500—to candidates who participate in the system.

New York *State* campaign finance laws, in contrast, include no spending limits, no matching funds, no ban on corporate contributions, and very high contribution ceilings that are easily and frequently evaded. In the late 1980s the New York State Commission on Government Integrity, led by then Fordham University Law School dean John Feerick, issued a scathing series of reports that exhaustively examined statewide campaign financing and recommended specific proposals for change. Upon completing the reports after years of work, Feerick wrote, "It would be a sad commentary on the history of these times if New York State, after commissioning a wide-ranging, nonpartisan examination of government ethical standards, were to squander this opportunity for meaningful reform." Yet squander it did. More than a decade later, nothing has happened.

In the 1998 gubernatorial campaign, Republican governor George Pataki, in a moment of unguarded candor, called the state's system "dreadful." In 1999, after winning reelection, the governor unveiled a reform bill—on the last day of the legislative session. It didn't even get introduced until 2000, when the state Democrats brought it to the floor of the Senate and the Republicans voted it down.

"The governor is all talk and no action," says Blair Horner, legislative director of the New York Public Interest Research Group (NYPIRG). "In 2001, because of redistricting, the governor was in a unique position to exert leverage over his Republican colleagues in the Senate. There were editorials all across the state, from the *New York Times* to the *Buffalo News,* calling on the governor to seize the opportunity to fix a horrendous system that needs top-to-bottom changes. But the governor didn't want his bill enough to do any work. He did nothing."

The Democratic-controlled state assembly passed a bill that differs from the governor's, but the two bills share many of the same elements. The assembly leadership said it would go to a conference committee to work out the differences if the Senate passed the governor's version. Nevertheless, says Horner, "the governor still wouldn't lift a finger to make it happen." It didn't, and nothing has changed in Albany.

As a lesson for Washington, it's useful to compare how each system affects five main areas: competition, fund-raising, expenditures, enforcement, and voter education.

Competition

New York City's 2001 elections were the first held under the new matching rate, and a record number of candidates ran for office. In the same year, term limits prevented most elected officials from seeking reelection, providing attractive opportunities to many first-time candidates. It is impossible to separate the two factors when considering the increased number of candidates, yet anecdotal information suggests that many candidates would not have run without the public funds program.

"Had there not been the availability of public matching funds," said Herb Berman, a veteran of the City Council and an unsuccessful candidate for city comptroller in 2001, "it would have been literally impossible for me to have run citywide. . . . I think [the city program] is probably the most creative form of the democratic process that I can think of, and it has literally enabled many people, as this past election has shown, to run for public office when otherwise they would have been totally incapable of doing it."

"The campaign finance program was a definitive factor in my decision to run for office," said Sandra Vassos, a first-time City Council candidate. "Both of my rivals were well known in the community. One rival was a virtual incumbent, having the same name, exactly, as his father, who was speaker of the City Council, and both had the capacity to raise substantial amounts of money. The campaign finance program made me competitive, and I'm very grateful for that."

"It works," concurred David Yassky, another first-time City Council candidate who won election in a race that featured several other competitive candidates. "I ran against somebody who had the capacity to raise much more money, and, in fact, did raise much more money than I did, but thanks to the system we spent roughly the same amount. I believe that the campaign was decided by ideas and message and campaigning rather than by sheer money. . . . People often have to spend a year, full-time, raising money, talking only to people who are able to write $1000 checks or $2000 checks. There is no question in my mind that that has an impact on how people see the world. I could spend my time talking to residents and the community leaders and activists in my district rather than spend all my time raising money."

While candidates chosen by the city's county leaders historically dominated elections, in 2001 term limits helped open the field to grassroots challengers; leveling it, however, required public funds and spending limits. New candidates could run with the knowledge that spending limits would protect them from being grossly outspent, and with the confidence that their community ties, if translated into small contributions, would provide them with the floor of public funds needed to be competitive. As a result, the campaign finance program energized the city's elections—quite a few of the City Council races featured five or more legitimate candidates—and enabled many challengers to defeat party favorites. Had such a campaign finance program been around in Boss Tweed's era, it would have put Tammany Hall out of business long before Judge Samuel Seabury and Thomas Nast's cartoons did.

Elections for the New York State legislature, on the other hand, are more of a formality than a competition. A report on the 2000 state legislative elections by Citizen Action of New York showed that incumbents rarely faced strong challengers and many faced no challenger at all: there were no major party contests in 40 percent of Senate elections and 27 percent of Assembly elections. Of the 202 incumbent officeholders who sought reelection, 3 lost in party primaries and 1 lost in the general election—a reelection rate of 98 percent.

Fund-Raising

Candidates who join the city's campaign finance program agree to contribution limits that are much lower than the state limits by which they would otherwise be bound. The limits for the citywide offices of mayor, public advocate, and comptroller are $4500, versus a state limit of $45,400 for nonparticipating candidates and for governor, attorney general, and state comptroller. Yet the state's extraordinarily high limit is actually no limit at all, because individuals and corporations— corporate contributions are allowed under state law but prohibited by the city's program—routinely give many times that amount by contributing to the state party.

For instance, a 2002 *Daily News* investigation revealed that various individuals and corporations—many of which do business with the state—contributed more than $200,000 each to Governor Pataki and the state GOP. The limit on direct corporate contributions to candidates is $5000, but state law treats corporate subsidies as separate entities, a major loophole that corporations routinely exploit. In the 2000 election, for example, when Anheuser-Busch hit the $5000 cap, each of its seventeen affiliated companies gave the max, or close to it—including Busch Entertainment Inc., operator of Sea World and Busch Gardens. The contribution surprised no one in Albany, but it did surprise Fred Jacobs, a spokesman for Busch Entertainment: "I was unaware that we had made any contributions to candidates outside the states in which we operate."

In the city's 2001 council elections, contributions of $100 or less accounted for 27 percent of total money raised, versus about 3 percent for the 2000 state legislative races. In addition, small matchable contributions ($250 or less), when added to the public funds they generated, accounted for 80 percent of all money available to City Council candidates. During the 1999–2000 legislative session, by contrast, New York State legislators raised 57 percent from contributions of $1000 or more—and 44 percent from sources who gave $10,000 or more. In New York City, over 80 percent of the total raised by council candidates came from individuals. At the state level, only 33 percent came from individuals; the rest came from corporations, unions, PACs, and other sources.

In the 2002 New York governor's race, three candidates—Governor George Pataki, Comptroller Carl McCall, and former Secretary of Housing and Urban Development Andrew Cuomo—collected over $26 million in the year before the election in amounts up to the $45,400 limit: 40 percent came from contributions of $10,000 or more while contributions of less than $100 made up only 2 percent of Pataki's contributions and less than 1 percent of Cuomo's and McCall's. Of the total money raised by the three candidates, 90 percent came from contributions of $1000 or more. Indeed, by the summer of 2002, Governor Pataki had raised an astonishing $32 million—already nearly triple what his predecessor Mario Cuomo spent in his 1994 loss to Pataki. During the election year, Pataki was breaking all records by raising $2 million a month, or about $100,000 per working day. It doesn't seem very complicated to understand why he proposes campaign finance reform—and then ensures that it's never enacted.

In contrast, in the New York City mayoral race, contributions of more than $1000 accounted for only 40 percent of the total available to candidates. Public matching funds ensured that each of the four major Democratic candidates had sufficient resources—about $5.5 million each—to compete on equal footing in the primary election. In state races, large special-interest contributions were dominant; in city races, matched gifts of moderate size were. Speaking as one of the Democrats in the mayoral primary, I recall never fretting that some big interest wouldn't contribute to me because (1) they couldn't give $45,400 anyway, and (2) with enough effort, I'd get to the ceiling with other gifts plus matching funds.

The New York City program cost city taxpayers about $40 million, which, over a four-year cycle, amounts to about $1.25 annually per New York City resident—a small investment to liberate candidates from being muscled by economic interests and to invite more talent to seek office. The program has been supported by voters in two different citywide referendums, and has enjoyed strong support from Democrats and Republicans alike. Mayor Giuliani participated in the program in each of his three mayoral bids and received over $4 million in public funds. As former Republican senator Alfonse D'Amato has said, "I think the city system is a pretty good one. It encourages people of modest means to run."

Spending

The New York City campaign finance program cannot, because of *Buckley,* offer candidates a level playing field to offset the spending power of a self-financing candidate. Yet its spending limits ensured a fair fight not only in the Democratic mayoral primary but also all across the city (since billionaires are apparently less interested in running for City Council or other lower-level offices). As a result the vast majority of serious candidates joined the program, and nearly every office was vigorously contested.

In New York State's 2000 legislative elections, however, there were few fights at all, and in most the challenger fought with one arm tied behind his or her back. According to the 2000 Citizen Action report, three-quarters of all assembly and senate races were landslides in which the winning candidate received more than 65 percent of the vote. In these races, winners on average outspent losers by twelve times in senate races and fourteen times in assembly races. Of the 211 races, only 15 were won with 55 percent or less of the vote. Six of these were Senate races where the winners outspent the losers by $1.1 million to $300,000, on average. In a recent study of legislative races in all fifty states, New York ranked first in dollars per vote, and twenty-ninth in voter turnout.

It was no surprise that a 2001 poll by the Marist Institute for Public Opinion found that 71 percent of New Yorkers said that they would support public financing if it came with limits on candidates' fund-raising.

Enforcement and Oversight

The New York City Campaign Finance Board is an independent city agency whose budget is given special protection in the City Charter to ensure that it is not hobbled by vengeful budget cuts. To prevent deadlocks, the nonpartisan board is composed of five members: two are appointed by the mayor, two by the speaker of the City Council, and the chairman of the board is appointed by the mayor in consultation with the speaker. The mayor's two appointees must come from different political parties, as is true for the speaker's.

The CFB audits every campaign to ensure compliance with the law, and only campaigns in compliance may receive public funds. When violations are uncovered, the board levies penalties in "real time"—during the election. In 1989, 1993, and 1997, the program's first three citywide election cycles, the CFB fined three sitting mayors: Ed Koch was fined $35,000 in 1989; David Dinkins, $320,000 in 1993; and Rudy Giuliani, $242,000 in 1997. The fines against Dinkins and Giuliani both came during the election. The fine against Dinkins, a Democrat, was particularly noteworthy because, at the time, the

Campaign Finance Board did not include a single Republican member. Each campaign paid the fine, and CFB has lived to tell the tale. Columnist Jack Newfield has written, "The CFB has been nonpartisan, impartial, independent, patronage-free, and fearless since its creation in 1989."

At the state level, however, the campaign finance laws are nearly as weak as the agency charged with enforcing them, the Board of Elections (BOE). The New York State BOE, in fact, makes the FEC look bold and aggressive. In a series of articles in 2000, *Newsday* reporter Liam Pleven exposed how some lawmakers used their campaign funds as personal slush funds—and got away with it. One senator, Serphin Maltese, spent $450 from campaign funds on cat food and a veterinarian's visit for his office cat. "If a bill comes in and there's money in my account," said Senator Maltese, "I pay for it out of my account. And if there's not then I pay for it myself."

Senator Maltese was by no means alone: Senate Majority Leader Joe Bruno spent $1300 in campaign cash on a pool cover for a pool at his home; Senator Ken La Valle spent over $800 on gifts for weddings and other occasions; Assemblyman Harvey Weisenberg spent $1500 in campaign cash at Albany restaurants in 1999, despite a public $116 per diem allowance and a $79,500 base salary for a legislative job that is part-time; Assemblyman Robert D'Andrea spent over $3000 from his campaign coffers for a private box at the Saratoga racetrack, which is in his district. The list goes on: legislators have used campaign money to pay for leased cars, trips abroad, and floral bouquets of celebration and sympathy.

New York State election law notes that campaign funds "shall not be converted by any person to a personal use which is unrelated to a political campaign or the holding of a public office or party position." The law has been interpreted so broadly that legislators can violate its spirit with impunity—and they do. Pleven's exposé did not result in a single enforcement action by the BOE. NYPIRG's Horner called the BOE's interpretation "insane," lamenting, "if you're an incumbent, anything goes." Complained a *Newsday* editorial: "Too many legislators use their campaign funds the way people in the private sector use expense accounts. And once they start doing that, the line between a campaign contribution and a bribe begins to look a bit blurry."

Voter Education

The New York City Charter mandates that the CFB produce a nonpartisan voter guide and distribute it to every household with a registered voter. Candidates submit biographical information and statements for inclusion in the guide, which also offers useful voting information. In addition, candidates for citywide office who receive public funds must agree to participate in public debates, ensuring that voters have the opportunity to see candidates in face-to-face meetings.

Again, contrast this with the failed state system, where no voter guide or debate program exists. In the 1994 and 1998 elections, not a single gubernatorial debate was held between the Democratic and Republican nominees. And governors have routinely appeared in state-financed "public service" advertisements during election years, a practice Governor Pataki took to unprecedented levels when, in his second term, he spent $50 million in ads featuring himself—nearly double what he and Mario Cuomo *spent combined* in their epic 1994 contest and $10 million more than New York City spent on the entire campaign finance program. It appears that Governor Pataki is a big supporter of taxpayer-financed campaigns, as long as they're financing his own. (In 1998, New York City eliminated this election law abuse.)

Although it can't be measured mathematically, the Albany big money chase appears to tolerate or incite far more unethical activities than can be found in New York City. "Albany is totally dysfunctional," says Rachel Leon, executive director of Common Cause New York. "So little gets done, and when an issue is put on the table, you see the money start pouring in. In 2001, there were two big deals that got done: a health care bill that was the most secretive, backward deal in the history of Albany, and a bill to allow gambling. The governor and the legislature agreed on those deals even though they never reached agreement on a budget!" The gambling and health care industries are two of the biggest givers in Albany, and both poured in millions of dollars in 2001. "Inside lobbying and outside cash—that's how Albany works," Leon says.

To believe defeatists who say that nothing will work is, in effect, to ratify the corrupt system of campaign financing at the state level, and to ignore the success that New York City has had in building a better democracy: more candidates less dependent on special interests; more small contributors involved in campaigns; more competitive races; more public debate; better disclosure; and real-time enforcement of laws with teeth.

Laboratories of Democracy

Supreme Court Justice Louis Brandeis conceived of the individual states as laboratories of democracy, where experiments in public policy could be conducted on a relatively small scale and used to inform federal legislation. Indeed, the federal government often looks to the states to learn their best practices and co-opt their successful programs. On the issue of campaign financing, however, Congress has refused to acknowledge the growing body of evidence accumulating in states and localities that reform works—and that the public wants it.

Currently more than a dozen states, as well as cities such as Los Angeles, San Francisco, Miami, and Cincinnati, have some form of direct public financing program in place. Although each program is different, most are based on two core elements: public funds and spending limits.

The best programs share much in common with New York City's: sufficiently high levels of public funds, reasonable spending limits, strict oversight, and budgetary protection. Candidates are rational actors who maximize their self-interest; if a reform program's benefit (public funding) does not outweigh its cost (spending limits), candidates will not participate.

Minnesota and Wisconsin, neighboring states that enacted similarly structured public funding programs in the 1970s, provide an illustration. Minnesota's program is fully funded through general revenue and other sources, including a $5 tax checkoff. Both its public funds and its spending limits have been adjusted to keep pace with inflation. Wisconsin's program, however, relies solely on a $1 tax checkoff that generates insufficient revenue, and its public funding and spending limits have remained frozen since 1986. In effect, candidates in Wisconsin are asked to pay a heavy price—unrealistically low spending limits—in exchange for the meager reward of limited public funds. As a result, candidate participation in Wisconsin's program has dropped steadily; it's now below 50 percent, while participation in Minnesota's program is nearly 100 percent. Not surprisingly, in the 1996 elections 78 percent of Wisconsin incumbents ran in noncompetitive races, compared with only 31 percent in Minnesota.

State and local experiments with partial public financing have taught many worthwhile lessons that merit attention.

Clean Money, Clean Elections

In 2000, Ed Youngblood, a first-time candidate for the Maine State Senate, challenged a powerful incumbent and won. At the same time in Arizona, another first-time candidate, a professor named Jay Blanchard, challenged the Arizona Speaker of the House—and also won. Neither Youngblood nor Blanchard would have begun their campaigns in the first place had they not been able to run "clean."

That year, candidates throughout Arizona and Maine participated in full public financing programs—dubbed "Clean Money, Clean Elections" by advocates—that voters had passed in referendums. Unlike public matching funds, full public financing provides a flat grant, equal to the spending limit, to candidates who collect a threshold number of $5 contributions. The idea is to eliminate fund-raising, except for the seed money that demonstrates community support, and to guarantee a level playing field by ensuring that every credible candidate has the same amount of money.

"It's a good way of giving government back to the people," said Youngblood. "It lets people who are not well connected run for the legislature." Peter Mills, a Republican incumbent Maine state senator who ran clean in 2000, said, "It was refreshing not to have to raise money. . . . I feel a certain independence from special-interest groups. It was nice to be able to say, 'Thanks for the thought, but I'm running clean.'"

The 2000 elections in Arizona and Maine were the first to be held under Clean Money laws, and although it is still too early to draw conclusions, the preliminary findings are encouraging. Compared with previous elections, in both states more candidates ran for office, had financially viable campaigns, and were competitive at the polls—and all for under seventy cents per resident.

In Arizona, where one quarter of candidates participated in the public financing program, contested races increased 62 percent from 1996. "We were able to find some really terrific people in seats that frankly would have been difficult to find good candidates [for] in the past," said Rick Bennett, the Republican president of the State Senate. "And in fact some seats where we had no candidates two years ago, people are running because the Clean Elections Act allowed them to be competitive."

In 1998, losing candidates for the Arizona State Senate raised on average 40 percent of the amounts raised by the winners. Yet with the advent of Clean Money in 2000, they raised slightly *more* than the winners—an astonishing fact. Losing candidates for the Arizona House of Representatives raised 78 percent of what winning candidates raised, compared with 51 percent in 1998. "Public funding appears to have really turned traditional trends upside down in Arizona's State Senate races while leveling the playing field significantly in the House races," said Samantha Sanchez, codirector of the National Institute on Money in State Politics, a nonpartisan research group.

In Maine, where nearly one-third of candidates participated in the Clean Money program, the results were similar: losing candidates in 2000 raised 78 percent of what the winners raised, versus only 53 percent in 1998. The number of competitive races, defined as those in which the winner's margin of victory was no more than 20 percent, rose 21 percent in Maine's Senate elections and 17 percent in its House elections. In addition, incumbents in both Maine and Arizona have traditionally enjoyed a 2-to-1 fund-raising advantage; however, in the 2000 election, challengers in Maine raised 78 percent as much as incumbents, and in Arizona, 77 percent.

Elections have become more competitive in Maine and Arizona, and candidates, freed from the money chase, have become more productive. By requiring that candidates raise a small amount of money from a large number of people—rather than a large amount from a small number—Clean Elections naturally blends fund-raising and campaigning into one activity. "I spent 90 percent of my time knocking on doors," said Don Gean, a former Maine House member and an unsuccessful candidate for Maine Senate in 2000. "This is where a candidate belongs, standing on porches."

In a survey of candidates who participated in Maine's program, nearly three-quarters responded that full public financing affected the way they campaigned—and by far the most important impact was that it allowed them to spend more time with voters. Senator David Peterson, an Arizona Republican, compared the old system with the new: "In previous campaigns, I would say that at least half or a third of the campaign was spent raising the dollars. In this campaign, the time I spent raising the dollars was actually in front of my constituents. It made me be more of a grassroots candidate."

Anecdotal evidence also suggests that residents in Maine and Arizona are also getting a more representative government. In January 2001, as the first Clean Money candidates took their seats in the Maine legislature, the Democratic leadership took up the issue of price controls for prescription drugs. "Historically, the pharmaceutical industry had given about equally to Republican and Democratic leadership committees," said Maine Senate Majority Leader Chellie Pingree. "When we raised the issue of price controls, we were immediately cut off. This year they are giving only to Republicans," a loss that Democrats might have felt much more keenly before clean money took the pressure off. "I think the passage of the Clean Elections Act freed up some of our legislators to feel less vulnerable about voting for the plan. One reason the prescription drug plan passed in Maine and not at the federal level is that money is less of a factor here."

Other legislators in Maine agreed. Before full public financing, Representative Paul Volenik had great difficulty getting support for his universal health care plan. But in the spring of 2001 Maine took the first steps toward such a system, and Volenik believes that public financing played a role: "The insurance industry's influence has been diminished, and a portion of that is due to Clean Elections." State representative Glenn Cummings, a Clean Money candidate, confirmed the transformation: "The business lobbyists left me alone. I think they assumed I was unapproachable. It sure made it easier to get through the hallways on the way to the vote!"

Public financing allows elected officials to operate independently. "Under the Clean Money option candidates will still get the money— but this time from the taxpaying public, who, providing the money, will be the boss," explained former congressman Cecil Heftel (D–HI) in his book *End Legalized Bribery*. "Instead of running filet mignon campaigns compliments of the rich and powerful, candidates will be forced to run pizza, hamburger, and spaghetti campaigns compliments of the American public."

ᶜ ᵍ

Two other states, Vermont and Massachusetts, have also passed Clean Money programs. Vermont was the first in the nation to enact Clean Money legislatively, while Massachusetts's legislature has fought it every step of the way.

In 1998, voters in Massachusetts approved a Clean Money referendum by a margin of 2 to 1. But the Speaker of the House, Democrat Thomas Finneran, opposes public financing and has refused to fund the law. In January 2002, the Massachusetts Supreme Court ruled that the legislature was violating the state's constitution and ordered it to fund or repeal the program. In March, after the legislature had failed to comply, the court ordered the state to sell off property, if necessary, to pay for the program. In July, less than two months before the 2002 primary elections, the legislature finally appropriated money. Unfortunately, it was too little and too late to fund the candidates who wanted to participate.

Adding insult to injury, Finneran and legislative leaders then agreed to place on the ballot a referendum question asking voters if they "support taxpayer money being used to fund political campaigns for public office in Massachusetts." This wording willfully and misleadingly fails to mention Clean Money's limits on spending and contributions. The legislature's obstinate disregard for the verdicts handed down by the voters and the court undermines public confidence in the democratic process—which, ironically, is precisely the problem that Clean Money is designed to combat.

It may be early to draw conclusions about Clean Money programs, nevertheless, some questions remain: Why did so few candidates (25 to 30 percent) join in Arizona and Maine? Are spending limits set too low? (In Vermont's 2000 elections, Governor Howard Dean opted not to run in the Clean Elections program, despite being a strong supporter of it, because he feared being outspent by an opponent.)

An important test of this approach will come in the fall of 2002, when Arizona and Maine hold their first statewide elections under their Clean Money systems.

Contribution Refunds

In 1986, Congress repealed a provision in the federal tax code that allowed for a nonrefundable tax credit of up to $50 for political contributions. The credit was intended to encourage small contributions, but fewer than 5 percent of taxpayers filed for it, and there was little protest when it was repealed. Currently, nine states provide some form of tax credit or deduction for political contributions, and a tenth, Minnesota, provides a more powerful incentive: a contribution refund.

Minnesota allows citizens to receive a refund of up to $50 for contributions made to candidates and parties that participate in the state's public financing program. Unlike a tax credit that takes over a year to materialize, the refund claim, once submitted to the state, takes only about six weeks to redeem. Compared with tax credits and deductions, the refund is quicker, better, and more financially attractive to working-class citizens. It also offers candidates a powerful fund-raising tool, but only if they accept spending limits. Minnesota thus offers candidates two bites at the carrot—public funding directly from the state and indirectly from citizens—for one thwack of the stick: spending limits. Nearly every candidate accepts the bargain—which, in total, costs Minnesotans about $1.25 a year each.

Contribution Limits

"Money buys many of the good things in life, but no one has cited any constitutional history suggesting that money is supposed to be the milk of politics or that large political contributions are a necessary ingredient of representative government protected by the Constitution. Constitutional history does not support the idea that laissez-faire economics is embodied in the First Amendment to assure the right to make large campaign contributions." These are not the words of a campaign reform advocate, but of a 2002 federal appeals court ruling, *Frank v. City of Akron,* which upheld contribution limits, ranging from $100 to $300, passed by voters in that Ohio city.

Since the Supreme Court's 2000 decision in *Nixon v. Shrink Missouri Government PAC* upholding Missouri's contribution limits, the courts have upheld contribution limits in Vermont and Montana that are the lowest in the nation. Vermont now caps contributions at $200 for legislative candidates and $400 for statewide candidates; Montana's limits are $100 and $400, respectively, for legislative and statewide races.

In the *Shrink* decision, Justice David Souter wrote for the majority: "Leave the perception of impropriety unanswered and the cynical assumption that large donors call the tune could jeopardize the willingness of voters to take part in democratic government. Democracy works 'only if the people have faith in those who govern, and that faith is bound to be shattered when high officials and their appointees engage in activities which arouse suspicions of malfeasance and corruption.' . . . There is little reason to doubt that sometimes large contributions will work actual corruption of our political system, and no reason to question the existence of a corresponding suspicion among voters." Justice Souter wrote that the test for contribution limits is whether they are "so radical in effect to render political association ineffective, [and thereby] drive the sound of a candidate's voice below the level of notice."

Currently, fourteen states have no contribution limits at all, and many others—such as New York—have limits so high as to render them almost meaningless. On the other hand, if the maximum is set too low it can restrict electoral competition and political speech—and force candidates to spend even more time fund-raising. But if contribution limits are tied to public financing, limits can be set at reasonably low levels without threatening the health of political speech. As a general rule of thumb, contribution limits should vary inversely—within a reasonable range—with levels of public funding.

States and cities have also experimented with restricting the source and timing of contributions. Candidates who participate in Los Angeles's public financing program must limit their aggregate PAC contributions to approximately 50 percent of the spending limit. In 1996, voters in Oregon passed a ballot measure banning out-of-state contributions, although it was later overturned in a 2–1 federal appeals court ruling. But the Alaska Supreme Court upheld a law passed by the Alaskan legislature severely restricting out-of-state contributions: gubernatorial candidates in Alaska may raise no more than $20,000 from out-of-state sources; candidates for Alaska state senator and representative may raise no more than $5000 and $3000, respectively. The U.S. Supreme Court refused to hear the Oregon and Alaska cases, leaving the future of out-of-state limits an open question.

On the issue of timing, Los Angeles's system prohibits fund-raising until two years before the election for citywide candidates and eighteen months before the election for City Council candidates. The ban is intended to reduce the fund-raising advantage that incumbents hold by virtue of their office, and to restrict the amount of time that fund-raising can occur simultaneously with city business. Minnesota, in order to diminish both the appearance of and potential for corruption, prohibits candidates from receiving contributions from PACs while the legislature is in session.

Finally, some jurisdictions have limited the amounts that candidates can lend to their own campaigns. When candidates get elected to office and then raise special-interest money to repay themselves, the already thin line between contribution and bribe is all but erased. In Kentucky, John Y. Brown, a Kentucky Fried Chicken magnate, lent his campaign for governor about $2 million. After he won election, he invited companies that did business with the state to fund-raising dinners and pocketed—because he was the one being paid back—the take, which wasn't chicken feed. Kentucky subsequently passed legislation limiting loans to no more than $50,000 per candidate, a law that has since been upheld by a federal court. New York City takes a different tack in addressing the same problem: candidates may receive unlimited loans, but those that are not repaid by election day constitute contributions. Thus any loan exceeding the contribution limit that isn't repaid by election day is a violation of the contribution limit and subject to financial penalties.

Other Countries

Since its founding, America has always viewed itself as the world's champion of democracy, and our soldiers continue to fight and die in its name. When it comes to free and fair elections, however, it appears increasingly that others have taken the lead in the fight for the Lincolnian ideal of "government of the people, by the people, and for the people."

In a recent study of sixty democracies, researchers found that 70 percent of countries—from Argentina to Zimbabwe—have some form of public financing of elections; nearly half have spending limits and offer tax incentives for contributions; and one-third provide free or subsidized printing or postage for campaign mailings. In addition, 88 percent of countries—from Botswana to Barbados and Ukraine to Uruguay—offer free political broadcasts. The few that do not are Ecuador, Honduras, Malaysia, Taiwan, Tanzania, Trinidad and Tobago . . . and the United States. For the country that gave the world Thomas Jefferson and James Madison, we're keeping some pretty strange company.

The free-market economist Joseph Schumpeter defined democracy as "free competition for a free vote." Most democratic countries understand that if the cost of competition is steep, elections are not free but very expensive. As a result, most countries offer the public airwaves for use in public elections. But not in America.

Among the chorus of critics is renowned investor Warren Buffett: "We should require broadcast stations—the beneficiaries of incredibly valuable licenses, courtesy of your federal government—to make available, prior to every election, modest amounts of time for political discourse. Let's add an ability to be heard to a right to speak."

On this issue the states are dependent on congressional action, because broadcasters hold federal licenses. This has not stopped Rhode

Island, however, from mandating free airtime on public television and community cable television for all candidates who participate in the state's public funding program.

In the British elections of 2001, parties were given five minutes a week of free airtime on both public television (BBC) and the commercial networks. In addition, there was no money chase to pay for an endless barrage of political commercials because there are no political commercials; Britain bans them. The defining unit of the American political campaign—thirty-second advertisements that sell images, attacks, and sound bites—simply does not exist in Britain. Free airtime and a ban on commercials offer two important benefits: they sharply reduce the demand for campaign cash, and they offer a higher level of public discourse at a cheaper price. In Britain's 2001 elections, the total cost of electing its 651-member House of Commons was $60 million—less than Jon Corzine spent winning *one* legislative seat.

Campaign finance scandals are not a uniquely American phenomenon, as influence peddlers can be found the world over.

For years European democracies have regarded influence-peddling campaign money as a peculiarly American problem, part of our wild western elections. Not anymore.

In 2000, for example, Prime Minister Tony Blair was tarnished when he backed the sale of a Romanian steel company to a London-based Indian businessman who had, weeks before, given $180,000 to Blair's Labor Party; the Conservative Party, attacked as the party of "sleaze" by the prime minister in the last election, has aggressively seized the issue. In Canada, leading newspapers have called for the resignation of Prime Minister Jean Chrétien because of what his opposition calls a pattern of how his ministers allegedly give big contracts to big contributors to his Liberal Party. And in Italy, the country's wealthiest man, Silvio Berlusconi, became its head of state due, in no small measure, to the power his money could purchase.

But while other democracies can no longer smugly chide our campaign finance scandals, unfortunately America still leads the way in size and sway of political money.

ᏇᏌ   ᏍᏅ

To retain its title as the world's preeminent democracy, the United States must confront head-on what has become the scourge of American politics: democracy for sale. If the international community perceives the American political system as corrupt, we lose the moral authority to preach the virtues of free elections. A great teacher is always surpassed by her pupils, and on the subject of democracy, it is now time for the United States to stop lecturing and start listening. We can still offer the world leadership on laws governing public campaigns and public disclosure, but we must recognize that other countries are bringing the spirit of Jefferson and Lincoln into the twenty-first century, and that we must too.

CHANGE, FOR GOOD
Who Owns Democracy—Enron or You?

"Who are to be the electors of the federal representatives? Not the rich, more than the poor . . . not the haughty heirs of distinguished names, more than the humble sons of obscure and unpropitious fortune."
—James Madison, *Federalist* 57, 1788

"We've got a real irony here. . . . We have politicians selling access to something we all own—our government. And then we have broadcasters selling access to something we all own— our airwaves. It's a terrible system."
—Newton Minow,
former Federal Communications Commission chairman, 2000

"Reform is not for the short-winded."
—Arthur Vanderbilt, New Jersey Supreme Court justice, 1949

The evidence, then, makes it clear: our campaign finance system is broken, citizens of all persuasions want change, and successful alternatives exist.

The alibis of apologists—change helps incumbents; money is speech; money doesn't buy votes—are shallow and unpersuasive. So now the defenders of the status quo have shifted to political and free-market arguments. Voters don't really care, they say; or, as Mitch McConnell argued in 2000, they assert that no candidate has ever been elected or defeated on the issue of campaign reform, and thus it can be safely ignored. Yet McConnell's Senate nemesis, John McCain, made campaign finance reform the heart and soul of his electrifying 2000 presidential campaign. Only by vastly outspending McCain did George

W. Bush squeak by him in a tight primary battle that was supposed to be a coronation—and not before soft money became a dinner-table conversation staple. That same year, Maria Cantwell believes, making campaign finance reform a centerpiece of her Washington State U.S. Senate race was a major reason for her squeaker of a victory.

Senators McCain and Cantwell ran against what big money buys for special interests—tax breaks and loopholes for big corporations, weakened environmental regulations for manufacturers, and price protections for drug companies. But they also ran against what those purchases cost Americans: higher taxes, more pollution, and expensive health care, respectively.

To be successful, a pro-democracy movement like campaign finance reform cannot be merely an abstract, good-government ideal. It must be tied to the issues that Americans care most about: affordable child care, education, health care, and housing; a clean environment and safe streets; and tax rates that are fair. Do we want children with lower rates of asthma? Then we need campaign finance reform. Do we want enough funds for smaller class sizes and qualified, well-paid teachers? Then we need campaign finance reform. Do we want seniors to have access to lifesaving medicine? Then we need campaign finance reform. Do we want to keep guns out of the hands of kids and criminals? Then we need campaign finance reform.

On nearly every issue, reform matters. It matters, first, because the public simply cannot get a fair shake from representatives who are forced to depend on money with strings attached. Voters need to know how money in politics is affecting their water and wallets, their schools and streets. And they need to know that there is a solution. As connections become more personal, support for the solution will become more pronounced.

Second, some critics of reform who disagreed with civil rights in the 1960s again argue for the free-market approach of a century ago. Disclosure is enough, they'll say; we don't need any campaign spending laws. If by this they mean that voters could "choose" between different candidates owned by different companies—perhaps each person seeking election wears a logo, as Wimbledon finalists show their Lacoste alligators or Nike swooshes. That's not about to happen, but if they are talking about the goals of efficiency, competitiveness, and productivity, I concur. As best articulated by Samuel Issacharoff and Richard Pildes in their 1988 *Stanford Law Review* article, "Politics as Markets," our political market should:

◄○► *Prevent monopolies.* We have long known that in the absence of antitrust laws, monopolies would dominate economic markets, drive up costs, and drive out competition. Similarly, rich candidates and interests can dominate political markets, drive up campaign costs, and drive out competition. In both, citizens are left with fewer choices. Federal laws should prevent money pursuing monopoly in our polity as well as our economy.

◄○► *Maximize efficiency.* As we've seen, too often public policies are bought by donors but paid for by voters. Special interests view campaign contributions as investments, and candidates know that without them, their own stock is likely to fall. As a result, special interests distort market decisions and receive many of the dividends to which the public is entitled—the core premise of Mancur Olson's classic book *The Rise and Decline of Nations.* Of course, not all subsidies are bad: public money can reduce pollution, expand health care, build essential transportation infrastructure, and invest in long-term research and development. But as a rule, minimizing market distortions leads to greater overall efficiency.

◄○► *Maximize accountability.* Corporate executives and board members serve shareholders whose private interests they rightly seek to maximize; elected officials serve citizens whose public interests they are supposed to protect. If shareholders are unsatisfied with a company's performance, they may take their money elsewhere. But what can voters do if *both* candidates in a campaign depend on special-interest money?

◄○► *Promote open markets.* In economic markets, we trade goods; in political markets, we trade ideas. In both, trade flourishes when barriers to entry are low and the cost of competition is affordable. The escalating cost of political campaigns is largely attributable to the high cost of TV advertising. For most would-be challengers, demand for the dollars to pay for political commercials is far outstripping supply, and thus many decide that they cannot compete in the political market.

➤◄◦► *Ensure market integrity.* When citizens lack confidence in the integrity of the nation's financial system, they put their money under their mattresses. When they lack confidence in the integrity of the nation's political system, they stay home on election day. It's time for change—for good.

Solutions

Both Republicans and Democrats came to agree that the problem with welfare was not necessarily the result of bad people but of a very bad system that—by paying more if a recipient had no work and no husband—discouraged employment and marriage. Ditto campaign finance. The sin is the *system.* How else can we explain how such provably honorable people as John Glenn, Alan Cranston, and John McCain felt it necessary to go to bat for the likes of a big, sleazy contributor like Charles Keating?

A comprehensive campaign finance reform program is ideally suited to achieve the conservative goals on which our economy and society are built—competition, efficiency, accountability, open markets, and market integrity. Specifically, four reforms would restore our electoral democracy by elevating voters over donors: spending limits, public financing, a restructured enforcement agency, and free broadcast time and mailings.

Buckley Must Be Overturned

Limits on campaign spending are an integral part of restoring our democracy; Congress understood this fact when it included expenditure limits in the 1971 and 1974 campaign finance laws. Furthermore, the experience of the last quarter century has taught us that without caps on campaign spending to complement contribution limits, money will always find ways back into the system. But as long as *Buckley v. Valeo* remains the law, the courts are likely to strike down any attempts to place limits on campaign spending.

As discussed in chapter 3, the Court in *Buckley* concluded that expenditures did not raise the problem of corruption in the same way contributions did. The Court's conclusion is based on two critical errors: (1) subjecting expenditure limits to a higher standard than contribution limits, and (2) considering only the anticorruption rationale while dismissing the other interests.

Why should campaign expenditures be entitled to much greater constitutional protection than campaign contributions? Neither expenditures nor contributions actually are speech; both merely facilitate expressive activities. And the argument that contributions pose a greater danger of quid pro quo corruption than expenditures seems ridiculous on its face: Are we really to believe that a $2000 contribution to a candidate will create a greater sense of obligation than millions of dollars in independent expenditures for that candidate?

And what makes preventing quid pro quo corruption so much more important than any other governmental interest? Of course, it is unacceptable for public officials to sell votes, access, or influence to the highest bidder. Why? Not because of the quid pro quo–ness of it all; we exchange money for goods and services all the time in our daily lives. Rather, it is because the sale of our government undermines the most fundamental principles of our democracy: competitive elections, effective government, and—most important of all—the guarantee that our public officials answer to their true constituents, not a handful of wealthy benefactors. Quid pro quo arrangements are surely egregious violations of these democratic norms, but they are not the only ones.

Some may argue that any effort to overturn *Buckley* is a pipe dream; and that even if the Court reconsiders *Buckley*, it will adopt an even harsher position on campaign finance regulation. However, if and when the Court finally breaks from *Buckley*, it will not be the first time the Court has overruled a long-standing precedent on an important constitutional issue. Chapter 1 reminded us that, while it took a century, *Dred Scott* was overturned by *Brown v. Board of Education* in 1954. As campaign finance expert Josh Rosenkranz has written, "There is good reason to be more sanguine." Here are three reasons:

◄○► *Not your father's Supreme Court.* The composition of the Court has changed dramatically since 1976; of the eight justices who decided *Buckley,* only Chief Justice William H. Rehnquist remains on the Court. This Supreme Court did not decide *Buckley*; it has merely inherited it from its predecessors.

◄○► *Hindsight is 20/20.* This Court has the benefit of a quarter century's worth of hindsight upon which to make its rulings. Along with the rest of America, this Court has seen the steady climb of campaign spending and the debilitating effects of the current system on our government and our democracy.

◄○► *Fool us once, shame on you. Fool us twice, shame on us.* The judiciary may be particularly hesitant to repeat *Buckley's* mistake of not developing an adequate factual record. Recently, Justices Anthony M. Kennedy and Stephen Breyer have each stressed the importance of looking at the real-world consequences of *Buckley.* Indeed, in setting the schedule to hear the challenge to McCain-Feingold, the D.C. Circuit Court of Appeals chose a timetable that allows for enough time to gather evidence.

Of course, the Second Circuit Court of Appeals decision in *Landell v. Sorrell* lays out the argument—if the Supreme Court needs a nudge or a rationale—of why the current money chase has such a "pernicious" effect on our democracy (to use its word). Indeed, in its own recent decisions, the Court has gradually been distancing itself from the artificial distinction between contributions and expenditures, and from the view that preventing corruption is the only justification for regulation.

Justice John Paul Stevens—who had just joined the Supreme Court when *Buckley* was handed down but did not take part in deciding the case—has been the most vocal advocate of the pro-reform position. In 1996, in *Colorado Republican Federal Campaign Committee v. FEC,* Stevens argued that "all money spent by a political party to secure the election of its candidate . . . should be considered a 'contribution' to his or her campaign," regardless of whether the expenditure was classified as "coordinated" or "independent." And in 2000, he went even further, arguing opinion in *Nixon v. Shrink Missouri Government PAC* that "money is property; it is not speech."

Shrink Missouri also saw Justices Breyer and Ruth Bader Ginsburg call for a significant reinterpretation of *Buckley,* advocating "making less absolute the contribution/expenditure line." Alternatively, if *"Buckley* denies the political branches sufficient leeway to enact comprehensive solutions to the problems posed by campaign finance," Breyer wrote, "the Constitution would require us to reconsider *Buckley."*

The Court's more conservative justices have also rejected *Buckley's* distinction. Justices Clarence Thomas and Antonin Scalia argued in *Shrink Missouri*—and reiterated the next year in a follow-up decision to *Colorado Republican*—that contribution and expenditure limits should both be evaluated under so-called strict scrutiny. Although Justice Kennedy joined Thomas's dissent in the *Shrink* case in 2000, Kennedy noted that "for now . . . I would leave open the possibility that Congress, or a state legislature, might devise a system in which there are some limits on both expenditures and contributions."

Only Chief Justice Rehnquist and Justices Souter and Sandra Day O'Connor continue to express endorsement of *Buckley's* distinction between contributions and expenditures, although *Shrink Missouri* suggests that at the very least they are not deaf to the cause of reform.

Meanwhile, the Court has recently embraced a broader range of permissible justifications for regulation. In *Austin v. Michigan State Chamber of Commerce,* the Court—with Justices Thomas, Scalia,

Kennedy, and O'Connor dissenting—upheld restrictions on the electoral activities of corporations to prevent "the corrosive and distorting effects of immense aggregations of wealth that are accumulated with the help of the corporate form and that have little or no correlation to the public's support for the corporation's political ideas." In *Shrink Missouri*, the Court's majority—now joined by O'Connor—noted that the anticorruption interest was "not confined to bribery of public officials, but extend[ed] to the broader threat from politicians too compliant with the wishes of large contributors."

The "new corruption" discussed in *Austin* and *Shrink Missouri*—by broadening the anticorruption interest to include a concern about "large, unequal expenditures"—reflects, as Columbia University law professor Richard Briffault writes, "the intermittent tendency of 'corruption' to morph into 'inequality.'" Justice Breyer has similarly observed that *Buckley* "cannot be taken literally" when it apparently rejects the equality interest; on the contrary, preserving "the integrity of the electoral process" is, according to Breyer, a constitutionally protected interest militating for regulation. As New Jersey Justice Arthur Vanderbilt wrote in an epigraph to this chapter, it may take a year—or ten or fifty—but the sheer illogic and antidemocratic consequences of *Buckley* are so blatant that it will, eventually, be overturned.

As an alternative to the judicial route, Senator Fritz Hollings has proposed overturning *Buckley* through a constitutional amendment. His proposed amendment states that "Congress shall have power to set reasonable limits on the amount of contributions that may be accepted by, and the amount of contributions that may be made by, in support of, or in opposition to, a candidate for nomination for election to, or for election to, Federal office."

But to amend the Constitution, a proposal must gain a two-thirds majority in both houses and be ratified in three quarters of the states. As any of the proponents of the ill-fated Equal Rights Amendment can attest, this is a very tall order; there have been only seventeen successful amendments since the original Bill of Rights. In 2001, Hollings's proposal was voted down in the Senate, though it picked up 40 votes. Senator Feingold opposes the Hollings amendment on the grounds that we ought to make changes to the freedoms enshrined in the Bill of Rights not by amendment but rather through the Supreme Court. But if President Bush (or his successor) manages to fill the Supreme Court with more justices who don't care whether democracy is for sale and who have never run for office and so cannot understand the problem—thereby making it virtually impossible to overturn *Buckley* through the courts—Senator Hollings's proposal may become more urgent and feasible.

As of now, twenty-six state attorneys general, forty senators, and two hundred constitutional scholars are on record urging that *Buckley* be overturned. Their numbers will only grow as campaigning for money intensifies.

Enact Public Financing

Many conservatives say they oppose a spending ceiling because it reduces speech. But that's an argument they can't use against voluntary public financing, which *increases* speech by subsidizing bona fide candidates. The very first legislation to propose using public funds in presidential elections was introduced in 1904 by Representative William Bourke Cockran, Democrat of New York. Presciently, he believed that "it might be possible for the government of the U.S. to do away with any excuse for soliciting large subscriptions of money by using public funds instead." When conservatives try to oppose public financing on non-free speech grounds, they betray their dirty little secret—that their opposition is not constitutional but political. The guiding principle of conservative Republicans—such as Mitch McConnell, chair of the National Republican Senatorial Committee from 1997 to 2001—is not free speech but the very expensive speech they benefit from every election cycle.

Because public financing enhances speech, promotes competition, levels the playing field, and reduces reliance on special-interest money, it is *the* essential reform of the next generation—along with overturning *Buckley.* So the question is, what form of public financing? The full public financing programs of Arizona, Maine, and Vermont are very attractive, promising experiments. But few elections have been held under Clean Money laws, and the body of evidence supporting them is limited. Because Clean Money is still in its infancy, it's hard to see Congress adopting it in the near future, which is precisely the reason that the movement's founding organizers focused their initial efforts in the states. They understood that you have to walk before you can run.

The bill that stands the best chance of both appealing to members of Congress and re-creating the large, diverse coalition behind McCain-Feingold is one built on a law that already has bipartisan support: public funding of presidential candidates. Qualifying presidential candidates who agree to accept spending limits receive public matching funds in the primary election and a flat grant in general election. No one can argue that the system protects incumbents: three of five incumbent presidents have been defeated running under it. Nor can anyone argue that it violates conservative principles: as noted, Ronald Reagan accepted over $90 million in public funding in his three presidential bids.

From lessons learned in presidential, state, and local campaigns, public financing for congressional candidates should include the following elements:

A GENEROUS MATCHING RATE. At the presidential level, the matching fund program provides a dollar-for-dollar match up to the first $250 contributed. New York City has shown that by increasing the matching rate to 4 to 1, candidates with grassroots community support can rely on small contributions and still raise the money needed to run competitive campaigns.

Although matching-fund programs aren't intended to eliminate fund-raising, as Clean Money aims to do, they can provide the bulk of funds available to candidates. There is no perfect matching rate, but none has proven more effective than New York City's in accomplishing the chief goals of reform: elections that are more competitive and candidates who are less dependent on special interests. For this reason, the congressional matching rate for public funds should be set at 4 to 1, up to the first $250 contributed by individuals (or more if a rich opponent opts out). Contributions from PACs should not be matched, nor should out-of-state contributions.

If candidates raise all of their money in small contributions, they should be able to receive public funds in amounts up to two-thirds of the spending limit. Most candidates will raise some of their money in amounts exceeding $250, and thus the average candidate will receive less than two-thirds of his or her money in public funds. But the 4 to 1 match, resulting in grants up to two-thirds of the spending cap, protects candidates with broad-based support in low-income communities from being significantly outspent by rivals with better financial connections.

REASONABLE QUALIFYING THRESHOLDS. For candidates to receive public funds, they must raise enough money from enough local residents to prove their viability. How much is enough? The trick in setting thresholds is to set them high enough to exclude frivolous campaigns, but low enough to include serious grassroots contenders. In Los Angeles, where City Council districts are about 40 percent as large as the average congressional district, council candidates must raise $25,000 from a total of at least 100 different contributors to qualify for public funds, and only the first $250 of a contribution applies toward this threshold. A report by the Center for Governmental Studies found that the thresholds are "appropriately set."

A comprehensive report on campaign finance reform by Professor Richard Briffault and the New York City Bar Association recommends the same qualifying threshold for congressional candidates. For Senate races, the Briffault report recommends that the House threshold apply to candidates in states with only one congressional district, and that $10,000 be added for each district thereafter, up to a maximum threshold of $75,000. In state-level public financing programs, the qualifying threshold for gubernatorial candidates ranges from $35,000 in contribution increments up to $50 (Minnesota), to $300,000 in increments up to $500 (Kentucky).

In my view, a House candidate should raise at least $25,000 in donations of $250 or under to meet the threshold, which means attracting 100 to 200 contributors at least. For Senate races the Briffault formula is sound, though with a higher cap of $150,000 for large states. In states like California and New York, where high spending limits will allow candidates to qualify for millions of dollars in public funds, a $150,000 threshold—again, with only the first $250 of each contribution counting toward it—is not an unreasonable precondition for such a large public investment. To ensure that a candidate is supported by his or her own constituents and not merely outside interests, only contributions from a House candidate's district and a Senate candidate's state should count toward the threshold. These are fair standards. Frivolous candidates will not meet them; serious candidates will.

SPENDING LIMITS. Until *Buckley* falls and a spending cap is found constitutional, funding limits can only be encouraged by offering public funds to candidates who voluntarily accept them. Only spending limits can end the arms race for campaign cash and reduce the power of war chests that incumbents build to scare off competition. And only the combination of spending limits and public funds can level the political playing field.

Spending limits that are set too high tend to favor incumbents, because few others can raise the resources to compete with them. Limits that are set too low, however, also favor incumbents, since challengers need to spend enough to overcome the natural advantages that accrue to incumbents through years of constituent service, free media, and use of the franking privilege. So the porridge must not be too hot or too cold. When weighing these two considerations, a third must also be taken into account: incumbents and the well-connected will not voluntarily join a public financing program if they feel its spending limits are significantly below what they could otherwise raise. If limits are too low, so too will be participation rates, and the program's purposes will be seriously compromised.

Of these three considerations, two point toward higher spending limits, which suggests that it is better to err on the side of caution. The average House winner spent $842,245 in 2000; the average candidate who challenged an incumbent spent just $143,685. In 1988, only 22 House campaigns hit the million-dollar mark; in 2000, the number reached 176. To control costs without discouraging participation or diminishing a challenger's ability to compete, House candidates should be held to inflation-adjusted spending limits of $900,000–$450,000 each for the primary and general election. A strong argument may be made that a $900,000 limit, which memorializes a level of spending that is about the current average, does not do enough to suppress campaign spending. But to undercut opponents who will use inadequate spending limits as an excuse to oppose reform, and to ensure that challengers can spend at significant levels, it is in the reform coalition's best interests to support limits around the current average cost of a winning campaign. By definition, this amount can't be too low or too high if it's the average amount it takes to win.

Senate candidates should be able to spend $1 million, plus fifty cents for each voting-age person in the state—which would come to about $8 million (for the primary and general election combined) in New York State, $7 million in Florida, $5 million in Ohio and Pennsylvania, and $2 million in Arkansas—or about one-fourth to one-half of what's recently been spent in these states. But in comparison to House contests, Senate races have higher profiles and receive significantly more media attention, making it harder for incumbents to dominate. Consequently, spending limits lower than current averages will protect challengers from the war chests that Senate incumbents can build over six years, and still ensure—because of free media coverage—that challengers will have ample opportunity to get their message out.

For instance, in Michigan's 2000 Senate race Debbie Stabenow spent $8 million in her victory over incumbent Senator Spencer Abraham, who spent $ 14.5 million. Under the spending-limit formula just outlined, both candidates would have been held to about $5 million. Similarly, in Pennsylvania, a $5 million limit would have helped challenger Ron Klink, who was outspent by nearly $10 million in his losing 2000 campaign against incumbent Senator Rick Santorum.

Separate limits for the primary and general election ensure that the winner of a hard-fought primary will not be placed at a disadvantage by facing a general-election opponent who suffered no primary challenge. To ensure equity, of course, candidates without primary election opponents should be allowed to spend up to the limit in the primary election period, although no public funds should be given to candidates without serious opponents, whether in primary or general elections.

A BONUS PROVISION. Again, so long as *Buckley* is the constitutional standard, legislation cannot prevent the super-rich from spending tens of millions of dollars on their campaigns. We can, however, help their opponents by eliminating the spending limit. It is unfair to keep a lid on a nonrich candidate when his or her opponent effectively says the sky's the limit.

Florida's public financing program attacks the issue head-on: candidates whose opponents reject spending limits are entitled to a dollar-for-dollar match up to the amount spent by their opponent. In 1994, Jeb Bush did not participate in the state's public financing program and exceeded its $5 million spending limit by $4 million. As a result, his opponent, Governor Lawton Chiles, received several million dollars more in public funding that allowed him to equal Bush's spending. Many observers cited the law as an important factor in Chiles's reelection. Indeed, after the 1994 election swept Republicans to power in Florida's legislature, they refused to renew the program.

It is unfair, however, to expect taxpayers to underwrite a spending battle with a billionaire. Had Florida's law been in effect in New York City in 2001, it would have entitled the Democratic nominee for mayor (yours truly) to an additional $58 million in public funds—an obscene amount to ask the taxpayers to spend on one mayoral candidate, particularly in a time of financial crisis. Currently, in New York City, the bonus for candidates who face big spenders is a bump in the matching rate from 4 to 1 to 5 to 1, which meant an additional $700,000 under this provision. But, if a $58 million increase is too gargantuan, given a $74 million campaign, an amount equal to only 1 percent of that total was insignificant.

One reasonable solution in the future is the approach of Maine's Clean Money program, which offers a participating candidate his or her opponent's theoretical share of public funds, times two. So if a rich person opts out and spends $5 million in Maine or $75 million in New York City, the complying candidate in a general election could receive a bonus up to a maximum of $850,000 in Maine and $8.5 million in New York City—amounts that would make a challenger more competitive.

CONTRIBUTION LIMITS. The passage of McCain-Feingold increased the contribution limit from $1000 per election to $2000, the first such increase in nearly thirty years. If Congress enacts a public financing program, these limits should ideally be returned to their original level for House races and left to stand for Senate races, reflecting the different fund-raising demands of each office.

Admittedly, going back to a $1000 maximum in hard money gifts may be a nearly impossible goal politically. A more promising avenue may be to bring PAC limits in line with individual limits, or to limit the total that may be raised from PAC contributions, as Los Angeles does (although some might question the constitutionality of such a move). Limits on total PAC giving would diminish the relative importance of any one PAC contribution, because each could be theoretically replaced with another, and reduce the incumbent's "temptation" when weighing legislatively interested PAC money against his or her own better judgment.

As for self-financing candidates, the Committee for Economic Development recommends a reasonable limit on personal contributions of $25,000—or $50,000 per couple. And to avoid the obvious loophole, personal loans should be regulated so that loans not repaid by election day are considered contributions, and subject to penalty if they exceed contribution limits.

Minnesota prohibits PAC fund-raising while the legislature is in session, and New York governor George Pataki has proposed a ban on fund-raising within twenty-five miles of the state capitol when the legislature is in session. If such a ban is good for state capitals, why not for our nation's capital? At the very least, it would mean a more productive workweek for members of Congress, who would not be dashing off to fund-raising cocktail parties and dinners several nights a week.

FUND-RAISING BLACKOUTS. In 2001, the Los Angeles City Council passed a bill tightening the city's previously mentioned fund-raising ban from eighteen months prior to elections to twelve for City Council candidates, and from twenty-four months to eighteen months for citywide candidates. The bill, which contained other provisions, was vetoed by Mayor Jim Hahn, but the shorter time allowed for fund-raising is likely to be resurrected in future legislation.

Non-election-year contributions overwhelmingly favor incumbents, and they usually come from special interests seeking to exert influence on legislation, not from citizens seeking to aid a candidate's election campaign. For both reasons, a blackout is a good idea. In addition, a fund-raising blackout in the years before elections would ease the perpetual campaign that now characterizes American politics. "Twenty years ago, you basically ran a Senate campaign in the last year of your term, if not the last six to nine months," said Frank Greer, a Democratic political consultant. "Now, senators who are elected have to begin planning for their next campaign right away." Greer made this remark in 1989; since then, as described in chapter 5, things have only gotten worse. Much worse.

Incumbents are already the huge favorites in the arms and ads race, so why should they also have a head start? Putting everyone on the same starting line would ensure that incumbents don't get halfway to the finish line before challengers hear the gun go off. And the next time you listen to elected officials call reform an "incumbent protection act," call their office and ask if they support a fund-raising blackout.

CONTRIBUTION REFUNDS. Tax refunds for small contributions offer several significant benefits. First, they encourage citizen participation, by providing a big incentive to contribute. Second, they encourage candidates to pursue a more broad-based community fund-raising strategy, reenforcing the purpose of public matching funds. And last, they provide an enormous incentive to candidates who might otherwise not accept spending limits. Only contributions to candidates who accept spending limits should be eligible for refunds, a requirement that may be the best tool available for inducing incumbents to limit their spending.

Critics charge that the refunds will go to those who would have given anyway and will merely subsidize wealthy contributors—and may drain scarce public funds away from the major reform of a matching public-funds system. Consequently, any such refunds should be limited to those contributors who give no more than the refundable amount, increasing the likelihood that the benefit will accrue to low- and middle-income citizens who otherwise would not give.

Restructure the Federal Election Commission

They should call it the Federal Election Omission. It has created what Fred Wertheimer calls "an anything goes, Wild West–show attitude about compliance with campaign finance" laws. Washington needs a new sheriff—badly. Other jurisdictions, such as New York City, have proven that law-and-order elections are possible. Here's what a restructured FEC should look like:

A NONPARTISAN MANDATE. As previously shown, the FEC's bipartisan structure means that enforcement cases are heard by partisan judges protecting political interests. The result is often deadlock. If an elections enforcement agency is to have any credibility, it must have the capacity to make decisions and to do so in a nonpartisan manner. This requires an odd number of commissioners and an appointment process that is removed, to the fullest extent possible, from partisan politics.

However the agency is structured, those nominated to lead it ideally should be chosen from a list of qualified and experienced candidates selected by a group of retired federal judges. While there are real constitutional questions whether a president can be limited to such a list, surely he or she can voluntarily commit to choose from such a list as often happens with merit judicial appointments. The commissioners should be protected from removal by the president or Congress and should serve a specific nonrenewable term, further insulating the agency from political pressure. The FBI Director serves a ten-year term, and the members of the Federal Reserve Board of Governors serve fourteen-year terms. Both agencies are designed to be above partisan politics, and so should any election enforcement agency.

INDEPENDENCE. Congress has repeatedly sought to undermine the FEC by stripping its powers and cutting its budgets. The result is an agency so understaffed and underfunded that it has had great difficulty carrying out even its highly limited mandate. To avoid such retaliation, the FEC should have special budgetary protections to ensure sufficient funding, perhaps by making its budget a fixed proportion of campaign spending, or of the total budget that members of Congress set for their own offices. It should also have the authority to litigate independently of the Justice Department, and to represent itself before the U.S. Supreme Court, a power it lost in the 1980s.

AUDIT AND ENFORCE. As Brooks Jackson noted, when Congress stripped the FEC of its authority to conduct random audits in 1979, it "put itself on the honor system." Congress never intended the honor system to work—and it hasn't. To restore a culture of respect for the law, it is essential for the FEC to have the authority to conduct random audits. Moreover, any penalties assessed after the election are meaningless to voters and nearly so to candidates. Real-time penalties assessed during an election would serve as an important deterrent to would-be violators of the law and provide voters with information about serious violations. Give the FEC the power to penalize violations—and candidates will comply more diligently.

THE POWER TO REVIEW, REFINE, AND RECOMMEND. The nature of competition is to seek advantage, and thus the search for loopholes will always be with us. As loopholes arise, however, it is the job of the FEC to close them, not codify them as it has so frequently done. Some loopholes can be closed by administrative decisions; others require statutory changes. In New York City, the City Charter requires that the Campaign Finance Board, following every citywide election, study the law's impact and make recommendations for change to the mayor and City Council. In this way, the law can rapidly adapt to changes in the political environment. A newly reconstituted FEC should be required to analyze the law's record of performance after each presidential election cycle, and submit legislative recommendations to Congress.

While there is an immediate need for each of these changes, it would multiply with public financing. With public dollars at stake, it would be absolutely critical to create an enforcement agency capable of, and dedicated to, protecting the treasury against fraud and abuse. Without such an agency, citizen support for public financing will quickly evaporate into an atmosphere fouled by a new breed of corruption scandal: the misuse of public campaign funds.

Free Broadcast Time and Mailings

The airwaves belong to us, the public. We provide broadcasters with federal licenses—for free—on the condition that they agree to serve "the public interest, convenience, and necessity." They have not lived up to their end of the bargain.

How have they gotten away with it? (You'll never guess.) The powerful broadcast industry vehemently opposes reforms affecting their bottom lines. The industry gave $6.8 million to candidates and parties in the presidential election year of 2000, with half coming in soft money. Their annual largesse has allowed them to skirt their public duty, and then some: despite a thirty-year-old law designed to hold down campaign ad rates, broadcasters routinely gouge candidates, as detailed in chapter 3. When the Senate included a provision in McCain-Feingold to close the loophole that allows for such price gouging, the industry went on the attack, showering both parties with hard and soft money. Their efforts paid off: the House stripped the provision from Shays-Meehan and the loophole remains.

Why is the broadcast industry unwilling to live up to its public service obligations? In the 2000 elections, broadcasters pulled down revenue from political commercials that approached $1 billion. Reducing that revenue would mean cutting into profit margins that average between 30 and 50 percent. So it makes perfect business sense for the industry to invest a relatively minute amount in contributions to candidates and parties, because the payoff is astronomical. Dan O'Connor, the general sales manager of WSYT-TV in Syracuse, New York, put it this way: Ad buyers for candidates "call you up and say, 'Can you clear $40,000 [in TV ad time] next week?' It's like, 'What? Am I dreaming? Of course I can clear that!' And they send you a check in the mail overnight. It's like Santa Claus came to town. It's a beautiful thing."

Paul Taylor, executive director of the Alliance for Better Campaigns, a nonpartisan group that advocates for free airtime, sums up the scam this way: "Let's follow the bouncing ball. Our government gives broadcasters free licenses to operate on the public airwaves on the condition that they serve the public interest. During the campaign season, broadcasters turn around and sell access to these airwaves to candidates at inflated prices. Meanwhile, many candidates sell access to the government in order to raise special-interest money to purchase access to the airwaves. It's a wonderful arrangement for the broadcasters, who reap windfall profits from political campaigns. It's a good system for incumbents, who prosper in the big-dollar, high-ante political culture of paid speech. But it's a lousy deal for the rest of us."

Walter Cronkite, the iconic American newsman, is chairman of the Alliance for Better Campaigns. According to Cronkite, "In the land of free speech, we've permitted a system of 'paid speech' to take hold during the political campaigns on the one medium we all own—our broadcast airwaves. It's long past time to turn that around. Free airtime would help free our democracy from the grip of the special interests." That's the way it is, and even Senator Mitch McConnell, the self-described Darth Vader of campaign finance reform, agrees that the broadcasters are not giving the public a fair shake. And for the rest of the world, this is a no-brainer. "America is almost alone among the Atlantic democracies in declining to provide political parties free prime time on television during elections," writes historian Arthur Schlesinger Jr. "[If it did so], it could do much both to bring inordinate campaign costs under control and revitalize the political parties."

It's time for electronic consumers to negotiate a better deal with those we give free licenses to. Cronkite's alliance is pushing an innovative and market-based proposal—first discussed in a 1982 monograph from the Democracy Project, *Independent Expenditures in Congressional Campaigns: The Electronic Solution*—that would provide free broadcast vouchers to candidates and parties. Here's how it would work: Qualifying candidates who win their parties' nominations would receive vouchers for use in their general election campaigns. Candidates, particularly those from urban areas who don't find it cost-effective to advertise on television or radio, could trade their vouchers to their party in exchange for funds to pay for direct mail or other forms of communication. Parties, in turn, could use the vouchers themselves or give them to other candidates. The system creates a market for broadcast vouchers that, because of pricing incentives, ensures their efficient distribution.

A comprehensive campaign finance reform program should provide candidates with a right of access to the public airwaves. Until then, the alliance's voucher proposal should be restricted to those candidates who accept spending limits. Whether vouchers were used for airtime or exchanged for party monies for direct mail, candidates would report them as expenditures. Under such a system, spending limits would retain their integrity. The value of the vouchers should be set at $250,000 for House candidates and vary by population for Senate candidates, with candidates in midsize states receiving up to $2.5 million in vouchers. As in public financing, candidates should be required to reach contribution thresholds to qualify for vouchers.

One might argue that vouchers would simply encourage the proliferation of slickly produced thirty-second advertisements. Yet the reality, for better or worse, is that political commercials are part of elections in America, and there's little chance that will change. The voucher proposal bows to that reality, but it also offers hope: candidates who accept the vouchers should be required to feature their own voices in at least 50 percent of all their ads—whether paid for by vouchers, private contributions, or public funds. There is a growing public distaste for anonymous negative advertising, and candidates, given free access to the airwaves, should be held accountable for their ads.

And there are other ways to promote civic discourse. Cronkite's alliance has put forth a complement to its voucher proposal, called "Voters' Time," that would require broadcasters to air a minimum of two hours a week of candidate discussion in the month preceding every election. At least half of the programs would have to be aired in prime time or drive time, and the formats—debates, interviews, town hall meetings—would be of the broadcasters' choosing. A voters' time requirement is necessary, because broadcasters are airing less and less campaign news and candidate discourse.

In the 2000 election campaign, despite the closest presidential election in a generation, ABC, CBS, and NBC devoted 28 percent less time to campaign coverage than in 1988. In a nationwide survey conducted two days prior to the 2000 elections, more than half the population could not answer basic questions about Bush's and Gore's positions on the issues. There are many factors contributing to that result, but two of them—the domination of election by big money interests, and the unwillingness of the broadcast industry to be a part of the solution—can be cured.

Mandating free airtime for candidates and candidate discussion would appropriately hold broadcasters to a minimal standard of what it means, under the Federal Communications Commission Act, to serve "the public interest, convenience, and necessity." But this will require a committed Congress standing up to an unusually powerful industry, one that gives big contributions and confers access to voters via the airwaves.

At a minimum, two other useful methods of encouraging civic discourse and facilitating candidate communication should be part of any reform bill. First, candidates who accept public funds should be required to debate. Kentucky, New Jersey, Los Angeles, and New York City all require debates of publicly funded candidates. Especially when the public has invested its money in public campaigns, it deserves to see the candidates in public face-to-face meetings. In March 2000, Al Gore proposed that he and George W. Bush eliminate campaign television advertisements and instead hold issue debates twice a week until the elections. Bush declined, but a CBS News poll showed that voters responded positively, with 65 percent calling it a "good idea."

Second, cities like New York and Seattle mail a voters' guide to registered voters before elections. The guides include candidate statements and biographical information, as well as information on voting. New York City's guide costs fifty cents a copy to publish and mail, a bargain by any standard. The federal government should do the same. Or it could create and promote a Web-based guide to serve as a clearinghouse for candidate and election information. Before voting, citizens could log on to the site, read statements by federal candidates, and find out information about their polling stations. In the age of information technology, democracy should not be left behind.

EPILOGUE: "IMAGINE..."

Dateline: October 1, 2008

Now that it's three years since the Supreme Court in 2005 upheld the Durbin-Shays campaign finance law of 2004—enacted after former Presidents Ford, Carter, Bush, and Clinton in an unprecedented joint statement agreed that "America deserves elections, not auctions"—we at DemocracyWorks *magazine believe it's time for an appraisal.*

The law—called "F&C" by its supporters, for "floors and ceilings"—made three major changes to the federal campaign finance laws. It built a floor under bona fide congressional candidates by providing (a) matching public funds for contributions up to $250 and (b) vouchers for candidates to convert into either 30 minutes of free TV ads or five free districtwide mailings; and (c) it built a ceiling over candidates by enacting an expenditure cap that the U.S. Supreme Court upheld in a 5–4 decision written by Justices Anthony Kennedy and Sandra Day O'Connor.

"We reverse the Buckley *decision," they wrote, "because the Court originally erred by not realizing the grossly undemocratic consequences that inevitably flowed from most candidates' living with contribution limits while those with great wealth—or great access to lobbyists eager to contribute—could spend unlimited amounts in a system where bigger spenders win 94 percent of the time. We were so concerned with corrupting contributions, which we rightly restricted, that we ignored the corrupting influence of the financial arms race, which a quarter century of experience has now exposed.*

"With ample expenditure limits, now both rich and average citizens can compete for high office based more on merit than money, since the public financing and free TV aspects of the law assure that all sides are heard.

How would it advance First Amendment values—which Judge Learned Hand wrote were based on 'the multiplicity of tongues'—if one side merely outspends and hence outshouts the other?

"If we did not take this step, we would be effectively condoning races that allowed one sprinter a 40-yard lead in a 100-yard dash. If we did not take this step, we'd be elevating the First Amendment right of a wealthy few to spend exorbitantly over the First Amendment rights of millions of citizens. If we did not take this step, then soon a Bill Gates could send not a piece of literature but a car with his name on it to every voter in the Iowa caucuses, and in his victory speech intone that 'the people have spoken.' "

The results of the law and ruling were immediately seen in the 2006 midterm elections. While only 25 seats had been truly competitive in 2004 (i.e., the margin of victory was under 10 percentage points and the winner did not outspend the loser by 2–1 or more), that number grew dramatically to 91 in 2006. And according to a Roll Call *survey, the percentage of time candidates spend fund-raising fell from 53 percent to 30 percent—and the percentage of all funds from $1000 or over donors fell by half owing to the encouragement of small gifts.*

DemocracyWorks *has found two participants in politics who believe they were helped by—and two who believe they were hurt by—the Durbin-Shays law and Kennedy-O'Connor decision:*

Susan Connolly *fell in love with politics and history listening to speeches by the late Congresswoman Barbara Jordan while a high school student in Ashtabula, Ohio, before going on to Ohio State University and Georgetown Law School.*

"I always dreamed of holding elective office to work on disability issues—my dad was confined to a wheelchair after a factory accident—but I assumed it was an impossible dream, since we weren't rich or connected to rich people," said the thirty-five-year-old Connolly in her campaign headquarters. "But with Durbin-Shays, I was able to raise enough public and matching funds from my network of school friends, church members, and fellow public interest lawyers—and knew no one could simply swamp me 10 to 1 at the end. And here I am, in a dead-heat race for the House against a five-term incumbent! Only in America."

Representative Bill Rodan *from California voted against Durbin-Shays but now lauds its impact. "As a Republican, I hated the idea of wasting taxpayer money on politicians. But now that I know I'll raise the maximum allowed, I'm not tempted to put my beliefs in escrow when the auto industry threatens to withdraw support if I vote for less-polluting cars. Now I campaign more, sit in a room dialing for dollars less, and can kick winking lobbyists out of my office since I don't need their tainted money to win. Congress really changed once the law passed and members understood this shift in power.*

"Remember that Yankees announcer Mel Allen, who would say in the 1950s 'Going, going, gone!' whenever someone hit a home run? Well, I can imagine him saying "Going, going" about our democracy—until Durbin-Shays made a leaping catch at the wall to save the game."

Harold Bayer *was angry. "I made my money legally and honorably," said the industrialist, whose fabric firm was number one in sales in the country for each of the past two years. "Why can't I spend my money my way? I had planned on running against Representative Rodan because we should run government more like a business.*

"And being a bottom-line businessman, my consultants and I figured that $3 million would be enough to drive up his negatives so he wouldn't be electable. But now that individuals can't spend more than $100,000 on their own campaigns, I'm not running. In 2004, I'd have run and won. But in 2008 there's no point."

Gus Vincent Bender *has been the PAC director at the American Petroleum Institute since its PAC took off in 1982. "Boy, have things changed. A decade ago I could get an appointment within a week with nearly any member—and I'd go to an average of three cocktail parties a night in the spring of an election year," he said, looking nostalgic and rueful.*

"But Durbin-Shays changed all that. Because candidates only need to raise the maximum allowed or the expenditure ceiling—and not a multiple of their opponent—we're getting fewer meetings and fewer invitations. The arms race mentality is over. And so is our advantage. God, how I miss the good old days."

ACKNOWLEDGMENTS

No book is an island.

In a sense *Selling Out* has been thirty years in the making, the culmination of both my investigative research and personal campaigning. What I learned from a decade working as a public interest lawyer in Washington in the 1970s, to a decade as the head of the Democracy Project and a decade plus as a New York City official—and of course six election campaigns—has provided me with a certain inside-out perspective on this subject.

So thank you, Ralph Nader, Gary Hart, David Dinkins, Bill Clinton, and innumerable other colleagues who educated me about the links between politics, business, and government. And over the past six months, six brilliant young scholars and researchers have been indispensable to producing *Selling Out:* Frank Barry, William Parker Baxter, Kevin Huyge, Ben Seigel, and Steve Yuhan—and, most significantly, the book's chief researcher, Blake Zeff. Any mistakes are mine and any credit must be shared.

A special thanks goes to Eric Alterman, since the idea for this book emerged from his commiserating at lunch with me in late 2001.

I am indebted to Dean John Sexton—and then Dean Ricky Revesz and Vice Dean Steve Gillers—for providing me a perfect environment to develop and write this book during my appointment as a Distinguished Visiting Lecturer at the New York University School of Law. Nor could this book have existed without the institutional support and home provided by the New Democracy Project, relaunched in mid-2002 by the author and a forty-six-member advisory board including, among others, David Boies and Russell Simmons.

Michelle Morazan, Linda Yunuzzi, Laura DeCarava, Leslie Jenkins, and Lina Perl were always upbeat associates, helping to produce and vet the manuscript. And I appreciate the valuable time provided by so many elected officials, on or off the record, as well as the special assistance of the offices of Representative Henry Waxman and Representative Carolyn Maloney (especially Ed Mills). Nor could the book have been completed without the special help and insights of people at Common Cause and Public Citizen.

I am hugely grateful for the time and care of three close friends and campaign finance experts who read drafts and offered invaluable suggestions: Joan Claybrook, John Siegel, and Michael Waldman. Complementing them was the advice of two colleagues and scholars of campaign finance issues, Professors Rick Pildes and Richard Briffault, of the New York University and Columbia University law schools respectively.

Of course, Judith Regan's and Cal Morgan's reputations as entrepreneurial and editing geniuses, respectively, were vindicated based on their contributions to this book. Their skill and smarts are appreciated—and were needed.

Finally, any book requires a large dose of something else to exist and excel—love. The love that allows creativity to flourish and hurdles to be leapt. I can't imagine a family more loving, supportive, and encouraging than mine, especially when the husband/father went directly from a political campaign to a writing campaign. Deni, Jenya, and Jonah, this is your book too, since you've also lived it.

Mark Green
August 2002

NOTES

1. The Evil of Access: An Introduction

1 **Shannon exchanges**: Interview with Rep. Shannon, May 1983.

3 **LBJ emerging**: Caro, Robert A., *Master of the Senate*. New York: Alfred A. Knopf, 2002; conversation with Caro, August 5, 2002.

3 **"political money from Enrons"**: Interview with Joan Claybrook, April 19, 2002.

4 **Skyrocketing prices of winning seats**: In 2002 dollars, $87,000 for a House seat in 1976 is $275,000 and $609,000 for a Senate seat is $1.9 million. So in real dollars, spending more than tripled from 1976 to 2000. Center for Responsive Politics, www.opensecrets.org; the Inflation Calculator, http://www.westegg.com/inflation/.

4 **"We're all tainted"**: Interview with Sen. McCain, May 9, 2002.

5 **Cheney-Lay meetings**: Nichols, John, "ENRON: What Dick Cheney Knew," *The Nation*, April 15, 2002, p. 14.

5 **"will pursue wrongdoers"**: Haigh, S., "Vice President Calls for Corporate Responsibility," AP wire story, July 15, 2002.

6 **Whitehead event**: Dicker, Fred, "Pay to Play: Ground Zero Czar Under Fire for GOP Fundraiser," *New York Post*, October 23, 2002, p. 1.

6 **Tobacco story**: Horner, Blair, and M. Stern, *Blowing Away the Smokescreen: The Case Against Big Tobacco*. New York: New York Public Interest Research Group, 2002, pp. 9–14.

7 ***Washington Post* and Norquist**: VanderHei, J., "GOP Monitoring Lobbyists' Politics," *Washington Post*, June 10, 2002, p. A1; "Reid Urges Bush to Condemn GOP Monitoring of Lobbyists," *Washington Post*, June 11, 2002, p. A5.

11 **Crain's analysis**: Lentz, Philip, "Election Day Attack on New York Unmakes Mayor Green," *Crain's New York Business*, March 4, 2002, p. 9.

11 **Garth's 16 points**: Siegel, Joel, "Feuding Pol Advisers in New Face-off," New York *Daily News*, January 14, 2002.

11 **"You know, we always talked"**: Cooper, Michael, "At $92.60 a Vote, Bloomberg Shatters an Election Record," *New York Times,* December 4, 2001, p. A1.

11 **Cunningham observation:** Ibid.

11 **" 'anemic' war-chest"**: Danis, Kirsten, "Mark His Words: Green to Pen Book on Politic$," *New York Post,* February 15, 2002, p. 9.

11 **"Buckley and very expensive campaigns"**: Green, Mark, "Financing Campaigns," *New York Times,* December 14, 1980, sec. 4, p. 21.

13 **First investigated pay scales**: Green, Mark, and Ralph Nader, "Crime in the Suites," *New Republic,* April 29, 1973, p. 17; Green, Mark, "Crime Up in Big Business Too, SEC Discovers," *New York Times,* May 11, 1975, p. 5; Green, Mark, "Richer Than All Their Tribe," *New Republic,* January 6 and 13, 1982, p. 23; Green, Mark, and John Berry. "The Waste of Fraud and Abuse," in *The Challenge of Hidden Profits,* New York: William Morrow, 1985, p. 254.

13 **Krugman and Phillips**: Krugman, Paul, "Plutocracy and Politics," *New York Times,* June 14, 2002, p. 37; Rich, Frank, "All the President's Enrons," *New York Times,* July 6, 2002, p. A13.

14 **"I view money . . ."**: Interview with Carl Levin, May 1, 2002.

14 **Maloney and NRA**: Interview with Carolyn Maloney, April 13, 2002.

15 **"I can't think"**: Rosenkranz, Josh, *Buckley Stops Here.* New York: Brennan Center for Justice, New York University School of Law, 1998, p. 63.

16 **"because Democrats become dependent"**: Reich, Robert, "Yes: Blame Election Funds," *New York Times,* October 12, 1989, p. A29.

16 **Democracy 21**: *Democracy Protection Money II: Corporate America's Top Soft Money Givers Over the Past Decade,* July 12, 2002.

17 **"Elite opinion is"**: Kettner, Robert, "A Tipping Point?," *American Prospect,* May 6, 2002, p. 3.

18 **"The problem with"**: Interview with Ellen Miller, April 19, 2002.

21 **" 'Values' can mean"**: Quoted in "Enron Values," *The Nation,* February 25, 2002, p. 3.

21 **"I felt like I needed"**: As related in an interview with Russ Feingold, May 3, 2002.

21 **"House members never"**: Schmitt, Mark, *Between McCain-Feingold and the Democratic Ideal: A Commentary on Campaign Finance Reform for Funders and Others.* Open Society Institute, March 2002.

22 **Tocqueville comments**: Quoted in Pildes, Richard, and Ricky Reverz, *Faculty Worship: When Is Forequality Perceived as an Injury? Tocqueville's Hypothesis Reconsidered.* New York: NYU Law School, March 25, 2002.

23 **"Winning McCain-Feingold"**: Interview with Fred Wertheimer, April 19, 2002.

24 **"freedom not to grovel"**: Editorial, "Sneak Attack on Campaign Finance," *New York Times,* June 3, 1985, p. A18.

25 **Jefferson to Washington**: Discussed in Greider, William, *Who Will Tell the People?* New York: Simon & Schuster, 1992, p. 246.

2. The History of Money in Politics

27 **"An honest politician"**: Mellen, Joan, "An Historic Inn in Pennsylvania," *New York Times,* September 15, 1985, p. 18.

27 **"Follow the money"**: Newfield, Jack, "Give Pataki Credit for Doing Nothing So Well," *Newsday,* August 1, 2002, p. A39.

27 **800,000 citizens**: Thayer, George, *Who Shakes the Money Tree? American Campaign Financing Practices from 1789 to the Present.* New York: Simon & Schuster, 1973, p. 25.

27 **Property requirements for office**: Zinn, Howard, *A People's History of the United States, 1492–Present.* New York: HarperCollins, 1995, p. 81.

28 **"Swilling the planters with Bumbo"**: Sydnor, Charles S., "Swilling the Planters with Bumbo," reprinted in Martin, James K., ed., *Interpreting Colonial America.* New York: Harper and Row, 1978, p. 348.

28 **Treating**: Overracker, Louise, *Money in Elections.* New York: Macmillan, 1932, p. 17.

29 **Washington's alcohol expenses**: Sydnor, "Swilling," p. 355. This practice is still popular today. During the 2000 Republican National Convention, House Majority Leader Richard Armey spent $400,000 on an extravagant gala featuring country music stars Brooks and Dunn.

29 **Washington's victory**: Clark, Harrison, *All Cloudless Glory: The Life of George Washington from Youth to Yorktown.* Washington, D.C.: Regnery Publishing, 1995, p. 129. See also Thayer, p. 75.

29 **Both friends and enemies**: Sydnor, "Swilling," p. 357.

29 **"I am extremely thankful"**: G. Washington to J. Wood, July 1758, on-line at the Library of Congress, http://memory.loc.gov/cgi-in/query/r?ammem/mgw:@field(DOCID+@lit(gw020174)).

29 **"the usage for the candidates"**: Ketcham, Ralph, *James Madison.* New York: Macmillan, 1971, p. 77.

30 **Burr's tactics**: Thayer, *Who Shakes,* p. 27.

30 **Party newspapers**: Alexander, Herbert E., *Financing Politics.* Washington, D.C.: CQ Press, 1984, pp. 5–6.

31 **Early election costs**: Dinkin, Robert J., *Campaigning in America.* New York: Greenwood Press, 1989, p. 40.

31 **"To pay money"**: Troy, Gil, "Money and Politics: The Oldest Connection," *Wilson Quarterly,* on-line at http://wwics.si.edu/OUTREACH/WQ/WQSELECT/TROY.HTM.

31 **Jackson campaigning**: Dinkin, *Campaigning,* pp. 42–43.

31 **Jacksonian patronage**: Thayer, *Who Shakes,* pp. 28–29; also Dinkin, *Campaigning,* p. 33.

31 **Six percent contribution**: Thayer, *Who Shakes,* pp. 28–29.

32 **Campaign developments**: Dinkin, *Campaigning,* pp. 32–33.

32 **Publicity campaign**: Thayer, *Who Shakes,* p. 29.

32 **"one of the greatest struggles"**: President Andrew Jackson's fifth State of the Union address, 1883, available on-line at http://odur.let.rug.nl/~usa/P/aj7/speeches/ajson5.htm.

32 **The price of a vote**: Thayer, *Who Shakes*, p. 29.

32 **Repeat voters**: Overracker, *Money*, p. 31.

33 **Lincoln campaign expenses**: Thayer, *Who Shakes*, pp. 32–33.

33 **"If we could demonstrate"**: Shannon, Jasper B., *Money and Politics*. New York: Random House, 1959, pp. 22–24.

33 **"in the near future a crisis approaching"**: Hertz, Emanuel, *Abraham Lincoln: A New Portrait*, vol. 2. New York: Viking Press, 1931, p. 954.

34 **Elections of 1868 and 1872**: Shannon, *Money and Politics*, pp. 25–26.

34 **"There is looming up a new and dark power"**: Ibid., pp. 34–35.

35 **Black Horse Cavalry**: Thayer, *Who Shakes*, p. 36.

35 **"I was a Republican"**: Troy, *Money.*

35 **Cameron bribe**: Thayer, *Who Shakes*, p. 44.

35 **"A regularly constituted agency"**: Ibid.

36 **Buying Senate seats**: Shannon, *Money and Politics*, p. 34.

36 **Millionaire senators**: Simon, R., "Income Disclosure Reports Reaffirm Senate's Rich Heritage," *Los Angeles Times*, June 12, 1999.

36 **"squeeze bills"**: Thayer, *Who Shakes*, p. 41.

36 **"I think I can say"**: Ibid.

36 **Vote buying**: Shannon, *Money and Politics*, pp. 32–34.

36 **Political machines**: Dinkin, *Campaigning*, p. 72.

37 **Tammany Hall assessment**: Overracker, *Money*, pp. 101–102.

37 **Pendleton Act**: Dinkin, *Campaigning*, p. 73.

37 **Boise Penrose**: Thayer, *Who Shakes*, p. 47.

38 **Standard Oil's returned contribution**: Overracker, *Money*, p. 33.

38 **1896 campaign**: Thayer, *Who Shakes*, p. 47.

38 **Hanna's scruples**: Overracker, *Money*, p. 33.

39 **"the politics of the country"**: Ibid.

39 **McKinley assassination**: Dinkin, *Campaigning*, p. 116; also Morris, E., *Theodore Rex.* New York: Random House, 2001, p. 30.

40 **Needed funds**: Morris, *Theodore Rex*, p. 359.

40 **TR and corporate contributions**: Thayer, *Who Shakes*, p. 52.

41 **"They are in a hole"**: Morris, *Theodore Rex*, p. 359.

41 **Depew scandal**: Overracker, *Money*, pp. 234–35.

41 **"Sooner or later"**: Morris, *Theodore Rex*, pp. 360–61.

41 **Vote buying**: Overracker, *Money*, pp. 32–33.

42 **"That is naturally what is involved"**: Thayer, *Who Shakes*, p. 53.

42 **"The need for collecting"**: Corrado, Anthony, *A History of Federal Campaign Finance Law*, on-line at http://www.brook.edu/gs/cf/sourcebk01/HistoryChap.pdf.

42 **Buying Senate seats**: Thayer, *Who Shakes,* pp. 54–55.

43 **1920 campaign**: Ibid., p. 57.

44 **Smith scandal**: Shannon, *Money and Politics,* p. 51, and Thayer, *Who Shakes,* p. 64.

44 **Vare campaign**: Thayer, *Who Shakes,* p. 63.

45 **1928 platforms**: Shannon, *Money and Politics,* p. 53.

45 *For Roosevelt Before Chicago*: Thayer, *Who Shakes,* p. 69.

45 **"The problem with the Democrats"**: Ibid.

46 **"economic royalists"**: Dinkin, *Campaigning,* pp. 151–52.

46 **1936 election**: Ibid., p. 140.

46 **Labor money**: Shannon, *Money and Politics,* p. 54.

46 **Convention ads**: Alexander, *Financing Politics,* p. 81.

46 **The Hatch Act**: Dinkin, *Campaigning,* pp. 142–43.

46 **The first PAC**: Ibid., p. 143.

47 **Fund-raising dinners**: Alexander, *Financing Politics,* p. 58.

47 **Radio spending**: Ibid., pp. 10–12.

48 **Television explosion**: "The History of Television," available on-line at: http://inventors.about.com/gi/dynamic/offsite.htm?site=http://www.rcc.ryerson.ca/schools/rta/brd038/clasmat/class1/tvhist. htm.

48 **Media spending**: Alexander, *Financing Politics,* p. 13.

48 **Sham issue ads**: "Buying Time," available on-line at http://www.brennancenter.org/programs/buyingtime2000.html.

48 **Campaign spending**: Nelson, Candice J., "Spending in the 2000 Elections," available on-line at http://www.brook.edu/gs/cf/Financing2000/ch02.pdf.

48 **Fat cats**: Alexander, *Financing Politics,* p. 59; Dinkin, *Campaigning,* p. 176; Thayer, *Who Shakes,* p. 106; and Adamany, David W., and George E. Agree, *Political Money.* Baltimore: Johns Hopkins University Press, 1991, p. 45.

49 **Self-financing**: Thayer, *Who Shakes,* p. 83.

49 **Bathroom deal**: Ibid., p. 91.

49 **"would not consider campaign contributions"**: Remarks at the Alfred E. Smith Memorial Dinner during the 1960 campaign, available on-line at http://www.chariscorp-wordgems.com/leadership.jfk.smith.html.

50 **Campaign Commission**: *Dollar Politics,* 3rd edition. Washington, D.C.: Congressional Quarterly, Inc., 1982.

51 **"there is not a Member of Congress"**: "Guide to the U.S. Congress," *Congressional Quarterly,* 1971, p. 488.

51 **Reporting requirement**: *Dollar Politics,* p. 676.

51 **FECA details**: Alexander, *Financing Politics,* pp. 35–36.

51 **Revenue act**: Ibid., pp. 37–38.

52 **Conduit system**: Thayer, *Who Shakes,* pp. 112–13.

52 **"Watergate is not"**: *Congressional Quarterly's Guide to U.S. Elections,* 2001, p. 14.

52 **Watergate money**: Ibid., pp. 110–11.

52 **Woodward and Bernstein**: Their articles on-line at http://www.washingtonpost. com/wp-srv/national/longterm/watergat e/articles/101072-1.htm.
52 **Pre-*Buckley* law**: Adamany, *Political Money,* p. 48.

3. Rules and Laws

55 **"Politics has gotten so expensive"**: Gunter, Linda, "Political Bill of Fare: What's on the Menu," *Birmingham Business Journal,* October 1990, p. 8.
55 **"[Buckley is] one of the most weakly reasoned"**: Green, Mark J., "Take the Money and Reform: Breaking a $3,000-a-Day Habit," *The New Republic,* May 14, 1990, p. 27.
55 **"You're more likely to see"**: Mitchell, Alison, "Bill to Overhaul Campaign Finance Survives in House," *New York Times,* August 1, 1998, p. A1.
55 **Buckley's section of 1974 law**: 2 U.S.C., sec. 437h.
56 **"Depended on a few people"**: Eisele, Albert, "Buckley, as in 'Buckley v. Valeo,'" Speaks Out," *The Hill,* March 28, 2001.
56 **"Initial credibility that gets the attention"**: Ibid.
56 **Valeo at the Supreme Court**: Keller, Amy, "Who Is Frank Valeo?" *Roll Call,* September 14, 1998; also "20 Years Later, Buckley and Valeo Still Disagree on Campaign Reform," *The Hill,* April 16, 1997.
56 **Fact-finding process**: Neuborne, Burt, *Campaign Finance Reform and the Constitution: A Critical Look at Buckley v. Valeo,* 1997, p. 2.
56 **Timing of lawsuit**: Homet, Roland S., Jr., "Fact-Finding in First Amendment Litigation: The Case of Campaign Finance Reform," *Oklahoma City University Law Review,* Spring 1996.
57 **"It takes the better part"**: Ibid.
57 **Opinion by committee**: Schwartz, Bernard, "Curiouser and Curiouser: The Supreme Court's Separation of Powers Wonderland," *Notre Dame Law Review,* 1990; also Rosenkranz, E. Joshua, *Buckley Stops Here,* 1998, p. 26; Nicholson, Marlene Arnold, "*Buckley v. Valeo:* The Constitutionality of the Federal Election Campaign Act Amendments of 1974," *Wisconsin Law Review,* 1977.
57 **"Virtually every means of communicating"**: *Buckley v. Valeo,* 424 U.S. 1, 19 (1976).
57 **"The concept that government may restrict"**: Ibid., at 48–49.
57 **"A general expression of support"**: Ibid., at 21.
57 **Disclosure requirements**: All campaigns and political committees are required to keep records of all contributions and expenditures, including the name and address of anyone who makes a single contribution over $50 or total contributions over $200; campaigns and political committees must also identify anyone who receives over $200. Briffault, Richard, *Dollars and Democracy: A Blueprint for Campaign Finance Reform.* New York: Fordham University Press, 2001, p. 23. The Court recognized that some would-be donors to controversial minor parties

might be scared off by the prospect of disclosure; the Court indicated that in such cases, the party would be exempted from the disclosure requirements. *Buckley,* at 68–74; also *Brown v. Socialist Workers '74 Campaign Committee,* 459 U.S. 87 (1982).

57 **"Helping voters to define"**: *Buckley,* at 81.

58 **"Furthered First Amendment values"**: Ibid., at 93, 96.

58 **Shifting majority**: Neuborne, p. 6. Justice Marshall thought expenditure limits were permissible only as applied to self-financing candidates. Chief Justice Burger thought requiring disclosure was permissible only as applied to large contributions.

58 **The Court's piecemeal approach**: *Buckley,* at 254–255 (Chief Justice Burger dissenting).

59 **It is property**: *Nixon v. Shrink Missouri PAC,* 528 U.S. 377, 398 (2000) (Justice Stevens dissenting).

60 **"Suppose I buy a bullhorn"**: Ely, John Hart, *Democracy and Distrust.* Boston: Harvard University Press, 1980, p. 110.

60 ***Buckley* as Dred Scott**: Turow, Scott, "The High Court's Twenty-Year-Old Mistake," *New York Times,* October 12, 1997.

61 **PACs defined**: 2 U.S.C., sec. 441b(b)(3); also Neuborne, Burt, "Is Money Different?" *Texas Law Review,* 1999.

61 **Section 611**: Green, Mark, "Political PAC-Man," *New Republic,* December 13, 1982.

62 **PAC contribution figures**: Briffault, *Dollars,* p. 64.

62 **"The public's whipping boys"**: Sorauf, Frank J. "What *Buckley* Wrought," in Rosenkranz, E. Joshua, ed., *If Buckley Fell.* New York: Brookings Institution Press, 1999, p. 13.

62 **"No one has ever shown"**: Green, Mark, "When Money Talks, Is It Democracy?" *The Nation,* September 15, 1984.

62 **"Members indignantly say"**: Interview with Jim Leach, April 19, 2002.

62 **"I wanted to go home"**: Jackson, Brooks, *Honest Graft.* New York: Alfred A. Knopf, 1988, p. 238.

63 **S. 2 summary**: http://www.pbs.org/newshour/campaign/issues/1988_retro.html.

63 **"To force the Republicans"**: http://www.pbs.org/newshour/realaudio/Jul.97/senate 2-24-88.ram.

64 **Guigni anecdotes**: Dewar, Helen, "Midnight Manhunt in the Senate," *Washington Post,* February 25, 1988.

65 **S. 3 summary**: Harshbarger, Scott, and Davis, Edwin, "Federal Campaign Finance Reform: The Long and Winding Road," *National Civic Review,* June 22, 2001.

65 **Bush veto**: Curran, Tim, "Dead Again: Senate Fails to Override Bush Veto of Campaign Finance Bill," *Roll Call,* May 14, 1992.

65 **"We have known exactly"**: Curran, Tim, "Veto Comes Next As Senate Passes Campaign Reform," *Roll Call,* May 4, 1992.

65 **Bush and public funds**: "A Retrogressive Veto," *Washington Post,* May 13, 1992.

66 **S&L PACs**: Waldman, Michael, *Who Robbed America? A Citizens' Guide to the Savings & Loan Scandal,* New York: Random House, 1990, pp. 60–65.

66 **S&L bailout costs**: Ibid., pp. 3–4.

67 **Meeting with regulators**: Muller, Bill, "Chapter V: The Keating Five," *Arizona Republic,* October 3, 1999, available on-line at http://www.arizonarepublic.com/special39/articles/1003mccainbook5 .html.

67 **Keating Five campaign contributions**: Waldman, *Who Robbed America,* pp. 94–95.

67 **"I want to say"**: Waldman, *POTUS Speaks,* pp. 94–95.

67 **Lincoln S&L collapse**: Muller, "The Keating Five."

68 **"To renew America"**: Bill Clinton's first inaugural address, available on-line at http://www.bartleby.com/124/pres64.html.

68 **1992 campaign spending**: Alexander, Herbert, and Anthony Corrado, eds., *Financing the 1992 Election.* Armonk, N.Y.: M. E. Sharpe, 1995, pp. 192–95.

68 **Cabinet room meeting**: Waldman, Michael, *POTUS Speaks: Finding the Words That Defined the Clinton Presidency.* New York: Simon & Schuster, 2000, pp. 48–49.

68 **"It was the high-water mark"**: Waldman, *POTUS Speaks,* pp. 48–49.

68 **"We are under close scrutiny"**: Ibid., p. 49.

68 **Foley PAC money**: Alexander and Corrado, *Financing 1992,* p. 267.

69 **Congress balked on reform**: Waldman, *POTUS Speaks,* pp. 48–52.

69 **Dole and Shilling**: Alexander and Corrado, *Financing 1992,* p. 270.

69 **Democratic reliance on PACs**: Ibid., pp. 268–69.

69 **"I talk to these members"**: Waldman, *POTUS Speaks,* p. 52.

69 **"They think they win or lose"**: Ibid., pp. 268–69.

69 **"So we passed bills"**: Interview with Fred Wertheimer, April 10, 2002.

70 **FEC soft money decisions**: Briffault, *Dollars,* pp. 45–46.

71 **Soft money explosion**: Lubenhow, Gerald C., ed., *A User's Guide to Campaign Finance Reform.* Lanham, Md.: Rowman & Littlefield, 2001, pp. 88–89.

71 **1980 statistics**: Corrado, Anthony, "Party Soft Money," in Lowenstein, Daniel Hays, and Richard L. Hasen, eds., *Election Law: Cases and Materials,* 2nd ed. Durham, N.C.: Carolina Academic Press, 2001, p. 908.

71 **1988 statistics**: Briffault, *Dollars,* p. 46.

71 **"Giving party organizations a clearer sense"**: Corrado, *Soft Money,* p. 909.

71 **1992 and 1996 statistics**: http://www.fec.gov/press/sftlong.htm.

71 **2000 statistics**: Holman, Craig B., and Luke P. McLoughlin, *Buying Time 2000: Television Advertising in the 2000 Federal Elections,* 2001, p. 61; C. Nelson, "Spending in the 2000 Elections," in Magleby, David, ed., *Financing the 2000 Elections.* Brookings Institution Press, 2002, p. 25.

71 **CPI calculation**: http://www.fec.gov/press/sftlong.htm; Holman and McLoughlin, *Buying Time;* "Consumer Prices Rise Just 0.2%," *San Francisco Chronicle,*

December 12, 1992; ftp://ftp.bls.gov/pub/news.release/History/cpi.12152000. news.

71 **Large contributors**: Briffault, *Dollars,* p. 49.

72 **1995–96 campaign spending**: Green, John C., ed., *Financing the 1996 Election.* Armonk, NY: M. E. Sharpe, 1999, p. 11.

72 **Democratic media blitz**: Ibid., p. 51.

72 **Early Republican spending**: Ibid.

73 **Trent Lott and the American way**: Seelye, Katharine Q., "Cash and Unlimited Gifts Are 'American Way,' Lott Says," *New York Times,* February 21, 1997, p. A26.

73 **Thompson hearings**: Drew, Elizabeth, *The Corruption of American Politics: What Went Wrong and Why.* New York: Overlook Press, 2000, p. 7.

73 **"If you want to build"**: Ibid., p. 173.

74 **"Then learn about it"**: Hunt, Al, "John McCain and Russell Feingold," in Kennedy, Caroline, ed., *Profiles in Courage for Our Time.* New York: Hyperion, 2002, p. 259.

74 **Description of S. 1219**: McBride, Ann, "A Golden Opportunity: With Public Pressure, Reform Will Succeed," Common Cause, Fall 1995; Rothenberg, Stuart, "McCain-Feingold 2002: A Pale Imitation of Authors' Original Plan," *Roll Call,* February 28, 2002.

74 **Ranking priorities**: Interview with Russ Feingold, May 3, 2002.

74 **"We will have campaign finance reform"**: Clymer, Adam, "Senate Kills Bill to Limit Spending in Congress Races," *New York Times,* June 26, 1996.

74 **Broadcast and mail subsidies**: Drew, *Corruption of American Politics,* p. 165.

74 **"You've put us"**: Ibid., p. 166.

75 **"This effort to put the government"**: Balz, Dan, "In Long Battle, Small Victories Added Up," *Washington Post,* March 21, 2002, p. A1.

75 **"I believe there will be more"**: Drew, *Corruption of American Politics,* p. 180.

75 **"A fair, bipartisan process"**: Fulwood, Sam, III, "Congress Plows Through Bills on Way to Adjournment," *Los Angeles Times,* November 14, 1997; Drew, *Corruption of American Politics,* p. 182.

76 **"There couldn't be a vote"**: Drew, *Corruption of American Politics,* p. 186.

76 **Farcical floor debate**: Dewar, Helen, "House Rejects GOP Campaign Finance Bill," *Washington Post,* March 31, 1998.

76 **Discharge petition**: Drew, *Corruption of American Politics,* p. 191.

76 **"To sow legislative chaos"**: "G.O.P. Trickery in the House," *New York Times,* June 8, 1998.

77 **"One of the things I find"**: Drew, *Corruption of American Politics,* pp. 199– 200.

77 **ACLU on Fossella**: Keller, Amy, "Campaign Reform Bill Starts Picking Up Steam," *Roll Call,* July 16, 1998.

77 **"You're more likely to see"**: Mitchell, "Bill to Overhaul," p. A1.

77 **"There will be"**: Chen, Edwin, "Clinton Under Fire; Senate Blocks Reform of Campaign Financing," *Los Angeles Times,* September 11, 1998.

78 **"Was killing us with kindness"**: Keller, Amy, "Shays, Meehan Worry GOP Will Kill Reform with Kindness," *Roll Call*, September 13, 1999.

78 **"I've had it"**: Interview with Russ Feingold, May 3, 2002.

78 **"With each change"**: Dewar, Helen, "'Millionaires' Amendment Added to Campaign Finance Legislation," *Washington Post*, March 21, 2001.

78 **"Severability is French"**: Balz, "Long Battle," p. A1.

78 **Daschle's efforts**: Lancaster, John, and Helen Dewar, "Luck, or Fate, Helped Guide Campaign Bill; Compromise Ruled Each Time McCain-Feingold Measure Seemed at Risk of Failing," *Washington Post*, March 31, 2001.

79 **Armageddon**: "Campaign Reform's 'Armageddon,'" *New York Times*, February 10, 2002.

79 **"Improve the system"**: Allen, Mike, and Dana Millbank, "President's Politics of Pragmatism Helped Undermine GOP Opposition," *Washington Post*, February 15, 2002.

79 **"It was an uphill climb"**: Lizza, Ryan, "O Pioneers!" *New Republic*, March 4, 2002.

80 **"An accurate factual record"**: Keller, Amy, "Reform Arguments Scheduled for December," *Roll Call*, April 25, 2002.

80 **"We would have gotten over"**: Interview with Russ Feingold, May 3, 2002.

80 **"Almost every one of them"**: Fineman, Howard, "Everything Will Change. Or Not," *Newsweek*, February 25, 2002.

81 **Details of law**: "New Campaign Finance Law Bans 'Soft Money' but Raises the Amounts Individuals May Contribute to Federal Candidates and National Political Parties," Willkie Farr & Gallagher client memorandum, April 30, 2002.

82 **"If the FEC doesn't aggressively"**: Beinart, Peter, "Oversight," *New Republic*, March 18, 2002.

82 **"Helps elite donors"**: Interview with Ellen Miller, April 19, 2002.

82 **"Many Democrats feel"**: Crowley, Michael, "Mourning After," *New Republic*, March 4, 2002.

82 **Potter figure**: Barnes, James A., "A New Blow to Public Financing," *National Journal*, April 20, 2002.

83 **"Follow the course of least resistance"**: Dewar, Helen, "Campaign Finance Bill Clears Big Hurdle," *Washington Post*, March 30, 2001.

83 **"This is only an incremental"**: Rothenberg, "McCain-Feingold 2002."

84 **"Tough Cop"**: Much of the FEC history presented in this section comes from a report by Project FEC, "No Bark, No Bite, No Point: The Case for Closing the Federal Election Commission and Establishing a New System for Enforcing the Nation's Campaign Finance Laws," April 2002. Project FEC was a task force of campaign finance experts led by Fred Wertheimer of Democracy 21. The report can be found on Democracy 21's Web site: www.democracy21.org.

84 **"Failure to Enforce Commission"**: Ibid., p. 5.

84 **1976 and big-spender figures**: Committee on Economic Development, *Invest-*

ing in the People's Business: A Business Proposal for Campaign Finance Reform (1999), p. 13.

84 **2000 figures**: http://www.opensecrets.org/overview/index.asp? Cycle=2000.

84 **Black-market effect**: Sullivan, Kathleen M., "Political Money and Freedom of Speech," *U.C. Davis Law Review,* 1997; Neuborne, Burt, "The Supreme Court: Love and a Question," *St. Louis Law Journal,* 1998; Weine, Kenneth, *The Flow of Money in Congressional Elections,* 1997, p. 1.

84 **Hard money figures**: http://www.publicampaign.org/hardfacts/.

84 **Contribution limits**: http://www.fec.gov/pages/contrib.htm; Willkie Farr Gallagher client memorandum.

84 **Jackson on FEC**: Project FEC, "No Bark, No Bite, No Point: The Case for Closing the Federal Election Commission and Establishing a New System for Enforcing the Nation's Campaign Finance Laws," April 2002; available at www.democracy21.org.

84 **"FEC epithets"**: Ibid.

84 **"Intense partisanship envelops"**: Ibid., p. 11.

85 **"The Federal Election Campaign Act means"**: Ibid., p. 79.

86 **Commissioners' professional background**: Ibid., p. 60.

86 **"The easiest way to gut regulation"**: Broder, David, "Watchdog Without a Bite?," *Washington Post,* February 12, 1995.

86 **"In effect, Congress put itself"**: Jackson, Brooks, *Broken Promise: Why the Federal Election Commission Failed.* New York: Priority Press, 1990, p. 30.

86 **"If I win an election:"** Project FEC, p. 6.

86 **The Federal Election Campaign Act**: Ibid., p. 79.

86 **FEC commissioners**: Ibid., pp. 60–61.

86 **Dismissed cases**: Ibid., p. 77.

87 **"Make it difficult"**: Ibid., p. 50.

87 **"You can put a tag"**: Ibid., p. 91.

87 **"The White House is like a subway"**: Ibid., p. 88.

87 **"Intellectual bankruptcy"**: Ibid., p. 18.

87 **"Anyone intent on circumventing"**: Drinkard, Jim, "Campaign Finance Law Appears Easy to Evade," *USA Today,* March 19, 2002.

87 **"[A]cted for all practical purposes"**: Hunt, Al, "Don't Stop at McCain-Feingold," *Wall Street Journal,* February 21, 2002.

88 **ITT Settlement**: Project FEC, pp. 105–110.

88 **Corporate contributions to 2000 conventions**: Ibid.

88 **"The definition has the potential"**: "Vote Broadens Use of Soft Money by State Parties," *Los Angeles Times,* June 20, 2002.

89 **"Election Law Coup d'Etat"**: "Election Law Coup d'Etat," *New York Times,* June 24, 2002.

89 **"Stop Opening Loopholes"**: "Stop Opening Loopholes," *Washington Post,* June 23, 2002.

89 **Student giving anecdotes**: Miller, Alan C., "Minor Loophole: Young Donors Are Increasingly Padding Political Coffers," *Los Angeles Times,* February 28, 1999.

90 **Student giving figures and Bainum fine**: Ibid.

90 **McCain-Feingold bundling ban**: Coyle, Marcia, "Squaring Off over Campaign Finance," *National Law Journal,* April 15, 2002. The American Center for Law and Justice has challenged the constitutionality of this restriction.

90 **"In which people or organizations"**: Malbin, Michael J., and Thomas L. Gais, *The Day After Reform: Sobering Campaign Finance Lessons from the American States.* Rockefeller Institute Press, 1998, p. 80.

90 **Corporate bundling**: Bonifaz, John C., Gregory Luke, and Brenda Wright, "Challenging *Buckley v. Valeo:* A Legal Strategy," *Akron Law Review,* 1999.

91 **1994 MBNA bundling**: Campbell, Steve, "Campaign System Riddled with Loopholes; They Render Existing Finance Restrictions Virtually Meaningless," *Portland Press Herald,* September 16, 1997; Zweifel, Dave, "Government for Sale Just Keeps on Going," *Capital Times,* July 5, 1996.

91 **2000 MBNA bundling**: Miller, Ellen, "Reform You Can Take to the Bank," *American Prospect,* May 7, 2001.

91 **EMILY's List**: Carney, Eliza Newton, "Stuffing Their Purses," *National Journal,* June 16, 2001.

91 **Fireman example**: Roeder, Edward, "Blank Check," *New Republic,* April 14, 1997; "Campaign financing. Fireman's bundle," *Economist,* July 27, 1996; Stephens, Joe, "Ill-Gotten Gains? Workers Say They Were Reimbursed for Dole Donations," *Kansas City Star,* April 21, 1996.

92 **"I don't know Mattingly"**: Stern, Philip M., *Still the Best Congress Money Can Buy.* Washington, D.C.: Regnery, 1992, p. 210. See also Edsall, Thomas B., "Campaign Skirts Rules by 'Bundling' Contributions," *Washington Post,* October 20, 1986; Wertheimer, Fred, and Susan Weiss Manes, "Campaign Finance Reform: The Key to Restoring the Health of Our Democracy," *Columbia Law Review,* 1994.

92 **"No way I would have sent"**: Stern, *Still the Best,* p. 210.

92 **"Did not deliberately violate"**: Ibid. But when a spokesman for the NRSC denied that it had directed the funds, he acknowledged that doing so "would be in violation of the law." Quoted in Edsall, "Campaign Skirts Rules."

92 **"Reigning champion"**: Quoted in Coile, Zachary, "Hunt Begins for Loopholes in Bill," *San Francisco Chronicle,* February 15, 2002.

92 **"Pioneers"**: Lizza, "O Pioneers!"; also http://www.tpj.org/pioneers/index.html for profiles of Bush's Pioneers.

92 **Potential bundling in 2004**: Lizza, "O Pioneers!"

93 **"Party committees are considered"**: *FEC v. Democratic Senatorial Campaign Committee,* 454 U.S. 27, 28 n.1 (1981).

93 **1972 and 1980 figures**: Schultz, David, "Revisiting *Buckley v. Valeo:* Eviscerating the Line Between Contributions and Independent Expenditures," *Journal of Law and Politics,* 1997.

94 **Colorado Republican unique**: Weine, *Flow of Money,* p. 10.

94 **1996 independent expenditures**: Lowenstein and Hasen, *Election Law,* p. 894.

94 **1980 NCPAC spending**: Wood, Daniel B., "Washington's PAC-Men," *Christian Science Monitor,* August 12, 1982; Shields, Mark, "NCPAC, PROPAC, DumbPAC," *Washington Post,* March 5, 1982; Broder, David S., and Bill Peterson, "Democrats to Push Probe of NCPAC's 'Independence,'" *Washington Post,* November 21, 1981; McPherson, Myra, "The New Right Brigade," *Washington Post,* August 10, 1980.

95 **"withdraw all radio and television ads"**: Kaiser, Robert G., "2 on Hill Call for Probe of NCPAC," *Washington Post,* July 30, 1981.

95 **NCPAC versus Moynihan**: "Striking Back at Nick-Pack," *New York Times,* June 1, 1986; "The FEC's Good News," *Washington Post,* May 22, 1986.

95 **"He showed me the piece"**: Eddings, Jerelyn, et al., "Hurting the One You Love," *U.S. News & World Report,* September 18, 1995; Jacoby, Mary, "Outside Expenditures not So 'Independent,' Packwood Diaries Say," *Roll Call,* September 14, 1995.

96 **Magic words**: *Buckley,* at 44, n. 52.

96 **"Names one or more individual candidates"**: Moramarco, Glenn, *Regulating Electioneering: Distinguishing Between "Express Advocacy" and "Issue Advocacy,"* p. 4 (1998).

97 **"Last year John McCain"**: Holman and McLoughlin, *Buying Time,* p. 25.

97 **"Who is Bill Yellowtail"**: Briffault, Richard, "Drawing the Line Between Elections and Politics," in Rosenkranz, *If Buckley Fell,* p. 121.

97 **Survey data**: Magleby, David, *Dictum Without Data: The Myth of Issue Advocacy and Party Building* (2001), p. 7.

98 **Four percent figure**: Holman and McLoughlin, *Buying Time,* p. 29.

98 **Top non-party spenders**: Slass, Lorie, "Spending on Issue Ads," *Issue Advertising in the 1999–2000 Election Cycle* (2001).

98 **Total spending**: Holman and McLoughlin, *Buying Time,* p. 29.

98 **Final 60 days**: Ibid., pp. 31, 73.

99 **McCain-Lieberman law**: Trister, Michael, "The Rise and Reform of Stealth PACs," *American Prospect,* September 24, 2000.

99 **Thomas-Brady bill**: Crabtree, Susan, "Foes Derail 527 Law Change," *Roll Call,* April 11, 2002.

100 **Rent control referendum**: Lee, Lester, "The Shattering of the Massachusetts Tenant Rights Movement," *Peacework* #264, 1994.

100 **Lauder and term limits**: Myers, Steven Lee, "New Yorkers Approve Limit of 2 Terms for City Officials," *New York Times,* November 3, 1993, p. B1.

101 **Honoraria**: Stern, *Still the Best,* p. 12.

101 **Honoraria figures**: Fritz, Sara, and Dwight Morris, "Lawmakers' Fees Exceed $8 Million," *Los Angeles Times,* June 15, 1991.

102 **"Provide special interest groups"**: Quoted in Stern, *Still the Best,* p. 195.

102 **Junkets**: Ibid., p. 194.
102 **Lott in Aspen**: Love, Alice, "An End to the Free Lunch?" *Washington Monthly,* April 1996.
102 **Dole fund-raising**: Simpson, Glenn R., "Senator Dole's Greatest Harvest," *American Prospect,* Summer 1995; Babcock, Charles R., and Ruth Marcus, "'Dole, Inc.': The Rise of a Money Machine," *Washington Post,* August 20, 1996.
102 **Democratic hopefuls' fund-raising**: Edsall, Thomas B., "Tactics Vary in Early Fundraising; Sens. Kerry, Edwards Lead Pack of '04 Presidential Prospects," *Washington Post,* July 17, 2002.
103 **Leadership PAC contributions**: Bolton, Alexander, "PAC Use Exploding," *The Hill,* February 6, 2002.

4. Campaigning for Money

105 **"I get elected"**: Kenworthy, Tom, "Are House Democrats Victims of Their Fund-raising Success?," *Washington Post,* October 30, 1989, p. A1.
105 **"Today's political campaigns"**: Minow, Newton M., "Television, More Vast than Ever, Turns Toxic," *USA Today,* May 9, 2001, p. 15A.
105 **"I'm not calling"**: Klein, Joe, "After Strom," *The New Yorker,* May 13, 2002, p. 38.
105 **"Today's political campaigns function as"**: Taylor, Paul, "The Case for Free Air Time," report prepared for the Alliance for Better Campaigns, March 2002, p. 7; available at www.bettercampaigns.org.
105 **"I'm not calling to ask"**: Klein, Joe, "After Strom, Can a Cracker-Barrel Fabulist Capture South Carolina's Senate Seat?" *The New Yorker,* May 13, 2002.
105 **"It's this incredible"**: Mannies, Jo, "Missouri Candidates Lament the Need to Keep Raising Money for Campaigns," *St. Louis-Post Dispatch,* October 4, 1998.
106 **"If you don't like raising"**: Interview with Carl Levin, May 1, 2002.
106 **Torricelli announcement**: Zengerle, Jason, "Clubbed: Are Bob Torricelli's Fellow Senators Happy to See Him Go?" *The New Republic,* May 7, 2001.
107 **Total campaign expenditures**: Federal Election Commission, http://www.fec.gov/press/051501congfinact/tables/allsenate2000.html and http://www.fec.gov/press/051501congfinact/tables/allhouse2000.html.
107 **"Television is dominant"**: Interview with Hank Sheinkopf, April 12, 2002.
108 **"In even-numbered election years"**: Taylor, Paul, "Gouging Democracy: How the Television Industry Profiteered on Campaign 2000," a report prepared for the Alliance for Better Campaigns, March 2001; available at www.bettercampaigns.org.
108 **Political ad sales**: Ibid.
110 **General Motors spending**: Thurber, James, and Candice Nelson, *Campaign Warriors.* Washington, D.C.: Brookings Institution Press, 2000, p. 43.
110 **Gross rating points**: Interview with Steve McMahon, May 21, 2002.
111 **"If you throw the dice"**: Ibid.

111 **Statewide markets**: Interview with Mark Mellman, June 10, 2002.

112 **"One of the big"**: Interview with East Coast media consultant, April 12, 2002.

112 **Candidates payments for ads**: Taylor, "Gouging Democracy."

112 **Supply and demand market**: Coco, Marie, "Broadcasters Are Getting Rich Off Campaign Ads," *Newsday,* February 26, 2002.

113 **"The most powerful industry"**: Drew, Elizabeth, *The Corruption of American Politics: What Went Wrong and Why.* New York: Overlook Press, 1999, p. 78.

113 **"Obviously, the broadcasting industry"**: Interview with Louise Slaughter, April 10, 2002.

113 **Station times**: Taylor, "Case for Free Air Time," p. 12.

114 **"For the vast majority"**: Faler, Brian, "Study Finds Most Political Debates Are Not Televised," *Washington Post,* May 20, 2002.

114 **"In the MTV age"**: Interview with Hank Sheinkopf, April 12, 2002.

114 **Owners of major media outlets**: "Goliath Getting Bigger," *American Prospect,* May 6, 2002.

114 **"Political advertising as a form"**: Interview with Paul Taylor, May 9, 2002.

115 **Attack ads**: Krasno, Jonathan S., and Daniel E. Seltz, *Buying Time: Television Advertising in the 1998 Congressional Elections.* New York: Brennan Center for Justice, NYU School of Law, 2000.

115 **Clinton/Lazio ads**: Denison, Dave, "Political Meatballs," *American Prospect,* December 4, 2000.

116 **Artur Davis ads**: Halbfinger, David M., "Generational Battle Turns Nasty in Alabama Primary," *New York Times,* June 3, 2002.

116 **"People don't like them"**: Interview with Steve McMahon, May 21, 2002.

116 **Voice broadcasting services**: Target Marketing USA, http://targetmarketingusa. com/automated<\>>politicalcallsystem.htm.

118 **"Vell, his system"**: Singer, Donald L., *Going Negative: The Smear Campaign Against Upton Sinclair,* Fortnightly Club of Redlands, California, October 19, 2000, http://www.redlandsfortnightly.org/singer00.htm.

118 **"stunt you can pull"**: Oreskes, Michael, "American Politics Loses Way as Polls Supplant Leadership," *New York Times,* March 18, 1990.

118 **"The central nervous system"**: Johnson, Dennis W., *No Place for Amateurs: How Political Consultants Are Reshaping Democracy.* London: Routledge, 2001, p. 90.

118 **Poll size and cost**: Interview with Mark Mellman, July 26, 2002.

119 **"If you can only afford"**: Interview with Mark Mellman, June 10, 2002.

119 **"Polling is at its best"**: Mellman, Mark, "Benchmark Basic and Beyond," *Campaigns and Elections,* May 1991.

119 **Oliver North campaign expenses**: Johnson, *No Place for Amateurs,* p. 176.

120 **Outspent winners**: *Almanac of American Politics, National Journal,* 2002, 2000, and 1998.

120 **"You go to the Democratic"**: Malone, Julia, "Cash Hunt Haunts Congress," *Atlanta Journal and Constitution,* March 25, 2001.

121 **"Kathy! Hi how are you"**: Berke, Richard L., "A Senate Candidate's Refrain: 'Could You Stretch It to $500,'" *New York Times,* June 8, 2002.

121 **"A powerful factor"**: Drew, *Corruption of American Politics,* p. 265.

121 **Scott Gale stories**: Interview with Scott Gale, April 20, 2002.

125 **"One day I walk in"**: Interview with Bob Abrams, April 30, 2002.

126 **"It is the Yin"**: Interview with Tara Ochman, April 10, 2002.

127 **Nussbaum pitch**: Interview with Bernard Nussbaum, 2001.

127 **"You become a pariah"**: Interview with Charlie King, May 2, 2002.

128 **Senator cash on hand**: Center for Responsive Politics, www.opensecrets.org.

129 **Three-state study**: Federal Election Commission, www.fec.gov.

130 **Boschwitz memo**: Jackson, Brooks, "A Senator's Advice: Don't Give Consent to Reelection Debate," *Wall Street Journal,* May 2, 1985.

131 **Challenger's paradox**: Jackson, *Honest Graft,* p. 187.

132 **"I don't give my people's"**: Stern, Philip M., *Still the Best Congress Money Can Buy.* Washington, D.C., Regnery, 1992, p. 28.

132 **"Early money is the most difficult"**: Interview with Adam Schiff, May 9, 2002.

134 **Committee for Economic Development study**: "Investing in the People's Business: A Business Proposal for Campaign Finance Reform," *Committee for Economic Development,* 1999, p. 19.

134 **"Even when I was spending"**: Interview with Ruth Messinger, May 1, 2002.

135 **"After I became an incumbent"**: Interview with Carolyn Maloney, April 13, 2002.

138 **Campaign receipts**: Federal Election Commission.

139 **"One of the primary reasons"**: Berke, "Senate Candidate's Refrain."

139 **Contributor breakdown,** Federal Election Commission.

139 **"I own a $25,000 Ford"**: Interview with Charlie King, May 2, 2002.

140 **"The sad thing about Enron"**: Interview with anonymous PAC manager, April 16, 2002.

140 **Enron PAC contributions**: Center for Responsive Politics, www.opensecrets. org.

140 **Number of PACs**: Federal Election Commission.

140 **Labor PACs**: Center for Responsive Politics, www.opensecrets.org.

141 **"When people help you get"**: Clawson, Neustadtl, and Scott, *Money Talks,* p. 65.

141 **PAC contributions**: Center for Responsive Politics, www.opensecrets.org.

142 **"After the 1982 election"**: Biersack, Robert, Paul S. Herrnson, and Clyde Wilcox, *Risky Business: PAC Decisionmaking in Congressional Elections.* New York: M. E. Sharpe, 1994, p. 241.

142 **House and Senate PAC contributions**: Center for Responsive Politics, www. opensecrets.org.

142 **House leaders**: Ibid.

142 **"PACs nationalize elections"**: Interview with Jim Leach, April 19, 2002.

143 **Common Cause study**: "If at First You Don't Succeed, Give, Give Again," *Common Cause News,* March 20, 1987.

143 **"These PACs obviously weren't"**: Ibid.

143 **"I doubt Enron held"**: Interview with labor union PAC manager, April 16, 2002.

144 **Retail PACs**: Center for Responsive Politics, www.opensecrets.org.

5. The Cost of Money

147 **"The day may come"**: Gunnison, R., "What Tammany Hall Can Tell Us About Sacramento," *San Francisco Chronicle,* July 6, 1997, p. 7/Z1.

147 **"I don't think we buy votes"**: McQueen, Michel, "PAC Attack: Big-Money Politics Must Face the Voters in California," *Wall Street Journal,* June 7, 1989, p 1.

147 **"I got $3,500"**: McGrory, M., "Enron's Political Potential," *Washington Post,* February 7, 2002, p. A25.

147 **Greenberg poll**: Democracy Corps, *Frequency Questionnaire,* April 2002, pp. 2, 10.

147 **University of Michigan poll**: The National Election Studies, Center for Political Studies, University of Michigan, Ann Arbor, 1995–2000. Electronic resources from the NES World Wide Web site, www.umich.edu/~nes.

148 **Ellen S. Miller study**: Berke, Richard, "Study Links Contributions to How Lawmakers Voted," *New York Times,* December 30, 1987, p. A10.

148 **"Let's be clear"**: Wertheimer, Fred, "Politician, Heal Thyself; Our Leaders Preach Values but Still Follow the Money," *Washington Post,* December 24, 1995, p. C1.

149 **"Every day there's a cadre"**: Interview with Matt Keller, May 15, 2002.

150 **International turnout data**: International Institute for Democracy and Electoral Assistance (IDEA), http://www.idea.int/voterturnout.

150–51 **U.S. turnout data**: Federal Election Commission (FEC), http://www.fec.gov/elections.html.

150 **Nebraska low turnout**: Napolitano, J., "Nebraska: Record Low Turnout," *New York Times,* May 16, 2002, p. A20.

150 **Press blames Le Pen victory on "absent voters"**: Editorial, "Apathy Is Not an Option," *Northern Echo,* April 24, 2002, p. 10.

150 **France's lowest turnout in four decades**: Noveck, J., "Far-Right Leader Gains Upset in France," *Boston Globe,* April 22, 2002, p. A8.

150 **Low U.S. turnout**: FEC.

150 **"The nation that prides itself"**: Gans, Curtis, "Table for One, Please," *Washington Monthly,* July/August 2000.

152 **"There is now a lower level"**: Interview with Curtis Gans, May 15, 2002.

152 **Gans on causes of less voting**: Ibid.

152 **EDR and turnout**: DEMOS, *Expanding the Vote: The Practice and Promise of Election Day Registration,* 2002, p. 12.

153 **Motor Voter Act**: Ibid., p. 5.

153 **Oregon, voting by mail**: Center for Voting and Democracy, http://www. fairvote.org/turnout/mail.htm.

153 **U.S. turnout by demographic breakdown**: DEMOS, p. 5.

153 **Data on money in federal elections 1992–2000**: "89 Percent of House Incumbents in Financially Uncompetitive Elections; House Candidates Enjoy Record $526 Million in Campaign Funds," Common Cause, November 2, 2000, pp. 1–5.

154 **Incumbent reelection data, 1998–2000**: "98 Percent of House Incumbents Win Reelection in 2000; 23 of Senate Incumbents Reelected; Incumbents Enjoy Huge Fundraising Advantage," Common Cause, November 14, 2000, pp. 1–4.

154 **Incumbent reelection data, 1960–1990**: Issacharoff, S., "In Real Elections, There Ought to Be Competition," *New York Times,* February 16, 2002, p. A19.

154 **Incumbents' spending, 2000**: "89 Percent of House Incumbents in Financially Uncompetitive Elections," pp. 2–3.

155 **"The problem is much worse"**: Interview with Ron Wyden, April 19, 2002.

156 **"I spend almost half my time"**: Interview with anonymous Congress member, April 12, 2002.

156 **"Of course I won't miss votes"**: Interview with Dick Durbin, April 2002.

156. **"Congressman, campaigner, fundraiser"**: Interview, April 19, 2002; Brown, Sherrod, *Congress from the Inside,* 1999.

156 **Byrd and Shields**: Shields, Mark, "Part-Time Legislators and Full-Time Fund-Raisers," *Washington Post,* May 1, 1987, p. A23.

156 **"On the proviso"**: Berke, Richard, "Raising 1990 Funds and Some Hackles," *New York Times,* February 23, 1987, p. B4.

157 **"At some point"**: Rosenkranz, E. J., *Buckley Stops Here.* New York: Twentieth-Century Fund, 1998, p. 43.

157 **"People are giving up"**: Interview with Paul Wellstone, April 2002.

157 **"I hoped to compensate"**: Milbank, D., "One-Time Rival Dole Basks in Bush Glow at GOP Fundraiser," *Washington Post,* February 28, 2002, p. A6.

157 **Askew drops out**: Filkins, Dexter, "For Senate Candidates, the Only Issue Is Money," *Washington Post,* May 25, 1988, p. A19.

158 **"Do you honestly think"**: Shields, "Part-Time Legislators," p. A23.

159 **Fitzgerald wealth**: Eckert, Toby, "Fitzgerald Votes 'Present' on Banking Bill," *State Journal-Register* (Springfield, IL), May 6, 1999, p. 22.

159 **Cost of seats in 2000**: "98 Percent of House Incumbents Win," pp. 1–4.

159 **"It's a growing solution"**: Interview with Carl Levin, April 2002.

159 **"Democratic leaders more eagerly"**: Interview with Jon Corzine, April 19, 2002.

160 **Huffington and illegal aliens**: Grove, L., "Natural Fibbers; In a Year of Lies,

Some Embroidery Came Apart at the Seams," *Washington Post,* December 17, 1997, p. D2.

160 **Checci and excessive advertising**: Lopez Baden, P., "Lack of Negativity in DFL Ads Might Work Against Candidates," *Minneapolis Star Tribune,* September 7, 1988, p. 1A.

160 **"The self-financed Democrats"**: Schmitt, Mark, *Between McCain-Feingold and the Democratic Ideal: A Commentary on Campaign Finance Reform for Funders and Others.* Open Society Institute, March 2002.

162 **"I think most people assume"**: Barlett, D., and J. Steele, "How the Little Guy Gets Crunched," *Time,* February 7, 2000, p. 38.

162 **Airlines, 1999 struggles**: "Left at the Gate: How the Airlines Beat Back Congress on Passenger Rights," *Common Cause,* 1999, pp. 1–5.

163 **"The industry is solely driven"**: Interview with Paul Hudson, May 16, 2002.

163 **Industry attempts to curb safety requirements**: "Delay, Dilute and Discard: How the Airline Industry and the FAA Have Stymied Aviation Security Recommendations," Public Citizen, 2000, p. 1.

164 **"That having been said"**: Interview with Con Hitchcock, May 15, 2002.

164 **"In the aviation debate"**: Interview with Paul Hudson, May 16, 2002.

164 **Airline industry and money**: "Left at the Gate," pp. 1–5.

165 **MIT study**: "Delay, Dilute and Discard." An FAA-funded study by a Massachusetts Institute of Technology professor showed that bag matching would only cause an average delay of seven minutes on 14 percent of flights and cost 25 cents to 52 cents per passenger.

165 **America uses 26 percent of world's oil**: Denny, J., "King of the Road," *Common Cause,* May/June 1991, p. 19.

165 **290 million barrels from Iraq and Kuwait**: Stern, Philip M., *Still the Best Congress Money Can Buy.* Washington, D.C.: Regnery, 1992, p. 173.

166 **U.S. oil imports**: Interview with Lowell Feld, Energy Information Administration, June 2002.

166 **"The fuel economy law passed"**: Denny, "King of the Road."

167 **Levin and Bond and auto money**: Nyhart, Nick, "Counting Reasons Congress Hates, Won't Back Fuel Efficiency," *Dodge City Daily Globe,* April 26, 2002.

167 **Kerrey-McCain**: Ibid.

167 **"They know that global warming"**: "Corporate Average Fuel Economy," Public Citizen, March 13, 2002, p. 1.

167 **"In 1985 Congress voted"**: Interview with John McCain, May 2002.

167 **"Farming's tough enough"**: Hakim, D., "Ads on Both Sides of Fuel Standards," *New York Times,* March 12, 2002, p. C1.

167 **"During the floor debate"**: "Corporate Fuel."

168 **"They would have to have"**: Brown, P., "Industry Whines Its Way to CAFÉ Victory," *Automotive News,* March 25, 2002, p. 16.

168 **Miller data**: Miller, Ellen, "Willful Error," *American Prospect,* May 17, 2002.

168 **"The current administration"**: Interview with Deanna White, May 16, 2002.

168 **"that was one of"**: Interview with anonymous senator, April 2002.

169 **"every fiber of my being"**: Pianin, Eric, "How Business Found Benefits in Wage Bill," *Washington Post,* February 11, 1997, p. A3.

170 **Tax breaks and contributions**: Ibid., pp. A1–2.

171 **"Members are only human"**: Ibid., p. A1.

171 **1999 bill yields $60 billion in lost tax revenues**: Common Cause Corporate Welfare Project, *Paying to Play* (1999), p. 1.

171 **"Republicans have great discipline"**: Interview with Robert McIntyre, May 15, 2002.

171 **AMT**: *Paying to Play,* p. 2.

172 **$22.2 million**: Ibid.

172 **"When candidates are forced"**: Cooper, M., "Campaign Finance Reform," *The CQ Researcher,* March 31, 2000.

172 **Multinationals**: *Paying to Play,* p. 2.

172 **"This administration is the worst"**: Interview with Robert McIntyre, May 15, 2002.

173 **Stimulus legislation**: Citizens for Tax Justice, "Latest GOP Corporate Tax-Giveaway 'Compromise' Looks Almost Identical to Original Bloated Plan," December 18, 2001, p. 1.

173 **Corporate rebates**: Citizens for Tax Justice, "House GOP 'Stimulus' Bill Offers 16 Large, Low-Tax Corporations $7.4 Billion in Instant Tax Rebates," October 26, 2001, p. 1.

173 **"pass the laugh test"**: McIntyre, Robert, "The $212 Billion Special-Interest Love Feast," *American Prospect,* October, 2001.

173 **Enacted compromise bill**: Citizens for Tax Justice, "Corporate Loophole Lobbying Conquers House," March 7, 2002, pp. 1–2.

174 **"The corporate guys"**: Interview with Robert McIntyre, May 15, 2002.

174 **Uses for $55 billion**: ITEP, CTJ & Public Campaign, *Buy Now, Save Later* (2001), p. 8.

174 **"Once again, we see"**: Sinclair, W., "Tobacco PACs' House Contributions Detailed," *Washington Post,* September 18, 1987, p. A4.

174 **Tobacco PAC contributions**: Ibid.

174 **"On the one hand"**: Ibid.

174 **Philip Morris interoffice documents**: "How It's Done," Common Cause, Winter 1992, p. 7.

175 **"back-room politics"**: Chen, E., "$50 Billion Tobacco Tax Break Rejected by Senate, 95–3," *Los Angeles Times,* September 11, 1997, p. 1.

175 **Tax revenues and $368 billion settlement**: Torry, S., "Tax Deal Reasserts Tobacco Industry's Clout," *Washington Post,* August 4, 1997, p. A6.

176 **"legislative orphan"**: Carlson, Margaret, "Where There's Smoke . . . There's Barbour. And Congress Still Reeks of Tobacco," *Time,* September 29, 1997, p. 29.

176 **"Joe Camel Tobacco Loophole"**: Torry, "Tax Deal."

176 **"an absolute outrage"**: Ibid.

176 **"When you consider"**: Ibid.

177 **Clinton files legal action**: Johnston, D., "In Shift, U.S. Opens Effort to Settle Tobacco Lawsuit," *New York Times,* June 20, 2001, p. A1.

177 **June 2000 suit, money, and votes**: Campaign for Tobacco-Free Kids, Common Cause, American Heart Association, and American Lung Association, *Buying Influence, Selling Death* (2001), p. 2.

177 **Republican tobacco money**: Ibid.

177 **"The administration is seeking"**: Johnston, "U.S. Opens Effort."

177 **"I worry about"**: Ibid.

177 **Bliley PAC money**: Kemper, V., "The Inhalers," *Common Cause,* Spring 1995, p. 20.

178 **Gingrich and Kessler**: Ibid.

178 **Members turned lobbyists**: Kemper, "The Inhalers," p. 22.

178 **McCain bill, money, and votes**: *Buying Influence,* p. 14.

178 **Foreign governments and Philip Morris**: Schapiro, M., "Big Tobacco," *The Nation,* May 6, 2002, pp. 11–20.

179 **Davis tobacco money**: Center for Responsive Politics, www.opensecrets.org.

180 **Senator Johnston and energy industry**: Corn, David, "Schilling in The Senate," *The Nation,* July 17, 1989, pp. 84–85.

180 **"politically foolish"**: Ibid., p. 84.

181 **"I'm very much playing"**: Ibid., p. 85.

181 **Energy industry contributions**: Center for Responsive Politics, www. opensecrets.org.

181 **"The industry in large part"**: Lutterbeck, Deborah, "Electric Shock," *Common Cause,* Fall 1995, p. 25.

182 **54 percent increase in profits**: Public Citizen, *Got Juice?,* February 2001, p. 2.

182 **Bush's Big Energy friends**: Ibid., p. 1.

183 **Energy contributions to California officials**: "Big Money and the Energy Crisis," *Common Cause,* 2001, pp. 2–3.

183 **"Nobody in the legislature"**: Ainsworth, Bill, "Effect of Political Money May Cloud Issue," *San Diego Union Tribune,* January 23, 2001.

183 **"The solution to the policy problem"**: "Big Money," p. 4.

184 **"The industry has an interest"**: Van Natta, Don, Jr., "A Company's Gain from Energy Report's Recommendation," *New York Times,* March 24, 2002, p. 1.

184 **Exelon $347,514 contributions**: Ibid.

184 **"the policy organization," NEI Web site**: http://www.nei.org/doc.asp?catnum=2&catid=136.

185 **"Because of the small market"**: "Patently Offensive: Congress Set to Extend Monopoly Patents for Cipro and Other Drugs," Public Citizen, www.citizen.org/print_article.cfm?ID=6435, 2001, p. 3.

185 **"This is an incentive"**: Ibid.

185 **Costs of pediatric tests vs. patent extension profits**: Ibid., p. 1.
186 **Drug industry and contributions**: Center for Responsive Politics, www. opensecrets.org.
186 **"uncontrolled drive"**: "Patently Offensive."
186 **Schering-Plough and Claritin**: "Schering-Plough Political Money Pushes Claritin Patent Extension," Public Citizen, www.citizen.org/printarticle. cfm?ID=1073, 2001, pp. 1–3.
187 **Torricelli, Hatch contributions**: Ibid.
187 **"What happens on a day-to-day scale"**: Interview with anonymous legislative directors, May 15, 2002.
187 **Breakdown of industry spending, 2000**: "Rx Industry Goes for KO: Drug Companies Spend Record Amount This Election Cycle," Public Citizen, www. citizen.org/print_article.cfm?ID=799, November 2000, pp. 1–8.
190 **"not so crass"**: Interview with Paul Wellstone, spring 2002.

6. The Players

193 **"Talking to politicians"**: Taylor, Paul, "PACs Proliferate as Debate Rages," *Washington Post,* March 30, 1982, p. A1.
193 **"In public policy"**: Stephens, Joe, "Bush 2000 Adviser Offered to Use Clout to Help Enron," *Washington Post,* February 17, 2002, p. A1.
193 **O'Neill and Enron**: "Enron on Its Own, Cabinet Members Say; White House Defends Inaction after Calls for Help," *San Francisco Chronicle,* January 14, 2002, p. A1.
194 **Fortune 500**: *Fortune,* April 16, 2001.
194 **Enron stats**: *Business Week,* August 15, 2001.
194 **Lay biography**: "How Enron's Chairman Changed the World," http://www. tompaine.com.
195 **Lay's parachute**: Strauss, Gary, "Enron CEO Exits Without Opening Golden Parachute," *USA Today,* November 14, 2001.
195 **"a supporter of Ann Richards"**: Oppel, Richard A., Jr., and Don Van Natta, "Enron's Collapse: The Relationships; Bush and Democrats Disputing Ties to Enron," *New York Times,* January 12, 2002, p. C1.
195 **Bush/Lay letters**: "The Bush-Lay Letters," http://www.thesmokinggun.com.
195 **State emergency**: Rosin, Hannah, "Bush-Lay Ties Based on Shared Priorities; Tex. Records on Ex-CEO of Enron Show a Mix of Lobbying, Friendship," *Washington Post,* March 24, 2002, p. A4.
196 **Enron to Bush perqs**: "Enron: Other Money in Politics Stats," http://www. opensecrets.org.
196 **Bush appointees**: Milbank, Dana, and Glenn Kessler, "Enron's Influence Reached Deep into Administration; Ties Touched Personnel and Policies," *Washington Post,* January 18, 2002, p. A1.

197 **White rebuke**: Reinert, Patty, "Senators Admonish Secretary of Army over Enron Holdings," *Houston Chronicle,* March 6, 2002.

197 **Lay's ultimatum to Hebert**: Bergman, Lowell, and Jeff J. Gerth, "Power Trader Tied to Bush Finds Washington All Ears," *New York Times,* May 25, 2002, p. A1.

198 **Lay recommended Wood**: Gordon, Marcy, "Enron on Bush Recommendation List: Lay Suggested Two Members of Bush Energy Commission," Associated Press, January 31, 2002.

198 **Abraham meetings**: Yost, Pete, "White House Defends Energy Meetings: Memos Show Industry's Access to Abraham; No Environmentalists Listed," *Detroit News,* March 27, 2002.

198 **More Abraham meetings**: Van Natta, Don, and Neela Banerjee, "Bush Energy Paper Followed Industry Push," *New York Times,* March 27, 2002, p. A20.

198 **Cheney's meetings**: Wallace, Kelly, "White House Pressed for More Enron Details," http//:www.cnn.com, January 9, 2002.

199 **"It was more like one"**: McGrory, Mary, "Diffident oilmen?," *Washington Post,* February 24, 2002, p. B7.

200 **$11,000 for Clinton**: Center for Responsive Politics, "Top Presidential Recipients of Enron Contributions, 1989–2001," http://www.opensecrets.org.

200 **NSC helps Enron**: Milbank, Dana, and Alan Sipress, "NSC Aided Enron's Efforts; Agency Sought Lay Meeting with Indians on Plant," *Washington Post,* January 25, 2002, p. A18.

200 **"there are U.S. laws"**: McNulty, Sheila, and K. Merchant, "Enron Issues Veiled Sanction Threat to India," *Financial Times* (London), August 24, 2001, p. 6.

200 **SEC subpoena**: Milbank, Dana, and Paul Blustein, "White House Aided Enron in Dispute; Cheney, Others Intervened over Indian Power Plant," *Washington Post,* January 19, 2002, p. A1.

200 **"a moment of truth"**: Newton, Christopher, "White House Shifted Carbon Dioxide Emissions Policy after Lobbyist's Letter," Associated Press, April 26, 2002.

201 **Enron contributions to members of Congress**: Center for Responsive Politics, http://www.opensecrets.org.

201 **Wendy Gramm biography**: http://www.pbs.org/wgbh/pages/frontline/president/players; shgramm.html.

201 **W. Gramm joins Enron**: "So You Want to Buy a President?," *Frontline* show 1410, PBS television, aired January 30, 1996.

201 **Enron explosion**: Giombetti, Rick, "Progressives for Enron? Utility Deregulation, Politics and Enronomics," *CounterPunch,* January 22, 2002.

202 **Enron strategies**: Oppel, Richard A., Jr., "Enron's Many Strands: The Strategies; How Enron Got California to Buy Power It Didn't Need," *New York Times,* May 8, 2002, p. C1.

202 **"Every time there is a shortage"**: *Frontline* interview with Kenneth Lay, PBS television, March 27, 2001.

203 **SEC chairman threatened**: *Frontline* interview with Arthur Levitt, PBS television, March 12, 2002.

202 **"reflects, to a great extent"**: Statement by SEC Chairman Arthur Levitt to the SEC Open Meeting on Market Structure Initiatives in the Options and Equities Markets, and Rules Governing Auditor Independence, November 15, 2000.

203 **"He is the most powerful"**: Mitchell, Alison, and Marc Lacey, "A Lawmaker Amasses Power, and Uses It," *New York Times,* October 16, 1999.

203 **"The Gestapo of government"**: Ivins, Molly, "The Exterminator Rep: Tom Delay Hates Clinton, Loves Lobbyists and Is the Big Winner in Washington's Saga of Sin," *Playboy,* May 1, 1999.

203 **"daycare, the teaching of evolution"**: *The Nation,* November 15, 1999.

203 **"They needed a Rottweiler"**: Dreyfuss, Robert, "DeLay, Incorporated," *Texas Observer,* February 4, 2000.

203 **Perks smorgasbord**: Milbank, Dana, "The Big Fence Party: On the Outside Looking in as Tom DeLay Whips up Some Fundraisers," *Washington Post,* August 2, 2000, p. C1.

204 **"Rep. J. C. Watts"**: Ibid.

204 **"If you want to play"**: Maraniss, David, and Michael Weisskopf, "Speaker and His Directors Make the Cash Flow Right," *Washington Post,* November 27, 1995, p. A1.

205 **"We're just following"**: Ibid.

205 **RICO suit**: McDonald, Greg, and Steve Lash, "Democrats' Lawsuit Takes Aim at Delay; Extortion, Money Laundering Alleged," *Houston Chronicle,* May 4, 2000, p. A1.

205 **"I am asking you"**: Associated Press, "Conservative Group Files a Complaint Against House GOP Whip; It Says Tom DeLay Promised Donors Access to Administration Officials," *St. Louis Post-Dispatch,* April 11, 2001, p. A7.

205 **"It is improper"**: Judicial Watch, www.judicialwatch.org/cases/75/delay/DeLayComplaint.htm.

206 **"I know the Gentleman"**: Staff writers, "Democrats Accuse DeLay of 'Grotesque' Remarks in Speech," *Houston Chronicle,* July 18, 1998, p. A6.

206 **"I feel terrible"**: Mitchell, Alison, "After Hours, Debate on Fund-Raising Rages," *New York Times,* July 20, 1998, p. A1.

206 **"Insult to the majority"**: See Dreyfuss, "DeLay, Incorporated."

207 **"The most investigated man"**: McDonald, Greg, "DeLay Says Democrats Zeroing In; He Sees Plot to Stir Up Accusations of Perjury," *Houston Chronicle,* February 10, 1999, p. A1.

207 **"money is not the root of all evil"**: Staff writers, "DeLay to Fight Fund-Raising Limits," *Washington Post,* May 15, 1998, p. A7.

207 **Enron figures**: Bresnahan, John, and Damon Chappie, "DeLay Advisers Reaped Enron Windfall," *Roll Call,* February 25, 2002.

207 **Won't return Enron money**: Hines, Cragg, "C'mon, Tom, Give up the Enron Spoils," *Houston Chronicle,* January 18, 2002.

207 **Big Tobacco gives**: "Congressional Leaders' Soft Money Accounts Show Need for Campaign Finance Reform Bills," Public Citizen, February 26, 2002, www. citizen.org.

207 **Big Tobacco action**: International Consortium of Investigative Journalists, Center for Public Integrity, www.icij.org/investigate/beelman.html.

208 **DeLay, Exterminator**: Perl, Peter, "Absolute Truth; Tom DeLay Is Certain That Christian Family Values Will Solve America's Problems," *Washington Post Magazine,* May 13, 2001, p. W12.

208 **More Exterminator**: Ibid.

208 **Enron meeting at DeLay's**: Bresnahan and Chappie, "DeLay Advisers."

208 **Marianas bid**: Roche, Walter F., Jr., "Enron Doused Island Electric Plant; Energy Giant Flexed All Its Muscle to Win Contract, Backed Out," *Baltimore Sun,* April 3, 2002, p. 1A.

209 **"Get off your butts"**: Zitner, Aaron, "Politicians Turn Up Heat on HMOs; Seen Making Reform of Health Plans a Major Campaign Issue," *Boston Globe,* July 10, 1998, p. E1.

209 **HBC and Lott**: "Senate Democrats Lose Early Patients' Rights Votes; Clinton Blasts 'Half-Hearted Protections'," http://www.cnn.com, July 13, 1999.

209 **"We are giving more"**: Public Citizen, "Holding Patients Hostage: The Unhealthy Alliance Between HMOs and Senate Leaders," April 5, 2000, p. 5.

209 **"the back-room tactic"**: Wright, Jim, "Time to Restore Power to the People," *Albany Times Union,* July 3, 2001, p. A7.

210 **"arbitrary and unfair"**: Victor, Kirk, "McCain's Evolution," *National Journal* 33, no. 32, August 8, 2001.

210 **"uncalled for"**: Ibid.

210 **"You know, you actually could"**: Fred Barnes interview with Senator Trent Lott, *Fox News Sunday,* July 15, 2001.

210 **Lott birth and upbringing**: Barone, Michael, and Richard E. Cohen, *The 2002 Almanac of American Politics.* Washington, D.C.: Gambit Publishers, 2002, pp. 859–62.

211 **"to touch his Pleistocene strands"**: Kamen, Al, "Texas Capital," *Washington Post,* July 25, 2001, p. A19.

211 **"coup of one"**: Barone and Cohen, *2002 Almanac,* p. 869.

211 **Lott and money from gambling industry**: Public Citizen, "Folding to the Casino Industry," www.citizen.org/print_article.cfm?ID=5771, 2001, pp. 1–14.

213 **"I mean, we're talking"**: Marinucci, Carla, and Lance Williams, "Davis' Non-Stop Cash Machine; Many Big Donors Have Interests in Governor's Decisions," *San Francisco Chronicle,* May 19, 2002, p. A1.

213 **"I don't think Gray"**: Ibid, p. A1.

214 **Proposition 34**: www.smartvoter.org/2000/11/07/ca/state/prop/34/.

214 **Pipe Trade Council**: Lucas, Greg, and Carla Marinucci, "Pipe Fitters' Gift Swells Governor's War Chest; Recent Ban on Plastic Is What Union Wanted," *San Francisco Chronicle,* May 14, 2002, p. A1.

214 **Second largest donor**: Gledhill, Lynda, "Plastic Pipe in Homes Still a Dream, but Unions Drop Objections to Flexible Gas Lines," *San Francisco Chronicle,* May 3, 2002, p. A7.

215 **Corrections contract**: Morain, Dan, "The State: Prison Guards' Labor Pact to Be Examined," *Los Angeles Times,* May 16, 2002, p. 8.

215 **Baheti contribution**: Staff writers, "Oracle Check, No-Bid Contract Haunt Governor," *St. Petersburg Times,* June 15, 2002, p. 5A.

215 **Auditor's report**: Salladay, Robert, "Auditors at Odds on Contract; Stark Contrasts on State's Oracle Deal," *San Francisco Chronicle,* June 6, 2002, p. A17.

216 **Davis solicits $1 million**: "Capitol Sausage: Unsavory Peek Inside," *Sacramento Bee,* May 19, 2002, p. E4.

216 **"Davis hit us up"**: Lopez, Steve, "Shameless Governor Is a Compulsive Money-Grubber," *Los Angeles Times,* May 15, 2002, p. 1.

216 **Davis can't recall**: Morain, Dan, "Davis Used Capitol to Seek Funds, Union Says," *Los Angeles Times,* May 12, 2002, p. 1.

216 **"This bill is a laser"**: Lucas, Greg, "GOP Bill Would Ban Capitol Fund Raising; Measure a Direct Attempt to Thwart Davis from Soliciting Donations in His Office," *San Francisco Chronicle,* May 22, 2002, p. A6.

217 **Multimillionaire candidates**: Berg, Steve, "Checchi's Lavish Spending May Not Fly in California," *Minneapolis Star Tribune,* May 31, 1998, p. 19A.

217 **Davis chooses Simon**: Barabak, Mark Z., "Daily Power Call Shapes Political Life of Gray Davis; Election: If It's 8:30 A.M., He's on the Phone with His Inner Circle, Sharing News and Strategy," *Los Angeles Times,* May 20, 2002, p. 1.

217 **"a difficult problem for voters"**: Editorial, "Bob Franks for the Senate," *New York Times,* October 25, 2000, p. 26.

217 **"a commendably compassionate liberal"**: Ibid.

218 **"outsized role of money"**: Ibid.

218, 219 **Corzine's birth and upbringing**: Kocieniewski, David, "A Contradictory Tycoon: Jon Stevens Corzine," *New York Times,* November 9, 2000, page 21.

218, 219 **Corzine at Goldman Sachs**: Halbfinger, David M., "Wall Street Rise Shows Corzine Was Iconoclast," *New York Times,* May 29, 2000, p. 1.

219 **"His use of money"**: Levy, Clifford J., and David M. Halbfinger, "Torrent of Campaign Cash Helped and Backfired," *New York Times,* November 9, 2000, p. 20.

219 **1999 spending**: Halbfinger, David M., "Senate Contender in New Jersey Finds His Money Attracts Others," *New York Times,* January 31, 2000, p. B1.

219 **"I raised $3 million"**: Interview with Jon Corzine, April 19, 2002.

220 **"It is utterly incomprehensible"**: Halbfinger, "Senate Contender in New Jersey," p. B2.

220 **"Bold ideas"**: Halbfinger, David M., "Florio Puts Corzine on Defensive in Their First Debate," *New York Times,* May 11, 2000, p. B1.

221 **"No one can tell him what to do"**: Jacobs, Andrew, "In Bayonne, Blue-Collar Backlash over Corzine's Spending," *New York Times,* June 1, 2000, p. B1.

222 **$7.4 million GOTV, homeless shelters**: Barone and Cohen, *2002 Almanac,* p. 979.

222 **margin of victory**: Peterson, Iver, "But for the Urban Core, It Could Have Been Senator Franks," *New York Times,* November 9, 2000, p. B21.

222 **$63 million**: Beiler, David, "Case Study: Mark Warner's Five-Year Plan," *Campaigns and Elections,* December 2001, p. 34.

222 **"I admit to being thin-skinned"**: Interview with Jon Corzine, April 19, 2002.

223 **"I was one of ten"**: Interview with Russ Feingold, May 3, 2002.

223 **Feingold electoral history**: Abramowitz, Michael, "The Foreseen Rise of Russ Feingold; Wisconsin's New Senator Knew His Offbeat Campaign Would Work—Just Ask Him," *Washington Post,* November 30, 1992, p. D1.

224 **"He comes out of"**: Kranish, Michael, "No Surprise Voiced at Feingold Break with Party," *Boston Globe,* January 28, 1999, p. A24.

224 **Ashcroft vote**: Gilbert, Craig, "Feingold Has No Regrets on Vote as He Clashes with Ashcroft," *Milwaukee Journal Sentinel,* December 9, 2001, p. 1A.

225 **"The Democratic party decided"**: Feingold interview with Matthew Rothschild, *Progressive,* May 2002.

225 **Hutchison amendment**: Gilbert, Craig, "Following the Money: Feingold's Push for Campaign Reform Angers Colleagues," *Milwaukee Journal Sentinel,* October 3, 1999, p. 1.

226 **Only two Republicans**: Chen, Edward, "Support Grows for Campaign Reform Bill, Backers Say; Legislation: Measure Banning 'Soft Money' Contributions Is Within 2 Votes of Senate Passage, Supporters Claim, but Opponents Are Unyielding," *Los Angeles Times,* September 12, 1997, p. 14.

227 **"members of Congress"**: Interview with Russ Feingold, May 3, 2002.

228 **Contribution limits**: Johnson, Dirk, "2 in a Wisconsin Race Put Limits on Coffers," *New York Times,* September 23, 1998, p. A16.

228 **"Get the hell out"**: Pianin, Eric, "Candidate's Costly Pledge on Donations," *Washington Post,* October 31, 1998, p. A1.

228 **Feingold wins**: Editorial, "A Principled Win," *Washington Post,* November 5, 1998, p. A22.

229 **Bush signs McCain-Feingold**: McQuillan, Laurence, and Jill Lawrence, "Bush Signs Campaign-Finance Bill," *USA Today,* March 28, 2002, p. 5A.

229 **"Now is the time"**: Interview with Russ Feingold, May 3, 2002.

229–232 **Ratner**: Barrett, Wayne, "GotterdamneRudy: Operatic Fundraiser Hits Low Note of Compromise," *Village Voice,* April 29, 1997.

233 **"I was the guy"**: Interview with James C. Callaway, May 6, 2002.

233 **"I was a fat cat"**: Suro, Robert, "Fundraiser Attacks the Practices He Thrived On," *New York Times,* June 5, 1989.

7. Reforms Don't Work

237 **"History is the"**: Asadullah, Samad A., "Between the Lines: Martin Luther King; Can His Legacy Get a 'True Witness'?," *Los Angeles Sentinel,* January 17, 2001, p. 7.

237 **"I spend this much"**: Jacobs, John, "A Rookie Powerbroker," *Orange County Register,* May 9, 1993, p. J4.

237 **"When these political action committees"**: Stern, Philip M., *Still the Best Congress Money Can Buy,* Washington, D.C.: Regnery, 1992, p. 107.

242 **"expanded givers tend to be"**: Edsall, Thomas, "As Cash Flows, Republicans Win, Survey Says," *Washington Post,* June 3, 2002, p. A4.

243 **2002 CBS poll**: CBS News Poll, January 15–17, 2002, as excerpted on www.nationaljournal.com.

243 **2001 ABC/*Washington Post* poll**: ABC News/*Washington Post* poll, March 22–25, 2001, as excerpted on www.pollingreport.com.

243 **2000 ABC/*Washington Post* poll**: ABC News/*Washington Post* poll, March 30–April 2, 2000, as excerpted on www.pollingreport.com.

243 **2000 Harris poll**: "Campaign Finance Reform Strongly Supported by Voters," Harris Poll Election 2000, February 2, 2000.

243 **2000 *New York Times*/CBS poll**: *New York Times*/CBS News poll, February 2000.

243 **2000 *Business Week* poll**: "Too Much Corporate Power?," *Business Week,* September 11, 2000.

244 **1999 *Newsweek* poll**: *Newsweek* poll, October 21–22, 1999, as excerpted on www.pollingreport.com.

244 **1997 *New York Times*/CBS poll**: *New York Times*/CBS News poll, April 8, 1997, as excerpted on www.publiccampaign.org.

244 **1996 Gallup poll**: Gallup poll, November 1996, as excerpted on www.publiccampaign.org.

244 **Center for Responsive Politics poll**: Center for Responsive Politics, "Individual Congressional Campaign Contributors: Wealthy, Conservative, and Reform-Minded," June 9, 1998.

245 **Report by CED**: Committee for Economic Development, "Investing in the People's Business: A Business Proposal for Campaign Finance Reform," 1999. The full report can be found at www.ced.org.

245 **"Reform is long overdue"**: Committee for Economic Development, press release, March 18, 1999.

245 **CED poll**: Committee for Economic Development, "Senior Business Executives Back Campaign Finance Reform," Press Release, October 18, 2000.

245 **"More executives are saying"**: "Campaign Reform's Time Has Come," *New York Times,* March 19, 2002.

245 **"[L]egislative action could happen"**: ibid.

245 **"[P]rofoundly undemocratic"**: Smith, Bradley A., "Campaign Finance Regulation, Faulty Assumptions and Undemocratic Consequences," Cato Institute, September 13, 1995.

245 **"When a law is in need"**: Smith, Bradley A., "Why Campaign Finance Reform Never Works," *Wall Street Journal,* March 19, 1997.

246 **"I think we should deregulate"**: Panel discussion interview, MSNBC, September 14, 1996, as excerpted by the Brennan Center for Justice at New York University School of Law, www.brennancenter.org.

246 **"Putting [Smith] in charge"**: Project FEC, "No Bark, No Bite, No Point: The Case for Closing the Federal Election Commission and Establishing a New System for Enforcing the Nation's Campaign Finance Laws," April 2002, pp. 67, 132.

246 **"Most of the problems"**: MSNBC panel discussion interview, September 14, 1996.

248 **"It would be a sad commentary"**: New York State Commission on Government Integrity, *Government Ethics Reform for the 1990s.* New York: Fordham University Press, 1991, p. 13.

248 **Pataki calls system "dreadful"**: Perez-Pena, Richard, "The 1998 Campaign: The Incumbent: Pataki Calls Campaign Financing 'Dreadful' but Has No Solution," *New York Times,* October 17, 1998.

248 **"The governor is all talk"**: Interview with Blair Horner, June 6, 2002.

249 **"Had there not been"**: Testimony of City Council member Herbert Berman before the New York City Campaign Finance Board, December 10, 2001.

249 **"The campaign finance program"**: Testimony of Sandra Vassos before the New York City Campaign Finance Board, December 11, 2001.

249 **"It works"**: Testimony of David Yassky before the New York City Campaign Finance Board, December 11, 2001.

250 **Report on the 2000 state legislative elections**: Citizen Action of New York, "The Wealth Primary: Spending in the 2000 New York State Legislative Elections," April 2001. The full report can be found at www.citizenactionny.org.

250 **Daily News investigation**: Blood, Michael R., "Big Donors Stuffing Gov's Coffers," *Daily News,* July 28, 2002.

251 **"I was unaware"**: Pleven, Liam, "Donor Cap Falls Flat: Beer Giant Legally Gave 85G in New York," *Newsday,* July 12, 2000.

251 **Contribution sizes in NYC and NYS**: Citizen Action of New York, "Capital Bargains, Capital Gains," October 2000. The full report can be found at www.citizenactionny.org. Data on contributions to city candidates provided by the New York City Campaign Finance Board.

251 **Contributions to NYS gubernatorial candidates**: Citizen Action of New York, "The Money Marathon: Big Bucks and the Race for Governor of New York," January 2002. The full report can be found at www.citizenactionny.org.

252 **Contributions to NYC mayoral candidates**: Data provided by the New York City Campaign Finance Board.

252 **"I think the city system"**: Former Senator Alfonse D'Amato (R–NY), New York University School of Law lecture, March 6, 2002.

253 **Spending by NYS legislative candidates.**: Citizen Action of New York, "The Wealth Primary."

253 **Dollars per vote**: Bender, Edwin, "How Much Does Your Vote Cost," National Institute on Money in State Politics, June 23, 2000.

253 **2001 Marist poll**: Odato, James M., "Poll: Pay for Campaigns, with a Limit," *Albany Times Union,* April 27, 2001.

254 **"The CFB has been nonpartisan"**: Newfield, Jack, "Time to Vote Out the Board of Elections," *New York Post,* September 24, 1997.

254 **Fines for Koch, Dinkins, Giuliani**: Interview with Frank Barry, New York City Campaign Finance Board, May 2002.

254 **"If a bill comes in"**: "In Albany, Many Uses for Campaign Cash," *Newsday,* May 10, 2000.

254 **Spending by state legislators**: Ibid.

254 **"Too many legislators"**: Editorial, "Free Lunch: Albany Must Close Loopholes That Let State Legislators Misuse Campaign Contributions," *Newsday,* August 14, 2000.

255 **$50 million in ads**: Perez-Pena, Richard, "Pataki's Presence in State Ads Is Campaign Tool, Critics Say," *New York Times*, April 4, 2002, p. B4.

255 **"Albany is totally dysfunctional"**: Interview with Rachel Leon, June 12, 2002.

256 **Comparison of Minnesota and Wisconsin**: Stern, Robert M., and Craig P. Holman, "Public Financing of Campaigns in the States," February 2002, p. 31. Report prepared for the American Bar Association.

257 **"It's a good way of"**: Public Campaign, "The Road to Clean Elections," 2001.

257 **"It was refreshing"**: Ibid.

258 **Contested races in Arizona**: Arizona Clean Elections Institute statistics, October 2001.

258 **"We were able to find"**: Breslow, Marc, Janet Groat, and Paul Saba, "Revitalizing Democracy: Clean Election Reform Shows the Way Forward," Money and Politics Implementation Project, January 2002. The report can be found at www.neaction.org.

258 **Spending in Arizona**: National Institute on Money in State Politics, "Public Funding Equals Contributions by Business Interests in 2000," press release, February 28, 2002.

258 **"Public funding appears to"**: Sanchez, Samantha, "First Returns on a Campaign Finance Reform Experiment: Maine, Arizona, and Full Public Funding," report prepared for the National Institute on Money in State Politics, March 26, 2001.

258 **Spending by winners and losers in Maine**: Ibid.

258 **Competitive races in Maine**: Breslow et al, "Revitalizing Democracy."

258 **Incumbents in Maine and Arizona**: Sanchez, "First Returns."

258 **"I spent 90 percent"**: Breslow et al., "Revitalizing Democracy."

259 **Survey of Maine participants**: Smith, Alison, "Clean Elections at Work: The Successful Debut of Maine's Public Funding System," Maine Citizens for Clean Elections, June 13, 2001.

259 **"In previous campaigns"**: Breslow et al., "Revitalizing Democracy."
259 **"Historically, the pharmaceutical industry"**: Green, Joshua, "Clean Money in Maine," *American Prospect,* September 24–October 2, 2000.
259 **"The insurance industry's influence"**: Sifry, Micah, "Donor-Free Democracy," *Mother Jones,* August 16, 2001.
259 **"The business lobbyists left me alone"**: Ibid.
260 **"Under the Clean Money option"**: Heftel, Cecil, *End Legalized Bribery: An Ex-Congressman's Proposal to Clean Up Congress.* Seven Locks Press, 1998.
261 **Tax credits**: Cressman, Derek, "Lone Star Election Laws: A Comparative Study of Texas's Campaign Finance System," U.S. Public Interest Research Group, July 2000.
261 **Out-of-state contribution limits**: Ibid.
263 **John Y. Brown's fund-raising**: Stern and Holman, "Public Financing of Campaigns," p. 53.
264 **Kentucky's loan limits**: Ibid.
264 **Study of sixty democracies**: Pinto-Duschinsky, Michael, "Handbook on Funding of Parties and Election Campaigns: Overview," prepared for the International Institute for Democracy and Electoral Assistance, 2001; available at www.idea.int.
264 **"[W]e should require broadcast stations"**: Taylor, Paul, "The Case for Free Air Time," report prepared for the Alliance for Better Campaigns, March 2002; available at www.bettercampaigns.org.
265 **Blair and Chrétien problems:** Hoge, Warren, "Dispute Involving Indian Businessman Tarnishes Blair's Image," *New York Times,* February 19, 2002; Krauss, Clifford, "Canadian Leader Attacked in a Loud Ethics Brouhaha," *New York Times,* May 31, 2002, p.A8.

8. Change, for Good

271 **Contribution-expenditure distinction**: Neuborne, Burt, *Campaign Finance Reform and the Constitution: A Critical Look at* Buckley v. Valeo. New York: Brennan Center for Justice at New York University School of Law, 1997, p. 9.
272 **"There is good reason"**: Rosenkranz, p. 19.
272 **Breyer and Kennedy on facts**: Briffault, Richard, "*Nixon v. Shrink Missouri Government PAC:* The Beginning of the End of the *Buckley* Era?" *Minnesota Law Review* 2001.
272 **Fact-finding timetable**: Keller, Amy, "Reform Arguments Scheduled for December," *Roll Call,* April 25, 2002.
273 **"All money spent by a political party"**: *Colorado Republican v. FEC,* 518 U.S. 604, 648 (1996) (Justice Stevens dissenting).
273 **"Money is property"**: *Nixon v. Shrink Missouri Government PAC,* 528 U.S. 377, 398 (2000) (Justice Stevens concurring).

273 **"Making less absolute"**: *Nixon v. Shrink Missouri,* at 405 (Justice Breyer concurring).

273 **Thomas and Scalia**: *Shrink Missouri,* at 413–418 (Justice Thomas dissenting); *FEC v. Colorado Republican,* 533 U.S. 431, 465–466 (Justice Thomas dissenting). See also *Colorado Republican,* at 635–644. (Justice Thomas concurring in judgment and dissenting in part).

273 **"For now I would leave open"**: See *Nixon v. Shrink Missouri,* 409 (Justice Kennedy dissenting).

273 ***Shrink Missouri* and *Buckley*:** Hasen, Richard L., "*Shrink Missouri,* Campaign Finance, and 'The Thing That Wouldn't Leave,'" *Constitutional Commentary* (2000).

274 **"The corrosive and distorting effects"**: *Austin v. Michigan State Chamber of Commerce,* 494 U.S. 652, 660 (1990).

274 **"Not confined to bribery"**: *Nixon v. Shrink Missouri,* at 389.

274 **"The intermittent tendency"**: Briffault, "*Nixon v. Shrink Missouri.*"

274 **"Cannot be taken literally"**: *Nixon v. Shrink Missouri,* at 401–402 (Justice Breyer concurring).

274 **"Congress shall have power"**: Witcover, Jules, "One Man's Futile Stab at Reform," *Baltimore Sun,* March 28, 2001.

274 **Feingold on Hollings amendment**: Interview with Russ Feingold, May 3, 2002.

275 **"it might be possible"**: *Congressional Quarterly's Guide to U.S. Elections,* 2001, p. 89.

277 **Study of Los Angeles system**: "Campaign Financing in the City of Los Angeles: Eleven Years of Reform: Many Successes—More to Be Done," prepared by Center for Governmental Studies, October 2001, p. 24; available at www.cgs.org.

277 **Briffault report**: Association of the Bar of the City of New York, Commission on Campaign Finance Reform, *Dollars and Democracy: A Blueprint for Campaign Finance Reform.* New York: Fordham University Press, 2000; available at www.abcny.org.

277 **Public funding qualifications**: Malbin, Michael J., and Thomas L. Gais, *The Day after Reform: Sobering Campaign Finance Lessons from the American States.* Albany, N.Y.: Rockefeller Institute Press, 1998, pp. 57–58.

278 **Spending in the 2000 elections**: Center for Responsive Politics, www.opensecrets.org.

282 **"Twenty years ago"**: Oreskes, Michael, "Modern Political Is Forcing Lawmakers to Devote More Time to Money," *New York Times,* July 11, 1989.

283 **"[A]n anything goes, Wild West"**: Nichols, John, "Campaign Finance: The Sequel," *The Nation,* April 29, 2002.

283 **An independent FEC**: Project FEC, "No Bark, No Bite, No Point: The Case for Closing the Federal Election Commission and Establishing a New System for Enforcing the Nation's Campaign Finance Laws," May 2002, p. 40.

284 **"Put itself on the honor system"**: Jackson, Brooks, *Broken Promise: Why the Federal Election Commission Failed,* a Twentieth-Century Fund Paper. New York: Priority Press, 1990, p. 30.

285 **"The public interest, convenience"**: Federal Communication Act of 1934.

285 **Broadcasters' contributions**: Alliance for Better Campaigns, "Broadcast Industry Flexes Its Lobbying Muscle to Remove Ad Rate Provision from Campaign Finance Bill," March 2002; available at www.bettercampaigns.org. See also the Center for Responsive Politics, www.opensecrets.org.

285 **"Call you up and say"**: Paul Taylor, "The Case for Free Air Time," a report prepared for the Alliance for Better Campaigns, March 2002. The discussion of free broadcast time draws heavily from the report, which can be found at www.bettercampaigns.org.

288 **Gore proposal to end ads**: CBS News poll, March 19–21, 2000, as excerpted on www.pollingreport.com.

INDEX